CREATIVITY AND INNOVATION IN ORGANIZATIONS

CREATIVITY AND INNOVATION IN ORGANIZATIONS

Applications and Exercises   Fourth Edition

DEAN C. DAUW

DePaul University

Waveland Press, Inc.

Prospect Heights, Illinois

For information about this book, write or call:

Waveland Press, Inc.
P.O. Box 400
Prospect Heights, Illinois 60070
(312) 634-0081

Copyright © 1971, 1974, 1976 by Dean C. Dauw and Alan J. Fredian
        © 1980 by Dean C. Dauw
Third Printing

ISBN 0-917974-42-5

Printed in the United States of America.

CONTENTS

PART IV

PART V

PART VI

PART VII

EXERCISES

Introduction

Part I of this volume includes some recent research and theory about creativity and innovation in executives, managers, and others working in the world of business and industry. Less research has been completed on these populations from which it is increasingly more difficult to isolate samples. The reason is obvious. These individuals are often engaged in profit-making ventures or in organizational climates that do not foster such investigations, whereas researchers have always been able to enlist captive populations of school children and college students.

Part II includes some of our ideas about organizational development.

Part III emphasizes the recent research and thinking about executive career change and development, which is another way to look at highly creative people in transition. Part IV considers some related issues, while Part V is one of the best methods for stimulating creative thinking.

The reader is invited to enhance his own creative growth by developing his own model, theory or framework within which these contributions may be even more fruitful.

"Management is, all things considered, the most creative of all arts. It is the art of arts. Because it is the organizer of talents."—Jean-Jacques Servan-Schreiber.

Dean C. Dauw, Ph.D.

PART I

A GUIDE TO MAXIMIZING LEARNING IN SMALL GROUPS

Do you want to increase learning, attendance, performance, and enjoyment in your group or class? You can do so by using the methods recommended in this guide.

Take care of the means and the end will take care of itself.
— M. Gandhi

If you give a man a fish, he will eat it and soon be hungry.
If you teach a man to fish he will never be hungry.
— Chinese Proverb

Fundamentals

Many people fail because they conclude that fundamentals simply do not apply in their case.
— M.L. Cichon

1. Learn each student's name. Get the students to learn each other's names. (Use name tags if you like.) Use first names when addressing each other.

A man's name is to him the sweetest and most important sound in any language.
— Dale Carnegie

2. Arrange the seating in a circle so that each student can maintain eye contact with the other students.

Pressed into service means pressed out of shape.
— Robert Frost

3. Seat the more talkative students opposite the more quiet ones.
4. Learn the students' concerns about the work of the group, i.e., is attendance required? Exactly what are we responsible for? Exactly how will we be evaluated? Are you a hard marker?

5. Disturbances and excitements must take precedence. If they are ignored you will lose the student as he/she will turn off. (Credit goes to Ruth C. Cohn for this important observation.)
6. (i) Find out early what the students' interests are in relation to the subject matter. Ask them to write their interests down. Give them as much time as they require to do this, down to the slowest student. Ask each student to voice his/her specific interests. Invite the students to inquire about each other's interests.
   (ii) Make the subject relevant to the students' interests. If you don't they will forget it all.

An effective leader establishes objectives that help individuals reach their personal goals.
— L. Peter

7. Learn how knowledgable the students are about the subject matter (no matter how many "prerequisites" they may have taken). Bring the less knowledgeable students up to the level of the more knowledgeable ones before proceeding further. Encourage peer teaching at this early stage.
8. Allow those students who are only interested in passing the course a way to do so which is fair to you, to them, and to the institution.
9. Be enthusiastic about the course material. Enthusiasm is contagious.

Nothing great was ever achieved without enthusiasm.
— Emerson

10. You may initiate a discussion by setting a problem, by asking an open-ended question, or by beginning with a controversy. Discussion is hindered when you ask questions that have right answers. Invite them to speculate. Allow them to play with ideas.

Learning depends on the process of discovery.

— Ruth C. Cohn

11. To increase participation talk less and listen more. Encourage the students to talk directly to one another instead of going through you each time. Try not to be the centre of attention most of the time.

Tis wisdom sometimes to seem a fool.

— English Proverb

12. Do not make decisions for the group. Decisions should be made co-operatively through discussion. This increases interest and involvement.
13. Assign readings periodically as they become relevant to the topic under discussion. Do not hand out a long reading list.
14. Allow the group freedom to progress at a pace comfortable to them and not to you.

He who treads softly goes far.

— Chinese Proverb

15. When the meeting is to span more than 75 minutes allow time for a short break.
16. Inform the students well in advance how they may prepare for a specific meeting. Make it easy for them to prepare by making the necessary materials readily available.
17. Clarify the goals or objectives for each meeting. Is today's goal subject matter mastery? Or is the goal to solve a problem? Or is the goal to discuss an issue?

H flung himself from the room, flung himself upon his horse and rode madly off in all directions.

— Stephen Leacock

18. If the goal of the group is *subject matter mastery*, the material should be pre-read and the following format may be adopted: clarification of terms, the author's message, major and minor themes, integration of the material with other knowledge, application of the material, and evaluation of the author's presentation.
19. If the goal of the group is *to solve a problem* the best results are obtained by first asking each individual to write down as many solutions as he/she can. Then bring the solutions in front of the whole group for discussion. Research has shown that this method produces the highest quality and the greatest number of solutions.

When we all think alike, no one thinks very much.

— W. Lippmann

20. Break up larger groups (8 to 30) into smaller units (1 to 5) from time to time.
21. Do not set yourself up as an authority (even though you may be one). This produces anxiety, discourages participation, and invites resentment.

The fish has no rights in the Comorant's beak.

— Hindu Proverb

22. Listen carefully to each student in order to learn his/her unique frame of reference. Half the time what you hear is not exactly what the student means. Ask the student to elaborate.

There is something that is much more scarce, something finer far, something rarer than ability. It is the ability to recognize ability.

— E. Hubbard

23. Don't rush in order to cover all of the course content. If you do they will quickly forget it. Don't be concerned if all of the content isn't covered. It is more important to be effective than efficient.

That carpenter is not the best who makes more chips than all the rest.
— A. Gutterman

24. Regard your students as mature, as individuals, and as experts in areas in which you are not.

Every man I meet is in some way my superior; and in that I can learn of him.

— Emerson

25. Recognize minority opinions. You can use them to upgrade the quality of discussion and increase cohesiveness.
26. Allow periods of silence to occur. The students may be thinking!

Deliberating is not delaying.

— Ecclesiasticus

Some Foundations and Other Considerations

a) **Existence.** Humans have a need to confirm their existence. We confirm our existence when we become mentally, emotionally, or physically aroused. You may help a student confirm his/her existence by getting him/her aroused through the methods recommended in this guide.

I think, therefore I am. — Descartes

b) **Worth (esteem)**. Humans have a need to affirm their worth. You can confirm a student's worth with rewards such as praise, grades, recognition (listening attentively, using his/her name) and by validating his/her thinking by agreeing with the student.

The deepest principle in human nature is the craving to be appreciated — William James

Learning will be more enjoyable and more permanent the more often the existence and worth needs are given satisfaction in the group.

We both exist and know that we exist, and rejoice in this existence and this knowledge.
— S. Butler

c) **Effectance**. Humans have a need to have an effect on their environment. You can help satisfy the students' needs for this by reacting to what they say and do. You can also allow them the freedom to affect the other students. Allow them to be productive, creative, critical, provocative, etc. The more that you allow students to affect you and the others in the group the more meaningful, lasting and satisfying will their learning be. Through effectance students confirm their existence and affirm their worth.

The bigger they are the harder they fall.
— Anonymous

d) **Reward and Punishment**. Social rewards such as praise and recognition lower anxiety, raise self-esteem, promote more active participation, and produce a comfortable climate in which more creative work emerges. Social punishment such as criticism produces anxiety, frustration and silence.

He that has been shipwrecked shudders at still waters. — Publius Oviaus Nasu

e) **Activate**. At all times try to get the students to be active (thinking, feeling, speaking) rather than passive (listening only). If they are not active they will not learn.

Learning is an active process. We learn by doing.
— Dale Carnegie

f) **Feedback**. Give the students many chances to improve. Set many mini-tasks. Give feedback constantly. The more feedback the faster the learning. The less feedback the greater the confusion.

g) **Allow them to Fail**. Establish a comfortable, non-threatening atmosphere in which the students can risk saying anything — can risk failing. Students need many opportunities to fail safely. Safe failing is conducive to learning and creativity. (Thomas Edison failed more than 2,000 times before he perfected the light bulb.)

The world ceases to be a pleasure when it ceases to be a speculation. — Balzac

h) **Leadership**. Groups with leaders function better than groups without leaders. However, do not monopolize the role. Allow students to occupy the role of leader often. Several leaders may emerge during the course of a single meeting.

I've got to follow them, I am their leader.
— Ledru-Rollin

i) **Resources**. For maximal performance the group should exploit the resources (skills, natural abilities, unique experiences, knowledge) of its members.

The variety of individual personalities is the world's highest richness. — J. Huxley

j) **Self-Disclose**. Be open about your background, your training, your knowledge and lack of it, and about your professional and personal biases. All of these will influence the functioning of the group (with or without your awareness). Self-disclosure promotes trust and produces disclosure in others.

He who persists in genuineness will increase in adequacy. — T. Lynch

k) **Use Spontaneous Humour**. Laugh at your subject and yourself when appropriate occasions present themselves.

l) **Don't lecture for more than a few minutes**. How much do you remember of what your professors told you? How much are you trying to tell your students? (It may be telling.)

The only thing to do with good advice is to pass it on, it is never of any use to oneself.

— Oscar Wilde

m) **Amount of structure in the group work.** Some is better than none. Less is better than more.

n) **Do not stress grades.** Dr. Donald Hoyt's (1965) review of 46 research studies concludes, "Present evidence strongly suggests that college grades bear little or no relationship to any measures of adult accomplishment." This was found to be true in all areas studied: business, teaching, engineering, medicine, scientific research, studies of eminence, miscellaneous occupations, and in non-vocational accomplishments. Do not stress grades. Foster involvement.

It is unfortunate that young people must go to school and interrupt their education.

— George Bernard Shaw

Reference

Hoyt, Donald, P. *The relationship between college grades and adult achievement: A review of the Literature*. Research Report No. 7, September 1965. Published by The Research and Development Division of The American Testing Program, P.O. Box 168, Iowa City, Iowa 52240.

SOME NOTES ON TEACHING

One of Our Goals for You

This university and this professor is concerned about your individual development. You may not even know some of your own goals—long-range or immediate—so that it should be important for you to take time and make the effort to find them. Then you can apply more readily all that's involved in this course to your own situation. In fact, if you do not try to apply the ideas taught in this course, you may be wasting your time and money.

Clairvoyance is no more of a gift for your professors than for you. So you have to tell a professor some of the things you want from a course, just as he'll tell you continually some of the values you should receive from a particular text or reading.

Involvement

In these days of the multiversity and large classes, students sometimes feel like animals herded from one class to the next along computer-printed paths. Students often ask for more personal contact and involvement, but are often reluctant to make the first step. We want you to become "ego-involved," which typically occurs in situations that threaten an individual's self-identity, feelings of importance or personal status.

Research shows that even students who had planned to do little work in a course will be concerned about a professor's opinion of him. Thus, to assist you in becoming ego-involved we encourage you to do certain exercises. These may not necessarily, in some cases, be big research projects, but rather small *action programs*. The criteria for action programs are three; they should be (1) fun (2) spontaneous and (3) able to succeed.

Motivation

Students work to earn high grades or avoid low grades. But grades are only extrinsic motivators and that means *work*. Intrinsic motivation is better. When students get turned on by any subject, they find learning to be exciting and enjoyable. Students get turned on when presented with ideas that are moderately stimulating or complex. These principles have been researched and described well by Schneirla (biphasic processes underlying approach and withdrawal), Walker (psychological complexity as a theory of motivation), and Leula (optimal stimulation).

The practical application of these principles presents a challenge. An idea that is moderately stimulating for one student may be too strong or complex for another and too weak or simple for a third. Our solution is to arrange assignments so that students have the freedom to respond to whatever attracts them. Instead of assigning an article that each person must read to understand an idea that we feel is important, we would prefer a better method. Each person should read a series of articles, making notes on those ideas to which they react. Never summarize, but rather write down comments about ideas that make you stop and think, upset you or provide insights. This assignment will be an enjoyable learning experience for almost every student.

Adult Relationships

To aid you in appreciating these concepts about goals, involvement and motivation, we propose adult relationships, according to Eric Berne's model. In *Games People Play*, Berne hypothesizes three ego states: Adult, Parent, or Child. A mother relates to her son as a parent to a child. Often a dominating wife may relate to an alcoholic husband as a parent to a child. Many professors prefer to overcontrol their students in a parent-child relationship.

We feel the best possible relationship is that of one adult toward another. We can at best provide some interest, motivation, inspiration or the like, but we cannot force a student to learn. He can only learn best when he assumes an increasingly more adult responsibility for his own self-support. Professors must relate as one adult to another adult-student, and not overly control them externally, but rather aid them in developing their own internal locus of motivation or self-support.

It is extremely important that both professors and students take advantage of a simple fact—for each person, the most important person in the world is himself. This can become an even more useful fact if only we could all use it to help us learn and apply knowledge to oneself.

One of the very best statements echoing our own beliefs on teaching comes from Henry P. Cole entitled "Tell Me, Teacher," published in the *Journal of Creative Behavior:*

TELL ME, TEACHER*

Teacher, teacher, tell me true,
Tell me what I ought to do!

Teacher, teacher, where's my book?
Tell me where I ought to look!

Tell me what to feel and how to think,
When to eat and what to drink.

Tell me what is good and what is bad
When I'm happy and when I'm sad.

Tell me, tell me, what to do,
Tell me, tell me, what is true.

Make me learn and make me know.
Watch me closely as I come and go.

For I am small and I am weak,
Without your permission I cannot speak.

I cannot learn except by your decree,
Please, I beg you, give knowledge to me.

I am stupid and you are bright.
I am wrong and you are right.

I am bad and you are good.
I must do what you say I should.

Oh teacher, teacher, look what you have done!
I don't believe I'm anyone.

Oh teacher, teacher, can't you see!
Look at what you've done to me!

As Cole explains well, there exist many real assumptions underlying educational practice. These assumptions include:

> Students cannot be trusted to pursue their own learning.
>
> Presentation (lecturing) equals learning.
>
> The truth is known.
>
> The goal of education is to accumulate brick upon brick of factual knowledge.
>
> Constructive and creative citizens develop from passive learners.
>
> The voice (and whims) of authority is to be trusted and valued more than independent judgment.
>
> Feelings are irrelevant in education.
>
> Discovering knowledge is beyond the power of students and is, in any case, none of their business or responsibility.
>
> Passive acceptance is a more desirable response to ideas than active criticism.

Many significant observers have confirmed that these assumptions, listed above, do exist and adversely affect educational practices. Various studies, especially those by E. Paul Torrance on Creativity, have shown that formal education frequently tends to inhibit or destroy a person's curiosity or desire to learn.

Henry Cole espouses *Process Education* as a means of helping to avoid the problems caused by "Tell Me, Teacher." Process education formally rejects as immoral, unhealthy, and completely inappropriate all educational practice that ignores the real development of unique individuals.

On the positive side, process education's assumptions demand the learner be active and expressive creator of knowledge and experience. The active learner desiring to grow and develop must make his own viable meaning from that knowledge and experience.

But students who are dominated, submissive and dependent will have little chance to reach such a goal and perhaps have little chance as adults to be very healthy and productive members of society.

Basic Concepts About a
Well-Functioning Individual

Elsewhere in this book is a chapter about "How to become more self-actualized." We list here, how-

"Tell Me Teacher" by Henry P. Cole. Published by *Journal of Creative Behavior*, Volume 6, Number 3, Third Quarter, 1972, pp. 204-208. Copyrighted by the Creative Education Foundation. Reprinted by permission.

ever, fourteen selected concepts that comprise the basic frame of reference for some of the teaching, learning, and behaving programs that are described in this volume.

1. Each individual has personality assets, physical and emotional strengths, and abilities gained from experience, some of which are identified and others unused.
2. Each individual has specific goals and long-range objectives that are meaningful to him.
3. All individuals, within themselves, have the desire to change and to grow.
4. The opportunity to design one's own learning situation provides additional motivation to develop and change.
5. Group encouragement and reinforcement assist in individual exploration and change.
6. The present can be altered and the future directed without explanation of the negative past.
7. Emotions may be affected by signs and symbols; they will respond to action.
8. Human behavior is strongly influenced by its present environment.
9. Meaningful education is a continuous process. It is, by and large, predicated on need and desire.
10. Peers learn best from peers when new information and experiences result from the relationship.
11. An individual learns success from those he selects as successful; the association is essential.
12. An individual continues to develop by completing a desired activity and moving to a new experience.
13. Each individual has a purpose within the universe. Identifying and pursuing this purpose is a vital part of fulfillment.
14. Learning occurs when an individual recognizes and accepts the differences between his failures and another's success and bases his next action on that information.

Carl Rogers, in his classic article "The Characteristics of a Helping Relationship," (in *On Becoming a Person,* Cambridge, Massachusetts: Riverside Press, 1961) describes a helping relationship as one "in which at least one of the parties has the intent of promoting the growth, development, maturity, improved functioning, improved coping with life of the other." This definition includes parent and child, teacher and students, manager and subordinates, therapist and patient, consultant and client, and many other less formally defined relationships. This concept is explained well by Rogers, and exemplified in the exercises of Kolb, Rubin, and McIntyre: *Organizational Psychology: An Experiential Approach.* (Englewood Cliffs, N.J.: Prentice-Hall, 1974). This is one of the goals of this book: to help you perceive and understand and become involved in a helping relationship as defined by the authors mentioned above.

MY CONVICTIONS
MY RELATIONSHIPS WITH OTHERS

(With thanks to Carl Rogers, Abe Maslow, Fritz Perls, and other important friends of the Association for Humanistic Psychology.)

You and I are involved in a relationship that I value and desire to keep. Each of us is still a very distinct individual with separate needs, which you have a right to try to meet. I will increasingly and continuously try to be genuine in accepting your behavior on every occasion, but especially when you are having problems meeting your needs or when my own feelings (being tired or anxious or frustrated) seem to get in the way.

When you share your feelings or problems with me, I will try as hard as I can to listen understandingly and acceptingly in a way that will facilitate your finding your own solutions. I believe in being other-directed in this way. (Rogers used the term client-centered but I mean it even if you are not a client.) So you can then develop your own solutions and not depend upon mine.

If you have a problem because my behavior is interfering with your meeting your needs, I will ask you to tell me openly and honestly how you feel. I will encourage candid confrontation. Then I will listen intently and decide whether to modify my own behavior.

On the other hand, if your behavior interferes with my meeting my own needs, and causes me to feel unaccepting of you, I will try to tell you as openly and honestly as I can exactly how I am feeling. Then I must trust you to respect my needs at least enough to listen. Whether you then choose to modify your behavior is another important matter.

At anytime when either of us cannot modify his behavior to meet the needs of the other, thus leading to conflict of needs in our relationship, let us try to make a commitment. I will honestly commit myself to resolve each conflict without ever resorting to the use of my power to win at the expense of your losing. I hope you will try to do the same. I do respect your needs, but I also must understand my own.

Hopefully, we might strive always to search for solutions to our inevitable conflicts that may be acceptable to both of us. Then your needs will be met and so will mine—no one will lose and both will win.

One hopefully good result will be that you will continue to develop as a person by meeting your needs, and so can I.

Our relationship may become increasingly healthier because it will be more mutually satisfying. You and I can each become what he is capable of being. We will continue to relate to one another in mutual respect, friendship, love and peace.

ON CONSULTATION AND THERAPY

These ideas are written in an effort to assist you in deciding about seeking help or about finding someone to share in your life, your feelings, and related problem-solving.

Most people do not really understand counseling and therapy. They often fail to realize the fine lines that distinguish all of consultation, counseling, therapy and education. These few pages, however, are not to define all the subtle differences. The scholarly reader who wishes to become a more active learner might be interested in reading one outstanding volume on therapy written by Everett Shostrom; *Actualizing Therapy*, San Diego: Edits Publishers, 92107, 1976; another good book on consultation is by Blake and Mouton, Reading, Mass: Addison-Wesley Publishing Company, 1976.

For myself, I would like to express here my own needs, wants, feelings, and expectations. Then, you can more easily decide if you want to work with me, get to know me better and permit us both to grow together, in a corporate consultation or personal therapy setting.

First, let me share with you some important issues in my life. Here are some ways in which I am constantly striving to grow and develop in an active way. (Perhaps you can make some similar statements now and/or in the near future). I want to learn how to accept myself more; to live life as it comes without fighting against the stream; to exhilarate more joyously; to become more tolerant and less blaming of myself for the foolishness and hassles of our daily existence. I need to accept emotional pain more gracefully.

The more I care about a person, the more I need to be less controlling and more accepting with a loving indifference: being with them without requiring them to be otherwise than they really are, here and now.

I want to get increasingly deeper into all my feelings, alive and alert to them. I need to thrill in their excitement, savoring their duration.

As I work at my personal growth and development, my own changes and transformations convince me all people are as strong or as weak as anyone. Everyone is vulnerable; any person can be hurt at any time. And everyone makes mistakes. Every person has delightful parts, things that can be found good in them, admired and appreciated. Perhaps we could all learn better to expect the unexpected; to accept what is still imperfect, understanding others as being truly responsible for their lives, without being blamed by us.

Self-actualization is the greatest goal for me to strive for and try to help others achieve. It requires breaking out of our safe, risk-shirking, familiar, old patterns in which we all too frequently submerge our lives, our joy and our growth. For me, in consultation and/or therapy, I need to offer a nurturing environment in which my client/friend and I get to know one another; in which I can disclose my own strengths or needs for growth, as an invitation for them to disclose their own. I only want to take on clients whom I like at the outset, so that then there is no need for me to try to change them. They can, therefore, on their own assume more responsibility for their own risking/changing/growing.

Whether in consultation or in therapy, I am still educated, trained, and disciplined to be a professional — to do my best, to be useful, to help someone grow, solve problems more effectively and efficiently, to become happier or whatever one wants to become. But I am not an authority insisting on how to define your happiness or growth. You run your life. I will work with you and care about you, while not judging your daily behavior.

Whatever you do in changing/risking/growing through therapy is not a measure of how well I am doing my job or fulfilling my role. We are not laying bricks, but you are choosing feely to build the mansions of your own happiness. Sometimes, when I am working very, very well, the client may not choose a certain risk/effort/outcome. On the other hand, when I may occasionally be feeling less than my best, the client may still get a great insight, invest the most energy, choose risking/changing/growing. For me to do my best work, I must reduce my anxieties about the results of your choices today or of your tomorrows.

Solving a present problem is something we can do together. But you do not have to have a problem to be in therapy with me. The more experienced I get at growing, the more I would like to aid others do likewise. Mostly, now, I believe I am happiest exploring the outer limits, far beyond present problem-solving, where most therapists seem to leave off. Perhaps you are one of the few who want to journey into that beyond.

More and More, I would ideally like to work with only those who have already been "cured" by other therapists.

You can begin to arrive at that place by viewing most emotional problems as problems of attention. If your increasing awareness can unleash you from that old place of attention, you can become unstuck and new things can begin to happen.

J.P. Guilford

CREATIVITY: YESTERDAY, TODAY, AND TOMORROW

The launching of a new journal devoted to the subject of creativity is an appropriate occasion for considering how the study of creativity has evolved, how matters in that subject stand, and what its future may be. The trail of the past is largely on the record, and also some aspects of the present status. The promise for the future can only be inferred from present trends found outside the field of creativity as well as within its borders. Interpretations and predictions are demanding mental exercises, and must inevitably reflect subjective impressions and judgments. And no one who undertakes these exercises is omniscient.

From Galton to 1950

Although geniuses in various fields of human affairs have always been recognized and usually highly valued, it was not until Galton's studies of men of genius (1869) that the eyes of natural science were turned upon them. Galton did not seriously attempt to understand the mental operations by which distinguished leaders produce their novel ideas, but rather he tried to understand the hereditary determination of creative performances. His study became a classic, but he failed to reach uncontestable conclusions.

Reaching an understanding of exceptionally creative people and of the mental operations by which creative productions are achieved should have been the responsibility of psychologists. But early scientific psychologists were having such difficulty with more simple mental events such as sensation, perception, and memory that they had neither time nor the courage to tackle problems of creativity. If anything at all related to the subject was mentioned in the textbooks, it was under the mysterious label of "imagination" or "creative imagination." Usually only passing mention was made of the concept. Then behaviorism swept the field of psychology—in the U.S.A. at least—and such mentalistic concepts were commonly forced off the pages of psychological writing. Only two writers (Schoen, 1930; Guilford, 1939, 1952), each devoting a chapter to the subject, have had much to say about creativity to the beginning student of psychology.

Psychometric Interests in Creativity

One kind of psychologist could not avoid the problem of creativity completely, for he dealt with the many characteristics in which one person differs from another. Among these characteristics are those that prepare some individuals for higher levels of performance, including invention and innovation. The first successful tests of intelligence, from Binet to Terman and others, were aimed at prediction of academic achievement at the elementary level, where almost no attention was given to self-initiated ideas when it came time to evaluate achievement. The selection of abilities to be measured in the first Stanford revision of the Binet scale omitted those especially relevant to the assessment of creative potential, due to an incidental result in a faulty experiment. Terman (1906) had administered to two extreme groups (of seven each, out of 500 subjects who had been ranked for brightness *versus* dullness by their teachers) a set of experimental tests, one of which he recognized as a test of ingenuity. The ingenuity test failed to discriminate the extreme groups, but all the other tests were successful in doing so. Thus, over the

Reprinted by permission of the author and publisher from *Journal of Creative Behavior*, 1967, 1, 1.

years, tests of creative qualities have been almost nonexistent in intelligence scales.

The lack of correlation between tests recognized as belonging in the creative category and tests common to intelligence scales had been noted in isolated studies over the years. Even before Terman's experience with an ingenuity test, Dearborn (1898) had found this relative independence to be true for his tests involving "productive imagination." Over the years, replications of such findings have been reported by Chassell (1916), Andrews (1930), and Welch (1946). Terman could have used Dearborn's finding as evidence supporting his own conclusion that inventive qualities were outside the realm of intelligence, where the latter pertains only to basic academic potential. Or he could have reached the more recently demonstrated conclusion that intelligence, broadly conceived, embraces several components, some of which, at least, do not correlate very much with others. But the prevailing notion was that intelligence was a monolithic ability, all-relevant and unanalyzable.

Anecdotal Studies of Creative Performance

While psychologists were doing very little to attempt to understand creative people and creative production, others, not willing to wait for enlightenment from that source, proceeded to do something about the matter. They recorded instances of discoveries in science, literary productions, and other examples of output from recognized creative geniuses. Samples of this kind of investigation may be seen in the books by Wallas (1945), Hadamard (1945), and Ghiselin (1952). Rossman (1931) made a more systematic study of inventors, utilizing a questionnaire approach.

The weaknesses of anecdotal methods for the purposes of extracting generalizations are well known. Still, such information can be fruitful by suggesting hypotheses that can be explored further by means of more rigorous scientific procedures. The most fruitful outcome of the study of creative episodes was a list of the stages of thinking that a creator typically exhibits in the total process, beginning with the realized need for creative effort and ending in "wrapping up" of the final product. Both Wallas and Rossman proposed steps that take place in the course of the total creative event—

Rossman for inventors, specifically, and Wallas for creative production in general.

Experimental Studies of Creation

A few, but very few, investigators took seriously the creative steps proposed by Wallas—preparation, incubation, illumination, and elaboration. One of them was the psychologist Patrick (1935, 1937, 1938, 1941), who attempted to determine by experiments, mostly within the psychological laboratory whether the Wallas processes could be identified, whether they run their courses in the given order, and what roles each of them play in a complete creative event. She found the process concepts relevant, but that the steps show many departures from the 1-2-3-4 order given by Wallas. The latter conclusion has been supported by similar findings of Eindhoven and Vinacke (1952).

Creative Production in Relation to Age

A more lively and more extensive area of investigation regarding creativity was that pertaining to the ages of life at which the highest quality of creative performances is most likely to occur, and to quantity of creative production as related to age. Studies by Lehman culminated in a book (Lehman, 1953). This kind of study has also been conducted by Dennis (1956).

This thumbnail sketch of the fate of the subject of creativity to midcentury has emphasized only a few points. The subject was almost entirely ignored by psychologists. Psychometric psychologists ruled creative potential out of intelligence, and behaviorists adopted a general viewpoint from which creativity could not be seen. Nonpsychologists made a few attempts to fill the gap, utilizing an anecdotal approach. One beneficial consequence was the suggestion of stages in creative production, which implied hypotheses that could and were investigated experimentally in a preliminary way. Genetic studies, utilizing biographical information, gave attention to the ages at which different degrees of quality and quantity of creative production occur. Almost nothing was learned about the nature of creative thinking itself, except that studies of such rare topics as insight have been shown to be relevant (Guilford, 1967).

14

Creativity Since 1950

Although the year 1950 is generally regarded as the turning point with respect to interest in creativity, and sometimes the writer's APA address (Guilford,1950) is cited as a stimulus, there were indications of other trends in our *Zeitgeist* that converged upon the same effects. The number of publications on the subject had shown some positive acceleration in the 30's and 40's, consistent with the explosive rate of activity of this sort since 1950.

A number of forces were undoubtedly at work. The Second World War had called forth great efforts toward innovation in research and development, culminating in the atomic bomb. The coming of peace that was no peace left us in the cold war, which called for ever-accelerating efforts in a contest of intellects. Inventive brains were at a premium, and there were never enough. We were on the eve of the space age, and rockets were already taking trial flights, stirring out imaginations of things to come. The stage was well set, then ready for the psychologist to play his proper role in trying to fathom the creative person and his creative processes.

As more tangible evidence of the stirrings of interest in creativity, Alex F. Osborn had written his book on *Applied Imagination,* which was ready for publication in 1953. The book was immediately popular, and has gone through numerous printings. The fact that it has been translated into a number of languages indicates that the new attention to the subject has become worldwide. Osborn also founded the *Creative Education Foundation* and the annual *Creative Problem-Solving Institute,* which has been held for twelve years at what is now the State University of New York at Buffalo. The Creative Education Foundation has initiated and is sponsoring the *Journal of Creative Behavior.*

New Investigations of Creativity

The lively research activity since 1950 has been variously motivated and has used several different approaches. There has been much theoretical interest, which leads to asking the questions of what, how, and why. There have been efforts to solve certain practical problems, some of them utilizing information derived from basic studies and some not.

Basic information on the nature of creativity. New research in an area where there has been little precedent is likely to be exploratory, involving little or no hypothesis testing. Such is the case with a number of investigations of the characteristics of people of recognized creative performance, as the study of outstanding scientists by Anne Roe (1952) and the studies of recognized creative writers, architects, and mathematicians, by MacKinnon and Barron, and their associates in the Institute for Personality Assessment and Research as the University of California in Berkeley (MacKinnon, 1960). With a psychoanalytic theoretical bias, these studies emphasized motivational and temperamental characteristics. Some of the salient findings were that highly creative persons, at least in the groups examined, are inclined to be strongly interested in esthetic and theoretical matters and that they tend to be highly intuitive and introverted. As to intellectual status, most of the individuals were in the upper ranges of IQ, and within this range there was practically no correlation between IQ and level of creative performance.

Another major approach, which has emphasized the intellectual qualities that might contribute to creative thinking and creative performance, has been made through application of multivariate methods of factor analysis. The locale of this research has been the Aptitudes Research Project at the University of Southern California, under the writer's direction. Rejecting the prevailing doctrine that intelligence is a single, monolithic ability, and also the view that creative talents are something outside the realm of intelligence, the studies began with the assumption that there are several, perhaps many, distinguishable abilities involved. It was also assumed that creative talents are not confined to a favored few individuals, but are probably widely distributed to different degrees throughout the population. Creative talents could therefore be investigated without being restricted to observation of the gifted few.

The initial factor analysis started with a prior hypothesis as to what distinctions were to be expected among abilities that should be relevant to creative performance. Most of the hypothesized abilities were demonstrated by a factor analysis (Wilson, *et al.,* 1954).

Within a setting of exploration of other

hypothesized intellectual abilities, a general theory of intelligence and its components known as the "structure of intellect" was developed. This theory forecast many distinguishable abilities yet to be demonstrated, many of which could be especially relevant for creative performance. Subsequent factor analyses have supported all the hypothesized abilities that have been investigated. The outcomes of all these studies are summarized, and their implications will be treated in the writer's forthcoming volume on *The Nature of Human Intelligence* (Guilford, 1967).

Briefly, the abilities believed to be most relevant for creative thinking are in two categories. One category is "divergent-production" (DP) abilities. DP abilities pertain to generation of ideas, as in solving a problem, where variety is important. Some DP abilities have been characterized as kinds of fluency, some as kinds of flexibility, and others as elaboration abilities. The varieties of abilities within the DP category depend upon the kind of information with which the person is dealing. This circumstance strongly suggests that creative talents depend upon the media in which the person is working—for example, whether he deals with lines and colors, sounds, or words, as in the various arts.

The other potential source of creative talents is in the category of "transformation" abilities, which pertain to revising what one experiences or knows, thereby producing new forms and patterns. Readiness to be flexible is a general characteristic of this group of talents, where flexibility leads to reinterpretations and reorganizations. Again, the variety of transformation abilities depends upon the kind of information or media with which creators deal.

An important advantage of analyzing creative disposition in terms of abilities is that kinds of abilities also imply kinds of mental functions. Having taken this logical step, we are ready to talk about the process of creative thinking, as such. Discovery of the intellectual factors or abilities answers the question what; applying these answers to operations that the individual performs answers questions of how. Thus, the study of how a creative thinker operates is opened to us, for we have the concepts that we need—the handles that we can grasp in further research efforts.

Some conditions of creative performance. Other traditional research approaches have been used for the problems of creative development and its promotion. Using tests of the kind developed through factor analysis, Torrance (1962) has examined the question of how creative potential changes as a function of age in children and adolescents. He has found that development does not occur at a uniform rate; the most significant departure is the "fourth-grade slump" at about the age of nine. Although the same tests show a leveling-off of averages in the late teens, other tests have shown further development even to the age of 30 (Trembly, 1964). The latter result supports the findings of Lehman, that quality of production commonly reaches its maximum in the early thirties. It is likely, however, that growth curves will be found to differ, depending upon which of the factorial abilities is being measured.

In line with the general optimism about improving abilities through favorable environmental conditions, some studies have been designed to assess improvement in creative activity as a result of various kinds of practice. From the factorial-theory viewpoint, we may regard the relevant abilities as being intellectual skills with some degree of generality. This means that exercises of appropriate kinds should yield improved performance in the abilities concerned. Most of the studies have shown that changes in performance can be assessed and that improvements with some degree of durability do occur. Many of these studies have been conducted by Sidney Parnes and his associates at SUNY Buffalo, and by Irving Maltzman and his associates at UC Los Angeles.

Other experiments have concerned the nature of creative thinking and problem solving, which extensively overlap, to say the least, and with the conditions affecting those phenomena. For example, Torrance and his associates have examined the effects of criticism and other conditions of motivation upon creative performances of school children (Torrance, 1965). Other experimental studies have examined conditions affecting insight or intuition.

As stated earlier, the relation of creative potential and creative production to the traditional IQ has been found close to zero where groups of superior IQ are concerned. This finding has been verified by a number of investigations (*e.g.*, Getzels and Jackson, 1961). But in the lower ranges of IQ there is a substantial correlation. When the whole range of IQ is included, say from 62 to 150, there is a characteristic scatter plot. This plot shows that when the IQ is low, scores on tests of creative potential can only be low. When the IQ is high, there can be a wide range in performance on creative tasks.

Assuming that IQ tests are very much confined to cognitive abilities (and this means essentially to amount of basic information possessed), IQ appears to set an upper limit on creative potential. The relationship described suggests that we have numerous creative underachievers but very few overachievers. A question of utmost educational import is whether ways can be found to bring creative underachievers up to cognitive potential, and whether the latter can also be raised by educational procedures. This is the great educational challenge of the immediate future.

Some Technological Problems

The pressing needs for more creative personnel, especially in the research and development arena, naturally directed considerable effort to finding more creative scientists and engineers, and to conditions in their working milieu that affect performance. The most outstanding example of this kind of effort has been the series of conferences on "The Identification of Creative Scientific Talent," sponsored by the University of Utah, under the leadership of Calvin W. Taylor. Six of these conferences have been held, culminating thus far in the publication of three books of proceedings (Taylor and Barron, 1963; Taylor, 1964; Taylor, 1966). The conferences included reports of basic research as well as technological matters. In pursuit of the main goal of these conferences, Taylor and his associates have tried to develop criteria for evaluating creative-research performance and to design a biographical-data scale for predicting research performance. McPherson and others have given much attention to the circumstances under which research scientists do their work, including problems of supervision.

Torrance and others have studied problems of creative teaching and procedures for developing creative behavior in the classroom. Getzels and Jackson (1961) and others have looked into the relation between scores on creative-thinking tests and measures of achievement in education. The problems of creativity in the educational setting are endless, and the scope of research in this area is rapidly spreading. . . .

Creativity's Future

There seems little doubt that considerable momentum has been generated in investigations of creativity and consequent implementations in education and elsewhere. So many new avenues of theory and ways of investigation have been opened that there should be little loss of momentum; there should, instead, be some continuation of the acceleration that has already been evident. Let us consider next some of the remaining problems, especially in the basic-research setting.

Needs for More Basic Research

Basic future investigations will probably take two major directions: toward a more detailed and complete understanding of the processes of creative thinking, and toward a survey of the conditions that influence creative thinking, positively or negatively.

The nature of creative thinking. It is desirable to conceptualize the roles of fluency, flexibility, and elaboration in the operations of creative production and problem solving in general, in ways that suggest investigative operations. Fluency, for example, is largely a matter of retrieval of information from one's memory store, and comes under the historical concept of recall of learned information. Psychologists have studied the storing of information intensively; they have given relatively little attention to the *uses* of stored information. What little effort has been evident treats only what this writer (Guilford, 1967) has called "replicative recall." Not much has been done with the much more important "transfer recall." How does one get at one's stored information and use it in new connections and in novel ways?

As a deduction from structure-of-intellect theory regarding mental functions, one kind of flexibility is a matter of transformations of information. How are transformations brought about? How is information reinterpreted or redefined so as to adapt it resourcefully to new uses? Another type of flexibility concerns reclassifications. No doubt the classification of items of learned information has much to do with their efficient retrieval. Class ideas determine the areas of search. Each item of information has its "address" or "addresses," to use computer terminology, which help to locate it. Failure to recall may be due to persistence in the use of wrong addresses, a persistence within wrong or too limited classes.

What are the processes of elaboration, and how may they be facilitated? Structure-of-intellect theory conceives of elaboration as a matter of producing implications. What are the various kinds of connections by which one item of information comes to imply another and produces chainlike thinking, each link bringing into view the next? This is really the old problem of association in new dress, envisaged in a way that should be more fruitful in accounting for thinking.

Transformations offer an important key to the understanding of insights or intuitions. The latter are often recognized as sudden changes, and changes are transformations. What are the principles or laws of transformation?

And what of the phenomenon of incubation, on which only one intentional study can be cited? Note that it is classed as a phenomenon rather than a process. It involves a period of relaxation of effort in the total event of solving a problem or producing a creative product. There is no doubt that the phenomenon exists and that some creators use it effectively. Why do some individuals keep a problem open, and keep coming back to it, when others regard early attempts as closed events? What kinds of mental processes occur during incubation? To say that unconscious thinking is going on tells us practically nothing. We have to infer what thinking events took place from the observed behavior of the individual before, during, and after the period of incubation.

Conditions affecting creative thinking. Some of the questions just raised imply that there are determining conditions that affect creative-thinking processes, by way of facilitation or inhibition. Effects of evaluation, critical or otherwise, were touched upon earlier. Absence of self-evaluation while generating ideas has been known as "deferred judgment." There is still much to be learned about when and where evaluation should be applied, for evaluation of some kind there must be, if the end product is to be satisfying in certain respects.

A general source of determination of creative events lies in the area of motivation. In general, what motivates individuals to creative production? To make the question somewhat more specific, which needs, interests, and attitudes help the individual to be productive creatively and which put blocks in his way? How do certain attitudes and emotions affect various steps in the entire creative event? What are their influences upon recall, insight, and elaboration? The answers to all such questions provide bases for increased control over creative events.

Social Consequences

The consequences on the future of mankind of present and future efforts to gain understanding and control of creative performances are incalculable. It is apparent that the solutions to numerous human problems are dependent upon education of the world's population, both extensively and intensively. An informed people, with skills in using its information, is a creative, problem-solving people. In a real sense, mankind is involved in a race between expanding education on the one hand, and threatened disaster, perhaps oblivion, on the other.

To live is to have problems, and to solve problems is to grow intellectually. It is probably safe to say that at no time has a larger number of informed and otherwise intellectually able individuals lived on this planet, yet the problems to be solved seem almost overwhelming—how to keep the peace, how to feed and clothe an expanding population, how to keep the population from expanding too rapidly, and how to educate it. Education in the more enlightened countries has been rather successful in transmitting to younger generations the accomplishments of older generations. But as Torrance (1962) has pointed out, teaching has been much too authoritative. It has not given the younger generation instruction in how to use information in creative ways, or even the opportunity to do so in many cases. Creative education, on the other hand, aims at a self-starting, resourceful, and confident person, ready to face personal, interpersonal and other kinds of problems. Because he is confident, he is also tolerant where there should be tolerance. A world of tolerant people would be one of peaceful and cooperative people. Thus creativity is the key to education in its fullest sense and to the solution of mankind's most serious problems.

References

1. Andrews, E.G. The development of imagination in the preschool child. *University of Iowa Studies in Character*, 1930, 3(4).
2. Chassell, L.M. Tests for originality. *Journal of Educational Psychology*, 1916, 7, 317-329.
3. Dearborn, G.V. A study of imagination. *American Journal of Psychology*, 1898, 5(9), 183.
4. Dennis, W. Age and productivity among scientists. *Science*, 1956, 123, 724-725.
5. Eindhoven, J.E., and Vinacke, W.E. Creative process in painting. *Journal of General Psychology*, 1952, 47, 139-164.
6. Galton, F. *Hereditary genius: An inquiry into its laws and consequences.* New York: Appleton, 1869.
7. Getzels, J.W., and Jackson, P.W. *Creativity and intelligence.* New York: Wiley, 1961.
8. Ghiselin, B. *The creative process.* Berkeley: Univ. of California Press, 1952; New York: Mentor, 1955.
9. Guilford, J.P. Creativity. *American Psychologist*, 1950, 5, 444-454.
10. ———.*General psychology.* Princeton, N.J.: D. Van Nostrand, 1939, 1952.
11. ———. *The nature of human intelligence.* New York: McGraw-Hill, 1967.
12. Hadamard, J.S. *An essay on the psychology on invention in the mathematical field.* Princeton, N.J.: Princeton Univ. Press, 1945.
13. Lehman, H.C. *Age and achievement.* Princeton, N.J.: Princeton Univ. Press, 1953.
14. MacKinnon, D.W. The highly effective individual. *Teachers College Record*, 1960, 61, 367-378.
15. McPherson, J.H. Environment and training for creativity. In C.W. Taylor (ed.), *Creativity: Progress and potential.* New York: McGraw-Hill, 1964, 130-153.
16. Osborn, A.F. *Applied imagination.* Rev. ed. New York: Scribners, 1963.
17. Patrick, C. Creative thought in poets. *Archives of Psychology*, New York, 1935, 26, 1-74.
18. ———. Creative thought in artists. *Journal of Psychology*, 1937, 4, 35-73.
19. ———. Scientific thought. *Journal of Psychology*, 1938, 5, 55-83.
20. ———. Whole and part relationship in creative thought, *American Journal of Psychology*, 1941, 54, 128-131.
21. Roe, Anne. *The making of a scientist.* New York: Dodd, Mead, 1952.
22. Rossman, J. *The psychology of the inventor.* Washington, D.C.: Inventors Publishing Co., 1931.
23. Schoen, M. *Human nature. A first book in psychology.* New York: Harper, 1930.
24. Taylor, C.W. (ed.) *Instructional media and creativity.* New York: Wiley, 1966.
25. ———. *Widening horizons in creativity.* New York: Wiley, 1964.
26. Taylor, C.W., and Barron, F. *Scientific creativity: Its recognition and development.* New York: Wiley, 1963.
27. Terman, L.M. Genius and stupidity: A study of some of the intellectual processes of seven "bright" and seven "stupid" boys. *Pedagogical Seminary*, 1906, 13, 307-373.
28. Torrance, E.P. *Guiding creative talent.* Englewood Cliffs, N.J.: Prentice-Hall, 1962.
29. ———. *Rewarding creative behavior.* Englewood Cliffs, N.J.: Prentice-Hall, 1965.
30. Trembly, D. Age and sex differences in creative thinking potential. *American Psychologist*, 1964, 19, 516. (Abstract)
31. Wallas, G. *The art of thought.* London: C.A. Watts, 1945.
32. Welch, L. Recombination of ideas in creative thinking. *Journal of Applied Psychology*, 1946, 30, 638-643.
33. Wilson, R.C., Guilford, J.P., Christensen, P.R., and Lewis, D.J. A factor analytic study of creative-thinking abilities. *Psychometrika*, 1954, 19, 297-311.

BRIDGING THE CREATIVITY-INNOVATION GAP

John Gardner (1965) has said: "Perhaps the most distinctive thing about innovation today is that we are beginning to pursue it systematically. . . . What may be most in need of innovation is the corporation itself. Perhaps what every corporation (and every other organization) needs is a department of continuous renewal that would view the whole organization as a system in need of continuing innovation." Fortunately, many corporations are now initiating programs in organizational development. Executives are seeing more clearly that they cannot maintain a system without innovation, nor innovate without maintaining the system. Organizations must face the challenge of balancing the maintenance demands and the innovation demands.

New Order

On the other hand, as Machiavelli has written, "There is nothing more difficult to carry out, nor more doubtful of success, nor more dangerous to handle, than to initiate a new order of things."

"Initiating a new order of things" is precisely what is involved in organizational innovation. Modern corporations and organizations of all kinds are finding that Machiavelli's words contain a truism more and more relevant to their daily ventures.

Fork in the Road

A large part of the problem is a result of divergence in research trends. One trend leads investigators to attempt the formulation of a theory of innovative behavior in organizations; another trend leads investigators into an analysis of individual creativity. On the surface, there appears to be no real divergence and one might wonder briefly why these trends should not in fact overlap. But let us urge a distinction between innovation and invention.

Invention is the product of an original, elaborating, highly creative thinker who can usually generate novel ideas rather fluently. (He cannot always translate them into action as easily, however, if he is able to do it at all.) Inventions need not occur within an organization by any means, and probably will not unless the organization has at least one original thinker.

Innovation, on the other hand, is an organizational or social process that usually follows invention but can be separated from it in time and place.

This, then, is the difference: invention is individual, innovation is organizational, or basically a cooperative group action. Becker and Whisler (1967), for instance, after reviewing the literature on innovation in organizations, define the term as the initial or early use of an idea by one of a set of organizations with similar goals.

Examining the Paths

Once innovation in defined in these terms, the theoretical problem is to explain what predisposes or equips an organization to become a leader. As stated, research to date has tended to keep separate these two characteristics—invention and innovation—and as a result we know a great deal more about creativity in individuals than we know about innovation in organizations.

Organizational Research

Why should this be so? Becker and Whisler reach a major conclusion after spotlighting various

Reprinted by permission of the publisher from *Journal of Creative Behavior*, spring, 1969, 3(2), 84-89.

research studies in organizational behavior (Shepard, 1967; Knight, 1967; Becker & Stafford, 1967; Evan & Black, 1967; and Carroll, 1967). Most previous empirical work was cross-sectional, where statistical relationships were established between selected inputs and outputs. The results have not been very encouraging. This is not too surprising because all four steps of the process are treated as an intervening variable: that is, the researchers look first at inputs across a number of organizations prior to the adoption of an innovation, and then they relate those inputs to the various outputs.

Innovation actually seems to be not a single variable but an attenuated, complex process in which many critical variables operate. Considering this, longitudinal analysis probably would be more productive, even at the level of single case studies.

Shepard (1967) makes motions toward bridging the gap between individual creativity and organizational innovation, but he does not really make the final point because his primary focus is actually on the organizations themselves. And, his concept of an innovator in innovation-resisting organizations is very like that highly original thinker described in the creativity research. Such a creative innovator needs a unique combination of qualities: an original yet pragmatic imagination; psychological security and autonomy; the gift of trusting and earning the trust of others; great and determined energy; sense of timing; organizing ability; and a willingness and skill to be Machiavellian when it is needed.

Other research has identified some relatively creative personalities employed in organizations and has also described at least one industry which has set up programs to identify and nurture highly original thinkers (Dauw, 1966, 1967, 1968 a, b). Yet it is not clearly known whether these original thinkers have been able to actually effect any innovations as distinct from inventions. Interestingly, the most certain fact known about them is that their turnover rates are at least twice as high as their less creative peers' (Dauw, 1967). One might conclude, then, that they have relatively little opportunity to perform much innovation. Future research will have to determine where these original thinkers eventually are able to find an environment that will nurture their creativity or whether their growing frustrations induce personality changes.

Their creative thinking abilities may tend to diminish or "ossify" before significant (or any) innovations can occur.

Individual Research

Now let us turn to the other research trend: most creativity research identifies and studies original inventors. The typical subjects range from eminent architects (MacKinnon, 1962) to highly creative grade schoolers (Torrance, 1962, 1965). Most of these individuals are isolated outside of organizations. Furthermore, a great many of the findings from these studies have been applied in the development of programs for improving individual creative problem-solving abilities; few findings have gone into the construction of programs for training individuals to be increasingly better innovators. That is, we can show engineers how to become more original, inventive thinkers who can churn out patents in the hot-house-nursery settings of various industrial laboratories, but so far we have not really been able to teach managers and executives how to innovate more effectively. (See, for example, Dauw's summary [1966] of the research on managerial creativity in organizations.) The problem is being approached indirectly by the entire human relations "sensitivity" movement, which helps managers better understand themselves and their impact on peer groups, so that they eventually can work more harmoniously together. (Bradford, *et al.,* 1964; Schein & Bennis, 1965; see also the *Journal of Applied Behavioral Science* literature on sensitivity training and T-grouping.)

The point, then, seems clear: creativity research has identified some original thinkers who are mostly—if not exclusively—in private practice or isolated settings; organization-innovations-theory has led to much related research and theorizing about innovations, but little, if any, parallel research on the personalities of successful innovators-in-organizations.

A Documentation

An example of this latter type of research is available in O'Connell's monograph (1968), which eminently chronicles a major innovation (some theorists might call it "change") in the insurance industry. The monograph details the work of a major consulting firm helping one of the world's largest insurance companies to reorganize their nationwide branch office structure.

O'Connell's first chapter tentatively approaches "a theory of organizational change." His next five chapters marshal the evidence. Finally, organization theorists can delight in his last two chapters concluding the "planning" and "controlling" of change.

One major element seems lacking, however. Apparently, no attempt was made to understand the personalities of the innovating consultants. Were they really creative? Or were they merely skillful manipulators who succeeded partly because of a corporation's desperate plight?

An Observation

These consultants may very well have been highly creative. On the other hand, my own employment experience with two management consulting firms (and my close friendship with consultants) has led me to observe that a high degree of creativity is rarely a characteristic of career consultants. Thus, it is a possiblity that the consultants' success in the project recorded by O'Connell may have resulted from the interaction of their Machiavellian skills; hard, honest labor; and an additional combination of organizational needs and attitudes.

Suggestions and Questions

Looking at O'Connell's evidence and taking into consideration other studies cited here, it would seem that one of the most necessary and fruitful areas of research to help bridge the creativity-innovation gap is the identification of really successful, innovating change agents. After identification, they should be studied as an experimental group—possibly using as a control group managers and executives with identical backgrounds, such as education, family, and so forth. Obviously, a longitudinal study of the kind that will eventually become possible because of "Project Talent"—type data would be more fruitful than a cross-section research plan.

Research for Growth and Progress

Such a study may enable us to understand more fully Shepard's (1967) hypotheses about in-

novating change agents. Perhaps their innovating talent is more of a "halo effect," or the result of various felicitous environmental circumstances. That is, possibly the most potent innovator is ineffective unless his work coincides with a crisis of series of crises that put people in a mood to accept innovation. If this is true, organizations should know it and they should also know what to look for in and expect from innovators.

Innovation is an organizational tool for growth and progress—for change, in other words—just as maintenance is a tool for continued existence. If an organization is to continue existing, however, it must do more than merely "maintain" itself; it must "keep up with the times," which means it has to change as society changes. It's doubtful that this can be done without research into the nature of innovation, action and change; and to date, industrial research has not commonly had as its goal the acquisition of new knowledge. Berry (1967) suggests that personnel researchers in industry, because of the nature of their function as *they seem* to define it, conduct studies to solve people problems and to make needed changes in the firm's behavior system. Although action and change should be among the goals of research and should be built into the research design, the investigators interviewed by Berry did not seem to consider implementation as a neccessary variable or goal. Because of this, the organizational utilization of the personnel research function has been restricted and limited. Berry concluded that until implementation is visualized as a research variable and is built into the research program, these departments will find their organizational growth rates and impact limited.

It may well be that this is exactly where the gap can be bridged. Innovation may be more readily accomplished by a creative person rather than by a typical change agent because he can build in the implementation phase. Since we already have so much literature on the creative person, particularly those outside of existing organizations, we need now to turn our research attention to innovations and the creative person's relationship to them. In other words, we already have a certain amount of information regarding the organization's impact on the creative personality; we now need, along with research into the nature of innovation as defined here, information regarding the impact of the creative individual on his organization. Business, industry, and society at large all are affected by change, and they should be equally interested in its agents.

References

1. Becker, S.W. and Stafford, F. Some determinants of organizational success. *J. of Business*, 1967, 40, 511-518.
2. Becker, S.W. and Whisler, T.L. The innovative organization: A selective view of current theory and research. *J. of Business*, 1967, 40, 462-469.
3. Berry, D.F. *Politics of personnel research.* Ann Arbor: Univ. of Michigan Press, 1967.
4. Bradford, L.P., Gibb, J.R., and Benne, K.D. *T-group theory and laboratory method.* New York: John Wiley & Sons, 1964.
5. Carroll, Jean. A note on departmental anatomy and innovation in medical schools. *J. of Business*, 1967, 40, 531-534.
6. Dauw, D.C. Creativity in organizations. *Personnel J.*, 1966, 45, 465-474.
7. ———. Vocational interests of highly creative computer personnel. *Personnel J.*, 1967, 46, 653-659.
8. ———. Creativity research on computer personnel. Life Office Management Association: *Personnel Quart.*, May, 1968a, 1-3.
9. ———. Creativity research on actuaries. *J. of Creat. Behav.*, 1968b, 2, 274-280.
10. Evan, W.M. and Black, G. Innovation in business organizations: Some factors associated with success or failure of staff proposals. *J. of Business*, 1967, 40, 519-530.
11. Gardner, J.W. *Self renewal.* New York: Harper & Row, 1965.
12. Knight, K.E. A description model of the intra-firm innovation process. *J. of Business*, 1967, 40, 478-498.
13. MacKinnon, D.W. The nature and nurture of creative talent. *Amer. Psychol.*, 1962, 17, 484-495.
14. O'Connell, J.J. *Managing organizational innovation.* Homewood, Ill.: R.D. Irwin, Inc., 1968.
15. Sapolsky, H.M. Organizational structure and innovation. *J. of Business*, 1967, 40, 497-510.
16. Schein, E.H. and Bennis, W.G. *Personal and organizational change through group methods.* New York: John Wiley & Sons, 1965.
17. Shepard, H.A. Innovation-resisting and innovation-producing organizations. *J. of Business*, 1967, 40, 470-477.
18. Torrance, E.P. *Rewarding creative behavior: Experiments in classroom creativity.* Englewood Cliffs, N.J.: Prentice-Hall, 1965.

CREATIVITY IN ORGANIZATIONS

The purpose of this article is threefold: first to review recent research about aiding individuals through deliberate training programs and personnel policies to function more creatively; second, to discuss the effectiveness of seminars to help business men liberate their creativity; and third, to analyze the psychometric science and art in predicting at least two kinds of creativity in business.

The President of Bell and Howell, P.G. Peterson, attending a seminar on creativity at the University of Chicago in 1962, stated:

> "Perhaps we should break down creativity into various types. Much of what goes on in business is not the creativity that many of these gentlemen (participants in the seminar) are talking about—not fundamental understanding, basic breakthroughs, etc., but just minor adaptations of things you know how to do. . . .90 percent of what business men would call creativity is really a different kind of creativity from what many of you have talked about."[1]

His statement has recently been confirmed by research where more than one type of creativity was hypothesized.[2] E. Paul Torrance's Tests of Creative Thinking[3] have successfully isolated two kinds of creativity, after years of research and validation that extended the initial impetus to study creativity provided by J.P. Guilford in his 1950 presidential address to the American-Psychological Association.

The movement toward developing creativity has been growing rapidly. Over 100,000 businessmen have taken at least one course in applied imagination in the U.S. during the last decade. Methods of applied imagination are known to have been taught in more than 150 courses at more than 200 colleges and universities.[4]

The need for increasing creativity in business has been felt for some time. Writing in the *Harvard Business Review* in 1955, F.D. Randall insisted that management "must learn to mine the creativity within its own ranks—the inventiveness and imagination buried by the pursuit of specialization, systematization and control." He further argued that executives, in their zeal to use the rare talents of a few imaginative men, often "tend to overlook a virtually untapped asset—the natural creativity of the average executive."[5]

The reasons vary within individuals and organizations as to just why executives' creativity is often untapped. One explanation was expressed well by A.H. Maslow of Brandeis University:

> "I had, like most other people, unconsciously confined creativeness to certain conventional areas of human endeavor. That is, I unconsciously assumed that any painter was leading a creative life—any poet, any composer. Theorists, artists, scientist, inventors, and writers could be creative. Nobody else could be. You were in or you were out, all or none, as if creativeness was the sole prerogative of certain professionals.[6]

This natural hesitancy on the part of psychologists to study creativity received an impetus from Guilford in 1950. Since then, at least seven national conferences on creativity have been sponsored by the National Science Foundation and the University of Utah, the results of which have been well summarized by C.W. Taylor.[7]

Definition of Creativity

Successful business entrepreneurs have been ably practicing the art of creativity for years, by continually seeking more innovative ways to do a job. They are actually functioning creatively without consciously viewing themselves as being original.

Reprinted by permission of *Personnel Journal*, September, 1966, 45 (8), 465-474.

If creativity and its growth are to be considered scientifically, however, as Torrance notes,[8] creativity has to be defined in a way that permits objective observation and measurement and is consonant with common, historical usage.

Some definitions are stated in terms of a product (*e.g.,* inventions); others, in terms of a process, a kind of person, or a set of conditions. Included in most definitions is the production of something new. Some writers define creativity as being different from conformity and as requiring nonhabitual rather than habitual behavior. Some insist that a creative contribution must be true, generalizing and surprising in the light of existing conditions. Some scholars argue that the term "creative" be reserved only for very rare or peculiar abilities, while others expand the concept to apply in a general way to all essentially healthy people. Still others suggested different levels of creativity, ranging from simple, expressive creativity, where skills and quality are nonessential, as in childrens' spontaneous scribblings, to a type of creativity that is manifested in a completely new principle or assumption from which entirely new developments flourish.

On the basis of these diverse analyses of creativity, Torrance initially focused his definition as:

> "the process of becoming sensitive to problems, deficiencies, gaps in knowledge, missing elements, disharmonies, and so on; identifying the difficulty; searching for solutions, making guesses or formulating hypotheses about the deficiencies; testing and retesting them; and finally communicating the results." [8]

Torrance's definition describes a natural human process. Intense personal needs are involved at each stage. If one senses any incompleteness or disharmonies, tensions are aroused. Because habitual behaviors are inadequate, one begins trying to avoid the common, obvious (but incorrect) solutions by investigating, manipulating, and making guesses or estimates. Until the hypotheses have been tested, modified and retested, one is still uncomfortable. Finally, the tension may remain unrelieved until the discovery is revealed to others.

Many other reasons for favoring this definition are presented by Torrance,[8] and pertinent objections against it are answered. One objection, for example, suggests that Torrance's definition does not distinguish between creativity or creative problem solving and other types of (intellectual) problem solving. Some hold that it equates creativity with all thinking. Obviously, one limitation of any brief definition is that only a few distinctions can be made explicit. Certainly implicit in Torrance's definition are those scholarly distinctions usually made between creative thinking and problem solving. Generally, creative thinking has been treated as one particular kind of problem solving. Newell, Shaw, and Simon maintain that any problem solving may be creative

> "to the extent that one or more of the following conditions are satisfied:
> 1. The product of the thinking has novelty and value.
> 2. The thinking is unconventional, requiring modior rejection of previous ideas.
> 3. The thinking requires high motivation and persistence over a long span of time (continuously or intermittently) or at high intensity.
> 4. The problem as initially posed was undefined, so that part of the task was to formulate the problem itself." [9]

The Creative Process

Surprising, if tentative, conclusions have resulted from research on the creative process in the past two decades. Perhaps the most startling finding is that there seems to be little correlation between creativity (divergent thinking) and scores on traditional intelligence and/or aptitude tests that measure convergent thinking. C.W. Taylor of the University of Utah stated:

> "Getzels and Jackson . . . at the University of Chicago and Torrance . . . at Minnesota have reported that if an IQ test is used to select top level talent, about 70% of the persons who have the highest 20% of the scores on a creativity test battery will be missed." [10]

In 1959, Guilford had identified "90 different" mental abilities in his structure of intellect model where 120 may actually exist. He concluded "IQ tests have concentrated on a very few factors in the structure of the intellect." [11]

A second research result is a corollary of the above. It is the hypothesis that nurturing creativity is not a question of increasing one's ability to score high on an IQ test, but a matter of improving one's mental attitudes and habits and cultivating creative skills that have lain dormant since childhood.

A third major research result found that differences in age, sex, and years of education have little effect on the capability of professional individuals to function creatively. [12]

Folklore seems to be upheld by research in that persistent effort is basic to creativity, especially when bolstered by long-term dreaming and believing in one's goal.

Roadblocks to Creativity

The need and value of developing proper attitudes and habits to nurture creativity is apparent when one harkens back to early childhood. Torrance's extensive research[13] showed that all children are born with a certain amount of creative thinking abilities. During nursery school or kindergarten, however, the child is forced more and more to conform to established patterns of thought and behavior. All these pressures of mass education and group activities develop inhibitions in the child that block some of his creative urges. Thus, many creative thinking abilities are either stultified completely or never developed beyond initial stages.

A brief overview of these mental blocks and inhibitions will lead into an analysis of actual training in industry. Arnold has called them perceptual blocks, cultural blocks and emotional blocks.[14]

The perceptual blocks are those inhibitions preventing one from getting valid, or relevant information from the persons, things, or situations observed. We always tend to see what we want to see. And one usually expects to see what he is in the habit of seeing. That is why one often feels like kicking himself for not having seen the answer sooner.

Consider as one example the nine dots problem in the following diagram.[15]

Problem

· · ·

· · ·

· · ·

(The solution can be found at the end of this article.)

Connect all nine dots with four consecutive movements of your pen without lifting it from the paper. Most people cannot solve it because they do not look at it in broad perspective. As soon as they let their pens go beyond the confines of the big square, they can get the solution quickly.

Cultural blocks are social inhibitions resulting from our culture that prevent one from being his independent, creative self. One example is the need or desire to conform to accepted patterns. Another example is the old maxim that it is a waste of time to indulge in fantasy. Or one may put too much faith in reason or logic.

Emotional blocks can be even more tragic. These are the fears and defense mechanisms presumably indulged in to make one's life more tolerable. Everyone fears making a mistake or making a fool of oneself. Too often one latches onto the first practical idea that comes to mind. Other emotional blocks may be anxiety, over-motivation, prejudice, and negativism. Within this category can be included Bower's[16] causes for the low birth rate of ideas.

This brief outline of the creative process and the blocks to it can be reassuring to the business executive aspiring to nurture creativity within his organization. The situation is not a job of converting ordinary executives and supervisors into geniuses. Rather, the task involves shifting attitudes and habits by providing the environment and training that can cultivate whatever innate talent business executives already possess.

Mental Tools

Various methods have been adapted to nurture the mental attitudes, skills and thinking habits of the creative person. Some of the most frequently used conceptual devices or tools, according to Whiting[17] are: the traditional scientific problem-solving framework, the principle of deferred (postponed) judgment, systematic self-questioning, the basic laws of association, analogous reasoning, morphological analysis, check lists, and forced relationship techniques.

A brief overview of the nature and interaction of the first three devices mentioned gives an idea of how such concepts are involved in the creative process.

Scientific Problem-Solving Procedures

The heart of the creative process is the traditional, scientific method of solving problems. The real answers to complex problems may not always (if ever) follow a vigorous sequence of steps, but visualizing the process as a series of steps facilitates efforts to integrate other tools of creative thinking into the process. One sequence is the following: problem recognition; problem definition; problem analysis (dissection); fact-finding; alternative solution-finding; solution selection; solution implementation and development; and solution cultivation or follow-up over a period of time. Thus, the foregoing outline can serve as a framework within which the other tools are useful.

Principle of Deferred Judgment

The popular press usually views it as a way to dream up alternative solutions to problems, but it is used to advantage at any or all steps in the problem-solving process. The idea is to "throw caution to the wind" momentarily while using check lists of questions to create large quantities of ideas. When the long list of ideas has been recorded or taped, the process of judging and developing the ideas is begun. This technique is often called "brainstorming" or "free-wheeling ideation." As a thought-starter, it is equally beneficial for individuals or groups but usually yields best results when individual thinking is supplemented with group ideation.

Osborn's four rules for this free-wheeling are:

1. *Postpone criticism* until after spontaneous ideation session.
2. *Try to free-wheel.* "The wilder the idea, the better; it is easier to tame down than tame up."
3. *Seek quantity.* "The greater the number of ideas, the more the likelihood of useful ideas."
4. *Seek combination and improvement.* "Participants should suggest how ideas of others can be turned into better ideas: or how two or more ideas can be joined into still another idea."[18]

The success of these techniques is partially explained by C.R. Rogers' theory of creativity. One of his main points is that people greatly fear ridicule. Because people consider it dangerous to be original, psychological safety and freedom are basic conditions for nurturing creativity.

> "For the individual to find himself in an atmosphere where he is not being evaluated, not being measured by some external standard, is enormously freeing. Evaluation is always a threat, always creates a need for defensiveness, always means that some portion of experience must be denied to awareness."[19]

A second reason for the extraordinary productivity of this device is its time-saving nature. By not discussing an idea until many have been produced, much time can be saved. Then only the most promising ideas need be discussed. Finally, one concept that is poor in itself might become practical when combined with a few others.

One final value of this deferment lies in what could be termed the principle of mental leverage. Imagine a problem as a weight to be lifted, and the mind as another weight on the opposite side of the fulcrum on the same lever. By dividing the problem solving (lifting the burden) into two parts—the creative and the judicial—and by focusing the whole mind on one task and then on the other, one's mind were shifted to a position farther from the fulcrum. Furthermore, team play in both brainstorming and judging can furnish even more leverage.

Systematic Self-Questioning

The self-query device employs check lists of idea-spurring questions to seek new viewpoints. In connection with deferred judgment and the three laws of association (continuity, similarity, and contrast), self-questioning is especially useful in prodding the mind to consider simple but basic possibilities, many of which may have been overlooked by authorities in the past. The approach (intimately connected with elaborative creativity to be discussed later) permits exploration of many aspects of a problem systematically and spontaneously.

J.G. Mason, a pioneer in applied imagination, identified[20] four different types of questions, each designed for a different kind of problem. The first type includes those that define or uncover problems. Examples are: Can we make it do more things? Can we eliminate excess parts? If so, new ways to improve the product are indicated.

A second category of questions is designed to get extra facts (or to indicate extra facts to look for) as one delves deeper into a problem. Examples are: Can we sell it? Can we make it ourselves? What investment is involved?

A third type of question leads to ideas. Osborn's[12] check list elaborates on questions like: modify? magnify? substitute? etc.

Decision-making questions form the fourth type of check list. Examples are: Does it improve safety? Does it reduce cost? Is it practical? Mason cautions one not to let the check list become a substitute for imagination, but rather be a spur to imagination.

Training Programs in Creative Thinking

Programs in creative problem solving function best as laboratory seminars where informality and humor prevail. Yet the learning is serious in nature, embracing difficult and important problems, real or hypothetical, that are used as the basis for challenging exercises applying the principles studied. Ideally, ten to twenty individuals comprise a seminar group. The flexible length of the course can vary from ten to fifty hours of learning time in a few days or spread over weeks. Courses have been offered for selected groups such as men in industry, education, etc. Some innovators, however, are now preparing seminars for groups within one company: *e.g.*, the engineers, the sales force and the like. In fact, research has already shown the better salesmen are much more creative than their less successful peers. Wallace[21] found that sales personnel ranking in the upper third on sales in a large department store scored significantly higher on tests of creative thinking than did those who ranked in the lower third. He also found that the more creative women had tended to gravitate to those departments judged by personnel managers as requiring more creativity.[22]

Seminar Objectives

A training program's goal is primarily to help an individual receive some benefits of creativity, rather than to make him a creative genius. A typical seminar includes these goals: (1) To survey the proven procedures; (2) To furnish individual and group experience; (3) To encourage a more open-minded attitude; (4) To initiate a lifetime of discovering, and using more of one's latent, creative powers.

Seminar Content

Training focuses on the traditional, scientific problem-solving process with various creative exercises spotlighting the innovative, adventurous spirit of science. Creative procedures, especially spontaneous ideation, are used at each step from problem recognition stage on through to implementation and follow-up. Each session involves both individual and group activities. Practice exercises highlight all the steps in the process. Additional exercises focus on just one or two phases of the procedure.

In the problem sensitivity stage, participants are encouraged within five minutes to name—a la brainstorming—all possible improvements on some object or situation. Then one of these suggested innovations can be selected for detailing as the next problem to be solved.

Using deferment-of-judgment, the problem is then outlined in different ways at various levels of abstraction. The most practical definition is selected and its sub-problems isolated, each of which may be analyzed by itself or in connection with other sub-problems.

The next stage includes grouping the tentative solutions, vetoing the unpromising ones and processing the remainder. Even at this evaluation stage, the principle of suspended judgment may be used to seek elaborations in some impractical but otherwise good ideas to make them workable. After the most promising solution has been chosen, a free-wheeling exercise might produce ways of testing or implementing it. Finally, all that remains is spontaneous ideation to develop a follow-up program that might lead to eventual success of the operation.

In actual business and professional life, however, the principle of suspended judgment is seldom employed at each stage. It may be required at only one or another step, if at all, in some problems; in others, conditions may warrant other devices or approaches. In the creative problem-solving seminar, however, suspended judgment is applied to all the steps so that the participant may learn to use it whenever needed in the future.

Seminar Materials

Osborn's[12] text leads the list of valuable materials available. The Creative Education Foundation (1614 Rand Building, Buffalo, N.Y.) also supplies a 152-page *Instructor's Manual* a 140-page *Student workbook, and a Supplementary Guide* containing 241 problems for participants' exercises.

The Validity and Value of Results

A business executive must evaluate a training program or seminar in creativity in the light of its possible influence on the mental health attitudes and morale of his employees, as well as on the long-range utility to his organization before committing himself to such a program. The creativity movement certainly is not a transitory educational fad that has attracted many only to fade out after the novelty has passed.

Look at some results that might be viewed as psychological and financial benefits.

Enhancement of Mental Abilities and Attitudes

Psychologists have scientifically researched these training courses during the past decade. Some of the best summaries are those by Taylor,[7, 23] Taylor and Barron,[24] Barron[25] and other volumes already cited.

Torrance[26] has especially emphasized how the development of the divergent thinking abilities helps one cope with stress constructively. These divergent abilities require flexibility. Flexibility is one of the hallmarks of the creative person, just as rigidity is a symptom of those suffering from emotional problems.

At Buffalo, Parnes[27] researched the increase of measured creativity, using large experimental and control groups. The tests investigated individual rather than group thinking.

> His more significant findings were that:
> 1. Creative imagination can be deliberately developed.
> 2. Courses in creative problem solving can measurably improve the ability of students with average intelligence to generate unique and useful ideas. They could produce 125% more good ideas.

Guilford[11] showed that the divergent thinking abilities measured by tests are in fact related to performance in everyday life.

Although few organizations have had professional psychologists to measure attitudes changed by such programs, improvements in morale, self-confidence, tolerance and leadership have been reported in most participants.

Profit Gains

Increased profits have been the most outstanding, consistent benefits of training programs in applied imagination. Sylvania Electronics Systems, for example, claimed that each dollar spent resulted in twenty dollars saved, after a course for 1,300 of the 7,000 engineers expected to enroll.[4] Similarly, Sikorsky Aircraft Corp. of Stratford, Conn. calculated fifteen dollars saved for every dollar spent on their 300 engineers. The U.S. Secretary of defense, Robert McNamara reportedly estimated savings in the defense budget that exceeded one hundred million dollars as a result of creative emphasis programs.[28] Many additional examples are detailed throughout the literature, and most recently by Bower.[16]

Limitations

Advantages however, like blessings, are seldom unmixed. The limitations of increases in applied imagination are obviously associated with all the benefits. The programs will rekindle whatever spark of creative talent is possessed by the participants. This spark could unfortunately be snuffed out by the wrong administrative environment. Top management must be solidly behind the program before positive results are realized. Employees contributing good ideas must be recognized, lest their efforts be diminished by frustration.

A second limitation results from the fact that increased rates of improvement in an organization inexorably mean an increased rate of change. Improvements can easily lead to jealousy and friction. Thus, top management and employees all need to be tolerant, self-confident, and flexible.

Third, sudden success can be dangerous. In the initial excitement over so many good ideas, businessmen might forget that no idea is valuable in the practical realm unless at least one idea is put into operation. There is a need for systematic evaluation, development and implementation.

Finally, in addition to the major mental blocks already mentioned, there also exists the special fear in employees of losing their jobs. Management must assure them that their enthusiastic ideas and savings will not eliminate their jobs. Here is where executives' creativity and flexibility can open up new jobs by increased sales and other means.

Predicting Creative Performance

In addition to liberating creativity in individuals and using it effectively, management also needs to attract new and more creative employees. Research in this area of predicting creative performance has been mounting steadily. Good summaries include those of Stein and Heinze,[29] Taylor and Holland,[30] and Steiner.[1]

The best general conclusion is that noticeable progress has been made, although many questions remain unanswered. The hallmarks of a creative individual, those personality characteristics that especially distinguish him, can be measured—at least in part—by simple paper and pencil test or other controlled observations. Although the instruments are admittedly imperfect, they are much more valid and reliable than an executive's casual judgment. Thus, as in all actuarial predictions of this kind, [31] the procedure becomes more valuable as the number of cases to be predicted increases. If many people are to be chosen, and it is necessary that some be highly creative, testing programs can improve the odds. Examples of this application include graduate students, research and development officers in the armed services or researchers in large industrial laboratories.

If only a few individuals are to be chosen, however, where each one must be highly creative (e.g., top executives; scientists to lead projects; etc.), careful personal appraisal and judgment can be used alone or in conjunction with psychometric instruments. In some instances, there is an undocumented suggestion that highly creative individuals may themselves be good judges of creativity in others. Advertising agency executives would put more credence in the considered judgment of another highly creative person who knew the candidate well. An ad-man naturally feels he can recognize original products as they fit into the context of his agency's programs. But, usually, in organizational recruiting, no one really knows the applicants well. So, this would be an advantage of the use of tests when large samples of people are available.[32]

The author has found one technique valuable. Ask an applicant without forewarning to outline any or all projects of special interest to him. Have him detail all innovations and elaborations he has privately thought about. The highly creative candidate who is fluent and flexible already has available many extracurricular interests in objects, situations, or projects along with original suggestions for improvement. (A phonograph record has also been developed that shows promise in both long-range research and prediction in current situations.)[33]   Approaches such as the above are especially valuable when the judge realizes creativity can be manifested in more than one way.

Originality and Elaboration

Here is precisely where recent research has indicated two distinct kinds of creativity: originality and elaboration, as measured by two scales of the Torrance Tests of Creative Thinking. Executives were not used in the study because their services are so difficult to enlist. From an initial population of 720 public high school seniors in a large Midwestern metropolis, Dauw[2] isolated those boys and girls who scored highest in originality; those highest in elaboration; and those highest in both abilities combined. These experimental groups were matched with adequate control groups who scored lowest in these abilities. (It was clearly established that creativity alone was being measured and not intelligence, by the very low positive correlations between the creativity tests and scholastic aptitude tests. In addition, there was a large proportion of highly intelligent students in the low creative groups, which supported the research already cited by Torrance and Getzels and Jackson.)

The highly original individuals were shown to have personality characteristics distinctly different from the highly elaborating persons.[34] These two groups of creative persons also manifested personalities that were different from those highest in both abilities combined. The interaction of both originality and elaboration together was evidenced clearly in the personalities of these individuals as distinguished from those who were only highly original or only highly elaborating.

These results were further confirmed by the histories of the creative individuals. The recollected life experiences of the highly original persons revealed that their parents had raised them in ways that clearly differed from the manner in which the highly elaborating individuals were raised.[35]

Thus, psychologists are now more aware of at least two kinds of highly creative personalities. They can better understand that the circumstances which induce an Edison to produce more of the same—to elaborate earlier inventions—may be quite distinct from those conditions that produce the initial innovations.

It may not at all be so much a question of the climate in a creative organization (whether one is creating productivity or producing creativity), but rather a question of just who are the really creative people and how do they differ from each other.

These differences in highly creative individuals have been apparent for sometime, but previously had not been researched. For example, Maslow[36] discussed primary and secondary creatives. Mackworth[37] called them problem-finders and problem-solvers. Leary[38] suggested creative-creators and reproductive-creators. Therefore, Dauw's research[34] seems to indicate that original thinkers may be very like the primary creatives, the problem-finders and the creative-creators. In the same way, the elaborating thinkers may be similar to the secondary creatives, the problem-solvers and the reproductive-creators. This research seems to answer some questions raised by executives as they seek or deal with more than one kind of highly creative individual.

Summary

This survey of applied creativity could leave the practical executive with a dilemma. In one respect, recent research has revealed the frontier-land of creativity to be rather risky because it includes new methods in problem-solving processes that may be unfamiliar to many businessmen. Psychologists researching in creativity do not consider it hunch-theology or risky in itself; but from the executives' viewpoint, it may be more risky than some of their other usual activities. (After all, most businesses were developed without the *conscious* use of creative techniques.) And creative techniques do not furnish ground-rules for dealing with vested interests, lack of information, and the usual suspicions accompanying new things.

Second, applied imagination certainly does not conflict with the age-old, scientific problem-solving principles, but rather enhances them by furnishing original insights into current business complexities. By not offering rigid rules to counter resistance, it especially unleashes the mental flexibility and adaptability needed in an organization's efforts to deal with the ineluctable advances of modern technology.

And in conclusion, recent research enables psychologists to help executives understand and deal with their various creative personnel. Creativity of two kinds can now be more readily predicted by psychologists, and more validly and reliably judged in particular individuals. These well-informed judgments then can aid businessmen in more creative productions and more eventual profit.

Solution

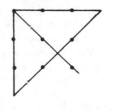

References

1. Steiner, G.A. (Ed.) *The creative organization.* Chicago: University of Chicago Press, 1965, p. 152.
2. Dauw, D.C. *Life experiences, vocational needs and choices of original thinkers and good elaborators.* Ann Arbor, Michigan: University Microfilms, Inc., 1965.
3. Torrance, E.P. *Guiding creative talent.* Englewood Cliffs, N.J.: Prentice-Hall, Inc., 1962.
4. Osborn, A.F. *The creative education movement* (as of 1964), Creative Education Foundation, 1614 Rand Building, Buffalo 3, N.Y.
5. Randall, F.D. Stimulate your executives to think creatively! *Harvard Business Review,* July-August, 1955, p.121.
6. Maslow, A.H. Emotional blocks to creativity. In S.J. Parnes and H.F. Harding (Eds.). *A source book for creative thinking.* New York: C. Scribner & Sons, 1962, p. 94.
7. Taylor, C.W. (Ed.). *Creativity: progress and potential.* New York: McGraw-Hill, 1964.
8. Torrance, E.P. Scientific views of creativity and factors affecting its growth. *Daedalus,* 1965, 94, pp. 663-682.
9. Newell, A., J.C. Shaw, and H.A. Simon. The processes of creative thinking. In H.E. Gruber, G. Terrell, and M. Wertheimer (Eds.). *Contemporary approaches to creative thinking.* New York: Atherton Press, 1962.

10. Taylor, C.W. A tentative description of the creative individual. In S.J. Parnes and H.F. Harding (Eds.). *A source book for creative thinking*. New York: C. Scribner & Sons, 1962.

11. Guilford, J.P. Creativity: its measurement and development. In S.J. Parnes and H.F. Harding (Eds.). *A source book for creative thinking*. New York: C. Scribner & Sons, 1962.

12. Osborn, A.F. *Applied imagination*. New York: C. Scribner & Sons, 1963.

13. Torrance, E.P. *Rewarding creative behavior: experiments in classroom creativity*. Englewood Cliffs, N.J.: Prentice-Hall, 1965.

14. Arnold, J.E. Education for innovation. In S.J. Parnes and H.F. Harding (Eds.). *A source book for creative thinking*. New York: C. Scribner & Sons, 1962, pp. 127-138.

15. Osborn, A.F. *Applied imagination*. New York: C. Scribner & Sons, 1963.

16. Bower, M. Nurturing innovation in an organization. In G.A. Steiner (Ed.). *The creative organization*. Chicago: University of Chicago Press, 1965, pp. 169-182.

17. Whiting, C.S. *Creative thinking*. New York: Reinhold, 1958.

18. Osborn, A.F. *Applied imagination*. New York: C. Scribner & Sons, 1963, p. 156.

19. Rogers, C.R. Toward a theory of creativity. In S.J. Parnes and H.F. Harding (Eds.). *A source book for creative thinking*. New York: C. Scribner & Sons, 1962.

20. Mason, J.G. You can ask creative questions. U.S. Chamber of Commerce: *Nation's Business*, Feb., 1962.

21. Wallace, H.R. Creative thinking: a factor in sales productivity. *Vocational Guidance Quarterly*, 1961, 9, pp. 23-226.

22. Wallace, H.R. Creative thinking: a factor in the performance of industrial salesmen. Doctoral dissertation, University of Minnesota, 1964.

23. Taylor, C.W. *Widening horizons in creativity*. New York: John Wiley & Sons, Inc., 1964.

24. Taylor, C.W., and F.X. Barron. *Scientific creativity: its recognition and development*. New York: John Wiley & Sons, Inc., 1963.

25. Barron, F.X. *Creativity and psychological health*. New York: D. Van Nostrand Co., 1963.

26. Torrance, E.P. *Constructive behavior: stress, personality, and mental health*. Belmont, Calif.: Wadsworth, 1965.

27. Parnes, S.J. Can creativity be increased? In S.J. Parnes and H.F. Harding (Eds.). *A source book for creative thinking*. New York: C. Scribner & Sons, 1962, pp. 186-191.

28. Stouffer, L. The biggest thing since mass production. *Reader's Digest*, Jan., 1964.

29. Stein, M.I., and Shirley J. Heinze. *Creativity and the individual*. Glencoe: The Free Press, 1960.

30. Taylor, C.W., and J. Holland. Predictors of creative performance. In C.W. Taylor (Ed.). *Creativity: progress and potential*. New York: McGraw-Hill, 1964.

31. Meehl, P.E. *Clinical versus statistical prediction*. Minneapolis: University of Minnesota Press, 1963.

32. McDermid, C.D. Some correlates of creativity in engineering personnel. *J. Applied Psychology*, Feb., 1965, 49, pp. 14-19.

33. Cunnington, B.F., and E.P. Torrance. *Sounds and images*. New York: Ginn & Co., 1965. (Imagicraft series.)

34. Dauw, D.C. Personality self-descriptions of original thinkers and good elaborators. *Psychology in the Schools*, 1966, 3, pp. 78-79.

35. Dauw, D.C. Life experiences of original thinkers and good elaborators. *Exceptional Children*, 1966, 32: pp. 433-443.

36. Maslow, A.H. *Motivation and personality*. New York: Harper, 1954.

37. Mackworth, N.H. Originality. *American Psychologist*, 1965, 20, pp. 51-66.

38. Leary, T. The effects of test score feedback on creative performance and of drugs on creative experience. In C.W. Taylor (Ed.). *Widening horizons in creativity*. New York: John Wiley & Sons, Inc., 1964, pp. 87-111.

CREATIVITY RESEARCH ON ACTUARIES

Definition

An actuary is a person who applies the theory of probability and statistics and the principles of finance to the problems of insurance, pensions, social security, vital statistics, and related fields. In the field of insurance, the actuary works with the probabilities of events such as death, sickness, disability, retirement, unemployment, property destruction, and so forth. He must combine these probabilities with the principles of finance and administration to determine premiums, reserves and other financial particulars which provide the basis for the sound and efficient operation of the company and the protection of the policyholder.

Actuarial Creativity

Since most authorities agree that one may be judged creative if he can invent original and useful processes or devices, the subject of creativity in actuaries is of interest to insurance executives. They have shown increasing interest, for example, in research (Dauw, 1966b; Dauw, 1966c) which has shown how creativity tests can isolate the personalities necessary to invent useful processes or original devices—that is, to identify those persons who can be expected to meet unusual events that might occur in industry or education, or in life itself, which fully covers the insurance business.

Dauw (1966a) has outlined a program of creativity research and development for organizations and has furnished a context wherein occurred a study of 69 actuaries employed by two different companies within a large insurance group. The actual statistics of the study appear at the end of this article.

Actuaries themselves feel that, since the social and financial world is always changing, they are continually meeting new problems for which they must be versatile, ingenious and aggressive. Casualty actuaries, for example, often have to deal with unexpected situations (such as hurricanes) where the data are inadequate, techniques are new, issues are not clearly defined, and political or regulatory influences are involved. They feel that their work places more demands on creativity because so little can be anticipated, each situation presenting a new challenge. Life actuaries, on the other hand, believe that their job requires more discipline and meticulous craftmanship in order to create more formal systems that are exactly reproducible by different men. They are faced with relatively predictable situations—death, for example, which happens with far greater statistical frequency than does the birth of destructive hurricanes.

In Comparison

Incidentally, using the criterion of statistical infrequency of choice, Dauw (1966d) found that the career of actuary itself was a "more creative one" than many others. He found, too, in other research (1967; 1968) that actuaries score much higher on all measures of the Torrance Tests of Creative Thinking (Torrance, 1966) than both Electronic Data Processing computer specialists and underwriters. In originality, for example, whereas the mean score for 69 actuaries was 109.13, the score for 86 EDP programmers was 95.87, for 65 EDP systems analysts 97.89 and for 38 underwriters 90.00. In elaboration, mean scores of 61.80 for programmers, 65.85 for systems analysts and 63.03 for underwriters were considerably lower than

Reprinted by permission of the publisher from *Journal of Creative Behavior*, fall, 1969, 2(4), 274-280.

those for life actuaries (84.88) and casualty actuaries (71.67). Table 1 at the end of this article reports all the highly significant *t* tests that reveal the superiority of actuaries over these other groups.

Elaboration Versus Originality

In his research, Dauw (1966a; 1966b; 1966c) has described good elaborators as those who are able to take an idea or task and spell out the detail. They can embroider a simple idea to make it fancy and attractive. Original thinkers, on the other hand, are those who are more able to get away from the obvious and break away from the beaten path. As innovators, they see relationships and think of ideas and solutions different from others. (Naturally, the most creatively gifted individuals may be outstanding in both of these divergent thinking abilities.) Analyzing the results of his research, Dauw found that, interestingly enough, life and casualty actuaries do not differ in originality; however, life actuaries are significantly more creative in elaboration than their casualty peers.

Table 1
Comparisons Between Actuaries, EDP-Specialists and Underwriters Using Fisher's Two-Tailed T-Tests

Actuaries		EDP-Programmers N = 86		SYS-Analysts N = 65		Underwriters N = 38	
		T	Sign.	T	Sign.	T	Sign.
LIFE	ORIG	3.101	<.005	2.893*	<.005	5.610	<.001
N=26	ELAB	7.576	<.001	5.711	<.001	5.949	<.001
CASUALTY	ORIG	4.740	<.001	4.496*	<.001	7.546	<.001
N=43	ELAB	3.766	<.001	2.013	<.050	2.606	<.020
ALL	ORIG	5.285	<.001	4.791*	<.001	7.846	<.001
COMBINED	ELAB	6.257	<.001	4.081	<.001	4.326	<.001
N=69							

* N=64

Obviously, in casualty and life actuarial careers the demands of the job determine who remains and who succeeds. A high response to originality is apparently necessary to casualty actuaries; and, if life actuaries do not have or develop strong elaborative abilities, they do not long remain in that type of work. In some cases at least, highly creative people

have a turnover rate more than twice as high as low creatives (Dauw, 1967; Dauw,1968).

Stability

Further comparison of these two groups of actuaries—using the Cattell (1962) Sixteen Personality Factor Inventory and the Pearson and Maddi (1966) Similes Preference Inventory—confirms other research (Barron, 1963) which indicates that highly creative individuals are much more affected by their feelings and emotions, experiencing them closer to the surface. That is, low creatives tend to submerge their feelings in order to attain greater calm and maturity, to keep in closer touch with reality. Not that low creatives are necessarily more "emotionally stable"; they merely do not feel as free as the high creatives do to express their feelings.

Implications

The implications for management seem clear. More extensive research needs to be done on the use of selection instruments (the SPI in particular). A person scoring high on creativity tests would be predictably a greater risk for repetitive kinds of work. Furthermore, the climate of a particular company may have much to do with high turnover rates. If, for instance, highly creative people are more emotionally labile, unhesitatingly expressing their feelings, managers may tend to lose patience with what appears to be emotional instability and, as a consequence, the more creative ones may feel that the environment is not sufficiently nurturant, that it is in fact frustrating and inhibiting.

So far as the management of actuaries is concerned, the major question becomes, how best can we manage original thinkers in contrast with elaborating thinkers? In the broader context of managing any creative individuals, the question becomes, Under what conditions do which methods work best with which kinds of men in what organizations?

Statistics of the Study

Within the home office of one of the country's largest insurance groups, all actuaries were invited to participate in this study. Of the 69 volunteers,

26 were life actuaries and 43 were casualty actuaries. There were 61 men (88%) and 8 women (12%). The mean age of the 43 casualty actuaries was 29.05 and the mean age of the 26 life actuaries was 26.27, a statistically significant difference ($p < .05$). In years of college, the casualty actuaries' mean was 4.53 compared with 4.15 for life actuaries. Since there were so few women (12%), sex differences did not affect the results of the data analysis. The research used the Torrance Tests of Creative Thinking (Torrance, 1966) to isolate the independent variables, the criterion groups.

The Tests and What They Measure

The Torrance test contain tasks that were constructed to be models of the creative process, and they are thus fairly complex, with features that make use of what we know about the nature of the creative thinking processes, the qualities of creative products, and creative personalities. The TTCT have verbal and figural forms. The number of relevant responses produced by a subject yields one measure of ideational fluency. The number of shifts in thinking or number of different categories or questions, causes or consequences gives one measure of flexibility. The statistical infrequency of these questions, causes or consequences or the extent to which the response represents a mental leap or departure from the obvious and commonplace gives one measure of originality. The detail and specificity incorporated into the questions and hypotheses provide one measure of the ability to elaborate.

The Scores

The total originality score used here was the normalized T-score combined from both the verbal and figural measures, whereas the elaboration score is the T-score from the figural subtests.

The more creative group (N=19) was selected from the top 27% of the scores; the less creative group (N=19) was designated from the lowest 27%. Thus, in terms of creativity test scores, 31 individuals who scored within the middle range were excluded from the analysis.

In originality, the mean scores were 110.12 for casualty actuaries, 107.50 for life actuaries, and 109.13 for all 69 actuaries. In elaboration, the mean scores were 84.88 for life actuaries and 71.67 for casualty actuaries. In isolating the top and bottom 27% into criterion groups for further analysis, the highly creative group (N=19) scored 123.16 on originality, whereas the low original group scored 94.74 ($p < .001$). Similarly, in elaboration, the good elaborators scored 83.42 and the poor elaborators scored 68.84 ($p < .02$). These criterion groups were also compared on two other measures, the Sixteen Personality Factor Inventory and the Similes Preference Inventory.

Other Comparisons

Pearson and Maddi (1966) developed the Similes Preference Inventory as a structured measure of the tendency toward variety. Their extensive evidence suggests that the SPI is a reliable, simple method to assess the intensity of the active, interoceptive tendency toward variety.

Correlations of .34 and .37 were reported (Pearson & Maddi, 1966) between the SPI and a measure of originality in two different samples. This present research reveals correlations of .42 and .32 between the same SPI and a different measure of originality (*TTTT*). (See Table 2.)

On the SPI, the mean scores were 18.46 for life actuaries and 16.37 for casualty actuaries ($p < .05$); 25.53 for the highly creative group, and 13.89 for the low creative group ($p < .02$). The Mann-Whitney nonparametric *t* test was used to test the statistical significance of these differences where the distributions were markedly non-normal (Siegel, 1956).

Table 2 reveals interesting correlations between the SPI and the various criterion groups. For example, among the more highly creative life actuaries, the correlation between originality scores and SPI is .42; among all the highest creative actuaries, .32; among all the actuaries, .31; and among the least creative actuaries, only .02.

The 16 P.F. Inventory (Cattell, 1962) measures 16 traits of personality that have been factor-analyzed into polar-opposite dimensions along a continuum. Although there are tendencies toward statistical significance, only one trait reveals extremely clear-cut diversity. On Factor C, the mean Sten score for highly creative actuaries was 4.42, compared with 6.21 for the low creative group ($p < .005$).

Table 2
Pearson Product-Memory Correlation Coefficients for Five Groups of Five Variables

HIGH CREATIVE GROUP
(N = 19)

	AGE	ED	ORIG	ELAB	SPI
AGE	1.00	.23	.02	−.10	−.13
ED		1.00	−.19	−.21	−.09
ORIG			1.00	.16	.32
ELAB				1.00	.12
SPI					1.00

LOW CREATIVE GROUP
(N = 19)

	AGE	ED	ORIG	ELAB	SPI
AGE	1.00	***.53	−.01	**−.49	−.28
ED		1.00	.29	*−.42	−.25
ORIG			1.00	.34	.02
ELAB				1.00	*.43
SPI					1.00

LIFE ACTUARIES
(N = 26)

	AGE	ED	ORIG	ELAB	SPI
AGE	1.00	.18	−.11	*−.32	−.02
ED		1.00	−.01	−.21	.15
ORIG			1.00	*.36	**.42
ELAB				1.00	▽.52
SPI					1.00

CASUALTY ACTUARIES
(N = 43)

	AGE	ED	ORIG	ELAB	SPI
AGE	1.00	***.37	−.03	−.02	*−.26
ED		1.00	.13	.09	.00
ORIG			1.00	▽▽▽.58	*.27
ELAB				1.00	.24
SPI					1.00

ALL ACTUARIES
(N = 69)

	AGE	ED	ORIG	ELAB	SPI
AGE	1.00	▽▽.35	−.03	−.19	*−.20
ED		1.00	.11	−.19	.02
ORIG			1.00	▽▽▽.41	▽.31
ELAB				1.00	▽.33
SPI					1.00

```
        * = < .100
       ** = < .050
      *** = < .020
        ▽ = < .010
      ▽ ▽ = < .005
    ▽ ▽ ▽ = < .001
```

Further analysis of scores on Factor C of the 16 P.F. supports the previous results and yields a biserial correlation coefficient of −.37, and an even more statistically significant lambda biserial of −.55 ($p < .001$). (See Clemans, 1958.) This biserial coefficient corrects for non-normality in the continuous variable whereas the regular biserial "r" does not. These correlational results clearly show that the more highly creative individuals tend to be less "emotionally stable" as measured by Factor C.

Table 3 reports the scores for all actuaries on all the variable, and serves as a good reference point in future research.

Table 3
Actuaries' Means and Standard Deviations on All Variables

	$\bar{X}$	s
AGE	28.00	6.08
EDUC	4.39	.92
ORIG	109.13	11.95
ELAB	76.65	16.04
SPI	17.16	13.26
A (16 P.F.)	4.91	1.91
B "	8.81	1.23
C "	5.51	1.94
E "	5.78	2.13
F "	5.61	2.29
G "	5.20	1.82
H "	5.19	1.51
I "	4.51	1.68
L	5.07	1.93
M	5.68	2.01
N	5.49	2.06
O	4.84	1.49
Q1	6.55	1.62
Q2	6.65	1.82
Q3	5.55	2.03
Q4 (16 P.F.)	5.52	1.88

References

1. Barron, F. *Creativity and psychological health.* Princeton, N.J.: Van Nostrand, 1963.
2. Cattell, R.B. *Sixteen Personality Factor Questionnaire.* Champaign, Ill.: Institute for Personality and Ability Testing, 1962.
3. Clemans, W.V. An index of item-criterion relationship. *Educ. & Psychol. Measurement,* 1958, 18, 167-172.
4. Dauw, D.C. Creativity in organizations. *Personnel J.,* 1966a, 45, 465-474.
5. ———. Personality self-descriptions of original thinkers and good elaborators. *Psychol. in Schools,* 1966b, 3, 78-79.
6. ———. Life experiences of original thinkers and good elaborators. *Except. Child.,* 1966c, 32, 433-443.
7. ———. Career choices of high and low creative thinkers. *Voca. Guid. Quart.,* 1966d, 15, 135-140.
8. ———. Vocational interests of highly creative computer personnel. *Personnel J.* 1967, 46, 653-659.
9. ———. Creativity research on computer personnel. Life Office Management Assoc.: *Personnel Quarterly,* 1968, May, 1-3.
10. Pearson, P.H., and Maddi, S.R. The Similies Preference Inventory. *J. of Cons. Psychol.,* 1966, 30, 301-308.
11. Siegel, S. *Nonparametric statistics.* New York: McGraw-Hill, 1956.
12. Torrance, E.P. *Torrance Tests of Creative Thinking.* Princeton, N.J.: Personnel Press, 1966. (See also The Minnesota studies of creative behavior: National and international extensions. *J. of Crea. Behav.,* 1967, 1 (2), 137-154.)

VOCATIONAL INTERESTS OF HIGHLY CREATIVE COMPUTER PERSONNEL

Can interest inventories help in the recruitment, selection and placement of computer personnel? The rapidly increasing use of computers in business and industry make this a vital question. This paper searches for means of identifying creative computer personnel.

According to executive trends, seers predict that the demand for computer programmers alone, not to mention systems analysts, will treble or quadruple by 1970. Today there are between 200,000 and 300,000 of these eagerly-sought specialists at work.[1] Thus, recruiting, selecting and training EDP personnel has become an important venture, because the computer is recognized as the most vital tool of management introduced in this generation. It increasingly affects not only business corporations, but government and education as well.

There are now perhaps 35,000 computers in use, and it has been estimated there will be 85,000 by 1975. Some idea of the mammoth size of the computer industry can be seen in IBM's five billion dollar gamble on the 360.[2]

As the computer industry expands and its personnel multiply,[3] some concepts apparently divide workers. Strachey,[4] for example, notes that confusion has developed about the naming of EDP concepts. Some programmers use the term "programming" for the second stage; others call the first stage "programming" and the second stage "coding." Still others lump both stages into programming, Strachey thinks the distinction between system analysis and programming is not a useful one. If the system analysis were carried out to a detailing of the program outline in a slightly more rigorous language than is presently used, it should be possible to relegate the whole of the remaining process of producing a detailed program in machine language to the computer itself.

If there is any difficulty in examining concepts, however, it may be semantic. Strachey[4] believes the process of stating a problem in language acceptable to a computer is primarily intuitive rather than formal. Yet others insist the primary skill needed is a logical approach to problem solving. Still others emphasize creativity as essential for success in EDP work.

Dauw[5] recently summarized research on creativity in organizations, and discussed various kinds of creative personalities, as well as new research techniques to discover such creative individuals. The research discussed here is an attempt to extend these concepts on creativity to computer personnel in general and more particularly, to investigate the vocational interests of computer personnel who are more creative in comparison with their less creative co-workers.

The Criterion Question

As in any research, the criterion can always be a problem. Taylor and Holland[6] emphasize how patents can be a most effective criterion. Authorities seem to agree that one can be judged creative if he can invent useful processes or devices that are truly original. Yet, industry, education and life itself cannot await the event, but must seek to foster it in advance. Thus, Torrance[7] clearly shows how psychological tests can measure creativity. Dauw[8,9] further showed how these creativity tests can isolate different creative personalities.

Vocational Interests

Vocational interests seem to be very definitely related to stability in a career, because job satisfac-

Reprinted by permission of *Personnel Journal*, November, 1967, 46(10), 653-659.

tion results from a basic interest that one has in his work. Presumably, then, an adequate measure of vocational interests could help predict whether one would be satisfied working as a programmer or systems analyst. Strong[10] was the first psychologist to develop and validate statistical measures that differentiate the vocational interests of workers in one career from those in another. Kuder[11] extended these concepts and developed his own interest inventory.[12]

The Kuder Occupational Interest Survey (KOIS)[13] is scored for 115 occupations and 33 college major subjects. Of these 148 scores, 99 are reported to male subjects and 81 to women. This inventory is especially valuable when a person is approaching the point of committing himself rather definitely to preparing for or entering a specific line of work. It may occur in late high school, early college, or very frequently, when an indecisive college graduate with a liberal arts major enters the world of work. Since only one interest inventory scale [14] is specifically validated now for computer-programmers, the present research was designed to seek clues and similarities in those major careers already measured and for creative personnel in particular. In other words, are the vocational interests of computer personnel more similar to those of professionals in some known career rather than in others?

Research Design

The present research used the Torrance Tests of Creative Thinking (TTCT)[15] to isolate the independent variables, that is, to determine the criterion groups—those computer personnel who were more creative in comparison with their less creative counterparts. Within the home office of one of the country's largest insurance groups, all programmers and systems analysts were invited to participate. Of the 151 volunteers, there were 115 men and 36 women; in the sample of 86 programmers, 64 were men and 22, women; of the 65 systems analysts, there were 51 men and 14 women. The more creative group (N=41) were selected from the top 27% of the scores, while the less creative group (N=41) were designated from the lowest 27% of the scores. Thus, in terms of creativity tests scores, 69 individuals who scored in the middle range, were excluded from the analysis.

The Torrance Tests were developed after ten years of research and validation that extended the initial impetus to study creativity provided by J.P. Guilford in his 1950 presidential address to the American Psychological Association. Deliberate attempts were made by Torrance to construct test tasks that would be models of the creative process, each involving different kinds of thinking and each contributing something unique to the batteries. Test tasks are thus fairly complex and have features that make use of what we know about the nature of the creative thinking processes, the qualities of creative products, and creative personalities. The TTCT have verbal and figural forms. The number of relevant responses produced by a subject yields one measure of ideational fluency. The number of shifts in thinking or number of different categories of questions, causes, or consequences gives one measure of flexibility. The statistical infrequency of these questions, causes or consequences or the extent to which the response represents a mental leap or departure from the obvious and commonplace, gives one measure of originality. The detail and specificity incorporated into the questions and hypotheses provide one measure of ability to elaborate.

Creativity Results

The basic criterion groups and the creativity test results are published elsewhere.[16] Briefly, computer personnel in general (N=151) scored much higher on the TTCT than other insurance workers in operating divisions (N=38) to a statistically significant degree (p<.01; i.e., the results could only happen by chance less than once in a hundred times). It was concluded that computer personnel were more creative than insurance workers in this sample. When considering originality scores, programmers (N=34) in a life insurance company were significantly more original than their peers (N=35) in a casualty company (p<.01).

Programmers and systems analysts scored equally well in originality, but differences appeared in elaboration scores. All 65 systems analysts in both companies scored higher than the 86 programmers in elaboration to a statistically significant degree (p<.01). It was concluded that, although programmers and systems analysts may be equal in originality, the latter are better elaborators.

Good elaborators[8, 9, 5] are able to take an idea or task and spell out the detail. They can "embroider" a simple idea and make it fancy and attractive. Original thinkers, on the other hand are those who are able to get away from the obvious and break away from the beaten path. As innovators they see relationships and think of ideas and solutions different from others. Naturally, the most creatively-gifted individuals may be outstanding in both of these divergent thinking abilities, both in real life as well as on psychological tests.

Further analysis showed no relationship between these TTCT scores and the IBM Aptitude test for programming personnel, so that it was concluded the TTCT were not measuring convergent thinking abilities, as on the P.A.T., but rather, divergent thinking abilities.

The criterion groups were composed of both programmers (mean age, 27) and systems analysts (mean age, 30) to obtain a better sample. Of the entire computer group (N=151), there were 36 women (23%). But in the more creative group (N=41), there were 14 women (34%), compared with only six women (15%) in the less creative group.

Table 1 shows the extreme separation of these criterion groups on the TTCT.

Table 1

Group	N	Originality		Elaboration	
EDP Personnel		Mean	S.D.	Mean	S.D.
More Creative	41	117.56[***]	12.29[a]	70.85[***]	13.60[b]
Less Creative	41	78.78	6.32	57.56	13.19

[***] $p < .001$
[a] = t-ratio = 25.35
[b] = t-ratio = 6.36

Vocational Interest Results

Tables 2 and 3 summarize those scales of the KOIS which had the most frequent high point scores in the sample. The three highest scales were arbitrarily chosen for each individual.

These results can be better understood in comparison with the data from Perry and Cannon.[14] They administered the Strong Vocational Interest Blank (SVIB) to 1378 male programmers. Programmers were considered to be especially interested in problem- and puzzle-solving activities, including all forms of mathematics, as well as mechanical activities. They tended to prefer varied, rather than routine, tasks and to dislike close personal interactions with people. Programmers' scores on existing occupational scales of the SVIB indicate an interaction of applied scientific and administrative interests, but none of the existing SVIB scales adequately represented the interests of programmers. Thus, Perry and Cannon developed a programmer interest key that was valid for differentiating between programmers and men in general.

In this sample, the KOIS results are interpreted as being very similar to those of Perry and Cannon on the SVIB, where the highest scales were: senior CPA, engineer, optometrist chemist, math-science teacher, and production manager. Table 2 indicates that the highest scales on the KOIS were CPA, statistician and six kinds of engineering specialties.

When comparing general interest patterns as measured by KOIS, programmers and systems analysts seem to be rather closely matched. Yet, there are very apparent differences between the highly creative and low creative groups of computer personnel. The highly creative group (N=27) scored higher on nine KOIS scales such as CPA, statistician and three engineering scales. The low creative group (N=35) scored higher in civil and electrical engineering, clinical psychologist and social group worker. But the most obvious differences could not be included in Table 2. The highly creative group had very homogeneous patterns, whereas the low creative group was very diverse with a wide variance in interest patterns. For example, the following 16 KOIS scales are highest scales for *only* the low creative group: psychology professor (2), forester (2), meteorologist (1), x-ray technician (1), plumber (2), building contractor (1), post-office clerk (1), buyer (1), optometrist (1), minister (2), university pastor (3), podiatrist (1), department storesalesman (1), real estate agent (1), TV repairman (1).

Female EDP personnel, like women in general, have interest patterns that differ significantly from male EDP workers, as shown in Table 3. These women in computer jobs have a much stronger orientation toward people than do their male peers, but in a definitely scientific (as in clinical

Table 2
Most Frequent Occupational Interest Scales (Including Three Highest For Each
Person) Of Male Computer Personnel Compared
With Highly Creative and Low Creative Male EDP Workers

KOIS Scale	Programmers (N = 57)		Systems Analysts (N = 51)		Highly Creative Group (N = 27)		Low Creative Group (N = 35)	
	N	%	N	%	N	%	N	%
C.P.A.	19	10.7	15	9.8	7	8.6	8	7.7
Engineer, Mechanical	16	9.0	8	5.2	7	8.6	6	6.1
Statistician	11	6.2	6	3.9	7	8.6	4	3.8
Engineer, Civil	9	5.1	8	5.2	3	3.7	6	6.1
Engineer, Industrial	7	4.0	8	5.2	5	6.1	3	2.8
Psychologist, Industrial	8	4.5	6	3.9	5	6.1	3	2.8
Engineer, Electrical	7	4.0	3	1.9	0	0	4	3.8
Engineer, Heat/ Air-Cond.	6	3.4	4	2.6	3	3.7	3	2.8
Sales Eng., Heat/ Air-Cond.	6	3.4	4	2.6	3	3.7	3	2.8
Auto Salesman	2	1.1	5	3.3	4	4.9	2	1.9
Architect	5	2.7	5	3.3	3	3.7	3	2.8
Psychologist, Clinical	6	3.4	4	2.6	1	1.2	5	4.7
Social Worker, Group	3	1.7	4	2.6	2	2.4	5	4.7

Table 3
Most Frequent Occupational Interest Scales (Including Three Highest For Each
Person) Of Female Computer Personnel Compared
With Highly Creative Female EDP Workers

KOIS Scale	Programmers (N = 21)		Systems Analysts (N = 14)		Highly Creative Group (N = 14)		Low Creative Group (N = 6)	
	N	%	N	%	N	%	N	%
Physical Therapist	8	12.7	3	7.1	5	11.9	2	1.1
Psychologist	7	11.1	7	16.7	6	16.2	1	.6
Psychologist, Clinical	5	7.9	6	14.3	5	11.9	2	1.1
Accountant	4	6.3	1	2.3	0	0	2	1.1
Science Teacher (High School)	4	6.3	2	4.7	3	7.1	0	0
Interior Decorator	3	4.8	4	9.5	2	4.5	3	1.6
Social Worker (Psychiatric)	2	3.1	5	11.9	3	7.1	1	.6
Occupational Therapist	3	4.8	2	4.7	5	11.9	0	0

psychology) as well as manipulative manner (physical and occupational therapy).

The interest patterns of female EDP workers are also more homogeneous than their male peers. Also, the highly creative females (like highly creative males) have more homogeneous patterns than their female counterparts in general and low creative females in particular. The large proportion of highly creative women among EDP females explains much of the similarity among these two groups, as contrasted with the males where there is a smaller proportion of highly creative people.

All these interest patterns of computer workers (both male and female, as well as highly creative groups among the sexes) stand out more clearly when contrasted to those of other insurance workers.

Interests of Other Insurance Men

Among operating insurance workers (N=38), occupational interest scales were analyzed for 17 long-range planners, and 21 nonplanners. (Using the three highest scales for each person, 51 and 63 scales were included.) The most frequently occurring interest scales of the planners were: industrial psychologist, eight (16%); personnel manager, five (10%); sales engineer, insurance agent, pharmaceutical salesman, C.P.A., and travel agent, each three (6%).

On the other hand, the interest scales were rather different for the nonplanners. Their most frequently occurring scales were: bookkeeper and department store salesman, each four (9%); real estate agent, insurance agent, and architect, each three (6%).

Long-range planners and nonplanners tend to have only one interest scale in common, insurance agent, which may be largely a function of interests developed in years on the job. When viewed as two separate groups, however, the interest patterns of long-range planners seem more cognitive, more people-oriented and less thing-oriented than the nonplanners. It is intriguing to note that planners tend to be high on C.P.A., whereas nonplanners tend to be more like bookkeepers. These differences may show commonalities in their respective methods and techniques may be overridden by their diverse orientations: that is, the nonplanners may be more maintenance-oriented like bookkeep-

ers, whereas the planners, like C.P.A.'s may be seeking meaning and interrelationships between the data in a more cognitive manner.

The most frequently rejected interest patterns of these computer workers (analyzing three lowest for each person) are doubtlessly similar to those rejected by white collar workers and managerial talent in general. The 108 EDP males have interests very dissimilar to mechanics (27), carpenters (27), truck drivers (22), ministers (18), interior decorators (16), university pastors (13), librarians (10), house painters (8), farmers (6), journalists (5), machinists (5), plumbers (5), and the like. The 35 female EDP workers most frequently rejected the career interests of department store saleswomen (14), office clerks (8), bank clerks (7), interior decorators (4), lawyer (4), religious education director (4), bookkeeper (3), and the like.

Discussion

Although this research, like that in all behavioral sciences, is not as strikingly clear as the most idealistic would prefer, it does furnish valuable results. And although this sample is much larger than that of many research projects, it does suggest that even larger samples could produce more significant conclusions.

(1) These results, coupled with those of Perry and Cannon, clearly show that interest inventories can be effectively used to help psychologists and managers recruit, select and place computer personnel in general.

(2) More specifically, these data indicate highly creative EDP personnel are a more homogeneous group on the basis of interests than are their less gifted peers. Thus, there is greater likelihood an applicant could function well in EDP work if his interests, whether indicated expressly in a college major or explicitly measured by inventories, are similar to the personnel in this sample. Briefly, the vocational interests of highly creative EDP males are more similar to those statisticians, mechanical and industrial engineers, and industrial psychologists rather than, as the less creative males, similar to civil and electrical engineers, clinical psychologists and social group workers. Similarly, highly creative females in EDP have interests more similar to clinical and other psychologists, and physical and occupational therapists.

(3) After selecting and placing these highly creative people, executives would do well to consider thoughtfully whether a technically proficient individual should be promoted to a managerial position. Knowing the job does not imply knowing how to lead others.

Nash[17] reviewed the literature on the vocational interests of effective managers. From his review, he identified four categories of interests that seem to have some consistent relation to managerial effectiveness: social service, people-oriented interests; persuasive, verbal interests; rejection of technical and scientific interests; and interest in business-type occupations.

Interests of effective managers, therefore, seem rather different from those of highly creative EDP workers. This suggests their creative talents might be more profitably engaged in technical rather than managerial pursuits.

(4) The use of special programmer keys can help college counselors stimulate an increased number of students to enter the data processing field.[18] A similar usefulness in business is more restricted because of a shortage of counselors or psychologists to *interpret* these refined instruments properly. Obviously, more efforts will be made by organizations like the National Employment Counselors Association.

(5) Research of this nature should help employment interviewers realize that there are few clear-cut decisions to be made in hiring applicants who verbally express an interest in a particular field. Instead of merely assigning an applicant to EDP work, all personnel men could intensify their efforts to help candidates understand their interests more fully in relationship to their work to increase satisfaction.

References

1. Editors, *Nation's Business*, "Executive Trends," 1966, p. 14 (Aug.).
2. Wise, T.A., "IBM's $5,000,000,000 Gamble." *Fortune*, 1966, 74:118-124 (Sept.).
3. Cassidy, C.E., Electronic Data Processing and the Personnel Function: The Present and the Future. *Personnel Journal*, 1966, 45:352-354.
4. Strachey, C., "System Analysis and Programming." *Scientific American*, 1966, 215:112-128.
5. Dauw, D.C., Creativity in Organizations. *Personnel Journal*, 1966, 45:465-474.
6. Taylor, C.W. and Holland J. "Predictors of Creative Performance." In C.W. Taylor (Ed.) *Creativity: Progress and Potential.* New York: McGraw-Hill, 1964.
7. Torrance, E.P., "Scientific Views of Creativity and Factors Affecting Its Growth." *Daedalus*, 1965, 94:663-682.
8. Dauw, D.C., "Personality Self-descriptions of Original Thinkers and Good Elaborators." *Psychology in the Schools*, 1966, 3:78-79.
9. ———, "Life Experiences of Original Thinkers and Good Elaborators." *Exceptional Children*, 1966, 32:433-443.
10. Strong, E.K., Jr., *Vocational Interests of Men and Women.* Stanford, California: Stanford University Press, 1943.
11. Kuder, G.F., A Rationale for Evaluating Interests. *Educ. and Psychol. Meas.*, 1963, 23:1-10.
12. ———, *Occupational Interest Survey General Manual.* Chicago: Science Research Associates, 1966.
13. ———, The Occupational Interest Survey. *Personnel and Guidance Journal*, 1966, 45:72-77.
14. Perry, D.K., and Cannon W.M. Vocational Interests of Computer Programmers. *Journal of Applied Psychology*, in press.
15. Torrance, E.P., *Torrance Tests of Creative Thinking.* Princeton, N.J. Personnel Press, Inc., 1966.
16. Dauw, D.C., Creativity Research on Computer Personnel. *Personnel Quarterly*, Life Office Management Association, New York, in press.
17. Nash, A.N., Vocational Interests of Effective Managers: A Review of the Literature. *Personnel Psychology*, 1965, 18:21-37.
18. Dauw, D.C., Career Choices of High and Low Creative Thinkers. *Vocational Guidance Quarterly*, 1966, 15:135-140.

CREATIVITY AND VOCATIONAL NEEDS OF CLERICAL PERSONNEL

Reduction of turnover among lowpaid female clerical personnel may be affected favorably, with a distinct saving of money, by consideration of the creativity and the vocational needs of such personnel as manifested in the results of certain tests. The implications as regards minority group personnel call for particular study.

Executives and EDP computer equipment are often considered to be among the most valuable and expensive assets of any corporation. The human resources movement in industry, however, is increasingly emphasizing the value of even the least paid file clerk for many reasons.

For one good financial reason, many managers often fail to realize that their companies may be paying out thousands of dollars annually just to recruit the least paid female clerks from employment agencies. Thus, better recruiting, selecting and placing of female clerical workers can save untold dollars as well as improve a corporation's productivity.

The present report is one attempt to research this issue from a novel viewpoint. Its goals are to study creativity and various vocational needs of these female clerical workers, both white and Negro, to discover clues that would help reduce turnover.

The racial issue is most recently prominent. The Equal Employment Opportunity Commission (EEOC) was one of the first federal agencies to consider disadvantaged groups in the labor market. Ash[1] has summarized the implications of the Civil Rights Act. Since early in 1967, the Office of Federal Contract Compliance (OFCC) of the Department of Labor has been drafting an order related to the use of psychological tests in industry.[2] Thus, it is becoming increasingly apparent that all employers must take care in hiring Negroes or other disadvantaged groups in any industry or job category.

In previous research on creativity, Dauw[3] has summarized issues and developed a continuing research program.[4,5,6] In extending the work of Torrance,[7] there was found to be more than one kind of highly creative individual who describes himself distinctly,[8] has had different life experiences,[9] makes unique career choices,[10] and has rapid turnover in some careers.[4,5,6] These creative individuals also have distinctive vocational needs[11] and interests.[5]

Research Design

Three measures were administered to the sample, and data were obtained from employee records on a fourth measure, the Short Employment Tests (Bennett and Gelink, 1956).

The Torrance Tests of Creative Thinking (TTCT) (Torrance, 1966)[7,12,13] were used to isolate the criterion groups, namely, those female clerical workers who were more creative in comparison with their less creative peers. Within the home office of one large insurance group, volunteers were sought from various administrative departments. Of the 193 volunteers, most were only high school graduates, and some were high school dropouts. Their mean age was 35.52, with a standard deviation of 16.18. For purposes of data analysis, they were divided into age groups of:

17-20 (N = 63, mean age = 18.67, S.D. 0.85);
21-25 (N = 27, mean age = 22.44, S.D. 1.51);
26-45 (N = 34, mean age = 38.97, S.D. 5.88);
46 & up (N = 69, mean age = 54.32, S.D. 5.29).

Reprinted by permission of *Personnel Journal,* December, 1968, 47(12), 870-876.

The more creative group (N = 38) was selected from those scoring highest in originality on the TTCT figural form B.[13] These originality scores ranged from 80 to 45, with a mean of 54.08, S.D. of 6.87. The mean age of this group was 28.18, S.D. 12.97. The low creative group (N = 38) has originality scores ranging from 30 to 20, with a mean of 26.05, S.D. 3.28. Their mean age was 36.24, S.D. 15.87. The difference in age between these two groups of more and less creative clerks was statistically significant (t = −2.389, Pp < .02); the more creative group was much younger.

The second instrument administered was the Minnesota Importance Questionnaire (Weis *et al.*, 1964),[14] a 100 item inventory with Likert-type scales measuring the intensity of 20 occupational needs. The satisfaction or fulfillment of these needs is considered to be important in determining job satisfaction (Dawis *et al.*, 1964).[15] One theory of work adjustment (Dawis, *et al.*, 1964) views two sets of variables—abilities and needs—as important to the description of work adjustment. An individual's abilities refer to his dimensions of response, while his needs refer to dimensions of reinforcement experience. Because response and reinforcement are separate concepts, abilities and needs are measured as independent, yet interacting, systems of variables.[14]

A third instrument was the Similes Preference Inventory (Pearson and Maddi, 1966),[16] a structured measure of the tendency toward variety. Extensive evidence suggests that SPI is a reliable, simple 54 item method to assess the intensity of the active interceptive tendency toward variety. Correlations of .34 and .37 were reported [16] between the SPI and a measure of orginality in two different samples. Dauw[6] (1967c, in press) found correlations of .42 and .32 between the same SPI and a different measure of originality (TTCT) that included both verbal and figural scores. In this sample, the SPI is correlated only with the figural scores from the TTCT.

The TTCT[13,7] were developed after many years of research and validation. Tasks were produced to be models of the creative process, each involving different kinds of thinking and each adding something new to the batteries. The tasks are thus rather complex, with features that use what we know about the nature of the creative thinking processes, the qualities of creative personalities. The TTCT have verbal and figural forms. The number of relevant responses produced by a subject yields one measure of ideational fluency. The number of shifts in thinking or number of different categories or questions, causes, or consequences gives one measure of flexibility. The statistical infrequency of these questions, causes, or consequences or the extent to which the response represents a mental leap or departure from the obvious and commonplace gives one measure of originality. The detail and specificity incorporated into the questions and hypotheses provide one measure of the ability to elaborate. The originality and elaboration scores used here are the normalized T-scores.

Data were obtained from the files of those employees who had taken the Short Employment Tests,[17] but no data was available on the longest-term employees.

The SET provides four scores, N,V,CA, and Total. The V score is a measure of the extent of vocabulary (the principal component of most so-called intelligence tests), while the N and CA tests measure the quantity of numerical and clerical aptitude production in fixed periods of time. The authors suggest the number of incorrect answers on the N and CA indicates the tendency of an individual toward erroneous or careless work.

Results

Data included in Table 1 and Figure 1 reflect the influence of age on creative thinking abilities (see also Torrance, 1962[12]). Considering only the four major groups, the general decline of scores with age is expected. It is not clearly evident, however, why the 21-25 age group should score so much higher than the 17-20 age group. Further research and replication may indicate whether these results are only due to local selection policies or whether more genetically, cultural or educationally influenced processed are operating.

Table 2 reveals statistically significant differences found on originality between the 17-20 and 46 and Up groups (p < .01); and between the 21-25 and 46 and Up groups (p < .001); and between the 26-45 and 46 and Up groups (p < .01); on elaboration between all the various group comparisons except the 17-20 and 21-25 groups.

Table 1

Means and Standard Deviations of Female Clerks in Low-Level Office Jobs on the TTCT (Figural Form B) and SPI, Listed by Ages and Race

Groups Age Groups	N	Originality X̄	Originality S.D.	Elaboration X̄	Elaboration S.D.	Age X̄	Age S.D.	SPI X̄	SPI S.D.
17-20	63	38.41	10.38	64.22	17.69	18.67	0.85	9.48	6.70
21-25	27	41.48	8.48	66.67	13.68	22.44	1.51	6.19	3.45
26-45	34	40.00	12.19	56.32	14.36	38.97	5.88	5.97	4.43
46 & Up	69	33.91	9.20	46.38	12.57	54.32	5.29	7.88	6.73
All Ages	193	37.51	10.48	56.79	17.08	35.52	16.18	7.83	6.12
High Creatives	38	54.08	6.87	73.08	16.11	28.18	12.97	8.68	7.28
Low Creatives	38	26.05	3.28	43.29	8.13	36.24	15.87	8.29	7.02
Negroes	28	39.46	7.60	61.96	15.55	23.00	5.59	8.36	6.83

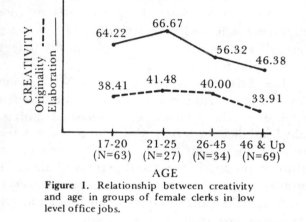

Figure 1. Relationship between creativity and age in groups of female clerks in low level office jobs.

When comparing the two major criterion groups, the more creative group is significantly younger. (t =− 2.389, p < .02), and scored significantly higher in originality (t = 22.403, p < .001), and elaboration (t = 9.714, p < .001).[20]

Table 2

Parametric T-Tests and Mann Whitney U Tests of Significance of Differences Between Groups on TTCT and SPI

Groups	Creativity Orig.	Elab.	SPI
High Creatives	22.403	9.714	.231
Low Creatives	<.001	<.001	
17-20	−1.340	−.634	2.392
21-25			<.02
17-20	−.668	2.213	2.684
26-45		<.05	<.01
17-20	2.619	6.674	1.301
46 & Up	<.01	<.001	
21-25	.528	2.806	.203
26-45		<.01	
21-25	3.664	6.863	−1.222
46 & Up	<.001	<.001	<.50
26-45	2.797	3.565	−1.447
46 & Up	<.01	<.001	

Interesting differences were also found between age groups on the SPI measuring a strong need for variety. Although the 21-25 and 26-45 groups are similar on the SPI, both of them score significantly higher than the 17-20 group. Yet this SPI measures no differences between the other age groups or the races. In this sample more significant differences and correlations would have been found between the SPI and originality, if both verbal and figural TTCT scores had been used (see Dauw, 1967c).[9] The Verbal tests were not used here because of time pressures and the fact that these jobs mostly require only numerical activities.

Table 3 contains significant correlations between age and creativity scores. It is interesting that, whereas age in all groups combined have a correlation of −.186 (p < .05) with originality, there is a steady progression through the distinct age groups. For example, in the 17-20 age group, age and originality correlate −.378 (p < .005); in the 21-25 group, −.122; in the 26-45 group, +.225; and in the 46 and Up group, +.105.

This progression emphasizes the data in Table 1 and Figure 1, and suggests that even in the 17-20 group, the youngest women have the highest originality scores.

Racial differences are manifested in many ways in the present research, doubtlessly resulting from local recruiting and manager's selection policies. The creativity scores for Negroes were compared with whites and corrected for age, so that any effects resulting from age would be partialed out. Negroes scored much higher than whites of the same age on originality (t = 1.274, p < .20) and elaboration (t = 1.121, p < .50).

46

Table 3
Pearson Product–Moment Correlation Matrices of Various Groups of Female Clerks on the SPI, Orig., and Elab. Scores of TTCT (Figural Form B)

Ages 17-20   *N=63

	Age	Elab.	SPI	Orig.
Age	1.000	−.307 (<.020)	−.144	−.378 (<.005)
Elab.		1.000	.048	.657 (<.001)
SPI			1.000	.173
Orig.				1.000

All Ages Combined   ****N=193

	Age	Elab.	SPI	Orig.
Age	1.000	−.489 (<.001)	−.092	−.186 (<.050)
Elab.		1.000	.000	.614 (<.001)
SPI			1.000	−.013
Orig.				1.000

Ages 21-25   N=27

	Age	Elab.	SPI	Orig.
Age	1.000	−.044	−.128	−.122
Elab.		1.000	.045	.370 (<.100)
SPI			1.000	−.161
Orig.				1.000

Negroes   N=28

	Age	Elab.	SPI	Orig.
Age	1.000	.010	−.343 (<.100)	.017
Elab.		1.000	.324 (<.100)	.366 (<.100)
SPI			1.000	.082
				1.000

Ages 26-46   **N=34

	Age	Elab.	SPI	Orig.
Age	1.000	−.139	−.015	.225
Elab.		1.000	.026	.580 (<.001)
SPI			1.000	−.036
				1.000

High Creative   *****N=38

	Age	Elab.	SPI	Orig.
Age	1.000	−.381 (<.020)	−.277 (<.100)	.409 (<.020)
Elab.		1.000	.194	.141
SPI			1.000	−.036
Orig.				1.000

Ages 46 and Up   ***N=69

	Age	Elab.	SPI	Orig.
Age	1.000	−.088	−.113	.105
Elab.		1.000	−.141	.621 (<.001)
SPI			1.000	−.120
Orig.				1.000

Low Creative   N=38

	Age	Elab.	SPI	Orig.
Age	1.000	−.285 (<.100)	.120	.205
Elab.		1.000	.107	−.174
SPI			1.000	.073
Orig.				1.000

*SPI N=62
**SPI N=33
***SPI N=59
****SPI N=181
*****SPI N=37

Similarly, the Negro girls scored significantly better than their white peers on the SET clerical aptitude scores (t = 3.101, p < .005). Although no significant racial differences existed on SET verbal or numerical scores, the SET total score tended to be much higher for Negroes (t = 1.246, p < .50).

The Negroes, however, scored significantly higher in clerical aptitude than their white peers (t = 3.101, p < .005), a fact doubtlessly reflecting selection policies.

Ability scores on the SET provide significant differences between age groups. Although none of the age groups differed from others on the SET numberical score, the 26-45 age groups scored higher than the 21-25 age group in verbal ability (t = −2.254, p < .05). In clerical aptitude the 46 and over group scored significantly lower than the 17-20 group (t = 3.091, p < .005), the 21-25 group (t = 3.701, p < .001), and the 26-45 group (t = 2.544, p < .02).

Vocational Needs

When comparing the high creatives with the low creatives on the MIQ, the more creative group scored higher on only one need scale: creativity (t = 2.854, p < .01). This result supports other research by Dauw (1966b)[11] and adds additional evidence to the validity of both the TTCT and MIQ. In this instance, as previously, the TTCT isolated the more original individuals, and the MIQ also measured their need for more creativity.

The 21-25 age group responds with the most clear-cut differences on five MIQ scales, undoubtedly reflecting their deeper job awareness. When comparing the 21-25 age group with the 26-45 age group, the younger individuals have significantly stronger needs for variety (t = 2.293, p < .05), creativity (t = 2.414, p < .02), ability utilization (t = 2.25, p < .05), achievement (t = 2.354, p < .05), and for more congenial co-workers (t = 2.824, p < .01). This 21-25 age group also scored significantly higher on the TTCT elaboration (t = 2.2806, p < .01), but lower than the 26-45 age group on the SET verbal (t = −2.254, p < .05).

The 17-20 age group provides a second very distinctive pattern of vocational needs. This youngest group has an even greater preference for variety as measured by the SPI (t = 2.395, p < .02) than the 21-25 group, but a lower need for autonomy (t = − 2.447, p < .02). The 17-20 age group when compared to the 26-45 group has much stronger needs for varity (t = 2.987, p < .005), ability utilization (t = 2.728, p < .01), advancement (t = 2.007, p < .05), and for more congenial co-workers (t = 2.345, p < .05). This youngest age group also scored much higher on the SET clerical aptitude (t = 3.091, p < .005), and on both TTCT measures of originality (t = 2.619, p < .01) and elaboration (t = 6.674, p < .001). However, this youngest age group felt a much lesser need for compensation than the 46 and over group (t = 3.052, p < .005). So also did the 26-45 age group feel a lesser need for compensation (t = −2.042, p < .05).

The Negro group (N = 28, mean age 23.00) has significantly stronger needs than the total white group (N = 193, mean age 35.52) for recognition (t = 2.270, p < .05), ability utilization (t = 2.046, p < .05), and for better working conditions and physical surroundings on the job (t = 2.138, p < .05). The Negroes also show a tendency toward a much stronger need for security (t = 1.464, p < .20). Perhaps these racial differences in voca-

tional needs may be associated with cultural factors more than age, ability, or selection policies.

Vocational Need-Age Curves

Intensive analysis of the vocational need scores by age revealed that 13 age curves were similar. The general pattern was a typical oscilloscope sinewave curve with distinct peaks and troughs. Figure 2 shows how the vocational need for achievement peaks out around age 25, is minimized around age 41, and rises steadily beyond age 55. Very similar patterns are found on the need for co-workers, responsibility, independence, social status, social service, advancement, security, autonomy, compensation, activity, recognition, and creativity. A second pattern is found for the need for working conditions, variety and ability utilization: both are highest at younger ages (17-20), decline sharply in a V-shape to age 41, and rise sharply again.

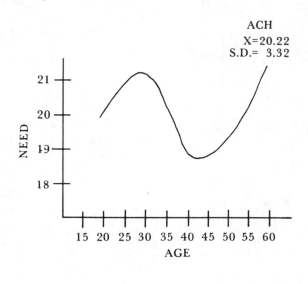

Figure 2. Vocational need for achievement plotted against age.

A third pattern is clear for the three needs of status, supervision-human relations, and company policies and practices. These needs are relatively high for the very youngest entering the work force, decline to the lowest around age 25, peak sharply up around age 45, and then level off toward retirement. Only one need—moral values—shows a most unique curve that is highest at age 17, drop lowest around age 25, and finally climbs very feebly around 45 where it levels off. All these need-age curves reveal startling insights that suggest supervisory practices for better motivation, human relations, and the like.

Discussion

When compared with professional actuaries, computer specialists, and underwriters,[4,5,6] these female clerks score extremely low in originality. On an individual basis, however, many clerks score higher, especially in elaboration, and this partially explains why they experience such a rapid job turnover.

Interestingly, the turnover among these more creative clerks is more than twice as high as the quit rate among the less creative group, a fact that prevails for other job categories already researched.[4,5,6] Future research on the SPI may also reveal its greater greater value as a predictor of turnover among those very high scorers manifesting a strong need for variety.

The Negro women generally scored better than their white peers when any possible differences due to age were ruled out. Many very talented girls from disadvantaged groups are being employed who will eagerly hope to win future promotions. In this sample, they had significantly better capabilities, as well as stronger needs for ability utilization, recognition and better working conditions that will doubtlessly require fulfillment if these girls are to remain satisfactorily employed.

Similarly, the various age groups especially require differential need fulfillment. In such distinct needs for variety, co-workers and ability utilization, the women in the 26-45 age group feel much more strongly than their peers in the 17-20 or 21-25 group, which suggests that potential supervisors may more readily be available in that group.

As was shown in the need-age curves, managers may be required to devote more time and attention to supervising the various age groups in different ways. There definitely exists a "middle-age" (or premenopausal) decline in need strength that reaches its depth between 40-45, on 13 occupational needs described above. These needs are significantly stronger as women enter the work force in the age range from 20-30, and steadily increase again as the workers approach retirement. There-

fore, to increase productivity, reduce turnover and achieve the goals of any organization, managers must concentrate more on satisfying the differential needs of these age groups.

Perhaps one method of motivating managers themselves is to introduce more sophisticated accounting techniques in the acquisition costs of new personnel. Each corporate division and department head might have costs of replacing employees more forcefully brought to his attention, by introducing a financial control mechanism. Apparently such a financial control would force managers to take a more definite look at higher turnover areas.

From the viewpoint of Civil Rights,[1] similar research can have educational implications for managers who must be made more aware of their local selection practices. Certainly it is possible that in some instances a Negro woman may have to produce significantly better results than white peers on test scores to be hired for similar positions.

In general of course, a deeper understanding[18,19] of how to manage more creative individuals, whether professionals or clerks, will become increasingly more necessary for all managers.

References

1. Ash, P. The implications of the Civil Rights Act of 1964 for psychological assessment in industry. *Amer. Psychol.*, 1966, 21:797-804.
2. Dunnette, M.D. President's Message to Division 14, American Psychological Association. *The Industrial Psychologist*, 1957, 4:1-8.
3. Dauw, D.C. Creativity in organizations. *Personnel Journal*, 1966, 45:465-474. (a)
4. ———. Creativity research on computer personnel. 1967, in press. (b)
5. ———. Vocational interests of highly creative computer personnel. *Personnel Journal*, 1967, 46: (Nov.) 653-659. (a)
6. ———. Creativity research on actuaries. 1967, in press. (c)
7. Torrance, E.P. The Minnesota Studies of Creative Behavior: National and International Extensions. *Journal of Creative Behavior*, 1967, 1:137-154.
8. Dauw, D.C. Personality self-descriptions of original thinkers and good elaborators. *Psychology in the Schools*, 1966, 3:78-79. (b)
9. ———. Life experiences of original thinkers and good elaborators. *Exceptional Children*, 1966, 32:433-443. (c)
10. ———. Career choices of high and low creative thinkers. *Vocational Guidance Quarterly*, 1966, 15:135-140. (d)

11. ———. Scholastic Aptitudes and Vocational Needs of Original Thinkers and Good Elaborators. *Personnel and Guidance Journal*, 1966, 45:171-176. (b)

12. Torrance, E.P. *Guiding Creative Talent*. Englewood Cliffs, N.J.: Prentice Hall, 1962.

13. ———.*Torrance Tests of Creative Thinking*. Princeton, N.J.: Personnel Press, Inc., 1966.

14. Weiss, D.J., Dawis, R.V., England, G.W., and Lofquist L. *Measurement of Vocational Needs*. Minnesota Studies in Vocational Rehabilitation: XVI. Industrial Relations Center, University of Minnesota, 1964.

15. Dawis, R.V., England, G.W., and Lofquist, L.H. *A Theory of Work Adjustment*. Minnesota Studies in Vocational Rehabilitations: XV. Industrial Relations Center, University of Minnesota, 1964.

16. Pearson, Pamela H. and Maddi, S.R. The Similes Preference Inventory. *Journal of Consulting Psychology*, 1966, 30:301-308.

17. Bennett, G.K., and Gelink Majorie. *Short Employment Tests*. New York: Psychological Corporation, 1956.

18. Barron, F.X. *Creativity and Psychological Health*. New York: D. Van Nostrand Co., 1963.

19. McPherson, J.H. *The Fate of an Idea*. Midland, Mich.: Hawkins Pub. Co., 1965.

20. Clemans, W.V. An index of item-criterion relationship. *Educational and Psychological Measurement*, 1958, 18:167-172.

FACTORS THAT AID AND HINDER CREATIVITY

In the part of our current *Zeitgeist* pertaining to psychology and education, no word has had more dramatic rise in popularity than "creativity." After generally ignoring the subject, psychologists have come to realize their backwardness in knowledge of this subject. Employers have been asking for more inventive scientists, engineers, and managers. Special courses on how to think creatively have been springing up by the score. Special institutes are being held on the subject. Teachers and educators are asking how they can make courses more stimulating and how they can arouse more productive thinking on the part of students.

The interest is international, as well it might be. The whole world faces two very critical problems—how to feed its exploding population and how to keep the peace. It has been estimated that in the next 20 years we shall need three times the number of scientists and engineers we now have, and they shall have to exercise all the ingenuity of which they are capable. We are reminded by the scriptures, however, that man does not live by bread alone. There is, I think, a very noticeable surgence of interest in the arts in all their forms. We wish to walk in beauty as well as in peace, freedom, and dignity. There is also good reason to desire increased creativity to achieve aesthetic goals.

Investigation of Creativity

My topic suggests that I give most consideration to the abilities and other traits of individuals that make some of them creative and some not. Knowing these traits should help us to recognize which persons are likely to have the potentialities of becoming creatively productive. The same knowledge should help us in taking steps that should increase creative output in ourselves and in others, and other steps that may remove obstacles in the way of creative productivity. Our primary concern, then, will be the basic facts concerning the nature of creative thinking and of the more creative persons, with reference to the application of this information.

Serious investigation of creativity by psychologists began only in recent years. For centuries the common idea had been that only the exceedingly rare person is genuinely creative and that creativity is a divine gift. As such, it was not to be investigated, or at best, there was little hope of understanding it. Even after Darwin came upon the scene, when creativity came to be regarded as some kind of rare, hereditary blessing, there was still little incentive to attempt to understand it because there was thought to be little that one could do about it. In addition to being very rare, the highly creative person's behavior is sometimes eccentric. This has sometimes branded him as being abnormal and even pathological. Mental pathology was similarly avoided as a subject of study by scientific investigators for a long time.

Creativity became an object of scientific study primarily because of the general interest in individual differences. This approach recognizes that individuals differ psychologically in traits or attributes that can be conceived as continua or dimensions— that there can be varying degrees of a quality possessed by different individuals. This concept was eventually applied to creativity, but in serious ways only about a dozen years ago. This new way of looking at the matter permitted us to think that not only a few peculiarly gifted persons but individuals in general possess some degree of the same creative trait or traits.

Reprinted by permission of the author and publisher from *Teachers College Record*, 1962, 63(5).

This conception has opened the door to many kinds of research. We need no longer study creativity by catching the rare persons who are recognized as having creativity to high degree; a multitude of subjects is now available to investigators. We can discover the various aspects of the phenomenon called "creativity." We can find out the conditions under which creative performance occurs or does not occur.

As in the case of all psychological characteristics that make up personality we may be forced to recognize that heredity establishes limits of development for an individual. But there is considerable faith among educators that rarely does an individual realize full development in any respect and that there is generally considerable room for improvement. This faith should also be applied to the creative aspects of personality.

Basic Traits and Creativity

There are a number of approaches to the investigation of the traits or characteristics in which creative individuals are most likely to excel. Some investigators appear to regard the phenomenon of creativity as a single dimension of personality. It is my view that the creative disposition is made up of many components and that its composition depends upon where you find it. Practically all investigators recognize that there are many potentially contributing conditions.

When the problem is approached from the standpoint of individual differences, the most natural scientific technique to apply is that of factor analysis. This is the approach that my associates and I have taken almost exclusively in the Aptitudes Project at the University of Southern California.

According to our original hypotheses[7] we expected to find the more creative individuals to think with greater fluency with more flexibility, and with greater originality. The tests designed to measure fluency present very simple tasks, and the quantity of output determines the scores. When told to produce a list of items of information of a certain kind, how many responses can the examinee give in a limited time? Quality does not count, but, of course, the responses must be appropriate.

Flexibility in thinking means a *change* of some kind—a change in the meaning, interpretation, or use of something, a change in understanding of the task, a change of strategy in doing the task, or a change in direction of thinking, which may mean a new interpretation of the goal.

There has been some debate concerning the meaning of "originality." In our research and in that of others, originality means the production of unusual, farfetched, remote, or clever responses. But there are some who say that an idea is not original or novel unless no human being has ever thought of it earlier. This conception is worthless to the scientist because there is no way of knowing that an idea has never existed before. It is somewhat better to say that a novel idea is a new one so far as the particular individual who has it is concerned. But unless we know the individual's past history of thinking, we cannot be sure of meeting this criterion either.

Fortunately, we can resort to empirical signs of novelty in terms of the statistical infrequency of a response among members of a certain population that is culturally relatively homogeneous. This gives us some workable operations for applying the criterion of unusualness. The index of unusualness can therefore be purely objective. As for the farfetched or remote associations and the clever responses we have as yet no way to avoid some degree of subjectivity of judgment in assessing test performance to obtain an index of origniality.

Another somewhat popular criterion of an original idea is that it is socially useful. Those who deal with practical affairs may be appropriately concerned about this aspect of produced ideas. But such a criterion involves us in values in a way that science cannot deal with directly; hence, the criterion of social usefulness can be quickly dismissed by the psychologist. This does not mean that as a person he is unconcerned about social usefulness. It does mean that as a scientist he cannot afford to be so concerned and so restricted.

Fluency Factors

We shall now give closer attention to the various factors of fluency, flexibility, and originality. It turns out that in verbal tests alone there are three differentiated fluency factors.[9] Ideational fluency has to do with the rate of generation of a quantity of ideas. The idea produced may be as simple as a single word, as complex as the title for a picture or a story, or as phrases and short sentences that convey unitary thoughts. In a test, we may ask the examinee to list all the things he can think of that are solid, flexible, and colored. He may respond with *cloth, leaf, rose petal, hair, skin, leather,* and so on. Any response that fulfills the specifications accepted and counts toward the total score. In other tests, we may ask the examinee to list the consequences of a certain action or event, the various uses of an object, or some appropriate titles for a given story. In all such tests, there are strict time limits.

It is easy to see where an operation such as that in tests of ideational fluency fit into problem solving of many kinds. Perhaps a problem situation, when interpreted in a certain way, calls for an object with a certain set of specifications in order to solve it. Once these specifications are realized, the person who can list pertinent possibilities most rapidly could, other things being equal, solve the problem most quickly.

Many a problem calls for a running through of the likely possibilities during the earlier stage of interpreting or structuring it as well as during the stage of finding solutions. This process also probably depends in some degree upon ideational fluency. Of course it is not necessary to run through *all* the logical possibilities in solving a problem. One can ignore the less promising ones. This point will be touched upon later.

Another kind of fluency is called "associational fluency." It pertains to the completion of relationships, in distinction from the factor of ideational fluency, which involves giving ideas that fit a class. As a test of associational fluency, we may ask the examinee to list all the words he can think of that mean the opposite, or nearly the opposite, of the word "good." He may respond with *bad, poor, sinful, defective, awful, terrible,* and so on. This ability is most obviously of use to the creative writer, who wants to find quickly a variety of verbal expressions without having to resort to a thesaurus.

The factor of associational fluency may have more general utility—for example, whenever we apply thinking by analogy as our strategy in solving problems. Thinking of a correlate is the completion of an analogy. Many solutions to new problems are

achieved by the practice of thinking by analogy. The success of certain kinds of engineers in their work has been predicted to a small extent by means of a test of associational fluency as found by Saunders (21, 1956).

A third kind of fluency is called "expressional fluency." It has to do with the facile construction of sentences. We ask the examinee to write as many four-word sentences as he can, all different, with no word used more than once. We may give the initial letters of the four words, the same four being specified for each sentence—for example, "W_____ c_____ e_____ n_____." To this task, he may reply "We can eat nuts," "Willie comes every night," "Wholesome carrots elevate nations," "Weary cats evade nothing," and so on. You will probably not be surprised when I tell you that in a ninth-grade sample, the girls obtained a higher mean score than the boys.

We do not know yet how much generality to attach to this factor, whether it is limited to tasks such as the writing of sentences or whether it is so broad as to pertain to organizing ideas into systems. If it is as broad as the latter suggestion, it should be of considerable consequence, perhaps in something as important as the trial-and-error development of a scientific theory. The factor has been found significantly related to ratings by psychologists of the creative performances of military officers.*

Flexibility Factors

One type of flexibility we first recognized as "spontaneous flexibility" because the tests that measure it do not even suggest that the examinee be flexible.[5] Without his knowing it, he can make a good score if he varies his *kinds* of responses. If we tell the examinee to list all the uses he can think of for a common brick, the total number of uses listed is a good score for his status on the factor of ideational fluency. But we also score his performance in terms of the number of times he changes *category* of uses. For example, the person who responds with *build a house, build a school, build a*

*From an unpublished study conducted jointly by the Aptitudes Project at the University of Southern California and the Institute for Personality Assessment and Research, University of California, Berkeley.

factory, etc., does not change his class of uses. Another person who responds with *make a paper weight, drive a nail, make baseball bases, throw at a cat, grind up for red powder, make a tombstone for a bird,* etc., changes class with each new response. He shows much more flexibility.

The person who makes a low spontaneous-flexibility score is rigid in the sense that he perseverates within one or a very few classes. As there are several kinds of flexibility in thinking, so there are several kinds of rigidity. When someone tells you that a certain person is rigid, beware of overgeneralization of the term. We do not find in normal (nonpathological) people a very general trait of rigidity vs. flexibility. We find several. This does not say that there are no individuals who are rigid in just about every respect, but the general rule is that they may be rigid in some respects and not in others, at least so far as thinking is concerned.

A new hypothesis may be considered in connection with the factor of spontaneous flexibility. Some advisers on how to think creatively suggest that in starting to solve a new problem, we keep our thinking at a rather high level of abstraction. We think of it first in very general terms. Thus, the person who goes from class to class in the Brick Uses test is operating within the frame of reference of a much broader class within which there are subclasses. A higher level of abstraction may mean thinking in terms of broader classes. This has the effect of broadening the scope of the scanning process in searching for information. Going from ony class to another in the Brick Uses test also means considering all the properties of a brick—its weight, its color, its texture, and so on. These are abstractions all lying within the class of the total nature of a brick. This is reminiscent of a stock method of practicing creative thinking, a method known as "attribute listing" and advocated by Crawford.[3]

A second kind of flexibility has been called "*adaptive* flexibility" for the reason that in tests in which it was first found, the examinee, to succeed, must make changes of some kind—changes in interpretation of the task, in approach or strategy, or in possible solutions. Our current interpretation of the factor of originality is that it is adaptive flexibility in dealing with verbal information.

We have a kind of test, called Plot Titles, in which the examinee is told a very short story and that he is to suggest as many appropriate titles for the story as he can. One of the stories is about a wife who is unable to speak until a specialist performs the appropriate surgery. Then her husband is driven to distraction by her incessant talking until another surgeon eliminates his hearing, when peace is restored in the family.

The number of commonplace titles given to the story may be used as a score for ideational fluency. Such titles include,

> A man and his wife
> Never satisfied
> Medicine triumphs
> A man's decisions
> Talking and hearing

The number of responses rated as "clever" serves as a score for originality. Such titles are exemplified by

> The deaf man and the dumb woman
> Happiness through deafness
> Operation—peace of mind
> Yack, yack, hack

Several other types of tests serve to indicate individual differences in the factor of originality.

Elaboration

In the course of our investigations of abilities involved in planning,[1] we found another kind of ability we have called "elaboration." In one test, given the bare outlines of a plan, the examinee is asked to produce the detailed steps needed to make the plan work. The more details he adds, the better is his score. We believe that the unique feature of this ability is that in tests for it, one item of information leads to another as a kind of extension or completion. In more technical language, we say that the examinee is producing a *variety of implications*.

It was eventually recognized that the abilities of fluency, flexibility (including originality), and elaboration are similar in that the tests of them call for a variety of answers. There is no right or fully determined answer in connection with the information given in the item. There are now parallel tests in which each item *does* have one right answer because it is fully determined by the information given or because there is one conventionally accepted answer. A distinction has therefore been made between *divergent* thinking and *convergent* thinking to represent the two classes of abilities. The abilities of which I have been speaking thus far belong in the divergent-thinking category. Because the individual has to generate his answer or answers, starting from given information, in both categories of abilities, we speak of devergent-*production* factors vs. convergent-*production* factors, respectively.

Quantity vs. Quality

Several questions arise concerning the relationship of quantity and quality of production. One debated and investigated hypothesis is that "quantity breeds quality." This hypothesis holds that if a person produces a greater total number of ideas, he also produces a greater number of high-quality ideas in a limited time. Another view is that a mental set for quantity is inefficient because if a person spends his time producing a lot of low-quality responses, he cannot produce so many good ones.

There is another aspect of this controversy. When a person is set to give "good" answers, he is applying judgment or evaluation as he goes along. On the one hand, it is believed that an evaluative or critical attitude is generally inhibiting to the flow of ideas, good and poor alike. On the other hand, it is believed that the application of evaluation as one proceeds has a selective effect, holding back the low-quality responses and letting the high-quality responses come through.

The well-known brainstorming technique, attributed to Alex Osborn[18] and employed by many others, conforms to the first of these two schools of thought. One of its chief claimed virtues is that the separation of production and evaluation—in other words, suspended judgment—is better procedure. As originally applied, of course, brainstorming has other features, which include thinking in small groups rather than thinking by individuals in seclusion.

The experimental results bearing upon the issue of suspended judgment are somewhat mixed. Meadow *et al.*,[16] report that with suspended judgment, the production of "good" answers was a little more than doubled. The problems were to suggest unusual uses for a wire coat hanger and for a broom. The criteria for "good" responses were "unique" and "useful."

In our Aptitudes Project,[2] we gave the Plot Titles test with and without the specific instruction to give clever titles. It was expected that the instruction for clever titles would entail more evaluation. The effects of this instruction were shown by a reduction in the number of low-quality responses, an increase in the number of high-quality responses, and a higher average rating of degree of cleverness.

Hyman[13] found that his subjects generated 68% more responses under quantity instructions, but that this increase in "good" responses, where "good" meant uncommon and of "high quality," failed to keep pace with the total output. Hyman is probably right when he concludes that quantity may breed quality for some types of problems but not for others. It is also probably true that the *kind* of evaluative attitude applied by the thinker has much to do with the quantity and quality of responses he produces.

Divergent thinking is a matter of scanning one' stored information to find answers to satisfy a special search model. Evaluation comes into the picture in determining whether or not the produced information fits the search model. Relaxed evaluation would permit a broadening of the base of the search, whereas an evaluative attitude with some degree of strictness should narrow the search. In doing so, however, it may lead more efficently to good answers. This should depend upon the clarity and accuracy of the search model. If the thinker has a good search model, the application of evaluation while he thinks should be helpful.

But if evaluation is of a more vague kind, such as that involving a fear of being unconventional, a fear of thinking socially unacceptable thoughts, or a fear of being wrong, it should be definitely better to suspend judgments based on such criteria. Evaluation incident to an overly strong desire for a quick solution would also be handicapping. But evaluation for the sake of efficient scanning, where there is good strategy in the scanning process, should be beneficial.

Hyman[13] has found that a general critical attitude can have rather broad transfer effects in solving problems. A group of engineers, in Hyman's experiment, read some previously given solutions to a certain practical problem under the instruction to list all the good points that they could see in those solutions. A second group was instructed to list all the faults they could see in the same solutions. Later, in solving the same problem and in solving a new one, the uncritical readers suggested solutions of their own that were rated higher on the average than those of the critical group. Thus, very general critical attitudes must be taken into account.

Group vs. Individual Thinking

The question of group thinking vs. individual thinking has received a great deal of attention. The virtue claimed for group thinking in brainstorming is that one person stimulates another. In support of this hypothesis, Osborn[19] reports that about a third of the ideas produced in group brainstorming are of the "hitchhiking" type. In such a case, one person's idea is based upon another person's idea.

There are results which do not support his hypothesis, however. Taylor *et al.*,[23] found a larger number of unrepeated ideas produced by individuals working alone than by those working in groups, where both kinds of thinkers were working under the condition of suspended judgment. Taylor points out that the group condition man have the effect of channeling thinking in similar directions, reducing the variety and therefore the quantity of unrepeated ideas.

Perhaps neither the group nor the isolation condition is best under all circumstances or for all individuals. It is quite possible that both can be applied to advantage. The preference of the thinker should have something to do with the choice of condition. A great deal is made of the point that the highly creative person is an independent thinker and that his creation may be a highly personal thing. Torrance[21] (1959) found that the more highly creative child (as indicated by his test scores) in a small group often works by himself or is somehow induced by the others to do so.

Whatever the outcome of brainstorming sessions in particular instances, experiments show that courses on creative thinking that are heavily weighted with brainstorming exercises seem to leave the students with beneficial results, and these results have some degree of permanence.[15,20] How much of the improvement to attribute to the brainstorming technique and to which aspects of it the improvement should be attributed are open questions.

Context of Creation

From the discussion thus far, one may conclude that creative performances are to be identified psychologically as a small number of divergent-production operations. Two different qualifications must be introduced. One exception is that two of the factors that we in the Aptitudes Project regarded from the first as being pertinent to creative thinking fall outside the divergent-production group. The other exception is that I have not yet told the whole story regarding the divergent-production factors. I shall make good on the latter omission first.

I have repeatedly stated that the tests on the factors thus far described are *verbal* tests. They pertain to verbally stated information. There are other kinds of information, and the question comes up whether the same person is usually equally creative in handling different kinds of information, material, or content. From our analytical results, we can say that it can happen, but we should rarely expect the same person to be equally capable of creativity in science, in the arts, mathematics, administration, and musical composition. Highly creative individuals in many of these different areas may have outstanding qualities in common, but psychological study indicates that they also have some marked differences.

In the area of divergent-production abilities alone, we find that individuals may vbe uneven in handling verbal vs. concrete vs. symbolic material. Symbolic material is the kind with which the mathematician deals—numbers and letters. Fluency, flexibility, and elaboration in dealing with concrete (perceived) material are probably of greater importance to the inventor of gadgets, the painter, and the composer, whereas the same kinds of abilities for dealing with verbal material or content are more important for the scientist. In other words, there are parallel abilities for dealing with concrete (or figural) material, symbolic material, and verbally meaningful (or semantic) material.

One of our earlier hypotheses[7] was that the unusually creative person has a high degree of sensitivity to problems. One person notices something wrong or in need of improvement, whereas another fails to observe defects, deficiencies, or errors. The observation of imperfections starts the creative person on his way to creative production. The observation of inadequacy of solutions also keeps the creative thinker at work on his problem.[17]

Factor analysis has consistently upheld this hypothesis by finding an ability common to a variety of tests calling for the noticing of defects and deficiencies in such things as common household appliances, social customs, or in solutions to problems. Such an ability, however, seems to fit better in the general category of evaluative factors than it does in that of divergent production.

Not being satisfied with things as they are is a matter of evaluation. We hear a great deal about the "divine discontent" of the creative person. It is said that Thomas A. Edison frequently admonished his workers with the comment, "There must be a better way. Go and find it." The uncreative, in contrast, are often willing to settle for half-way measures and tolerably successful solutions to problems.

Another of our initial hypotheses was that many an invention or new idea is the revision of something that is already known. But the revision is not an obvious one. It takes quite a change in the meaning, interpretation, or use of an object to achieve such an innovation. One of our tests, designed for such an ability, asks which of five objects or their parts could be most reasonably adapted to be used to start a fire when there are available the following items: a fountain pen, an onion, a pocket watch, a light bulb, and a bowling ball. The accepted answer is "pocket watch," since the cover of the watch face could be used as a condensing lens. Since this and other such tests call for one best answer, this factor falls logically in the convergent-production category. The feature that makes a contribution to creativity is that a transformation must occur; objects must be redefined. Individuals who are clever at improvising seem to show this kind of ability.

There are other abilities outside the divergent-production category that make some contribution to creative performances in their own ways. We have seen that one of the evaluative abilities—sensitivity to problems—has a function in getting the creative thinker started. Other evaluative abilities should have their uses, whether judgment is suspended or not, in determining whether the products of thinking are good, useful, suitable, adequate, or desirable. If the creator is to finish his job, he will eventually appraise his product, and he will revise it if he feels that revision is called for.

Cognition and Memory

Thus far I have spoken of three major categories of intellectual factors—abilities of divergent-production, convergent-production, and evaluation. There are two other major categories—cognitive abilities and memory abilities—all distinguished from those in the first-mentioned categories and from each other. Cognitive abilities have to do with discovery, recognition, or comprehension of information in various forms. Memory abilities have to do with storage or retention of information.

Many people, including some teachers, have for some reason disparaged memory and memory abilities. Some of them, who emphasize the importance of thinking, seem wrongly to believe that good thinking and good memory are incompatible qualities, perhaps even negatively correlated. Actually, good memory contributes to good thinking.

It is not a good, well-stocked memory, as such, that is bad, for even the most creative people have given due credit to stored information. It is the way in which storage is achieved and organized that makes the difference between the graduate who is sometimes described as "merely a walking encyclopedia" and the graduate who has a usable and fruitful fund of information. Memory abilities thus make their indirect but important contribution to creative performance.

The question often arises concerning the relation of creativity to intelligence. In connection with this question, the usual conception of "intelligence" is that which is measured by such tests as the Stanford Binet, the Wechsler scales, or the California Test of Mental Maturity.

In discussing abilities related to creativity, I have referred to them as intellectual factors. It is very doubtful whether these abilities, particularly those in the divergent-production category, are represented to any appreciable degree in standard IQ tests. IQ tests were designed to predict success in school learning, particularly in reading, arithmetic, and the subject-matter or informational courses. But we now know that there are many other kinds of intellectual abilities.

Studies of groups of research scientists and engineers[22] show that such groups have high average scores on IQ tests. They would need to have higher-than-average IQs to have passed all their academic hurdles, most of them including the PhD. But only a fraction of these are outstanding for creative performance. But within groups of scientists and engineers, the correlation found between IQ-test scores and creative performance is usually rather low. This is due in part to the restriction of range of IQ within such groups. The evidence seems to indicate that although the qualities in traditional IQ intelligence may be of some help to the creative scientist or engineer, they are by no means sufficient.

The low correlation between creativity and IQ is also found at younger age groups. In high school students, Getzels and Jackson[21] (1959) found that if the highest 20% of the subjects on IQ were selected as "gifted," 70% of those who stood in the highest 20% in terms of divergent-thinking tests would have been missed. Torrance [21] (1959) has reported a similar finding in the elementary grades. In both instances, it was reported that the teachers knew their high-IQ students better and like them better. The high-creative without high IQs were often regarded as nuisances, and they were somewhat estanged from other students. Those with both high IQ *and* high creativity were recognized as having unusual but sound ideas, to be good in planning and improvising, and effective in getting attention[21] (1959).*

Non-aptitude Traits

The assessment of traits of temperament, interest, and attitude in connection with creativity has been approached in various ways. One approach has been to find the most outstandingly creative individuals in different profession groups, such as architects, writers, and scientists, and to assess them quite thoroughly by methods that are available. If a creative group differs systematically from the general population or, better, some group outside the profession but matched with it for age, sex, and educational level, it is concluded that this creative group stands apart or is distinguished by the personality trait or traits in question.

There are obvious dangers in drawing conclu-sions from studies of this kind, unless an appropriate control group has been used. When it is found that creative architects, scientists, mathematicians, and writers alike tend to score highest on theoretical and esthetic interest on the Allport-Vernon-Lindzey *Study of Values,* this may occur just because any high-IQ group would do the same.[14] When it is found that the creative males tend to score relatively in the direction of femininity on the masculinity-femininity scale of the *Minnesota Multophasic Personality Inventory* scale, we remember that Terman and Miles[24] found that as members of the two sexes are more intelligent and better educated, they respond more alike to test items on masculinity vs. femininity. Nor should it be surprising that the creative groups just mentioned should tend to score high on the Strong *Vocational Interest Blank* scales for architect, psychologist, and author-journalist.

A somewhat better approach is to obtain two samples from the same profession, composed of highly creative and less creative individuals, respectively. The groups can then be compared with respect to various assessed qualities. Sometimes the groups are distinguished on the basis of judgments by their teachers.[4,12] In still other studies, subjects of mixed occupations but similar in IQ and educational level have been tested with measures of creative aptitude and of non-aptitude traits.[10]

Non-aptitude Differences

We have had to recognize that creative occupational groups share parallel but different exceptional abilities. We should expect the various groups to show some non-aptitude qualities in common and also to show some differences. One difference, for example, has been noted between creative students of art and of science. The more creative art student has been reported to be more of an observer than a participant in what is going on.[12] The more creative science student is reported to be more of a participant than the less creative student.[6] Such observations should prevent our generalizing conclusions obtained from one creative group to all other creative groups.

*For systematic treatments of a unified theory of intelligence see references (8, 11).

There are many ways in which creative people of many groups are alike, however. There is general agreement that the highly creative person, particularly the original person, is self-confident. Which comes first, originality or self-confidence? It is a little like the old hen-and-the-egg problem. Probably, it works both ways: Originality yields success and hence self-confidence, and self-confidence leads the individual to attempt to solve problems where others would give up. In some instances, self-confidence goes over into conceit, as we have all been aware. Sometimes this is fed by the adulations of admirers. Sometimes it may suggest an underlying hypersensitivity to criticism.

Along with self-confidence, there is usually self-assurance or social boldness. The creative person is especially confident about his own judgment and his own evaluations of his work. He is often described as an independent thinker, which includes having an independent set of values. If he thinks his product is good, he discounts the criticisms of others and may disparage their judgments.

Not only is he more or less independent of other people's judgments, he may be self-sufficient in that he can take people or he can let them alone. He is likely to find ideas more important than people, though he is not necessarily a social recluse. These qualities do not add to his popularity with others, so he is in danger of becoming estranged from his parents, his teachers, and his peers. Contributing to this state of affairs also is a lack of mutual understanding. The creative child and his associates may need special counseling to help smooth over some roughness in interpersonal relationships. This can be done without curbing development along creative lines.

We have found that young men who stand high in one or more kinds of fluency are likely to be somewhat impulsive, cheerful, and relaxed. Those who score high in tests of originality tend to have strong esthetic interests, and they like to indulge in divergent thinking. They do not feel much need for meticulousness or for discipline. Somewhat surprisingly, they show no particular dislike for conventional or socially approved behavior, nor do they show signs of neuroticism.

One of the striking traits found by Getzels and Jackson[21] (1959) among high school students who stand high in divergent-thinking tests is a strong sense of humor. This is shown particularly in the kinds of stories they tell in response to pictures. For example, one picture showed a young man working at his desk at six-thirty in the morning. A bright but less creative student wrote the following kind of story: "This young man is very ambitious to get ahead. He comes early every morning to impress his boss so he will be promoted." A more creative student told the following kind of story: "This picture is the office of a firm that manufactures breakfast cereals. It has just found a formula to produce a new kind of cereal that will bend, sag, and sway. The man is a private eye employed by a rival firm to obtain the formula. He thinks he has found it and copies it. It turns out to be the wrong formula, and the competitor's factory blows up."

Such stories usually involve some novel twist or transformation, such as the expression regarding the cereal that will "bend, sag, and sway." Many stories derive their humor from such a source. The person who makes up such stories is exhibiting verbal or semantic transformations, which is a sign that he has a fair degree of the factor of originality. Since this is a semantic ability, and since Getzels and Jackson's tests were verbal, we may well question whether the affiliation of humor and the ability to produce transformations extends to other kinds of content, figural or symbolic. It is probably true, however, that creative painters, composers, and mathematicians also experience a certain amount of enjoyment, if not amusement, in playfulness with their own kinds of materials.

Final Suggestions

Although the temperament and motivational qualities can help us somewhat in identifying potentially creative people, no one of them is a dependable sign, nor would all of them collectively be sufficient. Neither do these qualities help us very much in understanding the nature of the creative processes. On the whole, we have less chance of changing individuals with respect to these qualities in order to increase their creativity, except for changing certain attitudes.

Our chief hope, then, of either identifying the more creative persons or enhancing their creative performances lies with the aptitude factors. If we regard the intellectual factors as distinct but somewhat generalized thinking skills, this statement seems more reasonable. We develop skills by practicing them. The question, then, is one of what kinds of practice can best be applied and under what conditions.

An understanding of the nature of the skills is one of the most important steps either for the teacher or the student. When we know what kind of skill is to be developed, we have a more clearly defined goal toward which to work. Torrance[21] (1959) reports that even after 20 minutes of instruction on the nature of divergent-thinking processes, grade-school children showed a clearly observable improvement in performing tasks of this type.

Although special courses on creative thinking have proved beneficial, our whole educational system can be of greater help by giving more attention to this subject. There is abundant opportunity to teach almost any subject in ways that call for productive thinking rather than rote memory. Even the multiplication tables can be taught in ways that give the pupil insight into properties of the number system.

In some experimental courses at the University of Illinois in which mathematics is taught from the lower grades on by what is called a "discovery" method, instead of telling the child the axioms and other principles of mathematics, the teacher lets him discover them for himself by exposing him to appropriate examples. Also at the University of Illinois, science is being taught to children by a discovery method. Some natural phenomenon is demonstrated without explanations to the class, perhaps in motion-picture form. From then on, it is a matter of the students' asking questions, with minimum information being given by the teacher, until the student develops his own satisfactory hypothesis.

Education in this country has unfortunately been too much dominated by the learning theory based upon the stimulus-response model of Thorndike, Hull, and Skinner. People, after all, are not rats (with a few exceptions), and they are not pigeons (with similar exceptions). Let us make full use of the human brains that have been granted to us. Let us apply a psychology that recognizes the full range of human intellectual qualities. We must make more complete use of our most precious national resource—the intellectual abilities of our people, including their creative potentialities.

References

1. Berger, R.M., Guilford, J.P., and Christensen, P.R. A factor-analytic study of planning abilities. *Psychol. Monogr.*, 1957, 71, (Whole No. 435).
2. Christensen, P.R., Guilford, J.P., and Wilson, R.C. Relations of creative responses to working time and instructions. *J. exp. Psychol.*, 1957, 53, 82-88.
3. Crawford, R.P. *Techniques of creative thinking.* New York: Hawthorne Books, 1952.
4. Drevdahl, J.E. Factors of importance for creativity. *J. clin. Psychol.*, 1956, 12, 21-26.
5. Frick, J.W., Guilford, J.P., Christensen, P.R., and Merrifield, P.R. A factor-analytic study of flexibility in thinking. *Educ. psychol. Measmt.*, 1959, 19, 469-496.
6. Garwood, D.S. Some personality factors related to creativity in young scientists. Unpublished doctoral dissertation, Claremont Graduate School, 1961.
7. Guilford, J.P. Creativity. *Amer. Psychologist*, 1950, 5, 444-454.
8. ———. Three faces of intellect. *Amer. Psychologist*, 1959, 14, 469-479.
9. Guilford, J.P., and Christensen, P.R. A factor-analytic study of verbal fluency. *Rep. psychol. Lab.*, No. 17. Los Angeles: Univer. Southern Calfornia, 1957.
10. Guilford, J.P., Christensen, P.R., Frick, J.W., and Merrifield, P.R. The relations of creative-thinking aptitudes to non-aptitude personality traits. *Rep. psychol. Lab.*, No. 20. Los Angeles: Univer. Southern California, 1957.
11. Guilford, J.P., and Merrifield, P.R. The structure of intellect model: its uses and implications. *Rep. psychol. Lab.*, No. 24. Los Angeles: Univer. Southern California, 1960.
12. Hammer, E.F. *Creativity.* New York: Random House, 1961.
13. Hyman, H. *Some experiments in creativity.* New York: General Electric, Relations Services, 1960.
14. MacKinnon, D. What do we mean by talent and how do we use it? In *The search for talent.* New York: College Entrance Board, 1960.
15. Meadow, A., and Parnes, S.J. Evaluation of training in creative problem solving. *J. appl. Psychol.*, 1959, 43, 189-194.
16. Meadow, A., Parnes, S.J., and Reese, H. Influence of brainstorming instructions and problem sequence on a creative problem solving test. *J. appl. Psychol.*, 1959, 43, 413-416.
17. Merrifield, P.R., Guilford, J.P., Christensen, P.R., and Frick, J.W. A factor-analytical study of problem-solving abilities. *Rep. psychol. Lab.*, No. 22. Los Angeles: Univer. Southern California, 1960.
18. Osborn, A.F. *Applied imagination.* New York: Scribner's, 1953.
19. ———. *Development of creative education.* Buffalo, N.Y.: Creative Education Foundation, 1961.
20. Parnes, S.J., and Meadow, A. Evaluation of persistence of effects produced by a creative problem solving course. *Psychol. Reports*, 1960, 7, 357-361.

21. Taylor, C.W. (Ed.). *Research conference on the identification of creative scientific talent.* Salt Lake City, Utah: Univer. of Utah Press, 1956, 1958, 1959.

22. Taylor, D.W. Thinking and creativity. *Ann. N.Y. Acad. Sci.,* 1960, 91, 108-127.

23. Taylor, D.W., Berry, P.C., and Block, C.H. Does group participation when using brainstorming facilitate or inhibit creative thinking? *Admin. Sci. Quart.,* 1958, 3, 23-47.

24. Terman, L.M., and Miles, Catherine C. *Sex and personality.* New York: McGraw-Hill, 1936.

61

CREATIVITY AND INGENUITY: A RELATIONSHIP?

Some outstanding individuals are called creative and others are considered ingenious. Are these just synonyms for the same kinds of people, or are they really different? If so, how?

The purpose of this research project was to seek answers to these and other questions related to creativity and ingenuity.

E. Paul Torrance (1965) has defined creativity: "the process of becoming sensitive to problems, deficiencies, gaps in knowledge, missing elements, disharmonies, and so on; identifying the difficulty; searching for solutions, making guesses or formulating hypotheses about the deficiencies; testing and retesting these hypotheses and possibly modifying and retesting them; and finally communicating the results."

An exhaustive study of all the literature definitely reveals a great amount of research on creativity since 1950, but basically none on ingenuity (Buros, 1965).

The need for better understanding of creative people has been apparent for some time. Dauw (1965) has summarized much of the literature about creativity in organizations and in various settings (Dauw and Fredian, 1971).

METHOD. The data for this study were collected by administering three tests to 109 graduate and undergraduate students at two private universities. The students ranged in age from 21 to 51. All the graduate students were employed full-time in various jobs, half in private industry and half in careers with the Federal Government.

TESTS. Two tests measured creative abilities, the Similes Preference Inventory [Pearson and Maddi, (1966)] and the Torrance Tests of Creative Thinking (Torrance, 1966). The third test was designed to measure ingenuity, the Flanagan Industrial Test of Ingenuity (Flanagan, 1965).

The SPI was developed by Pearson and Maddi (1966) as a measure of the active, introceptive form of a tendency to variety. SPI's reflection of an active form of a tendency to variety has substantial positive relationship with originality of performance. In one research project, Dauw (1968) reported correlations of .42 + .32 between the SPI and a completely different measure of creativity, the Torrance Tests of Creative Thinking (1966).

The TTCT has both verbal and figural forms. Form B (Figural) was used here. This figural test has three subtests consisting of picture construction, incomplete figures and responding to incomplete circles. Both the SPI and TTCT have been shown to measure divergent thinking (Torrance, 1965).

The Flanagan Industrial Test of Ingenuity (1965) is considered a test of the ability to think of ingenious and effective ways of doing things. It consists of 20 problems that must be solved by providing the proper word or words. Clues are given for each problem consisting of the first and last letters of the word or words that must be used. The score is based on the number of correct solutions given. The F.I.T. test of ingenuity was correlated with the more detailed Flanagan Aptitude Classification Tests and the correlation on ingenuity was .531 (Flanagan, 1965).

Results

Table I reveals the various means and standard deviations of the groups of students. It shows a lack of significant correlations, suggesting there is no correlation between creativity and ingenuity as measured by these instruments.

Table II isolates the data just for the very highest and lowest scores on creativity to determine

Table I
Correlations Between Tests

	SPI	FIT	TTCT ORIG	TTCT ELAB	r.025 SPI-FIT	r.025 ORIG-FIT	r.025 ELAB-FIT
DGS(N = 45)					−.18	−.07	.1
$\overline{X}$	9.2	10.8	25.76	38.7	NS	NS	NS
S	8.6	3.9	8.8	16.2			
DGW (N = 25)					−.03	.21	.26
$\overline{X}$	9.7	11.2	27.7	39.9	NS	NS	NS
S	9.8	4.4	10.8	17.1			
DUS(N = 10)					.28	.78	.62
$\overline{X}$	14.4	9.7	23.9	33.4	NS	S	NS
S	12.4	4.7	8.2	13.8			
LUS(N = 29)					.09	.03	.06
$\overline{X}$	10.2	10.5	17.2	25.1	NS	NS	NS
S	10.6	3.5	7.4	10.1			
TOTAL(N = 109)					−.05	.1	.18
$\overline{X}$	10.1	10.7	24.2	34.9	NS	NS	NS
S	9.8	3.8	9.8	15.9			

DGS = DePaul Graduate Students
DGW = DePaul Graduate-Government Workers
DUS = DePaul Undergraduates
LUS = Loyola Undergraduates

Table II
High and Low Creative Correlations

High Creatives		N	$\overline{X}$	S	r.025
$X \overline{\geq} 17$	SPI	23	26.0	8.2	.09
	FIT	23	10.6	3.1	NS
$X \overline{\geq} 32$	ORIG	23	39.5	6.0	.36
	FIT	23	11.0	3.6	NS
$X \overline{\geq} 48$	ELAB	24	58.5	9.2	−.07
	FIT	24	11.5	4.2	NS

Low Creatives		N	$\overline{X}$	S	r.025
$X \overline{\geq} 2$	SPI	22	1.6	.6	.06
	FIT	22	11.1	3.7	NS
$X \overline{\leq} 15$	ORIG	23	11.5	8.1	.01
	FIT	23	10.1	14.4	NS
$X \overline{\leq} 21$	ELAB	22	16.8	3.8	−.29
	FIT	22	9.7	3.8	NS

whether significant differences existed among these subgroups. Again, no relationship existed.

Table III makes comparisons between the various groups of students, to determine whether any differences existed. Various statistical tests performed included the F-test of homogeneity (Freund and Williams, 1964) and the T-test (Chase, 1967). The only significant differences are revealed in Table III C and D where the De Paul University, Graduate and Undergraduate groups both scored significantly higher in creativity than the Loyola Undergraduate group.

Discussion

This research project seems to show there is no relationship between creativity and ingenuity as measured by these instruments. There certainly may exist people who are able to function both "creatively" and "ingeniously," and hopefully future research may lead to better instruments to assess these abilities.

Perhaps the crucial issues at stake here are the differences between divergent and convergent

Table III
Significance of Differences

A.	DGS (N = 45)					DGW (N = 25)		
	$\overline{X}$	S	S^2	F-Test (.05)	T-Test (.05)	$\overline{X}$	S	S^2
SPI	9.2	8.6	74	1.30 NS	.22 NS	9.7	9.8	96
FIT	10.8	3.9	15	1.26 NS	.37 NS	11.2	4.4	19
ORIG	25.8	8.8	77	1.52 NS	.76 NS	27.7	10.8	117
ELAB	38.7	16.2	262	1.11 NS	.29 NS	39.9	17.1	292

B.	DGS (N = 45)					DUS (N = 10)		
	$\overline{X}$	S	S^2	F-Test (.05)	T-Test (.05)	$\overline{X}$	S	S^2
SPI	9.2	8.6	74	2.08 NS	1.27 NS	14.4	12.4	154
FIT	10.8	3.9	15	1.47 NS	.69 NS	9.7	4.7	22
ORIG	25.8	8.8	77	1.15 NS	1.07 NS	28.9	8.2	17
ELAB	38.7	16.2	262	1.38 NS	1.06 NS	33.4	13.8	190

C.	LUS (N = 29)					DUS (N = 10)		
	$\overline{X}$	S	S^2	F-Test (.05)	T-Test (.05)	$\overline{X}$	S	S^2
SPI	10.2	10.6	112	1.38 NS	.95 NS	14.4	12.4	154
FIT	10.5	3.5	12	1.83 NS	.50 NS	9.7	4.7	22
ORIG	17.2	7.4	55	1.22 NS	4.03 S	28.9	8.2	67
ELAB	25.1	10.1	102	1.86 NS	1.75 NS.05 S.10	33.4	13.8	190

D.	DGS (N = 45)					LUS (N = 29)		
	$\overline{X}$	S	S^2	F-Test (.05)	T-Test (.05)	$\overline{X}$	S	S^2
SPI	9.2	8.6	74	1.51 NS	.42 NS	10.2	10.6	112
FIT	10.8	3.9	15	1.25 NS	.35 NS	10.5	3.5	12
ORIG	25.8	8.8	77	1.40 NS	4.55 S	17.2	7.4	55
ELAB	38.7	16.2	262	2.57 S	4.39 S	25.1	10.1	102

thinking. A close inspection of the ingenuity test suggests it may be measuring convergent thinking, whereas the Torrance tests definitely do measure divergent thinking abilities (Torrance, 1962, 1965, and 1966). Future research may also show more clearly what is the best definition of ingenuity and whether it is a convergent or divergent thinking ability.

Bibliography

Buros, O.K. *The Sixth Mental Measurements Yearbook.* Highland Park, N.J.: The Grayphon Press, 1965.

Chase, Clinton I. *Elementary Statistical Procedures.* New York: McGraw-Hill, 1967.

Dauw, Dean C. "Creativity in Organizations." *Personnel Journal.* Vol. 45, Number 8, September 1966, pp. 465-474.

———. "Creativity Research on Actuaries." *The Journal of Creative Behavior.* Vol. 2, Number 4, Fall 1968, pp. 274-280.

Dauw, Dean C. and Fredian, A.J. *Creativity and Innovation in Organizations.* Dubuque, Iowa: Kendall/Hunt Publishing Company, 1971.

Flanagan, John C. *Flanagan Industrial Tests Manual.* Chicago: Science Research Associates, 1965.

Freund, John E. and Williams, F.J. *Elementary Business Statistics: The Modern Approach.* Englewood Cliffs, N.J.: Prentice-Hall, Inc., 1964.

Pearson, Pamela H. and Maddi, S.J. "The Similies Preference Inventory." *Journal of Consulting Psychology.* Vol. 30, Number 4, 1966, pp. 301-308.

Torrance, E. Paul. Guiding Creative Talent. Englewood Cliffs, N.J.: Prentice-Hall, Inc., 1962, Chaps. 2, 3, Appendix.

———. *Rewording Creative Behavior: Experiments in Classroom Creativity.* Englewood Cliffs, N.J.: Prentice-Hall, Inc., 1965, Chap. 3 and Appendix A.

———. "Scientific Views of Creativity and Factors Affecting It's Growth." *Daedalus.* Summer 1965, pp. 94, 663-681.

———. *Torrance Tests of Creative Thinking.* Princeton: Personnel Press, Inc., 1966.

SCHOLASTIC APTITUDES AND VOCATIONAL NEEDS OF ORIGINAL THINKERS AND GOOD ELABORATORS

This study seeks to expand the concept of creativity by investigating the scholastic aptitudes and vocational needs of highly creative public high school seniors. Torrance's (1962) Minnesota Tests of Creative Thinking were administered to 708 seniors. Students scoring highest and lowest on two scales, originality and elaboration, were divided into 12 criterion groups (N = 311) among boys and girls. Significant differences were obtained on the Minnesota Scholastic Aptitude Test and the Minnesota Importance Questionnaire (MIQ) (Weiss, Dawis, England & Lofquist, 1964). Highly original seniors had significantly stronger needs than good elaborators on four MIQ scales. Students highest in both abilities had stronger needs than either high originals or good elaborators on five other MIQ scales.

Creativity and creative thinking abilities are being increasingly studied to improve the nation's scientific productivity, to understand man's cognitive functioning, and to aid counselors' perceptions of students' personality dynamics. The six national research conferences on creativity sponsored by the National Science Foundation and the University of Utah illustrate this trend (Taylor & Barron, 1963; Taylor, 1964a, 1964b).

Torrance (1962, 1965a, 1965b) has continually emphasized the need to understand creative abilities and to reward creative behavior. Previous research by Getzels & Jackson (1958) and Torrance (1962) revealed that highly creative students with lower IQ's achieved as well in school as highly intelligent students with IQ's higher by 20 points. Parloff and Datta (1964) spotlighted the personalities of highly creative high school seniors as being different from those of slightly less creative seniors scoring equally well in scholastic aptitude and science tests. Such personality characteristics were expected to associate with different career choices. Torrance and Gupta (1964) found that fourth grade children made more unconventional occupational choices under experimental conditions involving planned experiences in creative thinking. Perrone (1963) found boys choosing service occupations according to Roe's (1956) classification were less creative than boys choosing other categories of jobs.

Within all these studies, however, the primary focus was upon highly creative abilities, while little attention was given to the various kinds of creative thinking abilities. The present research was designed to test hypothesized differences among original thinkers and good elaborators: those students scoring highest on two scales (originality and elaboration) of Torrance's (1962) Minnesota Tests of Creative Thinking (MTCT). Each scale includes a verbal and nonverbal component added into a total score (Torrance, 1963). Tables for scoring are presented whereby, for example, originality denotes statistical infrequency of response. The figural and verbal measures assess different kinds of functioning. Thus, the two kinds of tests are combined so that the measures used would represent as broad a sampling as possible in a battery of this length.

Original thinkers (Torrance & Gupta, 1964) are those students who are able to get away from the obvious and break away from the beaten path. They see relationships and think of ideas and solutions different from others in the class. Good elaborators are able to take an idea or task and spell out the detail. They can "embroider" a simple idea and make it fancy and attractive. They are able to develop very detailed or thorough plans for projects.

The distinction between original thinkers and

good elaborators can also be inferred from other writers. Maslow (1954) described a primary and secondary creativity. Mackworth (1965) singled out "problem-finders" and "problem-solvers," while Leary (1964) termed them "creative-creators" and "reproductive-creators." Thus, original thinkers may possibly be analogous to the primary creatives, the problem-finders, and the creative creators. Elaborating thinkers may be similar to the secondary creatives, the problem-solvers, and the reproductive-creators.

Procedures

In one metropolitan Minnesota public high school in a middle-class area, 708 seniors were administered the MTCT. On the basis of scores on the two MTCT scales of originality and elaboration (approximately the highest and lowest 27 per cent), 12 groups of creative thinkers (N = 311) were designated—six in each of the sexes who were classified as high and low original thinkers, high and low elaborating thinkers, and students scoring highest and lowest in both abilities.

The 12 criterion groups were administered the Minnesota Importance Questionnaire (Weiss, Dawis, England & Lofquist, 1964) and asked to list their vocational choices. Other test scores were obtained from school files. Analysis of variance designs (creativity groups nested within sex-level classifications) and chi-square tests were made on the data.

Results

Sex and Creativity

Table 1 presents data revealing that senior girls scored significantly higher ($p < 01$) than boys in verbal, nonverbal, and total elaboration and in verbal originality. This is consistent with previous research where girls tend to have better developed verbal abilities. Apparently, they have also been better reinforced to develop their creative abilities (Torrance, 1965a). It is generally recognized that society expects girls and women to do a large share of its elaborating—working out the details of plans, making things fancy, and making the arrangements necessary to carry out ideas, but usually within certain limits. Most studies involving tests of ability, achievement and interest also show female superiority in the verbal area. Males have generally shown superiority over females on most tests of problem solving and originality, especially when verbal fluency is not an important factor in performance. Thus, it was reasoned and shown in this study that the girls excelled boys on all the creativity measures except nonverbal (figural) originality.

Aptitude Results

The mean scores on the Minnesota Scholastic Aptitude Test for all the high and low creative students by sex were significantly different at the .05 level by the analysis of variance. The 79 highly creative boys had a mean of 46.74 compared with a mean of 55.68 for 86 highly creative girls. But

Table 1

Means and Variances of 708 Senior Boys and Girls on the Originality and Elaboration Factors of the Minnesota Tests of Creative Thinking

Creativity Factors	Boys (N = 348)		Girls (N = 360)	
	X	S^2	X	S^2
Originality				
Nonverbal originality	14.49	41.12	15.19	38.13
Verbal originality	24.43	212.91	25.41**	201.27
Originality (total)	38.90	317.25	40.60	298.10
Elaboration				
Nonverbal elaboration	45.31	485.89	53.14***	537.83
Verbal elaboration	5.13	24.45	6.46**	34.65
Elaboration (total)	50.40	568.40	59.81***	610.34

***$p < .001$.
**$p < .01$.

66

the mean for the 66 low creative boys was 29.02, while the mean for the 80 low creative girls was 26.78. These results seem consistent with those presented in Table 1 where girls tend to score higher in verbal measures. In addition, the girls scoring highest in both originality and elaboration had significantly higher (p < .01.) scores than either highly elaborating or original girls on the MSAT (means were 74.71, 53.66, and 48.24). The difference of 5.42 between the latter means closely approached significance, supporting the tendency for highly elaborating girls to obtain better aptitude scores and also better grades.

Within the initial sample (N = 708), the Pearson product-moment correlation coefficient between MSAT and total creativity score was .32. Thus, only nine per cent of the variance in creativity scores can be accounted for by ability as measured by MSAT.

The MSAT results were also confirmed in high school rank (HSR), although no differences were significant between originnal thinkers and good elaborators. However, the 165 highly creative students achieved significantly higher (p < .01) school grades than the 146 low creative students (mean HSR was 63.04 compared with 44.29).

Vocational Need Results

Occupational choice data are presented in Tables 2 (boys) and 3 (girls) to place in focus the subsequent discussion of vocational needs. An association was found between levels of creative thinking ability and occupational choices for boys (p < .01) and girls (p < .001). More highly creative boys chose careers in Roe's categories of service, organization, general cultural and arts and entertainment, while low creative boys chose jobs in technology. More highly creative girls selected careers in categories of general cultural and arts and entertainment, while more low creative girls chose jobs in organization.

Even more significant differences are masked by the grouping of careers into categories. For example, many highly creative girls selected careers as psychologists, social workers, etc., in the service category, but these were offset by the many low creative girls choosing practical nursing within the same category. The results in Tables 2 and 3 cannot be explained by intelligence, as has been shown by Getzels & Jackson (1958), Torrance (1962, 1965a), and Perrone (1963).

Associated with these occupational choices were specific vocational needs measured by the Minnesota Importance Questionnaire. This instrument has 20 scales assessing such needs (or preferences for reinforcement in future jobs) as social service, moral values, responsibility, creativity, etc. In comparing the vocational needs of highly original and good elaborating thinkers, differences were found on four scales. Highly original girls mani-

Table 2

Proportions of High and Low Creative Thinkers Among 220 Senior Boys
Who Chose Careers Within Eight Occupational Groups

| Occupational Groups | Creative Thinking Boys | | | | | | Exq. Freq. |
| | Low | | High | | Total | % | |
	N	%	N	%			
Service	7	31.8	15	68.2*	22	10.0	11.0
Business Contact	2	66.6	1	33.4	3	1.4	1.5
Organization	8	33.4	16	66.6*	24	10.9	12.0
Technology	72	62.1**	44	37.9	116	52.7	58.0
Outdoor	7	53.8	6	46.2	13	5.9	6.5
Science	3	60.0	2	40.0	5	2.4	2.5
General Cultural	5	29.4	12	70.6*	17	7.7	8.5
Arts & Entertainment	6	30.0	14	70.0*	20	9.0	10.0
Total	110		110		220	100.0	110.0

Chi-square = 18.8
Chi-square (7df) = 18.5, p < .01

**p < .01.
*p < .05.

Table 3

Proportions of High and Low Creative Thinkers Among 220 Senior Girls
Who Chose Careers Within Eight Occupational Groups

Occupational Groups	Creative Thinking Girls						Exp. Freq.
	Low N	%	High N	%	Total	%	
Service	23	46.0	27	54.0	50	22.7	25.0
Business Contact	1	33.4	2	66.6	3	1.4	1.5
Organization	49	80.3**	12	19.7	61	27.7	30.5
Technology	3	60.0	2	40.0	5	2.4	2.5
Outdoor	0	0	0	0	0	0	0
Science	20	42.6	27	57.4	47	21.3	23.5
General Cultural	6	28.6	15	71.4**	21	9.5	10.5
Arts & Entertainment	7	21.2	26	78.8**	33	15.0	16.5
Total	110		110		220	100.0	110.0

Chi-square = 39.14
Chi-square (7df) = 24.3, p < .001

**p < .01.

fested significantly stronger vocational needs than highly elaborating girls for good working conditions ($p < .01$); while highly original boys had significantly stronger needs than highly elaborating boys for compensation ($p < .05$), moral values ($p<0.5$), and good employment practices and policies ($p<.05$).

The girls scoring highest in both creative thinking abilites had significantly stronger vocational needs than either highly original or elaborating girls for authority ($p < .01$) and creativity ($p < .01$). The highly creative boys in both abilities had significantly stronger needs than either highly original or elaborating boys for variety ($p < .01$), activity ($p < .01$ and responsibility ($p < .01$).

Interestingly, a validity check is provided for the two instruments. The MTCT isolated students as highly creative thinkers and the MIQ's scale for creativity measured their stronger vocational need for creativity. The 165 highly creative students had a creativity scale mean of 19.31 but the 146 low creatives only had a mean of 17.32—a difference significant beyond the .0005 level.

Discussion

Further development of the MIQ is described by Weiss, et al. (1964) to include a forced-choice technique that might provide clearer results. In this sample, a lack of more complete differentiation between groups of creative thinkers on the MIQ may be explained in the following way. These adolescents may not have as much vocational maturity as is needed to obtain the most adequate index by the MIQ. Thus, the highly creative students may have incomplete self-realizations of their creative abilities, of their vocational needs, or of the interaction of both needs and abilities. These seniors may have unrealistic attitudes toward the world of work and job requirements so that more experience may be required before they can respond adequately to an instrument like the MIQ.

Awareness of the study's results may influence counselors in interpreting test scores to clients, who should be apprised of intellecutal abilities other than those measured only by the standard aptitude tests. In these situations, Torrance's (1965a, 1965b) conclusions and recommendations seem to deserve consideration.

For example, more evidence is offered here that the divergent thinking abilities are, indeed, different from the convergent thinking abilities measured by intelligence and achievement tests. Further support is also added to the research cited by Taylor (1964a) that creativity tests can predict school grades with validities in the fifties and sixties, despite a low correlation between creativity and aptitude tests (*e.g.,r=.32*). This study also emphasizes that such creative abilities are associated with striking vocational needs.

Counselors can aid more creative students in attaining their more unconventional career choices, rather than merely introduce so-called "reality" factors militating against the attainment of creative students' cherished goals. Certainly the personalities and abilities of highly creative students may enable them to attain these goals more readily than the highly intelligent students.

Researchers may also wish to devise experiments within the primary grades to expand creative students' job horizons. Thus, the nation's creative talent might not be siphoned off into conventional careers, whereas a minimum of early identification of creative talent and proper reinforcement might utilize such talent more effectively. Such early identification and encouragement of creative talent might enable more creative individuals to enter those careers where they can contribute most to the commonweal. Certainly this is a new dimension added to Borow's (1964) compendium of vocational development theory.

Finally, implications from this study seem apparent for future research in different kinds of creativity. Although this exploratory study did not present the clearest portraits of these highly creative students, a basis is provided for expanding concepts of these individuals. One possible contamination may result from inclusion within the sample of those minority groups (about 15 per cent of the seniors were Negroes) from culturally deprived or economically disadvantaged homes.

PART II

HOW CAN WE COPE WITH FUTURE SHOCK?

In a Rapidly Changing World, Planned Organizational Development May be Business' Answer

The rate of change in society is increasing at a dizzying pace. Respected observers note milleniums of change being compressed into the next 30 to 40 years as a totally new civilization—"superindustrialism"—implodes into our midst. The new society will proffer fantastic varieties of choices with respect to products, culture, jobs, organizations and life styles. And the most important single characteristic of this new era will be its *pace*. Superindustrialism will in fact be a chain of temporary everything: evolving organizations, changing relationships and ground rules. People and especially organizations will be forced to learn, unlearn, relearn and delearn, adapt and readapt to a faster pace. Thus, top corporation executives are increasingly pondering these questions:

1. Can we cope with future shock? Are we keeping up with the changes in our industry? And responding quickly enough to these changes? Or are we usually just *reacting* to changes being made by other competitors?
2. Is our ability to solve problems keeping up with our growth in size?
3. Do we locate decision-making responsibilities as close to the information sources as possible?
4. Can we direct our competitive energy against external competitors within our industry, and make our internal competition more relevant to work goals? Do we need to maximize our collaborative efforts?
5. Can we improve our reward system to recognize both the achievement of our organization's goals (profits or services) and the development of people?
6. Can we help our managers to manage more effectively according to relevant objectives, rather than according to "past practices" or according to objectives that do not make sense for one's area of responsibility?
7. How can we increase self-control and self-direction for our workers?

As executives become more readily enabled to face these questions, they become more aware of the need for Organizational Development, which we shall call O.D.

O.D., briefly, is a response to change—the biggest topic in the world today. As these questions suggest, we are not coping adequately with all the change around us: change in our world and in our industry; change in the nature, location, and availability of jobs; changing relations between employers and workers, blacks and whites, professors and students, and between generations. Corporations, as human organizations, are susceptible, perhaps more than other social institutions, to changing times. Their successes and failures, rises and falls, all testify to their vulnerability. John W. Gardner, in his book *Self-Renewal* sums it up well:

> "What may be most in need of innovation is the corporation itself. Perhaps what every corporation (and every other organization) needs is a department of continuous renewal that could view the whole organization as a system in need of continuing innovation."

O.D. is a planned program to answer these needs, issues and questions. It is a complex educational strategy geared to change the beliefs, attitudes, values and structures of organizations, enabling them better to adapt to new technologies, market challenge, and rates of change.

Definitions of O.D.

In defining O.D., we imply efforts to find ways to change the organization from its current situation to a better developed state. O.D. then, is an effort (1) planned, (2) organization-wide, and (3) managed from the top, to (4) improve organiza-

Reprinted with permission from *Industrial Management*, September 1970, Vol. 12 No. 9, published by the Industrial Management Society, Chicago, Illinois 60611.

tional effectiveness and health, through (5) planned interventions in the organizational "processes" using behavioral science knowledge.

Look briefly at a deeper analysis of these points.

1. O.D. is a *planned change* effort, including a systematic diagnosis of the organization. A strategic plan for improvement is developed, and energies are enlisted to carry it out.
2. The total system is involved, such as in a change in the managerial strategies, reward systems or culture. In effect, however, this does not mean a *total* corporation, government or organization, as such, but rather emphasizes that the system must be relatively free in setting its own plans and future within only general environmental limitations.
3. O.D. must be managed from the top, because success depends upon total knowledge and commitment of top executives in the system.
4. O.D. is designed to increase organizational effectiveness and health. J.W. Gardner's writings cited above outline a set of rules for an effective organization. He emphasizes the need for an effective program to recruit and develop talent. But equally as important are the means of combatting the process by which men become prisoners of their procedures. (Defining effective organizations would require a complete book or article alone.)
5. O.D. includes planned interventions using behavioral science research. These interventions focus on such processes as individual motivation, power, communications, goal setting, interpersonal relationships, intergroup relationships, and conflict management.

There are four major interfaces or challenge areas, in which O.D. efforts must be conducted.

I. *Interface between Organization and Environment*—This is the process of developing the relationship or nature of the transactions between the organization and its wider environment. Relationships at this interface are called "planned transactions" to indicate there exists a definite strategy adopted by management to make more money, or as the case may be, to increase the resources of the organization. (In the insurance industry, for example, this may relate to entering the mutual fund field.)

II. *Interface between Groups within the Organization*—Groups or divisions develop their own unique task-related characteristics. Their differing points of view can complicate the coordination processes. Thus, destructive competition, hostilities and secretiveness develop.

III. *Interface between Individuals and the Organization*—Challenges are constantly arising in the psychological contract between company and employee. Does he seek a career or only a brief job?

IV. *Interface between Individuals*—How workers get along with each other, or bosses, is the subject of the whole human relations movement, and personnel administration—topics beyond the scope of this article.

Synergistic Effects

Another way to look at these challenge areas or interfaces is from the viewpoint of synergistic effects. A synergy results from the united actions and interactions of elements producing a greater effect than the results of these elements working independently. A common example of synergistic effects is 2 x 2 = 5, or the mixing of nitric acid and hydrochloric acid (1:3) to get "aqua regia" the corrosive, fuming yellow liquid that can dissolve gold or platinum. Taken separately, each cannot perform that function, but together they can synergistically create the action.

A good example from business could clearly illustrate the point. In the traditional line organization concept, the manager designs four separate jobs, wherein each worker independently does his own operation and passes the work on to the next person—almost in assembly line fashion. Presumably, because the system is laid out efficiently, the work will be done efficiently.

To benefit from the synergistic effect, however, the manager would merely assign his objectives or desired results to the whole group. Then, instead of each person simply working singly on his little segment, the people combine and unify their efforts from the total result—a synergistic effect.

A well designed O.D. program helps organizational systems to use synergistic effects for achieving the highest and best human talents. Then managers can offer an enterprise the best economic growth, social progress, human satisfaction and overall profitability.

Foundations of O.D.

During the past 50 years, many experiments and studies offered convincing proofs that organizations are not efficient in attaining the potential of their human resources, and that they operate on faulty assumptions concerning the nature of man, limiting the growth of people working in them. The increasing disaffection of college students for business careers seems to reinforce there findings. It appears natural in our society where basic animal needs of economic survival are no longer so urgent, that collegians would become increasingly more concerned with the fulfillment and development of their more human needs.

O.D. programs help all institutions to face these challenges—not only business organizations, but also government bodies, school systems, religious and volunteer associations, and the like.

By using behavioral science techniques and methods, O.D. integrates the individual's needs for growth and development with the systems' goals to make the organization more effective and productive. Thus, profitability is definitely increased.

Some Basic Research Findings

Underpinning the O.D. theory and method are these behavioral science hypotheses and research results:

1. Work can be arranged to meet individual needs as well as the system's prerequisites to produce synergistically results of highest quality and quantity.
2. When a person's basic animal and human needs are met, he does not seek a soft and secure situation. The motivation-hygiene research shows such men to be challenged by responsibility, expecting recognition and rewarding interpersonal relationships.
3. People have strong drives for growth and self-actualization.
4. When people experience in groups a managed process of greater openness about both negative and positive feelings, they strongly identify with the goals of the group and of its other members. Then they can more constructively deal with otherwise potentially disruptive issues.
5. Relationships that are honest, caring and nonmanipulative foster personal growth.
6. Innovations and constructive changes result from groups that feel a common identity and capability to influence their environment.

O.D. Methods

A basic O.D. program can be applied to any kind of organization or group association at any time in its life. It is especially appropriate to a functional team or department, or to a total institution, for current problems or long-range challenges. It can even be applied to beginning stages, as well as during mergers and acquisitions.

Although each O.D. program might be defined differently, one process has been conducted along these lines:

- Identify problems (or challenges).
- Rank problem priorities.
- Generate and share data about these problems. These data may range from systems and technology to interpersonal or personal factors.
- Planning action-oriented alternatives.
- Testing selected alternatives.
- Creative implementation or innovation of alternatives.
- Review and planning of follow-up actions.

Perhaps the most fundamental principle is to maximize the organization's own resources from the outset. The most effective outside consultations would share the initial responsibility, while aiding the organization to manage its own future, continuous program.

Process Consultation: One Method

In planning and working to cope with future shock, one of the best methods is to look at "process," as contrasted with structure. Process is defined as human interactions that mediate the various functions making up an organization. These human processes can never be overlooked in dealing with structure. The structure of an organization has historically been the primary focus of management. Managers have typically been more preoccupied with chains of command, spans of control, and the typical structural approach.

This approach has been incomplete. E. Schein suggests (*Process Consulation: Its Role in O.D.,* 1969) that existing management structures have been examined to increase productivity and effectiveness, yet the positions and roles defining the formal organizational structure are filled by people who put their personalities into getting the work done. Thus, each role occupant develops his own style and pattern of interacting with other people. And only by examining the processes happening between individuals can we understand the informal relationships, norms, traditions and environment suffusing the structure.

Process consultation involves the energies of a consultant helping the client comprehend and act upon the processes in the organization. The process consultant primarily focuses on aiding the client develop new skills to work out the organization's own solutions, rather than merely providing a project report.

This method can be best understood in comparison with other "models" of consultation.

A. *The Project Model*—consists in buying some information or service from a presumed expert. This most common method of consulting may range from market research to product planning to setting up a better wage and salary program. Among the crucial assumptions underlying this model are: (1) the executive has accurately diagnosed his problems; and (2) he has involved the expert consultant who can communicate best.

B. *Patient-Doctor Model*—The organizational unit believed to be the problem or needing improvement may not accept top management's diagnosis or cooperate in providing necessary information.

C. *Process-Consultation Model*—assumes the client must begin to comprehend the problem himself and become more *actively* immersed in solving it himself. Most importantly, the process-consultation consultant assumes the organization may know how to face its own challenges but may not know how to use all its own resources most effectively either in initial problem solution or in implementing solutions. Basically then, the process consultant aids an organization to solve its own problems by making it more aware of processes.

Processes: What are They?

There are basically six major topics viewed by most experts as the primary processes involved in organizations.

1. Communications
2. Functional roles of group members
3. Group problem solving and decision making
4. Group norms and growth
5. Intergroup processes
6. Authority and leadership

In summary, it can be seen that O.D. can answer the questions initially posed here, as the organization seeks to adapt to its ever changing world, and to become more profitable and effective in attaining its goals. The challenge suggested by John W. Gardner is a very real one that all top executives must face sooner or later.

THE CREATIVE THINKER AND HIS ORGANIZATION'S FUTURE

Dean C. Dauw received his B.S. degree from Spring Hill College, his M.A. degree from St. Thomas College, and his Ph.D. degree from the University of Minnesota.

After Dr. Dauw served as a Consulting Psychologist with various consulting firms, he was Director of Personnel Research with CNA Financial.

Dr. Alan J. Fredian was appointed Director of the Institute of Industrial Relations of Loyola University of Chicago in 1969.

As Director, he heads up the Institute's program which leads masters degrees in personnel management and industrial relations.

Fredian, a native Chicagoan, joined the Loyola faculty in 1967 as an Professor of Management. He later became Chairman of the Management Department.

Life and literature are replete with examples of successful entrepreneurs who became rich with a good idea. Walking down any street one can see innumerable examples of Edison's lights, Ford's cars and Bell's telephones.

These and many other inventions are classical examples of the original thinker or innovating genius.

Before 1950 there was relatively little scientific research into creativity. Some poets and philosophers and literary people had mused, philosophized and written on the subject, but psychologists had certainly done little formal research.

Then, J.P. Guilford made his address as president to the American Psychological Association in 1950, encouraging his colleagues to investigate the topic of creativity more thoroughly.

Since then the research and writing has become voluminous. The Journal of Creative Behavior was eventually born. National conferences have been held, inviting papers from some of the best researchers and authorities in the field.

Our colleagues have been able to consider the entire question of creative individuals and innovating organizations more completely. These are a few of the results we have learned.

1. *There is more than one kind of creative individual.*

All of the research done by Professor E. Paul Torrance, begun at the University of Minnesota and now continued by him at the University of Georgia suggests more
than one kind of creative thinker. One kind of person identified by his Torrance Tests of Creative Thinking may be a highly original thinker, while a second kind may be better as an elaborating thinker. Still a third person may be more gifted as both an original and an elaborating thinker. For example, an original thinker may dream up a light bulb, but an elaborating thinker may merely stretch that idea out into a neon bulb.

2. *Even ordinary folks can be educated to become more creative thinkers.*

The Creative Education Foundation of Buffalo, New York, has been teaching courses for many years on how to think more creatively. Their evidence suggests that any person, regardless of his I.Q. measure of convergent thinking, can learn to be more of a divergent thinker, which is really measured better by creativity tests.

Using many different methods now completely researched and clearly shown in various workbooks and sourcebooks, any person can unshackle his mind. This liberated thinker will no longer continue to see in ruts like a horse with blinders, but actually function more creatively in many ways.

3. *Organizations can select more creative people—if they can handle them.*

Much research has been done on how to select more creative people. Dauw and Fredian have recently compiled all their research published over a period of more than seven years in a book, *Creativity and Innovation in Organization*. (Dubuque: Kendall-Hunt, 1971.) It is well-known now that creative people can be validly and reliably screened and thus selected by psychological tests and appropriate interviewing techniques. The real challenge is not to get the creative people, in the first place, but rather to get companies and organizations to recruit and to select them in the proper manner and then use them in the best way.

There is naturally less research on how best to use all this creative talent because the research in time-consuming and costly. Many companies are especially reluctant to sponsor research on how to use their people more effectively because they blindly hynotize themselves into believing they are already doing that.

4. *Organizations can profit if they can select and handle creative employees.*

Some of the biggest companies have taught inventors how to think more creatively—and these men have produced more patents—better in quantity and quality. G.E., DuPont, Dow Chemical, to name just a few, have found it economically rewarding to teach new product developers how they can better develop new products. These studies have been well designed with adequate direct measuring instruments and even with unobtrusive measures to show how an experimental group with the training developed more patents than a matched control group without the training.

One has to ask: "How long will other executives in other companies avoid using these proven methods to increase their profitability?"

5. *Creative people are truly gifted and not really neurotic.*

Stories abound of gifted individuals like a Van Gogh who cut off his ear. Fact is, however, that most truly creative people are very normal in the sense of being mentally healthy. The real challenge facing most organizations—profit and non-profit alike—is not how to recruit, select, diagnose or whatever with creative people, but rather how to avoid giving most employees—creative or non-creative alike—some form of mental health problem. This is a result of meangingless work, poor supervision, inadequate communications, not providing proper motivations and the like.

6. *Even innovating organizations need to cope with future shock.*

Once one has begun to deal with creative individuals, one eventually considers the whole organization.

The rate of change in society is mounting at a dizzying pace. Respected observers note milleniums of change being compressed into the next 30 or 40 years as a totally new civilization—"super-industrialism"—implodes into our midst. The new society will proffer fantastic varieties of choices with respect to products, culture, jobs, organizations and life styles. And the most important single characteristic of this new era will be its pace. "Super-industrialism" will in fact be a chain of temporary everything; evolving organizations, changing relationships and ground rules. People and especially organizations will be forced to learn, unlearn, relearn and delearn, adapt and readapt to a faster pace. Thus, top corporation executives are increasingly pondering these questions:

(1) Can we cope with future shock? Are we keeping up with the changes in our industry? And responding quickly enough to these changes? Or are we usually just reacting to changes being made by other competitors?

(2) Is our ability to solve problems keeping up with our growth in size?

(3) Do we locate decision-making responsibilities as close to the information sources as possible?

(4) Can we direct our competitive energy against external competitiors within our industry, and make our internal competition more relevant to work goals? Do we need to maximize our collaborative efforts?

(5) Can we improve our reward system to recognize both the achievement of our organization's goals (profits or services) and the development of people?

(6) Can we help our managers to manage more effectively according to relevant objectives, rather than according to "past practices" or according to objectives that do not make sense for one's area of responsibility?

(7) How can we increase self-control and self-direction for our workers?

As executives become more readily enabled to face these questions, they become more aware of the need for Organizational Development, which we shall call O.D.

"Are we keeping up with changes in our industry? And responding quickly enough to these changes?"

O.D., briefly, is a response to change—the biggest topic on the work front today. As these questions suggest, we are not coping adequately with all the change around us; change in our world and in our industry; change in the nature, location, and availability of jobs; changing relations between employers and workers, blacks and whites, professors and students, and between generations. Corporations, as human organizations, are susceptible, perhaps more than other social institutions, to changing times. Their successes and failures, rises and falls, all testify to their vulnerability. John W. Gardner, in his book *Self-Renewal* sums it up well: "What may be most in need of innovation is the corporation itself. Perhaps what every corporation (and every other organization) needs is a department of continuous renewal that could view the whole organization as a system in need of continuing innovation."

O.D. is a planned program to answer these needs, issues and questions. It is a complex educational strategy geared to change the beliefs, attitudes, values and structures of organizations, enabling them better to adapt to new technologies, market challenge, and rates of change.

In defining O.D., we imply efforts to find ways to change the organization from its current situation to a better developed state. O.D. then, is an effort (1) planned, (2) organization-wide, and (3) managed from the top to (4) improve organizational effectiveness and health, through (5) planned interventions in the organizational "processes" using behavioral science knowledge.

Look briefly at a deeper analysis of these points:

(1) O.D. is a planned change effort, including a systematic diagnosis of the organization wherein a strategic plan for improvement is developed, and energies are enlisted to carry it out.

(2) The total system is involved, such as in a change in the managerial strategies, reward systems or culture. In effect, however, this does not mean a total corporation, government or organization, as such, but rather emphasizes that the system must be relatively free in setting its own plans and future within only general environmental limitations.

(3) O.D. must be managed from the top, because success depends upon total knowledge and commitment of top executives in the system.

(4) O.D. is designed to increase organizational effectiveness and health. J.W. Gardner's writings outline a set of rules for effective organizations. He emphasizes the need for a program to recruit and develop talent. But equally as important are the means of combating the process by which men become prisoners of their procedures (defining effective organizations would require a complete book or article alone).

(5) O.D. includes planned interventions using behavioral science research. These interventions focus on such processes as individual motivation, power, communications, goal setting, interpersonal relationships, intergroup relationships, and conflict management.

There are four major interfaces or challenge areas, in which O.D. efforts must be conducted.

I. *Interface between Organization and Environment*—This is the process of developing the relationship or nature of the transactions between the organization and its wider environment. Relationships at this interface are called "planned transactions" to indicate there exists a definite strategy adopted by management to make more money, or as the case may be, to increase the resources of the organization. (In the insurance industry, for example, this may relate to entering the mutual fund field.)

II. *Interface between Groups within the Organization*—Groups or divisions develop their own unique task-related characteristics. Their differing points of view can complicate the coordination processes. Thus, destructive competition, hostilities and secretiveness develop.

III. *Interface between Individuals and the Organization*—Challenges are constantly arising in the psychological contract between company and employee. Does he seek a career or only a brief job?

IV. *Interface between Individuals*—How workers get along with each other, or bosses, is the subject of the whole human relations movement, and personnel administration—topics beyond the scope of this article.

7. *Even creative people need help to grow and develop.*

This is a paramount view in "Humanistic Psychology," a term applied to the vast spectrum of approaches to human experience and behavior, all of which differ in their own ways from the more traditional emphasis of behaviorism and psychoanalysis. These various approaches have recently begun to become loosely affiliated.

In 1962 the Association for Humanistic Psychology (AHP) was formed to enable professional psychologists and others to meet in sharing their commitment to the fundamental uniqueness and importance of human life. Their most important conviction is that all human beings, are basically creative and that intentionality and values are basic determinants of human action.

While exponents of the humanistic orientation may often hold conflicting views, there is some unanimity on these four common elements:

(1) Attention centers on the experiencing person, with experience viewed as the primary phenomenon in the study of man. Overt behavior and theoretical explanations are both considered secondary to experience itself and to its meaning for the individual.

(2) There is an emphasis on such distinctively human qualities as creativity, choice, valuation and self-realization, as opposed to thinking about humans in mechanistic and reductionistic terms.

(3) Meaningfulness is desired in selecting problems for study and in research procedures. Primary emphasis is not placed on objectivity at the expense of significance.

(4) Humanistic psychologists are especially concerned with valuing the dignity and worth of man and developing the potential inherent in every person. Central in this viewpoint is the individual who is discovering his own being and relating to social groups.

The AHP believes in a broad conception of scientific method and is therefore open to new, relevant approaches, methods or significant aspects of human functioning. While the AHP is fundamentally committed to psychology as a science, it rejects only those philosophical assumptions that may restrict the field of inquiry and interfere with a more complete view of human experience. Because of this orientation, the AHP encourages attention to topics having a lesser place in previous systems, such as love, creativity, play, spontaneity, warmth, ego—transcendence, autonomy, responsibility, authenticity, meaning, transcendental experience and courage.

PEOPLE, PRODUCTIVITY AND PROFIT

Introduction

The following is a true story. It actually happened! A five-year old boy was walking along a busy highway leading to a viaduct, where much traffic criss-crossed in every direction. A large, semi-trailer truck drove under the viaduct. Much too large, it jammed up beneath. Havoc occured all around. Police re-routed the traffic. Highway engineers measured the height of the viaduct. Truck owners brought out acetylene torches to cut the truck apart.

The little lad tugged on the traffic engineer's shirt-sleeve and said: "I know how to solve your problem. Just let the air out of the tires and back the truck out from under the viaduct." The flabbergasted engineer replied: "Hey, kid, how could you solve the problem when all these well-paid engineers couldn't do it?"

The boy responded: "Well, maybe it's because I am so little, I'm closer to the tires."

This lad could solve the problem because he was creative, as you and I all were as youngsters. However, various school systems unfortunately taught us convergent thinking — arriving at the "correct" answers, such as $2 + 2 = 4$ — rather than divergent or creative thinking.

This example may hopefully help us understand that to become increasingly more effective and productive in our jobs, so that our companies can become more profitable, we need to learn to think and act more creatively. Fortunately, research shows there are many ways managers can unleash the creative power within themselves, and cope better with change.

"Change is avalanching down upon our heads, and most people are utterly unprepared to cope with it," says Alvin Toffler in *Future Shock*. Preparing managers to cope with today's accelerating rate of change is one of the major goals of modern behavioral sciences and personnel administration.

There are so many applications of behavioral sciences to today's corporations and modern personnel administration that it is difficult to pinpoint just a few. As an emerging discipline, the behavioral sciences aim at improving the effectiveness of the organization and its members by any means, including systematic change programs.

Management theorists and behavioral scientists note that the truly effective organization is one in which both the organization and the individual can grow and develop. Such an environment can be called a "healthy" organization. And this is one goal of successful personnel executives: making organizations healthier, more effective and more profitable.

Coping with change must be a systematic approach, differentiating between those features that are healthy and effective, and those that are not. (Parenthetically, your own MBO Program is an example of one effective intervention.)

Background

The tension or awareness that change is needed may arise in a variety of ways, but usually this awareness emerges from some problem that can no longer be ignored. This state of tension may result from internal growth or decline, or it may come from competitive, technological or social changes in the external environment. A few examples from other organizations may be helpful in clarification of this point.

At U.S. Steel, for example, CEOEdgar Speer implemented a reorganization because of an awareness that the organization was too slow to make decisions and too slow to move into new markets. ("A Steel Man Steps Up Pace At U.S. Steel." *Business Week,* March 9, 1974, page 154.)

At Allied Stores Corporation, a long history of stodgy management and dwindling profits caused Thomas M. Macioce, Chief Executive, to reorganize Allied's management structure. ("Allied Stores' Struggle With Profit Margins." *Business Week*, November 17, 1973, page 55.)

Analogous problems of slumping sales and reduced profits led to similar management reorganizations at General Foods Corporation and Unilever Ltd.

In the United States Navy, Admiral Elmo Zumwalt, Jr., then Chief of Naval Operations, implemented intensive human relations and command development programs after becoming aware of pandemic drug abuse, serious racial disturbances and low re-enlistment rates.

In Menlo Park, California, Saga Company, an institutional feeding contractor, had extremely high employee turnover rates. ("The Humanistic Way of Managing People." *Business Week*, July 22, 1972, page 46.)

All these incidents illustrate the interdependence of an organization and its environment, and the awareness of a need for change as an antecedent condition to any program of planned change.

Methodology

The behavioral sciences use many techniques to increase productivity and profits and in the process enhance the personnel function. Personnel executives can thereby more effectively show their contributions to the total organization's profitability.

This brief discussion here cannot possibly include all the information of a behavioral sciences text or even the Annual Review of Psychology's analysis of all the one-hundred-four relevant citations about organizational development in just the 1977 edition. But, because the thoughtful executive may wish a brief overview, the following analysis is included before citing some more specific techniques.

First, an organization must become aware of tension, future shock possibilities, or a need to manage change. Internal or external consultants must be called upon for aid. A relationship between the change agent and the client or client system must develop.

After the information-collecting phase, the diagnostic phase must work from symptoms to underlying causes. If the client system is sufficiently motivated to change so as to increase profits and productivity, then various strategies of intervention must be determined.

Usually, a change is made in the sturcture, the technology, or the people. Research suggests that it is easier to change the structure or the technology of the organization than it is to change the people.

Research suggests that there may be some important trends in the present that will aid your work in the future, and will continue to become more paramount.

(1) The *Prominence for Personnel Executives* (or sub-phrased by Larry Axline as "An Alternative To Carrying The Watermelon To The Company Picnic," in *The Industrial-Organizational Psychologist*, February, 1977) shows that "The personnel department has been represented on many a corporate organization chart as an orphaned box-one that came from nowhere and didn't seem to fit anywhere."

In critique of Herb Meyer's Personnel Directors are the New Corporate Heroes," (Fortune, February, 1976) Axline states that in the past and "...For far too long, personnel executives in many organizations have been cast as capable of 'broom and shovel' tasks such as scheduling coffee breaks and 'arrangements chairmen.' More often than not, 'charman' really meant the 'man/woman' who arranged the 'chairs' for higher ranking corporate officers who would tackle the bottom-line problems facing the firm."

The trend, however, as suggested by Herb Meyer's research is that "...the route of the most effective personnel directors can just as easily be to the top of the corporate pyramid, rather than into the oblivious role of counting its angles and filing the results in triplicate with an agency that insists that pyramids must be round. ...Recent evidence suggests a pronounced trend toward heavy reliance on personnel directors for corporate leadership."

All current predictors point to increased respect for the personnel discipline with corresponding opportunities for practitioners to contribute on a par with other business managers. As Herb Meyer's article suggests, "...The people who do the job (personnel directors) like to say that in the years to come, a tour of duty in the personnel department (more likely the division of human resources) will be mandatory for any executive who aims to be Chairman."

(2) The *Behavioral Sciences Techniques For Personal Growth*, shows even by a cursory glance at any popular bookstore, the explosion of personal

growth and self-help books. Individuals **are** becoming increasingly more aware of their needs to become more self-actualized. Executives are similarly becoming more aware of how to develop human resources — their greatest asset — for more productivity and profits.

There exist many behavioral science intervention techniques that focus on people and personal change. Whole libraries exist on only one method, such as psychotherapy (See Dauw, Mental Health in Managers," *Personnel Administration*, September, 1968.) When research was done for the above-cited article, a survey revealed that only a few in-house company counselors existed, and few of these were devoted to referring employees with problems to qualified therapists. A new survey just recently revealed that only ten personnel executives were involved in this activity in ten major corporations in a large, metropolitan city.

When the target system is personal or interpersonal development, intervention techniques include transactional analysis, gestalt learning, laboratory learning, career planning and outplacement and individual behavior modification. These will all be increasingly more useful methods and tools in the next quarter century.

(a) **Behavior Modification**, resulting from the work of early psychologists such as Thorndike and most recently studied by B.F. Skinner, has already proven very useful. A CRM film brochure asserts that Emery Air Freight has saved more than $2,000,000 in just the last three years.

The basis supporting behavior modification (or organizational behavior — O.B. modification, if you prefer) is B.F. Skinner's principle of operant conditioning. As applied in organizational change, it means providing positive reinforcement ('warm fuzzies' instead of 'cold pricklies') to improve performance and productivity and ultimately profit.

Skinner has emphasized the individual's behavior is determined or shaped by the environment and by any system of rewards that provide positive reinforcement. Skinner suggests the "maximum use of positive reinforcement that leaves the individual feeling controlled and coerced." ("Conversations with B.F. Skinner," *Organizational Dynamics*, I, No. 3, Winter, 1973, page 32.

Positive reinforcement is the rewarding of desired behavior, whereas negative reinforcement means punishing undesireable behavior. Positive rein-

forcement, then, involves rewarding each improved performance which then results in increasing the frequency of the desired response.

In any organization, positive reinforcement implies designing a method of communicating to the employee how well he is doing, and then rewarding improved performance, generally by approval and recognition. Edward T. Feeney, former Vice President of Emery Air Freight Corporation, innovated the use of these methods to improve efficiency. Feeney gave employees daily feedback on how their performance measured up to company goals. (E.J. Feeney, "At Emery Air Freight, Positive Reinforcement Boosts Performance," *Organizational Dynamics*, I, No. 3, Winter, 1973, pages 41-50.)

Feeney saw that a performance audit was first completed to establish performance standards and goals, followed by a system for providing individual employees with the basic data needed to show how well they were doing. Feeney devised a checklist so that each worker could show him/herself exactly how well he/she was achieving the job's goals. Finally, supervisors were trained to use the individuals' work record to praise the good performance of the employees. At Emery, each manager learned to provide recognition and rewards ranging from a smile or nod of encouragement all the way up the scale to detailed praise for a job well done. Emery adopted Skinner's principles: reinforcing specific behavior as quickly as possible and reinforcing frequently in the beginning, then less frequently and predictably.

Productivity allegedly improved up to ninety-five percent. Gerald A. Conners, former Senior Vice President at Emery stated: "They are setting a much higher standard for themselves than if we told them what they should be doing." ("New Tool: Reinforcement For Good Work." *Business Week*, December 18, 1971.)

In addition to Emery Air Freight, numerous other organizations have tried positive reinforcement programs, including Illinois Bell Telephone, IBM, IT&T, Procter and Gamble, plus United Airlines. (W.C. Hamner, "Worker Motivation Programs" in *Contemporary Problems In Personnel: Readings For The Seventies*. Edited by W.C. Hamner and F. Schmidt. Chicago: St. Clair Press, 1974, pages 280-401)

(b) **Outplacement** is always one effective behavioral science intervention technique if all else fails (see Dauw, *Up Your Career*, Prospect Heights: Waveland Press, 1980).

Most workers only get a pink slip when they are fired. Finally, however, some major corporations are using consultants as "outplacement" experts to de-hire higher-level executives.

The service is profitable to the company in the long run, especially if the consultants can make the departure non-disruptive. Human Resource Developers calls their program Executive Redirection. Its benefits to the company are: a. aids the company in the quick release of extra and/or ineffective managers or executives, b. as a constructive action, aids the about-to-be released executive and c. promotes good morale in the eyes of the remaining personnel or the public. The benefits to the individual executive are: a. provides the discharged man/woman with necessary first aid, b. gives him/her a proven program and career advancement expertise, c. offers a psychological assist in trying times and d. often avoids casualties and, the special plus, enhances self-actualization.

Some outplacement specialists refuse to help men with alcoholic and psychiatric problems as well as executives for whom the company refuses to provide a recommendation. (Chicago Daily News, Tuesday, September 3, 1974, page 25: "Consultants Hired to Fire Top Executives.") Most of the executives whom de-hiring specialists work with are displaced by economic cutbacks or management reorganizations, which are the "so-called" reasons for firing a man when you are too reluctant to tell him the **real** reason.

That is why a professional psychologist is needed to help the man face the real reason, which is a Herculean feat in itself. Most companies are too fearful of lawsuits to tell the real reason and a consultant may find it harder than pulling teeth, say, to get a man/woman to admit he has a drinking problem.

If these individuals do not get help, that is the real tragedy because such men/women are really the ones who need it most to keep them from the downward spiral that leads in a vicious circle to even greater problems.

The consultant's first job is to teach top executives how to fire a man. The unfortunate person must learn he is fired permanently and irrevo-

cably, which is an extremely difficult thing for a person to accept emotionally. Our research shows he may be aware of the decision intellectually, but thereafter four or five months of intensive counseling is needed for him to accept it emotionally. Executives who are unaware of this valuable service or who are not able to have it available, develop serious problems. Besides the typical depressions, self-doubts and anxieties, the usual lack of direction is followed by too many drinking bouts and other self-defeating behaviors. It is a rare executive who is fired and can find his own job in a reasonable period of time. "Reasonable" for him may seem to be a few weeks, or months, whereas "reasonable" to professional-expert-consultants may be twelve months to three years. And that is **even with** all best methods being used wisely and perserveringly. The outplacement program, then, is really a necessity for any individual.

(3) **MBO and Performance Appraisal** — Improved performance appraisals result from good use of behavioral modification as explained above and is intricately bound up in any MBO program. Because you have implemented such an effective program already, we need not discuss it here. Surely, MBO will become an increasingly greater tool for your productivity and profits, as you continue to make it even more effective.

(4) **Effective Strategies for Change** — Executives and managers at all levels will become increasingly more aware of strategies for change. Planned change, you will remember from our previous discussion, is necessary for personal growth and corporate profitability.

There are three basic strategies for planned change: empirical-rational, normative-reeducative, and power-coercive.

a. **Empirical-Rational**: The fundamental assumption here is that man is rational and will follow his self-interest once it is revealed to him. Points #(1) and #(2) above can be considered here.

b. **Normative-Reeducative** strategies believe man is guided in his actions and sociocultural norms and his commitment to these norms. Consequently, change in man is not exclusively at the cognitive (intellectual) level but is often at a more personal level: habits, attitudes and values. Behavioral science interventions are based on this strategy: the client identifies the changes he wishes to make, and with help from the change agent, they collaborate and work for solutions. MBO and Performance Appraisals (discussed in #(3) above) and better communicative programs can fall in this category.

c. **Power-Coercive** strategies are based on the assumption of compliance of those with less power to the will of those with more power. Power is evident in all human relationships and it is used in both of the preceding strategies (or, all of the above in this paper). For example, the empirical-rational strategies depend on knowledge as a source of power. The flow of power is from men who know to those who do not know through the process of education. Normative-reeducative strategies attempt to share their power, i.e., their knowledge of human behavior through and with the client system. These strategies are oriented against the use of coercive power on both moral and practical grounds. Power-coercive strategies, however, use both legitimate and illegitimate power.

The best or last book on power is yet to come, but hopefully you can read some of the present best sellers. Dr. Michael Maccoby has a book entitled *The Gamesman* which focuses on one whose main interest is in challenge, competitive activity where he can prove himself a winner. From a different viewpoint is Michael Korda's *Power*. He emphasizes power as a journey, not a destination, as the ability to control people, events, and oneself.

All executives in all companies will want to understand these issues because their daily lives and the future profits of their companies will greatly depend upon this understanding and how they utilize this knowledge.

(5) In the past ten years, much research has been done on *Job Enrichment*. (Fred Herzberg, "One More Time: How Do You Motivate Employees?" *Harvard Business Review*, January-February, 1968, page 53. And, Robert Ford, "Job Enrichment Lessons From AT&T," *Harvard Business Review*, January-February, 1973, page 96.)

Job Enrichment programs have been shown to increase profits significantly, if implemented correctly, by outside consultants who are wise enough to get firm evaluation commitments from top executives (J. Richard Hackman, "Is Job Enrichment Just A Fad?" *Harvard Business Review*, September-October, 1975, page 129.)

There are typically six major problem areas where problems may arise from organizations' redesign work, or at least may not resolve problems as it is supposed to:

(a) Rarely are the problems in the work system diagnosed before jobs are redesigned.

(b) Sometimes, the work itself is not even actually changed.

(c) Even when the work itself is substantially changed, anticipated gains are sometimes diminished or reversed because of unexpected effects on the surrounding work system.

(d) Rarely are the work redesign projects systematically evaluated.

(e) Line managers, consulting staff members and union officers do not obtain appropriate education in the theory, strategy and tactics of work redesign.

(f) Traditional bureaucratic practice creeps into the work design activities. Job enrichment projects offer employees an opportunity to become more autonomous and self-directed in carrying out the company's work.

According to job enrichment theory, managers assume that employees have the competence and sense of responsibility to seek appropriate assistance when they need it. And thus, they can work with a minimum of interference. Far too often, however, the process of implementing job enrichment is incongruent with this intended end. If pitfalls are avoided, job enrichment will significantly increase your profits.

A PARROT AND A BLONDE LIVE WITH ME, OR, WHAT THEORY X AND THEORY Y CAN DO FOR YOU

Yes, a parrot and a Blonde do live with me. And that is a good illustration of the main differences between Theory X and Theory Y.

You can manipulate, and easily punish a parrot (Theory X), depending upon how hostile or autocratic is your personality. But, you cannot do either with a Blonde (Theory Y), and expect to get away with it.

Please take just a minute and look at the formal definitions of the Theories X and Y, and then we can creatively suggest some implications and applications.

Douglas McGregor defined them in the following way:

Theory X

(1) Man inherently dislikes work and will avoid work (a parrot only eats, sleeps, and flies around).
(2) Because he dislikes work, man must be coerced, controlled, directed, threatened with punishment to get him to work toward achieving organizational goals. (A parrot must be caged and let out at its owner's whim, and trained not to do-do on the floor.)
(3) The average man prefers to be directed; he wishes to avoid responsibility; he has little ambition; he wants security. (A parrot wants to be fed.) Surprisingly, some parrot owners freely choose to teach parrots more than some bosses I have known want to inform employees.

Theory Y

(1) Work is as natural as play. ("Blondes do have more fun.")
(2) External control is not the only way for bringing about effort toward organizational goals. Man will exercise self-direction and self-control in the service of objectives to which he/she is committed, and committment is a function of rewards associated with goal achievement. (Blondes do exercise self-direction. As a management consulting psychologist to Playboy, while selecting Bunny-Mothers, I was very impressed how hard it is to control Bunnies — blondes, redheads or brunettes. Perhaps your own experiences with women are or have been even more convincing.)
(3) The average person seeks responsibility. His/her avoidance of it is generally a consequence of past frustration caused by poor management from above. The average person has a high degree of imagination and ingenuity which is rarely used in modern industrial life and this frustrates the individual. It leads one to rebel against the organization. (Every Blonde whom I have had the joy of knowing has seemingly fit this description.)

My research over many years has proved conclusively just how creative people can be. Unfortunately, the average executive does not understand or accept these facts, which is why there is so much trouble in organizations and why productivity could increase and why costs could decrease.

Instead of fantasizing about Blondes for one minute (which is what the research shows managers mostly do), please fantasize about how these theories could be extended to a Theory Z or beyond, completing the Circle and coming back again to another Theory A-B-C.

We need a Theory Z and A-B-C to implement X and Y. Too many managers are not aware of these assumptions, stated above, and how they influence their lives. We need to take Theory Y (The Blonde Theory) out of Theory and Fantasy and into Managerial Reality.

There is only one best way to accomplish this. It is called Organizational Development (O.D.). You can learn more about it in a host of O.D. books on the market.

Life and literature are replete with examples of successful entrepreneurs who became rich with a good idea. Walking down any street one can see innumerable examples of Edison's lights, Ford's cars and Bell's telephones.

These and many other inventions are classical examples of the original thinker or innovating genius.

Before 1950 there was relatively little scientific research on creativity. Some poets and philosophers and literary people had mused, philosophized and written on the subject, but psychologists had certainly done little formal research.

Then, J.P. Guilford made his address as president to the American Psychological Association in 1950, encouraging his colleagues to investigate the topic of creativity more thoroughly.

Since then the research and writing has become voluminous. The Journal of Creative Behavior was eventually born. National conferences have been held, inviting papers from some of the best researchers and authorities in the field.

Our colleagues have been able to consider the entire question of creative individuals and innovating organizations more completely. These are a few of the results we have learned.

Creative people are truly gifted and not really neurotic. Stories abound of gifted individuals like a VanGogh who cut off his ear. Fact is, however, that most truly creative people are very normal in the sense of being mentally healthy. The real challenge facing most organizations — profit and non-profit alike — is not how to recruit, select, diagnose or whatever with creative people, but rather how to avoid giving most employees — creative and non-creative alike — some form of mental health problems. This is a result of meaningless work, poor supervision, inadequate communications, not providing proper motivations and the like.

Even innovating organizations need to cope with future shock. Once one has begun to deal with creative individuals, one eventually considers the whole organization.

The rate of change in society is mounting at a dizzying pace. Respected observers note milleniums of change being compressed into the next thirty to forty years as a totally new civilization — "superin-dustrialism" — implodes into our midst. The new society will proffer fantastic varieties of choices with respect to products, culture, jobs, organizations and life styles. And the most important single characteristic of this new era will be its pace. "Super-industrialism" will in fact be a chain of temporary everything: evolving organizations, changing relationships and ground rules. People and especially organizations will be forced to learn, unlearn, relearn and delearn, adapt and readapt to a faster pace. Thus, top corporation executives are increasingly pondering these questions:

(1) Can we cope with future shock? Are we keeping up with the changes in our industry? And responding quickly enough to these changes? Or are we usually just reacting to changes being made by other competitors?

(2) Is our ability to solve problems keeping up with our growth in size?

(3) Do we locate decision-making responsibilities as close to the information source as possible?

(4) Can we direct our competitive energy against external competitors within our industry, and make our internal competition more relevant to work goals? Do we need to maximize our collaborative efforts?

(5) Can we improve our reward system to recognize both the achievement or our organization's goals (profits or services) and the development of people?

(6) Can we help our managers to manage more effectively according to relevant objectives, rather than according to "past practices" or according to objectives that do not make sense for one's area of responsibility?

(7) How can we increase self-control and self-direction for our workers?

As executives become more readily enabled to face these questions, they become more aware of the need for Organizational Development (O.D.).

O.D. briefly is a response to change — the biggest topic on the work front today. As these questions suggest, we are not coping adequately with all the change around us; change in our world and in our industry; change in the nature, location and availability of jobs; the changing relationships between employers and workers, blacks and whites, professors and students, and between generations. Corporations, as human organizations, are susceptible, perhaps more than other social institutions, to changing times. Their successes and failures, rises and falls, all testify to their vulnerability. John W. Gardner, in his book *Self-Renewal* sums it up well: "What may be most in need of innovation is the corporation itself. Perhaps what every corporation (and every other organization) needs is a department of continuous renewal that could view the whole organization as a system in need of continuing innovation."

O.D. is a planned program to answer these needs, issues and questions. It is a complex educational strategy geared to change the beliefs, attitudes, values and structures of organizations, enabling them better to adapt to new technologies, market challenge, and rates of change.

In defining O.D., we imply efforts to find ways to change the organization from its current situation to a better developed state. O.D. then, is an effort (1) planned, (2) organization-wide, (3) managed from the top to (4) improve organizational effectiveness and health, through (5) planned interventions in the organizational "processes" using behavioral science knowledge.

Look briefly at a deeper analysis of these points:

1. O.D. is a planned change effort, including a systematic diagnosis of the organization wherein a strategic plan for improvement is developed, and energies are enlisted to carry out.

2. The total system is involved, such as in a change in the managerial strategies, reward systems or culture. In effect, however, this does not mean a total corporation, government or organization, as such, but rather emphasis on the notion that the system must be relatively free in setting its own plans and future within only general environmental limitations.

3. O.D. must be managed from the top, because success depends upon total knowledge, and commitment of top executives in the system.

4. O.D. is designed to increase organizational effectiveness and health. J.W. Gardner's writings outline a set of rules for effective organizations. He emphasizes the need for a program to recruit and develop talent. But equally as important are the means of combating the process by which men become prisoners of their procedures (defining effective organizations would require a book alone.).

5. O.D. includes planned interventions using behavioral science research. These interventions focus on such processes as individual motivation, power,

communications, goal setting, interpersonal relationships, intergroup relationships, and conflict management.

There are four major interfaces or challenge areas, in which O.D. efforts must be conducted.

1. **Interface between organization and environment.** This is the process of developing the relationship or nature of the transactions between the organization and its wider environment. Relationships at this interface are called "planned transactions" to indicate there exists a definite strategy adopted by management to make more money or as the case may be, to increase the resources of the organization. (In the insurance industry for example, this may relate to entering the mutual fund field.)

2. **Interface between groups within the organization.** Groups or divisions develop their own unique task-related characteristics. Their differing points of view can complicate the coordination processes. Thus, destructive competition, hostilities and secretiveness develop.

3. **Interface between individuals and the organization.** Challenges are constantly arising in the psychological contract between company and employee. Does he seek a career or only a brief job?

4. **Interface between individuals.** How workers get along with each other, or bosses, is the subject of the whole human relations movement, and personnel administration — topics beyond the scope of this article.

Even creative people need help to grow and develop. This is a paramount view in "humanistic Psychology," a term applied to the vast spectrum of approaches to human behavior and experience, all of which differ in their own ways from the more traditional emphasis of behaviorism and psychoanalysis. These various approaches have recently begun to become loosely affiliated.

In 1962 the Association for Humanistic Psychology (AHP) was formed to enable professional psychologists to meet in sharing their commitment to the fundamental uniqueness and importance of human life. Their most important conviction is that all human beings are basically creative and that intentionality and values are basic determinants of human action.

While exponents of the humanistic orientation may often hold conflicting views, there is some unanimity on these four common elements:

(1) Attention centers on the experiencing person, with experience viewed as the primary phenomenon in the study of man. Overt behavior and theoretical explanations are both considered secondary to experience itself and to its meaning for the individual.
(2) There is an emphasis on such distinctively human qualities as creativity, choice, valuation, and self-realization, as opposed to thinking about humans in mechanistic and reductionistic terms.
(3) Meaningfulness is desired in selecting problems for study and in research procedures. Primary emphasis is not placed on objectivity at the expense of significance.
(4) Humanistic psychologists are especially concerned with valuing the dignity and worth of man and developing potential inherent in every person. Central in this viewpoint is the individual who is discovering hiw own being and relating to social groups.

The AHP believes in a broad conception of scientific method and is therefore open to new, relevant approaches, methods or significant aspects of human functioning. While the AHP is fundamentally committed to psychology as a science, it rejects only those philosophical assumptions that may restrict the field of inquiry and interfere with a more complete view of human experience. Because of this orientation, the AHP encourages attention to topics having a lesser place in previous systems, such as love, creativity, play, spontaneity, warmth, ego-transcendence, autonomy, responsibility, authenticity, meaning, transcendental experience, and courage.

Conclusion

Friends, thank you for your interest. My hope for you is that you may have less success with your parrots, and more joy with your Blondes.

Reference

McGregor, Douglas, *Human Side of Enterprises*. New York: McGraw-Hill, 1960.

PART III

EXECUTIVE CAREERS: MYTHS AND MECHANISMS

The president of a company recently fired his financial V.P., a Harvard MBA earning more than $70,000. Naturally, as one might expect of a Harvard MBA, it had nothing to do with his good knowledge and experience.

The president insisted it was solely because the man had never learned how to relate to people.

Research has clearly shown that interpersonal skills become increasingly more necessary as one ascends into higher postions, regardless of the setting.

My colleagues and research associates are searching to develop ways to understand this concept better and clarify it for managers. One primary reason why this is so difficult is because of the ways our parents raised us. For example, most kids are conditioned to realize pain in the tooth suggests one see a dentist. Pain in the stomach may lead one to his family physician. But no one hardly seems to understand that pain in the career should lead one to a career doctor.

Even as executives may become hopefully more aware of the need for a career checkup, they will continue to talk themselves out of it until it's too late.

My colleagues and I have not found, much relevant research yet on the issue, so we've tried to analyze some of the various defense mechanisms that keep both men and women from accepting the career guidance they need. Basically, these are various irrational, unfounded statements people keep telling themselves so that they can maintain their dependency and remain immobilized.

1. "I'm a procrastinator."

This person may often survive in putting off his administrative duties, but his "career clutch" can catch up. We know one man intimately who lost more than $200,000 in his first year, without even considering how much more he could have earned as president over the next 20 years of his career.

2. "I had a terrible childhood."

It's amazing how many otherwise apparently successful men (or women) managers reach a point where upward progress is blocked and this expression is their cop out.

3. "Well, that's the way I am."

One might more easily expect this of a woman secretary lacking in achievement motivation who really does not desire a better position. But it's heartbreaking when you hear it from a young MBA-type, who simultaneously wonders why he's not getting ahead.

4. "I'm a follower, not a leader."

Maybe. The person who says this, however, may have never really taken the initiative to test it out. It's amazing that some potentially great leaders just need someone to believe in him (her) then he (she) can begin to actualize his (her) potential. There are many outstanding, recent books by researchers in the human potential movement on this point.

5. "My family needs me"

is one favorite rationalization of women who lazily prefer kaffer-klatschs to a self-actualizing career. Many men have used the same defense mechanism to put off graduate school, or finding a more rewarding postion.

6. "I've been out of it too long,"

is a phrase more often used by women than men. It is psychologically related to the previous rationalization. We might expect such a statement from a divorced woman or a mother with all her children now in school. On the one hand, a recent divorce may be forcing her financially to return, but she still needs a great amount of consultation and support to get her to make the move. But we were once very surprised to hear it recently from a company president who had been fired. He had evaluated his best job alternative as returning to the full-time practice of a C.P.A. Then he ruled it out with this rationalization. Another man may be rigidly unable to even consider something different when a so-called "company reorganization" forced him out. A man ice said that to my colleagues then went home and shot himself.

7. "What will others think?"

This statement essentially makes other peoples' reactions overly important so that these projections override what the person really believes. Albert Ellis has written eloquently how such an over-reliance on the esteem of others can become the basis of neurosis. Essentially, he says, "I can be very happy and successful, even if there is one person out there who does not like me. So can you be equally real and worthwhile even if there is someone out there who dislikes you." Successful people who are well-integrated have learned to live their own lives regardless of the seemingly solicitous bad-advice of friends and relatives.

8. "Here I am, change me."

Many executives and administrators have been very highly conditioned to this attitude by their early grammar school experiences. So as adults, they get involved in workshops, classes, or counseling programs that have potential for change, but they defeat the purpose by putting the responsibility for change onto the program itself or the person leading the activity. Finding one fault in the program facilitator means they can focus on that excuse rather than their own personal responsibility for growth and development.

9. "My husband (wife) wouldn't like it."

This rationalization flows from the same assumptions as the previous one. Many individuals succumb to an overly strong need for approval or advice from authority figures, husband, wife, group leaders, bosses, psychologists, teachers or other experts. One heartbreaking case was a competent young wife whose husband refused to let her accept an outstanding postion because she would provide too much competition for his own insecure, inadequate self.

10. "I could try, but. . . ."

Never taking risks or trying the unknown is one of the biggest emotional and psychological blocks to creative behavior and personal growth. Much more research is needed for us to completely understand creative people and risk-taking behavior. Too many people misinterpret the fact that it took a lightening bolt to knock St. Paul off his ass. It would be interesting to know how many vast projects are begun with only half-vast ideas and still make it, just because someone was willing to take a small risk.

11. "How do I do it, who exactly do I call?"

This statement is okay if it is meant as one adult's question to another adult. Surprisingly, many people may know whom to call in a career crisis, but they'd rather cop out and just add this last excuse to one of the previous. Most people really know that for any crisis in life some aid is only a phone call away.

In summary, personal growth as shown in the examples of career crises and challenges is one of the most exciting ventures open to people. The human potential movement is beginning to show more clearly how people can reach the heights of human attainment in many ways. If only we can make the efforts!

One Suggestion for Universities

Once an alumnus (a) receives a degree, it often appears the only remaining ties to the university are financial, in the sense that alumni are asked to donate money. Universities might consider offering a "free" service that would really aid in the human growth and ultimate potential of their graduates. Professors might be encouraged to develop even more "personal, friendly" relations with graduates who would freely call or write once a year about their personal and career growth. By this method, the graduate would grow through more clearly formulating his own personal situation. In the process, the graduate would feel his university (or at least one friendly representative—a professor) was continuing to aid in his own growth and development which simultaneously would lead him to contribute more money. Both parties would gain, especially because the graduate would realize he is being contact not merely for another annual donation, but for an opportunity.

MENTAL HEALTH IN MANAGERS: A CORPORATE VIEW

A homosexual manager takes a bottle of sleeping bills because his roommate runs out on him. A senior executive is caught embezzling funds from an outside organization, is fired, and shoots himself. A female clerical worker hates her female boss and threatens to jump out of a window.

These problem cases are only a few examples of the situations that are daily faced by any consulting psychologist, psychiatrist or career worker in the helping professions. One real question is: Are there more appropriate preventive or therapeutic techniques available in industrial organizations to handle them?

Responsibilities Within Organizations

Various methods have been suggested. Bruce and Dutton[1] have recently summarized much of the relevant research. They concluded that the neurotic executive definitely needs to be helped by his organization, which should assume responsibility for him. *"Management obviously must recognize the neurotic executive before he can do irreparable damage.* Since the executive probably will have much to offer as a result of his experience on the job, it is only natural that management should try to place him elsewhere in the organization rather than dismiss him. Assigning him to a staff position where he would advise more than direct the activities of others seems to be a likely alternative. Altering the job assignments to fit the neurotic executive's qualifications would appear to be easier in some cases than changing the individual."[1] Bruce and Dutton argue that companies need to pay at least as much attention to the executive's psychological well-being as to his physical health. Additional evidence for this point of view is furnished by Trice and Belasco.[2]

Following the lead of the many authors cited by Bruce and Dutton, one could assume that future policies and situations could be improved merely by doing a better job under the current rules of the game. But the primary thesis of this article is that the previous policy which some corporations have used in dealing with their own lawyers and physicians is not necessarily the most appropriate policy for psychologists and psychiatrists in dealing with executive problem cases.

For example, a medical doctor employed by a corporation may have diagnosed a particular physical disorder, whether it be prior to hiring someone, or after he has been employed. Because of pressures within the medical profession that foster private practice fees of outsiders, among other reasons, the executive with any medical problem is often advised to see his personal physician. The situation has been similar with corporation lawyers, who may not charge a fee to a fellow employee or accept a private client from the same company. These policies may be quite valid, based on sound ethical, medical and legal practices, but they do not necessarily serve as the best model within which a behavioral scientist can apply his profession. Before specifying exactly all the reasons why this position should be taken, consideration needs to be given to an important assumption.

New Functions

Bennis recently described how organizations of the future will function.[3] He suggests that personnel and development directors will be fulfilling six new and different functions: (1) training for change, (2) systems counseling, (3) developing new

Reprinted by permission of the publisher from *Personnel Administration,* September/October, 1968, 31, 42-46.

incentives, (4) socializing adults, (5) building collaborative, problem-solving teams, and (6) developing supra-organizational goals and commitments.

Personnel executives will no longer be needed merely to handle maintenance and emergency chores, but will need to actively stimulate innovation.

One of the most important roles is that of aiding the institutional influences that society possesses to nurture good citizens. We have to accept the problem of continuing socialization; training in values, attitudes and ethics. In the past, these responsibilities have been primarily assumed by the family, school and church. It was falsely assumed that socialization stopped when the individual reached maturity. This assumption resulted partially from the fear of socialization for adults, as if it implies a dread, yet delayed childhood disease.

To be more specific, we do not deplore socialization, but rather the conscious and responsible control of it. In essence, organizations are very powerful, if undeliberate, forces of socialization. Companies, especially large ones, do in fact teach values, inculcate ethics, create norms, determine right and wrong, and influence attitudes required for success in that environment. Managers who succeed tend to be very well socialized. Men who do not succeed, whether fired or not, may have it said: "Smith was a good worker, but he never quite fit in around here." In non-business settings, such as universities, tenure may be granted to those men who most easily accept the values or norms, regardless of how openly the practice may be stated.

> Change at an every faster pace is the central feature of our life and the central problem of our day. The fantastic progress of science and technology has carried mankind headlong into a new era which is at once the most promising and the most difficult in all history.
>
> We know how to release nuclear energy, but not how to eliminate the possibility of nuclear warfare. We know how to prolong life, but not how to control the explosive growth of human population. We can build thriving industries, busy highways, and teeming cities, but we have not yet solved such plaguing, depressing problems as air and water pollution, death on the highway, and crime in the streets. —
>
> ARJAY MILLER
> Vice Chairman, Ford Motor Company.

Conscious Socialization

Bennis'[3] most important point is clear. "Taking conscious responsibility for the socialization process will become imperative in tomorrow's organization, and finding men with the right technical capability will not be nearly as difficult as finding men with the right set of values and attitudes. Of course, consciously guiding this process is a trying business, alive with problems, not the least being the ethical one: Do we have the right to shape attitudes and values? It can be proved that we really do not have a choice. Can we avoid it? How bosses lead and train subordinates, how individuals are treated, what and who gets rewarded, the subtle cues transmitted and learned without seeming recognition, occur spontaneously. What we can choose are the mechanisms of socialization—how coercive we are, how much individual freedom we give, how we transmit values. What will be impermissible is a denial to recognize that we find some values more desirable and to accept responsibility for consciously and openly communicating them.

Finally, a well-recognized authority like Bennis has stated it. At last, the often unspoken viewpoint is out in the open. *Corporations do teach ethics and values and attitudes within their organizational structure by means of rewards and punishments.* The logical question is: How does this relate to the mental health of managers?

The Internal Consultant

Until top executives are able or willing to accept Bennis' fundamental assumption, they will not be able to use behavioral scientists to their best therapeutic advantage. A psychologist's effectiveness may be seriously curtailed because managers do not employ the organizations' rewards or punishments to the most effective degree in motivating subordinates with mental health problems to engage in or follow through with counseling or therapy. Historically, men who did not adapt were fired, or asked to resign, which procedure poses no difficulties for the man who is sufficiently healthy or adaptable to find and cope with a new position. The focus narrows, however, if the problem-executive is rather valuable, or not sufficiently disturbed to be fired. What then?

A company psychologist or psychiatrist may diagnose the manager's behavioral difficulty and can locate a clinic or outside therapist for the client. This procedure follows the medical or legal model, wherein the company therapist merely diagnoses and refers the man outside. This is precisely where the difficulty arises and where Bennis' assumptions need to be accepted. Any outside lawyer can draw up a will, or any physician can set a broken arm, but a neurotic cannot talk to or relate to just any therapist. Most importantly, the manager with a mental health or behavioral problem does not always have the insight and motivation to accept the referral (no matter how adroitly it is made) *precisely because* of the problem itself. He can recognize a broken arm, but he often will *not* recognize an interpersonal, behavioral problem. Thus, nothing happens. Eventually, because his behavior has not improved, as the situation worsens, the higher level manager will naturally lose his patience or tolerance and encourage the problem-executive to leave.

When the problem-executive leaves, he often begins a downward job spiral. Other personnel interviewers may recognize his difficulty. Or they may not believe the reasons he gives for leaving his previous position. It often happens, then, that the problem-executive has his initial difficulty compounded by the anxieties and depression associated with all his efforts to seek a new position.

My argument is based on experience in following up many cases of problem-executives who were unable or unwilling to accept outside referral to clinics or therapists, and thus began a downward job spiral. These problem-executives may have been more easily rehabilitated within their own company, if they had received counseling or therapy from a company-employed or company-retained psychologist, psychiatrists, or psychiatric social worker *on the premises. The fact of being on the premises is very important for both motivational and practical reasons.* Regardless of who pays the therapist's fees, whether insurance fringe benefits or other company provisions, my research shows a problem-executive will often visit a therapist on the premises, but he will not as easily walk across the street to see someone else. Admittedly, some do, but the majority of neurotic, problem-executives will not do so, because of the nature of the difficulty itself.

If the problem-executive is still employed by the organization, appropriate measures can be employed to encourage him to counsel with the company's therapist. The client will know he must have his regular interviews or be fired. Thus, both practically (because of convenience) and motivationally (because of fear of being fired), the problem-executive will more readily accept either referrals or therapy.

In some cases, a company-employed therapist may not be the most appropriate personality to interact with the maladjusted manager. Existence within the company does not, in and of itself, insure the best ability to establish rapport with the client. However, the company psychologist or psychiatrist may at least start the therapy. Then he may later refer the client to an outside therapist, due to the nature of the problems encountered, his own personal desires, or other reasons. The argument here is not that a company-employed therapist alone should handle the case. Rather, it is that he needs to be present to make the appropriate referrals, using company pressures or possibility of dismissal if necessary.

Client-Employee Relationships

Closely allied to the need to influence a man to accept therapy is the issue of confidentiality. This need never become a problem. A company-employed therapist can maintain his professional ethics just as easily as an outside therapist. A company doctor who finds himself in a position of conflict has only himself to blame for not establishing the ground rules adequately. On the one hand, his professional ethics require a confidential relationship with his client. On the other hand, the company (e.g., the personnel department) may pressure him for information about the client-employee. If any client expresses misgivings about the conflict, he can be assured no conflict exists. If the client still does not believe it, he may be the most appropriate person to be referred to an outside therapist. The important point is that any potential risks of ethical conflicts need to be taken as a means of initiating the rehabilitation process.

Further advantages are enjoyed by a company-employed or in-house consultant. He can often dissipate the client's anxieties more easily upon the first visit when initial determination was made that the client needed help. The client then recognizes that therapists can be warm, understanding and accepting. In the referral process for a disturbed person who has never even seen a mental health specialist outside of a few stereotypes on TV, this recognition is a serious hurdle. Once this initial hurdle has been passed, the company therapist can decide whether to work with the client himself or refer him outside. Some clients are unable to generalize this acceptance sufficiently to be convinced that the therapist across the street is equally accepting.

These issues are also treated by Thomas Szasz in "The Psychiatrist as Double Agent."[4] He concludes that:

> "The college psychiatrist doubly misrepresents himself and his role-first, by claiming that his work is like that of the nonpsychiatric physician, when, in fact, he deals not with the diseases of a sick person but with the social problems of the college campus; and second, by implying that he is agent simultaneously of the student-patient whose personal confidences he respects and of the school administration whose needs for social control he fulfills. In fact, he is a double agent, serving both parties in a conflict but owing real loyalty to neither."

Szasz's view of a double agent role may be true in university mental hygiene clinics, where many psychologists have worked as interns, but double-agent dealings need not occur in industry, because the therapist owes and gives primary allegiance to the patient only. Thus, if the patient does not decide to try for a job transfer, the company may still profit by gaining a well-adjusted manager.

Economically, the company may profit even more. Insurance fringe benefits that will pay for an employee's outpatient therapy by an outside psychologist or psychiatrist are becoming more prevalent. Larger corporations may find that a psychologist's salary may be much less expensive than the insurance claim costs that would have been made by outside therapists. However, this argument may well become merely academic because of the shortage of qualified mental health professionals.

Timely Action Needed

In conclusion, this position is based upon Bennis' outline of how organizations actually do socialize. Secondly, it is based upon the need for organizations to accept more responsibility to aid in society's problems. Witness, for example, in the aftermath of the 1967 race riots how the larger life insurance companies pledged $2,000,000,000 in mortgage money. President Lyndon B. Johnson acknowledged this gesture as a significant step forward in social responsibility. Similarly, any company, regardless of its size or its health insurance fringe benefits, can provide professionals on the premises to aid the psychological health of the employees. By doing so, the organization will be more effectively preserving and using its good talent and, more importantly will be rehabilitating problem-executives rather than forcing them into a downward job spiral and very possibly to an eventually permanent residence in a hospital.

As managers become more sophisticated psychologically, they may be better able to spot the problem-executive before it is too late. Regardless of how effective the preventive measures may be, the actual methods of therapeutic referral are the most crucial.

Argyris[5] has argued that the needs of the employee are basically in conflict with the needs of the organization and that this conflict is a major reason for the widespread problems of mental health in industry. However, as better research is done on all the issues at hand, Bennis' position may become more readily accepted. Then executives may become more aware that by accepting greater responsibility for aiding neurotic or other problem-executives, they will be decreasing future tax needs. The need to help these problem-people in order to improve job performance is evident.[6]

References

1. Bruce, G.D., and Dutton, R.E., "The Neurotic Executive." *Personnel Administration*, 1967, 30, 25-31.
2. Trice, H.M., and Belasco, J.A., "Job Absenteeism and Drinking Behavior." *Management of Personnel Quarterly*, 1967, 6:7-11.
3. Bennis, W., "Organizations of the Future." *Personnel Administration*, 1967, 30, 6-19.
4. Szasz, T.S., "Psychiatrist as Double Agent." *Trans-Action*, 1967, 4:16-25.
5. Argyris, C., *Understanding Organizational Behavior.* Homewood, Ill.: Dorsey, 1960.
6. Dickson, W.J., and Roethlisberger, F.J., *Counseling in an Organization.* Boston: Harvard Press, 1966.

EXECUTIVE CAREER GUIDANCE

Suppose you seek a new job. Whether you are fresh out of college, or a highly-experienced, well-paid executive vice president, there are three methods or avenues of approach that you can use.

If your father is president of a corporation, or you own a great amount of stock, you are a shoo-in for an easy job seeking adventure. But for the majority of men, seeking a new job or trying to advance one's own career may be very traumatic. For these men, three methods may be of assistance.

Employment Agencies: Referral

Because of their large number and some of their practices, many authorities feel employment agencies have the least value and prestige. Such agencies typically charge a referral fee to any company that decides to hire a candidate referred by the employment agency counselor.

Because employment agency counselors are paid strictly on a commission basis, receiving about half of the placement fee, they are highly motivated to place as many candidates as quickly as possible. Within this motivation and incentive structure, such an employment agency counselor often may be impelled to "shade the facts." Thus, a candidate may seek a very desirable job announced in the ads to induce him to visit ABC agency instead of XYZ agency, that lists less desirable ads. If, however, the candidate is not suitable (lacking a degree or any other qualification) or is not impressive (poorly dressed, long hair) or is somehow not attractive for some other reason, the counselor must still, for monetary considerations, try to interest the candidate in some different job opening. Thus, the counselor may be forced, by the ecomomics of the situation, to convince the candidate to rule out public relations or modeling (presumably very intriguing careers) in favor of insurance underwriting or technical writing (presumably very boring jobs).

Financially, then, the reward structure set up by society, corporations, and employment agencies does not lend itself to assisting the candidate to get any really professional guidance, but rather, just to get another job. Vast improvements have been made, however, by the certification procedures of the National Employment Association. (NEA).

Executive Recruiting Firms: Search

Executive recruiting firms, or "search firms," are retained by their client companies to find a higher-level manager or executive than is either available or currently being offered by employment agencies. Search firms usually charge from 15% to 30% of the candidate's first year salary, with the typical fee around 25%. Many search firms are highly professional and belong to the Association of Executive Recruiting Consultants (AERC) which requires stiff screening and ethics on the part of its members.

One very important hallmark of the executive recruiting firm is the motto: "Don't call us, we'll call you." It points up a curcial assumption—not really proven by research—that their ideal candidate is already happily employed elsewhere, so that the recruiters' function is merely to woo him away from his present employer. This feat is accomplished by offering the candidate more challenges, authority, responsibility, autonomy (the "motivating" factors), and not just more money and better titles (the "hygiene" factors).

Reprinted by permission of the publisher from *Personnel Administration*, Spring, 1971.

Executive Consulting Firms: Career Guidance

Because of the real limitations of these two sources—that recruiting firms most often want persons not actively looking; and that employment agencies do not offer professional guidance—the youngest part of the employment industry has recently developed: firms offering executive career guidance.

Executive career guidance is performed by executive consulting firms, which, in most cases, are retained by the manager himself to aid him in choosing his career, resolving any questions about it, and ultimately to advance his career. Executive consulting firms are not typically recruiters, although some organizations may have one division or department for each activity.

The executive career guidance section of the industry is least well known, because it is the newest. For example, a large metropolitan area such as Chicago has 1,000 or more employment agencies, 100 search firms, but only seven executive consulting firms. One major firm in executive guidance has had some amount of adverse publicity and these firms are now attempting to establish their own professional organization to set standards and a code of ethics, The International Association of Executive Consultants (IAEC).

Executive career guidance firms advertise to attract an executive to visit their offices. Then the first of three phases of the career guidance work begins. The managing director or another consultant explains the various programs, primarily designed to aid an individual (1) choose the right career, (2) the proper company, and (3) help him prepare for, enter into, and progress to even higher executive levels.

Executive consultants feel that almost any person may confront career problems which he cannot resolve alone. Thus, just as one may see a lawyer for a legal problem or a physician for a medical problem, going to an executive consultant is a way to resolve a career problem.

The fundamental assumption on which executive consulting rests may be summed up in this way:

> Every executive, manager, and professional man has available to him the best position for his talents and achievements. It may or may not be in the company for whom he presently works; it may or may not be in his present field; it may or may not be at his present level. But the position exists. Our goal is to find that "Best" position for each client, then see that he moves into it.

After a client decides to go through a career guidance program, he works with a professional psychologist for the second phase of the program. After and during a series of depth interviews, a battery of psychological tests, various homework assignments between consulting sessions, and guided readings from texts and journals, the client is led to make decisions about his career progress. One crucial decision concerns his next career move.

Once this career goal or objective is set, the third phase of the program begins: marketing.

Marketing a client progresses by various means, depending, for the most part, upon the specific career goal and level of position desired. Obviously, the methods used will be different if a client chooses a position in social work, or if he is already a vice president in a firm. Marketing methods may differ for each client, but the goal is almost always reached in helping the client achieve a better, more satisfying, and more rewarding position.

Clientele for Executive Career Guidance

Among the typical clients of an executive consulting firm, one might well find the following: (1) a 27-year-old MBA who does not want to continue being a stockbroker, realizing it was a poor choice to suit his needs; (2) a 61-year-old vice-president with a law degree whose corporation is going bankrupt; (3) a 45-year-old production superintendent with an engineering degree who seeks a change from business to a more meaningful career in social work; (4) a clergyman leaving the ministry because he wants more meaningful work outside of religion and who also wants to be married.

Clergymen are among the most numerous client groups of executive consulting firms. One such firm has been contacted by more than 200 clergymen within six months.

Clergymen pose a special challenge, however, to anyone attempting to aid them in seeking employment, and the nature of this challenge illustrates the desirability of the executive career guidance approach. The difficulty results from two faulty stereotypes—invalid perceptions on the part of employers, who cannot translate a clergyman's previous education and skills into business terms, and invalid perceptions by clergymen of both themselves and the business world.

There are basically two main directions toward which a clergyman could be guided: the non-profit world of government, teaching, or social welfare, or the profit-making world of business and industry. Once that decision is made, a much more specific direction can be taken. This decision, fortunately, is not and need not be irrevocable. Because personalities are dynamic and because value systems and attitudes may change, the idealistic clergyman might choose the non-profit area first, but later opt for business. In fact, many clergymen initially may seek social work because they feel it is the closest to what they like and need, often basing their choice on a low level of self-esteem. (Holland, for example, defines level of occupational choice as a combination of intelligence and self-esteem.)

Later on, as financial needs and desires rise, the former clergyman may decide to seek a better paying position within the business world.

The dynamics of career change of clergymen illustrates some of the factors which must be taken into consideration in executive career guidance. A recent doctoral dissertation by Dr. Edgar Mills analyzed such dynamics. Field interviews were held with 60 men who had recently moved from United Presbyterian Church pastorates. Four groups of 15 were selected to represent four types of career movement: to secular work, to church executive service, to graduate study, and to another pastorate. The findings constitute correlates of career change in the ministry, but it is difficult to attribute causality to them in any firm way. Mills found ten themes:

1. The long-range plan (e.g., pastors who returned to graduate school used this as a means to advance their career).
2. The attractive job (those choosing secular life found more challenging work).
3. Inability to relocate (into a more suitable ministerial job).
4. Church conflicts.
5. Restlessness (or loss of interest in one's position).
6. Sense of hopelessness (frustration or personal inadequacy).
7. Acute marital crisis (from breakdown of communication and loss of respect).
8. Acute family needs.

9. Health breakdown.
10. Need of a moratorium (a desire to step back and reflect upon it).

Application of Allport's "Lens Model" to Analysis for Career Decisions

Many variables interact with one another in a multicausal process of career change. One conceptual framework explaining this complex picture that has emerged is the "lens model" used by Gordon W. Allport (1950) for his analysis of causation in social psychology.

Allport regarded any social issue as accessible to several different but equally valid levels of analysis—in terms of (1) the stimulus object, (2) the phenomenal field, (3) the dynamics and structure of the individual life, (4) the surrounding situation, (5) the underlying cultural norms and laws of social structure and action, and (6) the total relevant historical context.

Executive career guidance seeks to apply Allport's six levels of analysis to career decisions. In this case, the stimulus object is the prospect of changing occupation or position. The phenomenal field includes an internal process that "represents the convergence of many etiological factors, and defines the immediate regancy that leads to specific acts of behavior" (Allport, 1950). The remaining levels (3) to (6) from characteristics of the individual to historical context, represent the field of force within which the executive works out his decisions.

Challenges in Executive Career Guidance

One of the biggest challenges in the practice of executive career guidance is found in psychological blocks of potential clients. Some have always been used to a free ride or had a job handed them on a silver platter. After being spoon-fed in school, they have often been spoon-fed into a job, or they may fall into, or even back into, a particular job because nothing more attractive came along. Sooner or later they find that their career adjustment becomes unglued.

Professor Alan N. Schoonmaker has recently analyzed this problem well in the California Management Review. He concludes:

The opportunities for individualism and independence in our society have become very limited, because most of us are employees and will always be employees.

Individualism and independence are worthwhile goals in and of themselves.

Without independence a man can't be truly satisfied with himself.

Popular proposals to increase independence have not been successful in the past and will not be successful in the future.

The best way for a manager to be independent is to take control over his own career.

In order to control his own career a man must accept his essential aloneness, analyze himself and his situation, and carefully plan his career.

Another great challenge in executive career guidance is that too many clients come too late. (A comparable medical analogy would be the terminal cancer patient, who should have been referred, diagnosed, and treated much earlier.) Consider, for example, the president of a large firm, who was fired. Thereafter, before proper consultation, he invested heavily in the wrong franchise for him. In this particular individual, certain psychological factors led to his firing, then to his not seeking the next position in the best manner, then to panicking into a franchise where he could never succeed. He could not have succeeded in this particular franchise because certain personality traits prevented him: i.e., as a former president he could not bring himself to make all the insistently persistent phone calls needed in a fledgling employment agency franchise seeking new business. It all cost him at least $100,000 in lost wages and bad investments, whereas a few dollars invested in career counseling may have prevented such troubles. Cases such as these are legion.

Interestingly, ancient Greeks believed anxiety to be a disease of their gods. The authorities ruling today at the corporate zenith are no less vulnerable to feelings of anxiety and failure than subordinates who often mistakenly tend to regard them as more successful.

Perhaps the biggest challenge for everyone— business and industry, professional consulting psychologists, and all their employees and clients is more research on the nature of work, career development, and all the interactions involved.

References

1. Flory, C.D., *Managers For Tomorrow*, Mentor M0746, paperback, 95¢.
2. ———, *Managing Through Insight*, New American Library, 1968, $5.95.
3. Neff, W.S., *Work and Human Behavior*, Atherton Press, 1968.
4. Holland, J.L., "Major Programs of Research on Vocational Behavior," *Man In A World At Work*, Borow, H. (Ed.), Boston: Houghton Mifflin Co., 1964.
5. Mills, E.W., "Career Change in the Protestant Ministry," *Ministry Studies*, 1969, 3:5-21.
6. Allport, G.W., The Individual In his Religion: *Psychological Interpretation*, New York: McMillian Company, 1950.
7. Schoonmaker, A.N., *California Management Reivew*, 1968, 11, No. 2, Winter, 9-22.
8. Levinson, H., *The Exceptional Executive*, Harvard University Press, 1968. $6.95.
9. Leavitt, H.J., *Managerial Psychology*, University of Chicago Press, 1968. $2.75.
10. Jennings, E.E., *Executive Success: Stresses, Problems, and Adjustment*, Appleton-Century-Crofts, 1967.

CAREER CHANGES OF CREATIVE CLERGYMEN

Work is a central fact in human life. And people are often judged by the work they do, just as they judge themselves by their own work. The way people perceive their own job, then, is surely related to the way they perceive themselves and the careers of others.

Creative people are certainly a good example of these key propositions or assumptions. Some research has been done on these issues (Dauw, 1966a, b, c, d, e, 1967, 1968a, b, 1969, and Dauw and Fredian, 1970a), but a great more needs to be known about how creative individuals look at themselves, their jobs and their work environment.

This research project studied the creative thinking abilities and job choices of former clergymen who were switching into some other career. The sample consisted of the first 81 former clerics with completed files who became clients of an executive career guidance firm (Dauw and Fredian, 1970b). This firm's consultants assisted the clergymen-clients to evaluate themselves, explore their possibly job choices, and eventually at the end of the program help them get their choices.

There is little research on the topic of executive career guidance (Dauw and Fredian, 1970b), and even less on clergymen who switch careers. Mentus' recent thesis (1970) reviewed the literature and investigated the topic. Some other research inquiries include those by Dauw (1966), Menges and Dittes (1965), Jud et al. (1970) and O'Brien (1969).

Sample

Statistical analyses were performed on 81 clergymen who had completed most of the program (testing and consultation), but major analyses were on the first 64 who had already been placed in a new job at a definite salary. Their age range was: 12 between 25-29; 20 between 30-34; 23 between 34-39; 19 between 40-44; 5 between 45-49; 1 between 50-54; and 1 between 55-60.

All Protestant denominations were represented by 12 men. Roman Catholics included 33 from religious orders and 36 from the various Midwestern dioceses. Of the first 81 clients considered, 38 held at least the bachelor's degree, 39 had the M.A., and 4 had Ph.D.'s. The majority (49) had been ordained before 1959, but 23 were ordained between 1950-1964, and 9 between 1965-1969.

Occupational Mobility: Statistics

Mentus (1970) was interested in the former clergymens' occupational mobility. The North-Hatt scale (Hodge et al., 1964) was used to measure occupational prestige. Initially devised in 1947, and replicated in 1963, it is the most recently published information on ranking occupations according to prestige. It ranks occupations according to "the way they are articulated into the division of labor, the amount of power and influence implied in the activities of the occupations by the characteristics of the incumbent and the amount of resources which society places at the disposal of incumbents."

Occupational mobility is determined on this scale by locating the rank assigned to clergymen and using that score as a fixed point from which to judge ascending or descending movement. The lower the numerical rank on the scale, the higher the job prestige. The ranking for ministers is 17.5 and the rank for the Roman Catholic priest is 22.5. When the final job placement is scored on the prestige scale, it is then compared with the former clergymen's ranking.

If the new rank is numerically larger, then the individual is given a minus score of the exact number of points he has descended from his fixed position down to his new position. If the new rank is numerically smaller, then he has risen in prestige and the clergymen's score indicates the number of points he has moved up the scale.

A difficulty with the North-Hatt scale concerns the new technology jobs, such as EDP systems analyst, not found on the scale. This inadequacy was resolved by consulting the 1960 Census Alphabetical Index of Occupations and Industries. A new rank was obtained by finding a comparable position. For example, an EDP programmer was given the same rank as a civil engineer (21.5). In another case, a position in "administrative management" (35.5) was located by averaging the highest and lowest ranks of a range such as factory owner (31.5) to agricultural agent (39.0).

Since it is not sufficient to determine the mobility of clerics by prestige only, a second scale was chosen to provide socioeconomic rank. The Duncan scale (Robinson et al., 1969) measures occupations by the amount of education and income inherent in a position. The Duncan values are the reverse of the North-Hatt numbers. The larger the numerical value of a position, the more income and education assigned to it.

Results

Table 1 summarizes the occupational mobility data. There is a significant correlation between age and socioeconomic change, (r = .24, significant at .05 level). When clergymen were assigned their socioeconomic change score, 63 of the 64 had improved their status and received a plus score on the Duncan scale indicating upward mobility. The scores ranged from a plus 9 to a plus 32. The fact that all but one of these former clergymen gained in status was predictable because the Duncan scale is based on the amount of education income inherent in a position. The important finding is not that former clergymen in general gained in status but that the older men had a greater increase than the younger men reflecting the possible fact that the older men had more experiences that were transferrable assets.

In Table 1, the analysis of variance was significant between types of work performed in the clergy and socioeconomic status. These results are clar-

Table 1

Summary of Analyses

Predictors of Occupational Mobility		Indicators of Mobility	
		Duncan Scale Socio-Economic Change Scores	North-Hatt Prestige Scale Change Scores
Age	n=64	r=.24*	r=.08
Time in the clergy	n=64	r=.20	r=.14
Similes Preference Inventory (Creativity)	n=64	r=.05	r=.23
Duncan Socio-Economic Scale			r=.001
Education	d.f.=2/61	F=.47	F=2.67
Type of work done in clergy	d.f.=6/57	F=2.41*	F=1.45
Religious group	d.f.=2/61	F=2.15	F=1.40

*Indicates significance at the .05 level. (Table 1 attempts to show the significant relationships between the six variables and the socio-economic change scores as measured by the Duncan Scale and the prestige change scores as measured by the North-Hatt Scale. The "r" indicates coefficient of correlation test and the "F" means the analysis of variance results. There are two significant associations and they are pointed out by an asterisk.)

ified in Table 2, where the mean scores are ranked by type of work performed.

Three variables—age, time in clergy, and type of work done in the church—have a bearing on the former clergyman's socioeconomic change score. The fact that they are associated seems to result from a number of factors. Organizationally, the church needs administrators to raise funds, maintain buildings, supervise new construction and direct educational services. These businessmen of the church have certain experiences they can carry over.

Table 2 reveals that certain groups of clergymen attained higher mean scores on the socioeconomic scale. Positions available in the three top groups, religious order officials, pastors and chancery officials, are relatively few, so that competition results. Age and time in the clergy are related since it is logical that the longer someone remains in the clergy he will grow older. By the mere fact of more time in rank, an individual increases his chances of obtaining one of these influential positions. Hence, the businessman of the church will be older than many other members. As a result of

Table 2

Ranked Mean Scores of the Groups Which Indicate
the Type of Work Done in the Clergy

Groups—Type of Work Done			Mean Scores
Group E	Religious Order Officials	n=7	x=28
Group A	Pastors	n=14	x=22.71
Group D	Chancery Officials	n=2	x=21
Group C	Teachers	n=15	x=20.8
Group F	Educational Directorship (seminary or secular)	n=4	x=20
Group G	Missionary—Chaplains	n=8	x=15.75
Group B	Assistant Pastors	n=14	x=15.29

*These mean scores are ranked from the highest to the lowest.

their education qualifications and general interactions with the business community some of these older clerics have developed a certain self-confidence. This self-assurance and related socializing skills enable them to move almost immediately into an upwardly mobile occupation.

The other indicator of occupational mobility as shown in Table 1 is the North-Hatt prestige scale. This scale measures occupational prestige in terms of how people view a certain job in relation to other occupations. The North-Hatt scale ranks priests at 21.5 and ministers at 17.5 of the 64 cases under study, 63 dropped in prestige—a reversal of the Duncan scale results where almost all the clergy gained in socioeconomic status.

Table 1 shows that none of the six variables are significantly related to the North-Hatt prestige score. The latter, however, is almost significantly (r = .23) related to the creativity (SPI) score. The more creative individuals obtained the better and more pretigious positions. The fact that none of the six variables are related suggests that despite a general decrease, there is no relationship between the variables and loss of prestige.

Table 3 shows the distributions by age of the former clergymen related to job placement and scale scores discussed above. Although a wider variety of jobs were obtained, it was necessary to categorize them in six groups for this analysis. The older clergymen achieved more upward mobility than their younger peers in socioeconomic status.

Table 4 compares the results of various psychological tests scores for the clergymen comparable data on creative actuaries (Dauw, 1968). The SPI score is explained at greater length elsewhere (Dauw, 1968; Pearson and Maddi, 1966).

Pearson and Maddi (1966) developed the Similes Preference Inventory, as a structured measure of the tendency toward variety. Their extensive evidence suggests that the SPI is a reliable, simple method to assess the intensity of the active, interoceptive tendency toward variety.

Correlations of .34 and .37 were reported (Pearson and Maddi, 1966) between the SPI and a measure of originality in two different samples. This present research reveals correlations of .42 and .32 between the same SPI and a different measure of originality (TTCT).

There were no significant differences between the clergymen and actuaries on the SPI. While

Table 3

Age Distribution of Ex-Clerics* Related to the Type
of Occupation Received After Final Job Replacement

Final Job Placement	Duncan Scale Rank	North-Hatt Scale Rank	Distribution Age	Frequency
1. Systems Analyst or Computer Programmer	62	21.5	25-29	1
			30-34	3
			35-39	4
			40-44	3
2. Management Positions	80**	35.5*	25-29	1
			30-34	7
			35-39	7
			40-48	8
			45-49	3
			50-54	1
3. Sales	61/65/66**	51.5/57**	25-29	1
			30-34	4
			35-39	4
			40-44	1
4. Social Work	64	44	25-29	1
			30-34	1
			40-44	1
			50-54	1
5. Public Relations and Personnel Work	84	35.5**	35-39	5
			40-44	2
			45-49	1
6. Teaching	72	27.5	30-34	2
			35-39	1

*Indicates that the size of the sample of ex-clerics used for this table had to be reduced to 63 ex-clerics. One of the men was dropped because his occupation did not warrant the establishment of a new category. He is a foreman at U.S. Steel and his age is 28 years.

**These scores were arbitrarily chosen because they were the most common rank in that particular category. The difference, however, was never more than 5 points as is demonstrated by the three scores for sales positions:

Wholesale sales—61
Manufacturing sales—65
Insurance sales—66

Table 4
Clergy Means and Standard Deviations
Compared with Actuaries

| | Clergy | | Actuaries | | |
	x	s	x	s	t(test)
SPI	15.00	13.12	17.16	13.26	
A (16 P.F.)	6.75	1.76	4.91	1.91	+6.29**
B (16 P.F.)	6.79	1.64	8.81	1.23	−8.77**
C (16 P.F.)	6.01	1.86	5.51	1.94	
E (16 P.F.)	5.52	1.98	5.78	2.13	
F (16 P.F.)	5.73	2.14	5.61	2.29	
G (16 P.F.)	3.76	2.01	5.20	1.82	−4.71**
H (16 P.F.)	5.52	1.97	5.19	1.51	
I (16 P.F.)	7.37	2.14	4.51	1.68	+9.29**
L (16 P.F.)	5.91	2.09	5.07	1.93	+2.63**
M (16 P.F.)	7.73	1.74	5.68	2.01	+6.82**
N (16 P.F.)	6.32	1.66	5.49	2.06	+2.76**
O (16 P.F.)	5.32	1.69	4.84	1.49	
Q1 (16 P.F.)	7.16	1.95	6.55	1.62	+2.41*
Q2 (16 P.F.)	4.55	1.58	6.65	1.82	−7.74**
Q3 (16 P.F.)	5.30	2.08	5.55	2.03	
Q4 (16 P.F.)	5.06	2.08	5.52	1.88	

*.05
**.01

there were a number of very highly creative clerics in this study, who did receive the best jobs, they were still lower in creativity than the highly creative actuaries (Dauw, 1968).

Very many statistically significant differences appear, however, when comparing the clergymen with the actuaries on the 16 P.F. Questionnaire (Cattell, 1962). The 16 P.F. measures 16 traits of personality that have been factor-analyzed into polar opposite dimensions along a continuum.

The clergymen are significantly more social extroverted; more tender-minded, dependent, overprotected and sensitive; more conscientious and rule-bound; more suspicious and self-opinionated; more wrapped up in their own inner urgencies; more group-dependent; more experimenting and critical; more shrewd and calculating.

By contrast, the actuaries described themselves as being much more resourceful and self-sufficient. The actuaries were significantly more intelligent, and abstract thinking, with higher scholastic mental capacity. The clergymen were less intelligent, concrete-thinkers.

Discussion and Implications

The overwhelming feeling on the part of the researchers was that these clergymen were making some creative career choices. The subjects of this study described themselves as self-actualized individuals striving for more challenging assignments, more responsibility, and more opportunities for achievement. They were seeking more creative behavior according to their own terms.

Despite their lower mean score on the SPI, many clergymen scored very high individually. Those who scored highest on the SPI received the highest level job with the best salaries.

The implications for management and organizations seem clear. It is very difficult for a creative individual to find the one right job that can most effectively use all his talents and abilities. Managers need to understand their creative employees better and use all their talents more effectively.

References

1. Cattell, R.B., *Sixteen Personality Factor Questionnaire*, Champaign, Illinois: Institute for Personality and Ability Testing, 1962.
2. Dauw, D.C., "Creativity in Organizations," *Personnel Journal*, 1966a, 45, 465-474.
3. ———, "Personality Self-Descriptions of Original Thinkers and Good Elaborators," *Psychol. in Schools*, 1966b, 3, 78-79.
4. ———, "Life Experiences of Original Thinkers and Good Elaborators, *Except. Child.*, 1966c, 32, 433-443.
5. ———, "Career Choices of High and Low Creative Thinkers," *Voca. Guid. Quart.*, 1966d, 15, 135-140.
6. ———, "Research on Religious Careers," *Insight*, 1966e, 5, 24-30.
7. ———, "Vocational Interests of Highly Creative Computer Personnel," *Personnel J.*, 1967, 46, 653-659.
8. ———, "Creativity Research on Computer Personnel," Life Office Management Association: *Personnel Quarterly*, 1968, May, 1-3.
9. ———, "Creativity on Actuaries," *Journal of Creative Behavior*, 1968, 2, 274-280.
10. ———, "Bridging the Creativity-Innovation Gap," *Journal of Creative Behavior*, 1969, 3, 84-89.
11. Dauw, D.C. and Fredian, A.J., *Innovation and Creativity in Organizations*, New York, Simon and Schuster, 1970a.

12. ———. "Executive Career Guidance," *Personnel Admin. istration*, in press, (1970b).

13. Hodge, Robert W., and Seigel, Paul M., and Rossi, Peter H., "Occupational Prestige in the United States, 1925-1963," *American Journal of Sociology*, 70 (November 1964), 286-302.

14. Jud, G.J., Mills, E.W., Jr., and Burch G., *Ex-Pastors*, Philadelphia, Pilgrim Press, 1970.

15. Menges, R.J. and Dittes, J.E., *Psychological Studies of Clergymen*, New York, Thomas Nelson and Sons, 1965.

16. Mentus, S.J., "A Study of the Occupational Movements of Ex-Clergymen into Secular Positions." Unpublished Master's Thesis, DePaul University, 1970.

17. O'Brien, John A., ed., *Why Priests Leave*, New York, Herder and Herder, 1965.

18. Pearson, P.H. and Maddi, S.R., "The Similes Preference Inventory," *Journal of Cons. Psychol.*, 1966, 30, 301-308.

19. Robinson, John P., Athanasiou, Robert, and Head, Kendra B., *Occupational Measures of Occupational Attitudes and Occupational Characteristics* (Survey Research Center, Institute for Social Research, University of Michigan, 1969), 335-356.

SELF-ACTUALIZATION OF PROFESSIONAL CAREER WOMEN IN A RELIGIOUS SETTING

Abstract

A measure of self-actualization was administered to 42 religious sisters and a control group of 76 male grad students. The mean self-actualization score was lower for the religious career women. The discussion suggests self-actualization is difficult for these women to achieve because of their career situation, and possibly difficult to measure for them. Implications are discussed for future research.

Introduction

The human potential movement in recent years increasingly used the concept of self-actualization to help understand individual growth as well as to explain behavior in complex organization. Since its origins in Goldstein's (1939 pages 197-198) discussion of drives, the concept was refined by Maslow (1945, 1954). Today the concept is being used extensively by many behavioral scientists, including Argyris (1957, 1964, 1970) and Shostrom (1966).

The self-actualized person according to Shostrom is "one who is more fully functioning and lives a more enriched life than does the average person. Such a person is seen as developing and using all his unique capabilities or potentialities, free of inhibitions and emotional turmoil of those less self-actualized." (Shostrom, 1966).

Argyris suggests self-actualization is present when organizational members believe their work-role-demands permit relatively full expression of their individual potential as well as opportunities to enhance this potential (Argyris, 1964, page 32).

According to Argyris, individuals seeking self-actualization want work settings that permit them self-determination, independence, variety, challenge, a long time perspective, an equal or superordinate position relative to their peers, and awareness and control over self (Argyris, 1957, pages 49-51). The degree in which the work setting permits the expression of any of these predispositions (their potency varying from individual to individual and perhaps by work settings) is the degree in which the setting permits self-actualization.

Where there is no congruence between the individual and the organization, (that is, where individual needs and organizational demands are not in harmony) low actualization is expected to cause forms of adaptive behavior including:

1. Leaving the organization.
2. Climbing the organizational ladder.
3. Manifesting defense reactions such as daydreaming, aggression, ambivalence, regression, projection, and so on.
4. Becoming apathetic and disinterested toward the organization, its make-up and goals. This leads to the following phenomena:
   (a) Employees reduce the number and potency of the needs they expect to fulfill while at work.
   (b) Employees goldbrick, set rates, restrict quotas, make errors, cheat, slow down, and so on.
5. Creating informal groups to sanction the defense reactions and apathy, disinterest, and the lack of self-involvement.
6. Formalizing the informal groups.
7. Evolving group norms that perpetuate the behavior outlined in 3, 4, 5 and 6 above.
8. Evolving a psychological set that human or nonmaterial factors are becomingly increasingly unimportant while material factors become increasingly important.
9. Acculturating the youth to accept the norms discussed in 7 and 8 (Argyris, 1960, pages 16-17).

Measuring the concept of self-actualization is of paramount concern to both behavioral scientists and practical managers or superordinates for personnel selection and placement techniques. By assessing employees' relative self-actualization, the manager or superior could better predict turnover, absenteeism, slow downs, and hopefully identify possible "trouble spots" before they occur.

Method

Following the research of Argyris, Bonjean and Vance (1968) developed a short form measure of self-actualization, that might be a more effective technique than a semistructured research interview. They validated their short measure by (a) comparing the data yielded by it with the data yielded by the semistructured form of Argyris (1957, 1960) and (b) by showing that the scores yielded by the structured technique are associated with the same phenomena as scores yielded by the semistructured technique.

In this present study, an adaptation of the Bonjean and Vance (1968) instrument was administered to 42 religious sisters who were participating in an organizational development program. (See Figure 1.) Their mean age was 43 with a range from 22 to 74. Of the 42 sisters who were primarily involved in full-time teaching positions, with only a few among them working as administrators, 17 had bachelor's degrees, 23 had Master's degrees, and 2 had the Ph.D.

Results

The instruments were scored according to the Bonjean and Vance (1968) method. The data revealed a mean score of .80, with the range from .52 to 1.00.

Intensive depth interviews did not reveal a consistent pattern that could be readily interpreted within the framework of the Bonjean and Vance (1968) research. For example, according to the Bonjean and Vance research, the high scorers would tend to be more self-actualized and have fewer forms of adaptive behavior, such as thinking of getting another job.

Yet in this sample, at least two of the highest scorers were known to be seriously considering a resignation from religious life. Some of those nuns judged to be among the most self-actualized by ratings during intensive depth interviews did in fact

score rather low, and certainly much lower than the .79 cutoff score used in the Bonjean and Vance (1968) research.

Control Group

For comparison purposes, the Dauw and Fredian adaptation of the Bonjean and Vance instrument (1968), shown in Figure 1, was also administered to 76 male graduate students. These men, ranging in age from 23 to 55, were all employed full time during the day in regular jobs while studying for the MBA during the evening. Their mean score was 91, with the range from .66 to .99.

Only one item differed in the instrument: #7. The amount of money I make. This item was used for the businessmen but not for the religious women, as explained in the following discussion.

Discussion

A major issue involved in the religious life of these professional career women may have been a factor in these results. Most working people in any career situation view their job-related activities as major factors contributing to their S.A. ultimately leading to more satisfaction at home. Diagrammatically, the lines of force would be from JOB → Home.

Many women living in religious life tend to view this question differently from that of other people. Because religious women put so much emphasis on love and peace in their living environment their lines of force would diagrammatically be from House (i.e., religious life in total) → JOB. Thus, it may be that the total emphasis of this kind of S.A. measure would appear somewhat inappropriate to them. Money is not an issue for religious women. The item about money, therefore, was interpreted to mean "receptivity," having supervisors and superiors who are receptive to their creative ideas.

Other factors or items of sufficient importance that the sisters wrote them into the S.A. measure. Some examples were:

(1) Opportunity to help in planning the work.
(2) Being involved in goal setting for the organization.
(3) Finding new ways to satisfy one's needs.
(4) Being involved in work that matters and helps others.
(5) Being part of something really significant.

CAREER ANALYSIS: PRESENT AND IDEAL
(CAPI)

by Dean C. Dauw, Ph.D
Alan J. Fredian, Ph.D

PART I: IDEAL

're is a list of conditions indicating what other people have felt to be the most important aspects of an ideal job. I should like to find out which of these are important to you. If you were looking for work, within the field for which you are qualified, which of these items would you consider most important?

Please put a "4" in front of any items you consider *most important.*

If there is any item NOT ON THIS list, which you consider MOST IMPORTANT, please write it in at spaces 13 or 14.

Which items would you rank next in importance?

Please place a "2" by these items or write one in at spaces 13 or 14.

Finally, are there any other items that make little or no difference? Please place a "1" by these least important items.

ITEM

_____ 1. Being alone while at work

_____ 2. Being with other people while at work

_____ 3. Directing other people's activities

_____ 4. Having a supervisor who is available and who tells me what I should do

_____ 5. Having new and varied tasks from day to day

_____ 6. Having similar tasks from day to day

_____ 7. The amount of money I make

_____ . 8. Having a job that is secure

_____ 9. Having responsibility and being important to the company

_____ 10. Doing my work in my own way

_____ 11. The physical surroundings where I work

_____ 12. Having the opportunity to do quality work

_____ 13. Other:

_____ 14. Other:

TOTALS

Figure 1.

Adapted from *Jabs*, 1968, 4:299-312.

PART II: PRESENT

In this section we focus on your present job. We would like to find out some things about the work you are actually doing right now. Please check or circle the response under each item that seems appropriate.

1. WOULD YOU SAY THAT YOU ARE:
   0. never alone while at work?
   1. rarely alone?
   2. alone sometimes, but not enough?
   3. alone as long as you want?

2. WOULD YOU SAY THAT YOU ARE:
   0. never with other people?
   1. rarely with others?
   2. with others sometimes but not enough?
   3. with others as often as you want?

3. WOULD YOU SAY THAT YOU:
   0. never direct the activities of others?
   1. rarely direct the activities of others?
   2. sometimes direct but not enough?
   3. direct others as often as you want?

4. WOULD YOU SAY THAT YOUR SUPERVISOR IS:
   0. never available to tell you what you should do?
   1. rarely available?
   2. available sometimes but not often enough?
   3. always available to tell you what you should do?

5. WOULD YOU SAY THAT:
   0. there is no variety in the tasks you perform?
   1. there is little variety?
   2. there is some variety but not enough?
   3. you have all the variety you want?

6. WOULD YOU SAY THAT:
   0. you do no routine work at all?
   1. there is very little routine in your work?
   2. there is some routine but not so much as you would like?
   3. you get as much routine in your work as you would like?

7. WOULD YOU SAY THAT:
   0. the amount of money you make is completely unsatisfactory?
   1. the amount is poor but acceptable?
   2. the amount is fair but you should be making more?
   3. you are satisfied that the money you make is good for similar work in this area?

8. WOULD YOU SAY THAT YOU:
   0. have no job security at all?
   1. have very little job security?
   2. have some job security but not enough?
   3. have all the job security you want?

9. WOULD YOU SAY THAT YOU:
   0. have no responsibility and are not important to your company?
   1. have very little responsibility or importance?
   2. have some responsibility and importance you want?
   3. have all the responsibility and importance you want?

10. WOULD YOU SAY THAT:
   0. you are never able to do your work in your own way?
   1. you are rarely able to do your work in your own way?
   2. you are able sometimes but not often enough?
   3. you do your work in your own way as much as you would like?

11. WOULD YOU SAY THAT:
   0. the physical surroundings in your work are highly unsatisfactory?
   1. the surroundings are barely satisfactory?
   2. satisfactory but should be better?
   3. completely satisfactory?

12. WOULD YOU SAY THAT YOU:
   0. never have the opportunity to do quality work?
   1. rarely have the opportunity?
   2. have some opportunity but not enough?
   3. have as much opportunity as you would like?

Figure 1. (cont.)

These items and many others spontaneously written in seem to suggest a different focus in the perceptions of these religious sisters. Certainly it does imply a different thrust in their orientation that could be more meaningfully measured by a revised instrument. Future research might lead to the development of a more meaningful instrument, that could include additional, more relevant variables.

The present research results could be interpreted as being consistent with the results of "Career Changes of Creative Clergymen" (in Dauw and Fredian, 1971). In that study the data suggested that many of the clergymen switching careers from religious to secular life were highly creative as measured by the tests of creative thinking abilities. Here it is suggested that at least two of the highest SA scores were produced by respondents who confided plans of leaving the community. There is not sufficient evidence here as was found in the previous Dauw and Fredian study (1971), but a tendency may appear that leads to certain hypotheses. In ordinary business life (Bonjean and Vance, 1968) a low SA score does suggest adaptive behavior leading to a job change. In religious life, a high SA score may suggest adaptive behavior leading to a career change away from community religious life.

These hypotheses, if supported by future research, may suggest that the S.A. concept needs to be interpreted differently in religious life primary as far as one form of adaptive behavior is concerned: a decision to leave community religious life.

Summary and Conclusion

Self-Actualization was discussed as an important concept in the lives of career people, including professional women teachers in religious life. An instrument measuring S.A. was administered to 42 sisters whose results were inconclusive. Suggestions were made for future research.

BIBLIOGRAPHY

Argyris, C. *Integrating the Individual and the Organization.* N.Y. Wiley, 1964.

Argyris, C. *Intervention Theory and Method.* Reading, Maws. Addision-Wesley Publishing Company, 1970.

Argyris, C. *Personality and Organization.* N.Y. Harper, 1957.

Argyris, C. *Understanding Organizational Behavior.* Homewood, Ill.: Dorsey Press, 1960.

Bonjean, C.M. and Vance, B.B. A Short Form Measure of Self-Actualization. *J. Applied Behavioral Science*, 1968, 299-312.

Dauw, D.C. and Fredian, J.J. *Creativity and Innovation in Organizations.* Dubuque: Kendall/Hunt Publishing Company, 1971.

Goldstein, K. *The Organism: A Holistic Approach to Biology.* N.Y. American Book Co., 1939.

Maslow, A.H. *A Theory of Human Motivation.* Psychological Review, 1943, 50, 370-396.

Maslow, A.H. *Motivation and Personality.* N.Y. Harper, 1954.

Shostrom, E.L. *Manual for Personal Orientation Inventory.* San Diego: Educational and Industrial Testing Service, 1966.

HOW TO BECOME MORE SELF-ACTUALIZED

The self-actualized person has been called by many names, since he was first clearly described by Abe Maslow. Carl Rogers wrote about the "fully-functioning person"; Marie Jahoda the "mentally healthy"; Sidney Jourard, the "disclosed self"; Charles Morris, the "open self"; and Ted Landsman, "the beautiful and noble person."

At the same time, there has been much research on truly creative people by men like Don MacKinnon, Calvin Taylor and E. Paul Torrance.

Regardless of whose system or what adjectives, the self-actualized person is surely someone who has risen to his full stature emotionally. He is truly in touch with his own feelings and is therefore better enabled to understand and accept the feelings of others. Because he's more in touch with reality, he's able to be more perceptive an accepting of himself and the world. He can be unconventional and spontaneous without calling too much attention to the differences.

An individual so "centered" receives much satisfaction from inside himself, enabling him to appreciate solitude more than other people do.

Although he is typically able to along well with others, he does not really need them and is self-directed. He may be typically free of the need to impress others or be liked by them.

Because the self-actualized person has a great ability to love, he is very open, spontaneous and giving in his love relationship. A creative person, he is divergent in his thought process rather than convergent or constricted. Experiencing a deep empathy, he can enjoy profound relationships with others.

Perhaps one of his most endearing traits is his continuing wonder with life—being able to enjoy almost ecstatically each new rainbow, sunrise or sunset.

Although the above description is not perfect (you would have to paraphrase all the above mentioned authors for the most complete picture), it does give some idea of the individual.

How can one become more self-actualized? Maslow suggested at least eight ways you can begin, and briefly paraphrased here:

(1) Make a great effort to experience totally each and every single moment. Try to get "into" it as unselfconsciously as a young child, becoming fully absorbed in it to the exclusion of all else. You may occasionally be having such intense moments now. But you *can* make them happen more often and prolong them. "At this moment of experiencing," said Maslow, "the person is wholly and fully human. . . . This is a moment when the self is actualizing itself.

This especially means living in the here and now. It is surprising how many people are usually re-living the past or worrying about the future. They forget we make our future out of fully-functioning HERE AND NOW.

(2) View life as a "process of choices, one after another." Everyone has to make myriads of choices daily. Each time you are actually deciding to progress or regress; to really be developing and growing or falling back on habits or fears. Try to be more and more making growth choices. According to Maslow, "self-actualization is an ongoing process." By making a growth choice instead of a fear choice dozens of times daily, you can "move a dozen times a day toward self-actualization."

(3) Really listen to the "impulse voices" within yourself. Look inside yourself for your own decisions, tastes and interests. Maslow explained: "Most of us listen not to ourselves but to Mommy's introjected voice or Daddy's voice or to the voice of the Establishment, or of the elders, of

authority or of tradition." It's actually more healthy to concentrate on how you yourself really feel about something, not on how you think you are expected to feel.

(4) "When in doubt, be honest rather than not." Most people are really full-fledged game players. (See E. Berne's *Games People Play* and T. Harris' *I'm Okay, You're Okay.*) Or they seek discretion and diplomacy rather than honesty and openness.

A truly honest person, however, will be looking to himself for answers and will be taking responsibility for whatever he finds in himself. And each time you take responsibility for yourself, you are taking a greater step toward actualizing yourself.

(5) Be a courageous risk-taker. Dare to be unique. Risk making even a seemingly unpopular statement if that is how you really feel. Maslow noted that even in the so-called avant-garde art world, a conformity of taste is demanded. Many people try too hard to make sophisticated pronouncements about something they really may not understand or even like. A self-actualized person may admit "that puzzles me. I'll have to think about." A person who is willing to take a risk can more often than not succeed because it becomes a positive, self-fulfilling prophecy. It's surprising how a risk-taker can be more successful than someone considered a dishonest phoney.

(6) Discover what you *really, really* want to do, and work hard to do it very well. Become as out-standing as you really can. This may mean, of course, going thru an arduous period of education or self-preparation. Executive consultants have found, by researching their clients in a management consulting firm, that there are large numbers of top executives and men on the way up seeking some career guidance as a means of becoming more self-actualized.

(7) Open yourself up to peak experiences— "little moments of ecstasy"—for they are fleeting glimpses of self-actualization. Try to set up conditions in which peak experiences may be most likely to happen, and treasure them when they do occur, as in # 1 above. Maslow became convinced almost everyone had a few peak experiences, but "some people wave these small mystical experiences aside" and deny them.

(8) Try to identify your defenses. (This relates to #4 and 5 above, too.) These are self-defeating behavior patterns you have developed over the years, mostly as a result of our total previous environment and because of not following the seven previous routes to self-actualization. Although it may be painful, it surely is necessary—repressing or supressing a problem won't solve it.

If you can make the daily efforts to follow these suggestions—especially toward finding out who you really are, what you really like, what you can become—then you are on the road to self-actualization.

Louis T. Brusatti, c.m.

JOURNEY TOWARD SELF-ACTUALIZATION: ABRAHAM MASLOW

Introduction

This study of Abraham H. Maslow begins with general background questions: Who is Abraham H. Maslow? To what school of psychology does he subscribe? How is this school to be understood in relation to the whole of psychology?

Abraham Maslow, born in Brooklyn, New York on April 1, 1908, was an internationally known educator and psychologist. he received his B.A., M.A., and Ph.D. (1934) degrees from the University of Wisconsin. Dr. Maslow taught and lectured at major colleges and universities throughout the United States, Canada and Mexico during his career. In 1951 Maslow went to Brandeis University where he served as Chairman of the psychology department for ten years. In 1967-68 his outstanding accomplishments and contributions to the field of psychology were honored through his election to the presidency of the American Psychological Association. In 1969 Maslow took a four year leave of absence from Brandeis University to accept a grant from the W.P. Laughlin Foundation in Menlo Park, California. After only one year work on this project he died of a heart attack on June 8, 1970.[1]

In addition to his classic work in motivation theory *Motivation and Personality*, Maslow's major publications include: *Toward a Psychology of Being; Religions, Values, and Peak-Experiences; The Farther Reaches of Human Nature; The Psychology of Science; Eupsychian Management;* and a work titled *New Knowledge in Human Values*. Maslow was on the editorial boards of many leading journals and his articles appear in a great variety of publications. A full bibliography of Maslow's works can be found in Appendix E of *The Farther Reaches of Human Nature*.

Where does Maslow fit into the psychological enterprise? Without question Maslow is one of the founding fathers of a growing school of psychology called the "Third Force." Maslow situates this school.

Two comprehensive theories of human nature most influencing psychology until recently have been the Freudian and the experimentalist-positivist-behaviorist. All other theories were less comprehensive and their adherents formed many splinter groups. In the past few years, however, these various groups have rapidly been coalescing into a third and comprehensive theory of human nature, into what might be called a "Third Force."[2]

This "Third Force" is a vigorous protest against the limited and limiting conceptions of humankind found in the two traditional schools. Maslow further specifies the meaning of this school in saying, "It derives most directly from clinical experience. This theory is, I think, in the functionalistic tradition of James and Dewey, and is fused with the holism of Wertheimer, Goldstein and the Gestalt psychology, and with the dynamicism of Freud, Fromm, Horney, Reich, Jung and Adler."[3] This synthesis has been termed a holistic-dynamic theory. It presents a philosophical program placing the human person and his/her experience at the center of its concern.

At the outset I want to note Maslow's seeming "religious" orientation. From his writings, especially *Religions, Values and Peak-Experiences*, it is evident Maslow is a naturalist following the tradition of John Dewey. Part of his concern is to demonstrate that spiritual values have a naturalistic meaning, that they do not need supernatural concepts to validate them. He links what he calls a "positive naturalistic faith" with the "common faith" of Dewey and the "humanistic faith" of Fromm and other humanistic psychologists.[5]

This "Third Force" psychology stands on respect for the worth of persons, respect for differences of approach, openmindedness as to acceptable methods, and interests in the exploration of new aspects of human behavior. "It concerns itself with topics having little place in existing theories and systems; e.g., love, creativity, self, growth, organism, basic need gratification, self-actualization, higher values, being, becoming, play, humor, affection...and related concepts."[6]

Who can be said to belong to this "Third Force" school of psychology? Maslow presents something of a who's who in the "Third Force:"

> This group includes the Adlerians, Rankians and Jungians as well as the Neo-Freudians (or Neo-Adlerians) and the Post-Freudians (psychoanalytic, ego-psychologists as well as writers like Marcuse, Wheelis, Erikson, Marmor, Szasz, N. Brown, H. Lynd and Schachtel, who are taking over from the Talmudic psychoanalysts).

> In addition, the influence of Kurt Goldstein and organismic-psychology is steadily growing. So also is that of Gestalt therapy, of the Gestalt Lewinian psychologists, of the general-semanticists and of such personality psychologists as G. Allport, G. Murphy, J. Moreno and H.A. Murray.[7]

Before moving on to an exploration of Maslow's theory of personality and motivation, please note that in terms of Salvatore Madi's personality theory classification Maslow fits into the fulfillment category. As this paper progresses my claim will become obvious.[8]

Section One

Maslow's concept of a healthy personality is deeply embedded in the matrix of intrinsic human nature and its potential for growth. The human person has an essential inner nature which is instinctoid, intrinsic, given and natural. It includes instinctoid basic needs, capacities, talents, anatomical equipment, psychological or tempermental balances, prenatal and natal injuries, and tramauta to the neonate.[9] It also includes a higher and transcendent nature with its values and motivations, a nature rooted in our biological essence as members of the species from which we came. Because of this grounding, human nature, our innate nature limits us. "Man is his own project and does make himself. But also there are limits upon what he can make himself into. The 'project' is pre-determined for all men; it is to become man."[10] The human project is to move forward or upward toward self-actualization or full humanness, to become the person we are potentially at the process of conception. This inner nature has species-wide or universal, as well as idiosyncratic or individualizing features.[11]

Maslow maintains our innate or human nature has been sold short, has been degraded and underestimated over the centuries. Our intrinsic nature is not evil or bad as was once believed and taught.[12] Human nature seems **not** to be intrinsically, primarily, necessarily or biologically evil.[13] Rather, it appears this basic nature, this core of the person, in itself is either neutral, pre-moral or positively good. Yet, despite this innate goodness, neutrality or pre-morality — whichever word is your preference — the inner nature is not strong, overpowering and unmistakable like the instincts of other animals. "It is weak, delicate, subtle and is easily overcome by habit, cultural pressure and wrong attitudes toward it."[14] This nature of the human person must be encouraged in order to allow human potentialities room for development and growth, for actualization, for movement from lower to higher forms of need gratification. Central to Maslow's developmental or actualizing approach is his position that by permitting our interior nature to guide our life, the individual will grow to become a happy, healthy and fruitful person.[15] If this biologically grounded interpretation of this inner/intrinsic self is correct, it would seem intrinsic guilt is a consequence of denying one's own inner nature or self, a turning off the path of/to self-actualization, an attempt at being what one is not.[16]

SECTION TWO

Maslow presents the pursuit of life and development or self-actualization in the context of an instinctoid need hierarchy covering the full range of human desire and potential (See Appendix A). Satisfaction of these basic or instinctoid needs is crucial for the human person. "The basic needs stand in a special psychological and biological status.... They must be satisfied or else we get sick."[17] Maslow outlines seven characteristics of a basic or instinctoid need:

1. Its absence breeds illness.
2. Its presence prevents illness.
3. Its restoration cures illness.
4. Under certain (very complex) free choice situations, it is preferred by the deprived person over the other satisfactions.
5. It is found to be inactive, at a low ebb, or functionally absent in the healthy person.

Two additional characteristics are subjective ones, namely:

6. Conscious or unconscious yearning and desire
7. Feeling of lack or deficiency, as of something missing, on the one hand, and on the other, palatability.[18]

These needs are in some sense and to some appreciable degree constitutional or hereditary in their determination. As has been noted our basic or instinctoid needs are biologically rooted.[19]

In Chapter Four of *Motivation and Personality*, Maslow specifically discusses the basic or instinctoid needs of the person. I have attempted in the following to summarize his presentation:

The Physiological Needs

In order for biological/physical survival the human organism **must** have certain needs satisfied, e.g., food, shelter, clothing, etc. "It seems impossible as well as useless to make a list of the fundamental physiological needs, for they can come to almost any number one might wish depending upon the degree of specificity of description."[20] These physiological needs are in a dynamic and interactional relationship to each other. Physiological needs will dominate the organism unless sufficiently satisfied or gratified. When these basic needs are not satisfied higher needs are pushed into the background or simply become non-existent. Gratification of a lower need releases an organism from domination by the lower need (physiological need) and allows the emergence of a higher need (social need). "A gratified need ceases to exist as an active determinant or organizer of behavior."[21]

The Safety Needs

Once the physiological needs are relatively well satisfied this set of safety needs arises. It includes: security, stability, dependence, protection, freedom from fear, from anxiety and chaos; need for structure, order, law, limits, strength in the protector and so on.[22] This need is clearly demonstrated in infants and children: Illness may lead to nightmares, fear and an intense need for protection. The child needs an organized and structured world. Confronting a child with new, strange stimuli or situations may often elicit a danger or terror reaction.

From an adult perspective: "The average adult in our society generally prefers a safe, orderly, predictable, lawful, organized world which he can count on and in which unexpected, unmanagable, chaotic or other dangerous things do not happen, and in which, in any case, he has powerful parents or protectors who shield him from harm."[23]

The Belongingness and Love Needs

"If both the physiological and safety needs are fairly well gratified there will emerge the love, affection and belongingness needs.[24] The desire to belong, to be part of, to have friends, family, wife or husband is an intense experience of receiving and giving love and affection, of the common life, of creating and belonging. The person feels sharply the pangs of loneliness, estracism, rejection, friendlessness and rootlessness. While litte scientific data are available the thwarting of these needs is the most commonly found core in cases of maladjustments and more severe pathology.[25]

The Esteem Needs

All people have a desire for a stable, firmly based, usually high evaluation of themselves, for self-respect, for self-esteem and for the esteem of others."[26] The most healthy or useful self-esteem is based on deserved respect from others rather than on external or internal unwarranted adulation and fame. In terms of self, strength, achievement, adequacy, mastery and competence, independence and freedom are important qualities. In terms of the social reality, reputation, status prestige, fame and glory, dominance, recognition, attention, importance and dignity are sought after characteristics. If these needs are not fulfilled feelings of inferiority, weakness and helplessness result.

The Need of Self-Actualization

This need refers to a person's desire for self-fulfillment, namely, to the tendency for him/her to become actualized in his or her potentiality. The clear emergence of this need is dependent on the previous satisfaction of the physiological, safety, belonging and self esteem needs.[27]

These five basic needs usually arrange themselves in a fairly definite hierarchy based on a principle of relative potency. This heirarchy of needs is not absolutely fixed. For example, developmental conditionings may place self-esteem needs before love needs, thus indicating the one most likely to be loved is a strong or powerful person. Those who were starved for love in early development may experience a permanent loss of the love "need." Finally, people who have been made secure and strong during their earliest years tend to remain so in the face of any threatening events. It also needs to be noted that there are clearly relative degrees of need satisfaction. Thus, in our society most members are partially satisfied in their basic needs and partially unsatisfied.[28]

The "higher" and "lower" needs mentioned under physiological needs require further attention. "There are real and operational differences between those needs called 'higher' and those needs called 'lower'."[29] In Chapter Seven of *Motivation and Personality*, Maslow unpacks this difference. I list below his sixteen differentiating characteristics.

1. The higher need is a later phyletic or evolutionary development.
2. Higher needs are later ontogenetic developments.
3. The higher the need the less imperative it is for sheer survival, the longer gratification can be postponed, and the easier it is for the need to disappear permanently.
4. Living at the higher need level means greater biological efficiency, greater longevity, less disease, better sleep, etc.
5. Higher needs are less urgent subjectively.
6. Higher need gratifications produce more desirable subjective results.
7. Pursuit and gratification of higher needs represent a general healthward trend, a trend away from psychopathology.
8. The higher need has more preconditions.

9. Higher needs require better outside conditions to make them possible.
10. A greater value is usually placed upon the higher needs than upon the lower by those who have been gratified in both.
11. The higher the need level, the wider is the circle of love identification.
12. The pursuit and the gratification of the higher needs have desirable civic and social consequences.
13. Satisfaction of higher needs is closer to self-actualization than is lower need satisfaction.
14. The pursuit and gratification of the higher needs leads to greater, stronger and truer individualism.
15. The higher the need level the easier and more effective psychotherapy can be.
16. The lower needs are far more localized, more tangible, and more limited than are the higher needs.[30]

As has been noted, the chief principle of organization in human motivational life is the arrangement of basic needs in a hierarchy of less or greater priority or potency. The unfolding of the human potential for growth is viewed from a perspective of progressive need gratification. Human growth and/or change takes place when a lower satiated need is submerged (gratified) and a new and higher need emerges. Maslow points to a number of consequences resulting from this progressive need satisfaction.

1. There develops an independence and certain disdain for the old satisfiers while a new dependence grows toward the new satisfiers which to this point were of no real importance for the individual.
2. With this change in need focus comes a change(s) in cognitive capacities.
3. Gratification of any need helps to determine character formation — it improves, strengthens and contributes to the healthy development of the individual.[31]

Section Three

What has been presented thus far can be focused into a theory of growth and health. Maslow's theory is based on two fundamental premises already discussed: 1) the nature of the human organism and 2) the progressive gratification of basic, instinctoid or deficiency needs. Within the human person there is innate a growth tendency, a tendency for self-actualization or self-perfection. As the human person moves from the gratification of one need to a higher need, there is a general healthward trend. Growth, the unfolding of personality, can be seen as a twofold process: *the discovery* or uncovering of innate qualities and tendencies, and *the creation* of the person in the social environment — "The person insofar as he is a real person is his own main determinant."[32]

What part does the social environment play in the growth of the human? Obviously human growth or activity does not actualize itself in behavior except in relation to the social situation. "The sources of growth and of humanness are essentially within the human person and are **not** created or invented by society which can only help or hinder the development of humanness; yet, culture is the sine qua non for the actualization of humanness itself."[33] Environment then simply provides a context which will either help or hinder the person with his/her human development; environment and culture are absolutely necessary yet not a/the primary determining factor. How then is an environment to be defined which fosters health or self-actualization? Maslow theorizes the point:

> A good environment is one that offers all necessary raw materials and then goes and gets out of the way and stands aside to let the (average) organism itself utter its wishes and demands and make its choices (always remembering that it often chooses delay, renunciation in favor of others, etc., and that other people also have demands and wishes).[34]

Maslow does list some basic environmental preconditions for any further need gratification. "Freedom to speak, to do what one wishes so long as no harm is done to others, freedom to express oneself, to investigate and seek for information, freedom to defend oneself, justice, fairness, honesty, orderliness in the group — these are examples.[35]

With regard to the individual's relationship to his/her own innate qualities or tendencies Maslow is also clear. No psychological health is possible unless the essential core of the person is fundamentally accepted, loved and respected by the self and others.[36] Essential to this is an awareness and gratification of the basic needs especially the physiological, security and self-esteem needs. Trust of the organism is crucial to development in Maslow. "In the normal development of the healthy child, it is now believed, much of the time, if he is given a really free choice, he will choose what is good for his growth."[37] All of this points and confirms that the health and self-fulfillment of a person is achieved via need-gratification. For this to optimally take place it is necessary to understand that capacities of organs and organ systems press to function, to express themselves, to be used and exercised and that such use is satisfying and disuse irritating.[38]

Attention has been paid to the general capacities of health, the how of growth or progressive need gratification; attention must also be paid to "the defensive maneuvers of crippled spirits" or the evasion(s) of growth. In his book, *The Farther Reaches of Human Nature* Maslow indicates, "It is reasonable to assume in every human being, and certainly in almost every new born baby, that there is an active will toward health, an impulse toward growth or toward the actualization of human potentialities."[39] If indeed this is true, what accounts for basic need frustration, for a lack of full humanness, of self-actualization? What accounts for this evasion of growth?

Our basic nature, despite its goodness, its tendency toward full humanness, is weak.[40] It is easy for the person to be taken in by the attractions of security and safety. It is easy for the organism to protect itself against pain, fear, loss and threat and to ignore the need for courage in the face of growth, to be manipulated by environmental pressures. This basic, internal or core weakness must not be equated with depravity, impoverishment or "evil." A lack of growth or full humanness (neurosis) is not part of our inner core; rather, it is a defense against or an evasion of it, as well as a distorted expression of it. Ordinarily this lack is a compromise between the effort to seek basic need gratification in a covert or disguised or self-defeating way and a fear of these needs, gratifications and motivated behaviors.[41]

This innate weakness can be seen as enlivening a dialectic between growth producing and growth discouraging forces. Maslow further elaborates these forces:

> Every human being has two sets of forces within him:

1. One set clings to safety and defensiveness out of fear, tending to regress backward, hanging on to the past, afraid to grow away from the primitive communication with the mother's uterus and breast and afraid to take chances, afraid to jeopardize what he already has, afraid of independence, freedom and separateness.
2. The other set of forces impels him forward toward wholeness of self, and uniqueness of self, toward full functioning of all his capacities, toward confidence in the face of the external world at the same time that he can accept his deepest, real, unconscius self.[42]

In light of these forces we can classify various mechanisms of growth as those:

a) Enhancing the growthward vectors, e.g., making growth more attractive and delight producing.
b) Minimizing the fears of growth.
c) Minimizing the safety vectors, i.e., making it less attractive.
d) Maximizing the fears of safety, defensiveness, pathology, regression.[43]

The above can be diagrammed:

Enhance the Dangers   **Enhance the Attractions**

    safety   (person)   **growth**

Minimize the Attractions   **Minimize the Dangers**

The human person is confronted with a never ending series of free choices and situations. Choices are made between safety and growth, dependence and independence, regression and progress, immaturity and maturity. "Safety has both anxieties and delights; growth has both anxieties and delights. We grow forward when the delights of growth and the anxieties of safety are greater than the anxieties of growth and the delights of safety."[44] We move forward because we feel safe and secure to do so. Our safety needs must be gratified.

Beyond need gratification or frustration Maslow speaks of the Jonah complex or the evasion of growth.[45] We fear our own greatness; we run from our own best talents and destiny; we fear our own God-like qualities. "We are generally afraid to become that which we can glimpse in our most perfect moments, under the most perfect conditions, under conditions of greatest courage."[46] This evasion of growth can also arise with a fear of paranoia — pride or overconfidence in the face of no or a lacking talent. "For some this evasion of one's own growth, setting low levels of aspiration, the fear of doing what one is capable of doing, voluntary self-crippling, pseudo-stupidity, mock humility are in fact defenses against grandiosity, arrogance, sinful pride, hubris."[47] The only true remedy for the Jonah complex would seem to be the graceful integration between humility and pride.

Our task is to become fully human or self-actualized, to fully activate the potential within us. Can this state of self-actualization be further specified? Maslow writes in many places about the complex meaning of self-actualization.[48] Chapter Three of *The Farther Reaches of Human Nature* ("Self-Actualization and Beyond") presents a brief summary of Maslow's thought on the subject. "Self-actualizing people are, without one single exception, involved in a cause outside their own skin, in something outside of themselves."[49] Such persons are involved in the search for the "being-values" (B-values) or intrinsic, ultimate values (see Appendix B) These B-values act or behave like needs and thus involve meta-needs.[50] Meta-need deprivation results in meta-pathology or a sickness of the soul, a value starvation (see Appendix B).

Maslow describes a number of characteristics of the self-actualizing person.

1. Self-actualization means experiencing fully, vividly, selflessly, with full concentration and total absorption.
2. Self actualization means an ongoing process; it means making each of the many single single choices about whether to lie or be honest, whether to steal or not to steal at a particular point, and it means making each of these choices as a growth choice.
3. Self-actualization means that there is a self to be actualized.
4. Self-actualization means being honest rather than not — taking responsibility for what I/you do.
5. Self-actualization means not only an end state but also the process of actualizing one's potentialities at any time, at any moment.
6. Self-actualization means listening to the self, to the impulse voices from within.

120

7. Self-actualization means transient moments called peak experiences — more will be said of these later.

8. Self-actualization means identifying defenses and finding the courage to give them up.[51]

This section can be concluded by observing that health/self-actualization/full-humanness is achieved by/with an articulation and actualization of one's innate and biologically grounded value system. The higher values, the B-values, instinctoid basic needs and a sensitivity to human nature (the humanness of human nature to quote Haring) are involved here. The major expressions of such actualization is to be found in the peak-experience, an issue I will deal with in the next section. What has been said implies a naturalistic system of values, a byproduct of the empirical description of the deepest tendencies of the human species and specific individuals.[52]

Section Four

Maslow's religious orientation is naturalistic. "The so called, spiritual or value life or 'higher' life, is on the same continuum with the life of the flesh, or the body, i.e., the animal life, the material life, the lower life....The spiritual life is part of our biological life....The spiritual life is part of the human essence....Our 'highest nature' is also our 'deepest nature'."[53] Spiritual values have naturalistic meaning and rooting. Because of this we may be able to accept the basic religious questions, questions of ultimate meaning as the proper part of the jurisdiction of science, that is, a science broadened and re-defined.[54]

In terms of his naturalism Maslow has come to see "revelations and mystical illuminations" as coming under the category of peak-experiences or self-transcendant experiences. In general everything that happens in the peak-experience can be listed under the heading of religious happening. Eighteen characteristics of a peak-experience, an experience of B-cognition, can be listed.[55]

1. In B-cognition the experience of the object tends to be seen as a whole, as a complete unit, detached from relations, from possible usefulness, from expediency, and from purpose.

2. When there is a B-cognition, the precept is exclusively and fully attended to.

3. B-cognition because it makes human irrelevance more possible, enables us to thereby see more truly the nature of the object in itself.

4. B-cognizing seems to make the perception richer.

5. B-cognition allows perception to be relatively ego-transcending, self-forgetful, egoless.

6. The peak-experience is felt as a self-validating, self-justifying moment which carries its own intrinsic value with it.

7. In all the common peak-experiences which I have studied, there is a very characteristic disorientation in time and space.

8. The peak-experience is only good and desirable, and is never experienced as evil or undesirable.

9. Peak experiences are perceived and reacted to as if they were in themselves, 'out there,' as if they were perceptions of a reality independent of man and persisting beyond his life.

10. B-cognition is much more passive and receptive than active.

11. The emotional reaction in the peak experience has a special flavor of wonder, awe, of reverence, of humility and surrender before the experience as before something great.

12. In some reports, particularly of the mystic experience or the religious experience or philosophical experience, the whole of the world is seen as unity, as a single rich live entity. In other of the peak experiences, most particularly the love experience and the aesthetic experience, one small part of the world is perceived as if it were for the moment all of the world.

13. In the peak-experiences can be found simultaneously the ability to abstract without giving up concreteness and the ability to be concrete without giving up abstractness.

14. At the higher levels of human naturation, many dichotomies, polarities, and conflicts are fused, transcended or resolved.

15. The person at the peak is godlike not only in senses that have already been touched upon but in certain other ways as well, particularly in the complete, loving, uncondemning compassionate and perhaps amused acceptance of the world and of the person.

16. Perception in the peak moment tends strongly to be idiographic and non-classificatory.

17. One aspect of the peak-experience is a complete, though momentary, loss of fear, anxiety, inhibition, defense and control, a giving up of renunciation, delay and restraint.

18. In the peak experience there seems to be a kind of dynamic parallelism or isomorphism between the inner and the outer. This is to say that as the essential Being of the world is perceived by the person, so also does he concurrently come closer to his own Being.

In psychoanalytic terminology Maslow summarizes the peak experience:

...It may be seen as a fusion of the ego, id, super-ego, and ego-ideal, of conscious, preconscious and unconscious, of primary and secondary processes, a synthesizing of pleasure principle with reality principle, a healthy regression without fear in the service of greatest maturity, a true integration of the person at all levels.[56]

In light of this Maslow hypothesizes: "To the extent that all mystical or peak experiences are the same in their essence and have always been the same, all religions are the same in their essence and always have been the same."[57] The peak-experience may well be the model of religious revelation or the religious illumination or conversion which has played so great a role in the history of religions.[58]

Using the peak experience as the basic model for religious experience leads to the conclusion that religious or transcendent realities are totally private and personal experiences that can rarely be shared. "From the point of view of the peak-experiencer, each person has his own private religion which he develops out of his own private myths and symbols, rituals and ceremonials, which may be of the profoundest meaning to him personally yet completely idiosyncratic."[59] In light of this does Maslow see any place for organized religion in his developmental approach?

Maslow's harshness toward organized religion is tempered in the Preface to the second edition of his work *Religions, Values and Peak Experiences*. "I now consider that the book was too imbalanced toward the individualistic and too hard on groups, organizations and communities....Basic human needs can be fulfilled only by and through other human beings, i.e., society."[60] Even with this in mind Maslow offers three serious critiques to organized religion(s).

1. For most people conventional religions dichotomize life into secular and sacred segments. The holy becomes only that which takes place in Church and the rest of life is something to tolerate.[61]

2. Conventional religion through its dogma, ritual and formulae may be used as a defense against and resistence to the shaking experience of transcendence.[62]

3. Familiarization makes it unnecessary to attend, to think, to feel, to live fully, to experience richly.[63]

Maslow's conclusion indicates, "If organized religion has any ultimate effects at all it is through its power to shake the individual in his deepest insides."[64]

Section Five

In order to concretize and to reflect on Maslow's progressive need gratification approach to human development I will look at three distinct happenings/events in my life. I choose these three because they highlight specific elements of Maslow's approach.

I A Night Alone — Security or Growth

I made a decision to leave the college seminary after my second year, thus ending immediate association with people I had been going to school with for the previous six years. It was a decision made in security: my parents were supportive, my spiritual director was encouraging and the vast majority of my friends were understanding. It was a decision made in the name of growth and development, an effort to expand my horizon and world view. I choose to attend a large state university, to live far from home, to strike out alone in a new environment. In this environment my security was gone. The initial experience was disasterous: I became reclusive and anti-social, avoiding people and having no desire to meet new people.

From my dorm window on a lonely Saturday night early in the semester, I could hear the music of an outdoor dance down the street. I walked over to check things out. As I was standing, listening to the music, I was completely driven inside myself. I remember someone walking up and talking to me — I was unable to respond. I simply could not speak. Realizing — for the first time — how bad off I was I returned to my dorm, bought a candy bar and went to my room. At that point I reviewed why I came to this school, why I had left the seminary and what I believed I was all about. I decided it was time to break out of my shell and stop feeling sorry for myself. After a few minutes I went back to the dance. It was as if the night had just begun. I had overcome my fears and took the first step outside myself.

Reflection: This illustration clearly brings out the continuing dialectic between the growth and safety forces. The decision to leave the seminary was made in personal and environmental security. It was a decision to move out of my small world, a decision for growth. The turning inside myself was a decision to run from that growth, to turn to my own diminishing security. The final decision to again move out of myself was based in something of an awareness of who I am at the core — a fun-loving, social person.

II *A First Night in Jail — A Peak-Experience*

What follows is a small section of a journal I wrote during Holy Week, 1972 while doing five days in jail for an act of civil disobedience done in protest at the trial of the Harrisburg Seven.

"...I was taken to my cell — this really is quite a monastic place. Three walls and bars, a bed, sink and throne over which is a small shelf — clearly no chance of escape. Alone at last, locked behind bars, a five day criminal — can they really reform me? My presence here makes a lot of people really wonder about me. I quickly made my bed in hope of getting some sleep. As I lay back in bed my mind continues to spin in circles and a million other directions. I opened my pocket Good News to 2 Timothy and began to pray. Locked behind bars I could not help but smile. Never before have I felt so free and Spirit filled. The smile I could feel on my face manifested well the happiness and content, the peace, I am filled with. I could not sleep; rather, I just lay between the two sheets full of life, enjoying the presence of God as I seemed to transcend every wall and bar around me. The Lord is responsible for me. No bars can change that — I am free. They can put my body in prison but no jail can hold in the word living within me. Sleep is long in coming but finally..."

Reflection: I define this experience as a peak-experience. Maslow writes an excellent description of what I felt was happening.

We may define it as an episode, or a spurt in which the powers of the person come together in a particularly efficient and intensely enjoyable way, in which he is more integrated and less split, more open for experience, more idiosyncratic, more perfectly expressive or spontaneous, or fully functioning, more creative, more humorous, more ego-transcending, more independent of his own lower needs, etc. He becomes in these episodes more truly himself, more perfectly actualizing his potentialities, closer to the core of his Being, more fully human.[65]

If the reader will note the eighteen characteristics of a peak-experience previously listed in this paper, other similarities will be evident.

III *The Sunday After Easter Decision — 1972.*

For the most part my first two years in the major seminary (Kenrick in St. Louis) were racked with indecision — I could come to no decision about celibacy. I wanted the priesthood but I also wanted a married life. The inability to make a decision was consuming more and more of my time and energy — study and ministry were suffering. My spiritual director and I had been working on the "problem" for some time. Before I went home for Easter I decided to make a decision over the holiday and report back the Sunday after Easter. A week and a half later I walked into my director's room, closed and locked the door, sat down and said, "I didn't make a decision and I'm not leaving this room until I do!" That was 10:00 p.m. For the next four hours we went over everything we had talked about for the past ten months. I finally said, "You know, ultimately it doesn't make a damn bit of difference what I do. I can be happy with either decision but I know I can't be happy living on the fence." We sat there in silence for a good amount of time. Finally I said, "I want to be a celibate priest." With that a good bottle of scotch appeared and a celebration was had by the two of us.

Reflection: This decision making process heightens in my own mind Maslow's contention that the growth process or the self-actualizing process is long, difficult and a matter of small progressive steps. It was only when the state of being committed to nothing became so burdensome, so oppressive and so crippling that I was able to make a growth oriented decision. In this case it was a decision to limit the available options for my life-style. Yet the decision to limit my options tremendously opened to me possibilities within the chosen option, possibilities which ultimately could work toward my own self-actualization. This decision also points out the relationship between the person and his/her environment. My decision for a celibate priesthood was made in a social contect. At the same time, the decision was made independent of that context. My director functioned to heighten my own awareness of what was happening within me and what alternatives I could freely choose. I was responding to my core, to the deepest part of my person in making that decision. It was a self-determining decision made in the context of a supportive environment.

Conclusions

1. I am in fundamental agreement with Maslow's concept of human nature as innately neutral, pre-moral or positively good when seen with a corresponding innate human weakness.

2. I think Maslow underplays the role of environmental factors in development.

3. Maslow sets the ground for what I think could be a rich theology of the Incarnation.

4. I disagree with Maslow's ultimate boiling down of all religious experience to empirically explanable phenomenon.

5. I disagree with Maslow's religious naturalism which seems to deny a personal God who reveals himself as other than human desire and aspiration.

6. Maslow does not deal specifically with the development of the child and thus it is difficult to make applications, i.e., applications such as can be made in light of Erickson's stages. One of his great contributions is in dealing with the "higher" forms of human development, e.g., self-actualization.

7. In order to form a comprehensive theory of development from birth to death it would be useful to supplement what Maslow says with what other "Third Force" people are saying.

8. The whole concept of self-actualization must be seen in more relational terms, e.g., other-actualization.

Appendix A

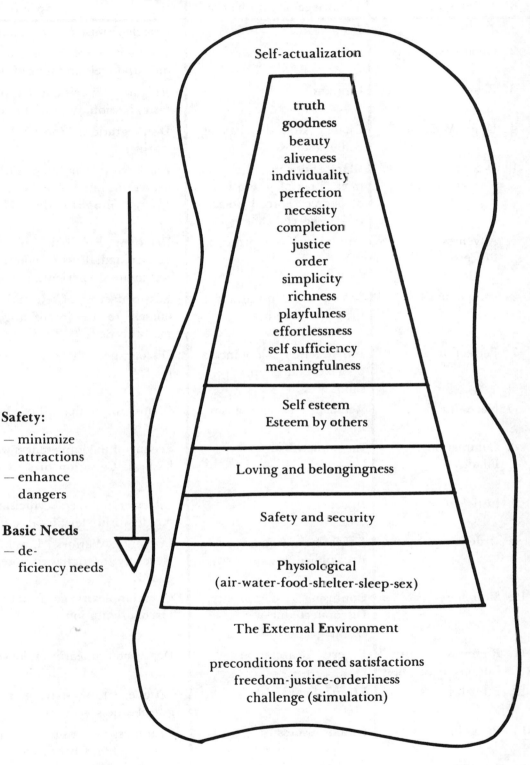

Growth:

— enhance
  attractions
— minimize
  dangers

Growth Needs*

— being-values
— metaneeds
— meta-
  motivations

Safety:

— minimize
  attractions
— enhance
  dangers

Basic Needs

— de-
  ficiency needs

Abraham Maslow's Hierarchy of Needs**

*Growth needs are all of equal importance. They are **not** in a hierarchical order.
**This is my variation of a chart presented by Frank Goble in *The Third Force*, p. 52.

B-Values	Pathogenic Deprivation	Specific Metapathologies
1. Truth	Dishonesty	Disbelief; mistrust; cynicism; skepticism; suspicion.
2. Goodness	Evil	Utter selfishness, hatred; repulsion; disgust. Reliance only upon self and for self. Nihilism. Cynicism.
3. Beauty	Ugliness	Vulgarity. Specific unhappiness, restlessness, loss of taste, tension, fatigue. Philoistinism, bleakness.
4. Unity; Wholeness	Chaos, Atomism, loss of connectedness.	Disintegration; "the world is falling apart." Arbitrariness.
4a Dichotomy-Transcendence	Black and white, dichotomies. Loss of gradations, of degree. Forced polarization. Forced choices.	Black-white thinking. Either/or thinking. Seeing everything as a duel or a war or a conflict. Low synergy. Simplistic view of life.
5. Aliveness; Process.	Deadness. Mechanizing of life.	Deadness. Robotizing. Feeling oneself to be totally determined. Loss of emotion. Boredom (?); loss of zest in life. Experiential emptiness.
6. Uniqueness	Sameness; uniformity; interchangeability.	Loss of feeling of self and of individuality. Feeling oneself to be interchangeable, anonymous, not really needed.
7. Perfection	Imperfection; sloppiness; poor workmanship, shoddiness.	Discouragement (?); hopelessness; nothing to work for.
7a Necessity	Accident; occasionalism; inconsistency.	Chaos; unpredictability. Loss of safety. Vigilance.
8. Completion; Finality.	Incompleteness	Feeling of incompleteness with perseveration. Hopelessness. Cessation of striving and coping. No use trying.
9. Justice	Injustice	Insecurity; anger, cynicism; mistrust; lawlessness; jungle world-view; total selfishness.
9a Order	Lawlessness. Chaos; Breakdown of authority.	Insecurity. Wariness. Loss of safety, of predictability. Necessity for vigilance, altetness, tension, being on guard.
10. Simplicity	Confusing complexity; Disconnectedness. Disintegration.	Overcomplexity; confusion; bewilderment, conflict, loss of orientation.
11. Richness; Totality; Comprehensiveness.	Poverty. Coarctation.	Depression; uneasiness; loss of interest in world.
12. Effortlessness	Effortfulness.	Fatigue, strain, striving, clumsiness, awkwardness, gracelessness, stiffness.
13. Playfulness	Humorlessness	Grimness; depression; paranoid humorlessness; loss of zest in life. Cheerlessness. Loss of ability to enjoy.
14. Self-sufficiency	Contingency; accident; occasionalism.	Dependence upon (?) the perceiver (?). It becomes his responsibility.
15. Meaningfulness	Meaninglessness	Meaninglessness. Despair. Senselessness of life.

This table is taken from *The Farther Reaches of Human Nature* by Abraham H. Maslow, pp. 318-19.

Bibliography

Corsini, Raymond, ed., *Current Psychotherapies*. Itasca: F.E. Peacock Publishers, 1973.

Fick, Willard. *Humanistic Psychology*. Columbus: Charles E. Merril, 1971.

Goble, Frank G. *The Third Force*. New York: Pocket Books, 1970.

Maslow, Abraham H., ed., *New Knowledge in Human Values*. Chicago: Henry Regnery Company, 1959.

---. *Toward a Psychology of Being*, (second edition). New York: D. Van Nostrand Company, 1968.

---. *Religions, Values and Peak-Experiences*. New York: The Viking Press, 1964.

---. *The Farther Reaches of Human Nature*. New York: The Viking Press, 1971.

---. *Motivation and Personality*, (second edition). New York: Harper & Row, 1954.

---. *Eupsychian Management*. Homewood: The Dorsey Press, 1965.

Ruitenbeek, Hendrik M., ed. *Varieties of Personality Theory*. New York: E.P. Dutton & Co., 1964.

Footnotes

[1]This brief biographical sketch is substantively taken from Willard Fick, *Humanistic Psycholgy*, (Columbus: Charles E. Merril, 1971), pp. 182-186.

[2]Abraham H. Maslow, *Toward a Psychology of Being*, (New York: D. Van Nostrand Company, 1962), p. ix. In this paper I will be using the terms "Third Force" psychology and Humanistic Psychology as interchangeable.

[3]Abraham H. Maslow, *Motivation and Personality*, (New York: Harper & Row, 1970), p. 35. In order to get a clearer perspective on the holistic-dynamic approach let me briefly define the three schools mentioned in this quotation. *Functionalism* concerns itself with mental operations rather than structures of the mind, thus dealing with the processes of adjustment, adaptation, intelligent behavior and purposeful activities of human beings. *(The Encyclopedia America*, Volume 12, p. 160*)*. *Holism* demotes part functions from the central investigative focus in favor of studying the whole person and how he/she moves through life. From the external observer's viewpoint all part functions are subordinate functions to the individual's goals, his/her style of life. (*Current Psychotherapies*, edited by Raymond Corsini, (Itasca: Peacock Publishing, 1973, p. 39). *Dynamicism* maintains processes and activities in progress, not static mental states, are the subjects which psychologists should investigate. There is a great emphasis on the concrete.

(The Encyclopedia America, Volume 9, p. 454-55.)

[4]Abraham H. Maslow, *Religions, Values and Peak-Experiences*, (Columbus: Ohio State University Press, 1964), p. 4.

[5]*Ibid.*, p. 39.

[6]*Ibid.*, p. 70 as quoted in the *Journal of Humanistic Psychology*, (no specific reference is given by Maslow.

[7]Maslow, *Toward a Psychology of Being*, p. ix.

[8]Salvatore R. Maddi, *Personality Theories: A Comparative Analysis*, (Homewood: The Dorsey Press, 1972).

[9]Maslow, *The Psychology of Being*, p. 190.

[10]Abraham H. Maslow, *The Farther Reaches of Human Nature*, (New York: The Viking Press, 1971), p. 315-16.

[11]Maslow, *The Psychology of Being*, p. 191.

[12]Maslow seems to lay blame at the door of the Church for overemphasizing the depravity of the person while ignoring human goodness.

[13]Maslow, *Psychology of Being*, p. 193. See also, Maslow, *Motivation and Personality*, p. 118.

[14]Maslow, *Psychology of Being*, p. 164.

[15]*Ibid.*, p. 4.

[16]Maslow, *The Farther Reaches of Human Nature*, p. 339. See also, Maslow, *Psychology of Being, p. 193*.

[17]Abraham H. Maslow, *Motivation and Personality*, (New York: Harper & Row, 1954), p. 92.

[18]Maslow, *Psychology of Being*, p. 22. See Appendix D of *The Farther Reaches of Human Nature* for a more developed and technical position on the subject.

[19]See Chapter Six of *Motivation and Personality*.

[20]Maslow. *Motivation and Personality*, p. 36.

[21]*Ibid.*, p. 38.

[22]*Ibid.*, p. 29.

[23]*Ibid.*, p. 41.

[24]*Ibid.*, p. 43.

[25]*Ibid.*, p. 44.

[26]*Ibid.*, p. 45.

[27]*Ibid.*, p. 46.

[28]*Ibid.*, pp. 53-4.

[29]*Ibid.*, pp. 98-100.

[30]*Ibid.*, pp. 98-100.

[31]*Ibid.*, pp. 60-62.

[32]Maslow, *Toward a Psychology of Being*, p. 193.

[33]*Ibid.*, p. 211.

[34]Maslow, *Motivation and Personality*, p. 277.

[35]*Ibid.*, p. 47.

[36]Maslow, *Toward a Psychology of Being*, p. 196.

[37]*Ibid.*, p. 198.

[38]*Ibid.*, p. 201.

[39]Maslow, *The Farther Reaches of Human Nature*, p. 25.

[40]Maslow, *Toward a Psychology of Being*, p. 191.

[41]*Ibid.*, p. 205.

[42]*Ibid.*, p. 46.

[43]*Ibid.*, p. 47.

[44]*Ibid.*, p. 47.

[45]Maslow, *The Farther Reaches of Human Nature*, p. 35.

[46]*Ibid.*

[47]*Ibid.*, p. 39.

[48]See: Appendix A of Maslow's *Religions, Values, and Peak-Experiences*; Chapters 11 and 12 of Maslow's *Motivation and Personality*; and, Chapter 10 of Maslow's *Toward A Psychology of Being*.

[49]Maslow, *The Farther Reaches of Human Nature*, p. 43.

[50]*Ibid.*, p. 44.

[51]*Ibid.*, pp. 45-50. What is presented here is a summary of these pages.

[52]Maslow, *Toward a Psychology of Being*, p. 205.

[53]Maslow, *The Farther Reaches of Human Nature*, pp. 224-5.

[53]Maslow, *Religions, Values, and Peak-Experiences*, p. 11. See also, Maslow, *Motivation and Personality*, Chapters 1 and 2.

[55]Maslow, *Toward a Psychology of Being*, pp. 71-96. The material here is also treated in Appendix D of *Religions, Values and Peak-Experiences*.

[56]Maslow, *Toward a Psychology of Being*, p. 96.

[57]Maslow, *Religions, Values and Peak-Experiences*, p. 20.

[58]*Ibid.*, p. 26.

[59]*Ibid.*, p. 28.

[60]*Ibid.*, p. xiii.

[61]*Ibid.*, p. 30.

[62]*Ibid.*, p. 33.

[63]*Ibid.*, p. 34.

[64]*Ibid.*

[65]Maslow, *Toward a Psychology of Being*, p. 97.

Roy E. Horton　　**J. Patrick Murphy**
Alan J. Fredian　　**Dean C. Dauw**

SELF-ACTUALIZATION AND CREATIVITY

Introduction

Are creative people highly self-actualized? And conversely, are self-actualized people highly creative? Many authors seem to use these terms synonymously. This research project is an attempt to unerstand and define these two concepts more clearly, and to answer the above questions.

Review of the Literature

Weisskopf (1959) explains Maslow's interpretation of self-actualization as being identified with integration, psychological health, individuation, autonomy, creativity, and productivity. Self-actualization is the ultimate human goal of man who constantly tends toward growth.

Maslow (1959) says there is within the human being "a pressure toward unity of personality, toward spontaneous expressiveness, toward full individuality and identity, toward seeing the truth rather than being blind, toward being creative, toward being good." All these forms of self-actualization imply "good values, serenity, kindness, courage, honesty, love, unselfishness, and goodness."

Maslow seems to include creativity as one way of expressing self-actualization. Weisskopf's interpretation states that the concepts of self-actualization and psychological health contain value elements. He asks why such generally recognized virtues as kindness, love, and unselfishness are the result of self-actualization and why Maslow excludes such obvious phenomena of *self-realization* as aggression, destruction, hostility, domination, egotism? Weisskopf suggests a criterion of higher logical order is needed to separate the positive from the negative strands in self-actualization. Maslow does not use the term self-actualization to mean simply living out any and all tendencies in the human person; he discriminates between good and bad tendencies.

Maslow (1968) explicity states that self-actualization is an uncommon achievement attained only in late maturity. This list of characteristics may indicate why. Self-actualizing people possess:

superior perception of reality;
increased acceptance of self, of others, of nature;
increased spontaneity;
increase in problem centering;
increased detachment and desire for privacy;
increased autonomy, and resistance to enculturation, greater freshness of appreciation, and richness of emotional reaction, higher frequency of peak experiences;
increased identification with the human species;
changed (the clinician would say, improved) interpersonal relations;
more democratic character structure;
greatly increased creativeness;
certain changes in the value system

Smith (1973) summarized many aspects of Maslow's doctrine of self-actualization and emphasized the *process* of self-actualization. He interpreted self-actualization as the congruence of a person's actions and experiences with his existing self.

Shostrom (1967) defines self-defeating behavior as manipulative behavior, and creative behavior as actualizing behavior. Actualizing behavior is simply manipulative behavior expressed more creatively. Shostrom accepts Perl's statement that each person has two sides, a *top-dog* and an *under-dog*. *Top-dog* is the active side in that it is more energetic, commanding, and authoritative. The *under-dog* is the passive side in that it is compliant and submissive. Each of these sides can be expressed in either a manipulative or a creative, actualizing way.

The Journal of Creative Behavior, on the other hand, devotes much space to creativity, but does not seem to subsume *creativity* under self-actualization. Only one major article in this journal seems to tie the concepts together.

Foster (1968) emphasizes "self-actualization, like true psychological health, requires both creativity and human relatedness. Deprivation of either reduces the individual to less than his true self." In sum, her article seems to echo many others where creativity and self-actualization are synonymous.

Dauw and Fredian (1974) have summarized much of the research on creativity and creative personalities. But at this time no research has been found that explicitly spells out the psychometric relationship, if any, between creativity and self-actualization.

Torrance (1962) initially pointed out differences between people who are highly creative in originality or elaboration. Good elaborators are those who are able to take an idea or task and spell out the detail. They can embroider a simple idea to make it fancy and attractive. Original thinkers, on the other hand, are those who are more able to get away from the obvious and break away from the beaten path. Being more innovative than the elaborating thinkers, they see relationships and think of ideas and solutions different from others. (Naturally, the most creatively gifted individuals may be outstanding in both of these divergent thinking abilities.) Extensive research by Dauw (1974) has substantiated the differences between these original thinkers and good elaborators.

The Tests and What They Measure

Shostrom (1964) has developed an instrument, the Personal Orientation Inventory (POI), to measure self-actualization as currently conceived in humanistic existential psychology. Shostrom (1966) defines the self-actualized person as "one who is more fully functioning and lives a more enriched life than does the average person. Such a person is seen as developing and using all his unique capabilities, or potentialities, free of inhibitions and emotional turmoil of those less self-actualized."

Various research projects on the POI have shown it is reliable (Ilardi & May, 1968); resistant to faking good (Warehime & Foulds, 1973); and has been factor-analyzed with good results (Tosi & Hoffman, 1972).

The Torrance Tests of Creative Thinking (TTCT) have verbal and figural forms. The number of relevant responses produced by a subject yields one measure of identical fluency. The number of shifts in thinking or number of different categories or questions, causes, or consequences gives one measure of flexibility. The statistical infrequency of these questions, causes, or consequences, or the extent to which the response represents a mental leap or departure from the obvious and commonplace gives one measure of originality. The detail and specificity incorporated into the questions and hypotheses provide one measure of the ability to elaborate.

Pearson and Maddi (1966) developed the Similes Preference Inventory (SPI) as a structured measure of the tendency toward variety. Their extensive evidence suggests that the SPI is a reliable, simple method to assess the intensity of the active, interoceptive tendency toward variety (creativity).

Correlations of .34 and .37 were reported (Pearson & Maddi, 1966) between the SPI and a measure of originality in two different samples. Dauw's research (1969) revealed correlations of .42 and .32 between the same SPI and a different measure of originality (TTCT).

Lafferty's (1973) Life Style checklist is a self-description inventory consisting of some 240 adjectives and phrases of two to seven words that are scored on twelve scales, one of which is the self-actualization scale. The instrument is based on the theory that interpersonal relationships are a "field" of tensions and needs produced by people attempting to satisfy their basic concerns. That is why Lafferty's (1973) Life Styles are based on a field theory of interpersonal relations.

The Sample

The data for this project was collected by administering the four tests to 177 graduate and undergraduate students. Half of the students were Vincentian seminary (C.M.) students. The undergraduate seminarians ranged in age from 18 to 24 and were majoring in philosophy. The graduate seminarians ranged in age from 22 to 36, and were doing graduate work in theology. All seminarians were full-time students.

The rest of the sample consisted of undergraduate students who were employed full time in various jobs throughout private industry, their age range being from 22 to 42.

Results

In this project, some statistical results are very significant, while others are less clear. Using two different measures for both creativity and self-actualization, strong positive correlations were found between both creativity measures and both self-actualization inventories. But no strong relationships were found, as initially hypothesized, between creativity and self-actualization.

The 88 seminary students were much more creative to a statistically significant degree than the 89 university students (p. < .005), on both the Torrance Test of Creative Thinking (TTCT) originality and the TTCT elaboration variables.

On one self-actualization measure, the university business students were more highly self-actualized to a significant degree (p. < .01). And when 35 seminary graudate students were compared with just the 38 university graduate (MBA) business students, the seminary graduate students were much more creative, to a statistically significant degree (p. < .001). But on the two self-actualization variables, no differences were significant.

The same pattern is true on creativity measures when the 53 undergraduate seminary students were compared with the 51 university undergraduates (p. < .001). However, the latter were much more self-actualized than the seminarians (p. < .005).

All possible statistical tests were run, including the F ratio for the Multivariate Test of Equality of Mean Vectors for the five major variables; however, they are not reported here in tabular form.

Only one of all the variables on all the tests analyzed by diverse statistical techniques was significant as far as the creativity-self-actualization relationship is concerned. Those scoring as High Elaborators on the TTCT creativity tests also scored high on self-actualization (p. < .01) to a significant degree.

If there were in reality a highly significant relationship between these two concepts, one might expect it to be evidenced regardless of how they were measured. They may not be clearly unified traits. Rather, self-actualization may be a larger, global concept, whereas creativity as measured by the Torrance Test of Creative Thinking may be a more clearly defined trait in the realm of intellectual abilities.

Discussion

The fact that there are no extremely clear-cut differences on the POI self-actualization variable scales between groups may be explained by the following statements.

Shostrom and Knapp (1966) had previously reported significant negative correlations between the Depression, Psychasthenia, and Social Introversion scales of the MMPI and the scales of the POI. Therefore, Foulds (1969) concludes that the Personal Orientation Inventory (POI) "purports to assess particular personality variables commonly associated with self-actualization, positive mental health, or psychological well-being — terms that Shostrom appears to use synonymously." The self-actualized person is one who is functioning more fully than the average individual and is living a more enriched life.

Thus, this research may really be measuring not highly self-actualized people in Maslow's optimum sense of the term, but rather ordinary people who just have good, positive mental health.

Perhaps, if a more obviously creative group had been sampled, such as exceptionally creative artists, architects, and the like, then more significant differences might have been found. The sample here may have simply been from the relatively undistinguished middle range of the population that did not include enough individuals who are in fact more highly creative or more highly self-actualized.

Finally, the instruments selected here may not be measuring the concepts as clearly as possible. It seems likely that the creativity (TTCT) tests are spelling out intellectual differences more distinctly than the self-actualization measures, which are measuring personality variables.

In conclusion, the data seem to suggest highly creative people may be more self-actualized and that highly self-actualized people may be creative but neither hypothesis is measured in this sample.

References

Alwan, A.J. & Parisi, D.G. *Quantitative methods for decision making.* Morristown, NJ: General Learning Press, 1974.

Dauw, D.C. Creativity research on actuaries. *Journal of Creative Behavior,* 1968, 2(4).

Dauw, D.C. & Fredian, A.J. *Creativity and innovation in organizations,* Dubuque, IA: Kendall-Hunt, 1974.

Foster, E.P. The human relationships of creative individuals. *Journal of Creative Behavior,* 1968, 2(2).

Foulds, M.L. Self-actualization and level of counselor inter-personal functioning. *Journal of Humanistic Psychology,* 1969, 11.

Ilardi, R.L. & May, W.T. A reliability study of Shostrom's personal orientation in inventory. *Journal of Humanistic Psychology,* 1968, 8.

Lafferty, J.C. *Evaluation systems: life styles.* Plymouth, MI: Human Synergistics, 1973.

Maslow, A.H. (ed.). *New knowledge in human values.* Chicago: Henry Regnery, 1959.

Maslow, A.H. A theory of meta-motivation: the biological rooting of the value life. *Journal of Humanistic Psychology,* 1967. 7.

Maslow, A.H. *Toward a psychology of being.* (2nd ed.). Princeton, NJ: Van Nostrand, 1968.

Pearson, P.H. & Maddi, S.R. The similes preference inventory. *Journal of Consulting Psychology,* 1966, 30.

Shostrom, E.L. A test for the measurement of self-actualization. *Educational and Psychological Measurement,* 1964, 24.

Shostrom, E.L. *Manual for personal orientation inventory.* San Diego: Educational & Industrial Testing Services, 1966.

Shostrom, E.L. *Man, the manipulator.* NYC: Bantam Books, 1967.

Shostrom, E.L. & Knapp, R. The relationship of a measure of self-actualization (POI) to a measure of pathology (MMPI) and to therapeutic growth. *American Journal of Psychotherapy,* 1966, 20.

Smith, M.B. On self-actualization: a transambivalent examination of a focal theme in Maslow's psychology. *Journal of Humanistic Psychology*, 1973, 13.

Torrance, E.P. *Guiding creative talents*. Englewood Cliffs, NJ: Personnel Press, 1966.

Tosi, D.J. & Hoffman, S. A factor analysis of the personal orientation inventory. *Journal of Humanistic Psychology*, 1972, 12.

Warehime, R.G. & Foulds, M.L. Social desirability response sets and a measure of self-actualization. *Journal of Humanistic Psychology*, 1973, 13.

Weisskopf, W.A. In Maslow, A.H. (ed.), *New knowledge in human values*, Chicago: Henry Regnery, 1959.

J. Patrick Murphy, Management Department
Address: DePaul University, 25 East Jackson Boulevard, Chicago, Illinois 60604

Dean C. Dauw, Associate Professor, DePaul University.
Address: President, Human Resource Developers, Inc. 112 West Oak Street, Chicago, Illinois 60610

Roy E. Horton, Associate Professor.
Address: DePaul University, 25 East Jackson Boulevard, Chicago, Illinois 60604

Alan J. Fredian, Director, Institute of Industrial Relations.
Address: Loyola University, Chicago, Illinois 60626.

CREATIVITY, PERSONAL AND ORGANIZATIONAL GROWTH

Top executives and CEO's of corporations are constantly stating in speeches and being quoted in business publications as echoing certain major themes.

Some of these themes are:

1. "What's good for General Motors is good for the U.S.A."

2. "Corporations must become more profitable and return a fair dividend to shareholders."

3. "We must fight inflation to help companies become more profitable."

After paying homage to the "Almighty Dollar" and offering tribute to her handmaidens, "Corporate Profitability," and "Reducing Costs," somewhere along the line these executives will slip in corollary statements. "Yes, we want creative employees." "We must find the best managers to help us run our organizations."

These sentiments are even carried over into Wall Street Journal ads for "XYC Co. is searching for an **aggressive** controller." In one recent research study we conducted, over one half of all WSJ ads begged for 'an *"aggressive"* person, whether in marketing, finance, accounting, engineering or any field. (Parenthetically, English scholars and psychologists will quarrel on many levels with the word "aggressive" in recruiting ads. In the dictionary, "agressive" means "hostile." What they really mean to say is, we want a manager who is "achievement-oriented" or even perhaps "creative.")

Some executives state in commencement addresses at universities that they want "creative" employees. (The stated desire for "creative" employees even creeps into WSJ ads on occasion.) Idealistic young graduates believe that Commencement Speakers really mean it.

The perfect way to assess whether top executives truly mean what they say is to look around you where you work. Does your company training center or management development program ever offer a course in Creative Problem Solving? Does your Company President or Training Director retain consultants to aid employees develop their creative thinking abilities? Does your company reward creative thinkers? Record your answer here:

Recent research proves conclusively we can educate managers and supervisors on all levels to become more creative problem solvers. The evidence shows companies and even non-profit organizations can significantly increase productivity and reduce costs by training employees to learn more creative methods to do their jobs. You could even do a simple, controlled experiment today in your organization to prove it. (See Dauw's book on Creativity and myriads of other citations in any library.)

CEO's will also repeatedly verbalize their desire for personal growth and the development of their employees. After all, they say, we have "Management Development" programs. Millions are spent annually on these MD programs. They are helpful. Industrial psychologists have proven they save money. Pick up any textbook on personnel management or industrial psychology, if you doubt it. Yet, if you query any consulting psychologist in industry, she will say little progress is being made. Stress is increasing. Mental health in managers is continuously deteriorating. Alcoholism rates are increasing. Today, at lunch, 10 million alcoholics will drink too much. One recent study showed corporations lose a minimum of $26 billion annually because of alcoholic employees. And alcoholism is only *one category* in any text about Abnormal Psychology.

Consider the costs of Drug Abuse. A recent estimate revealed marijuana is the U.S.A.'s third largest industry, after Exxon and General Motors. Certainly, it will increase, whether regulated or not. More than one secretary referred to me for counseling admits she lights up a joint upon leaving for work, so she can tolerate her boss. More than one boss referred to me for career development admitted he smoked pot at lunch time. The topic is so involved that volumes could be written on that subject alone. The point is, CEO's and companies are not yet *sufficiently committed to* the personal growth and development of employees, which is the first fundamental bedrock of organizational growth. (See Dean C. Dauw: *Up Your Career*. 3rd edition. Waveland Press, Prospect Heights, Illinois 60070.)

Organizational growth is the dream and goal of every entrepreneur and most high-level bureaucrats. It is written between the lines on every page of the Harvard Business Review, WSJ, Forbes, Business Week and the like. Just as success is the same for both men and women, so also is success similar for the individual and the organization. Few people understand or appreciate that statement. An individual must do certain things to grow, develop, and become more productive. For example, an alcoholic and her boss both need to understand games alcoholics play. Similarly, an organization must do certain things to grow, develop, and become more profitable, A CEO needs to understand, for example, the need to reduce bureaucracy and increase employees' creative thinking abilities.

In summary, then, consider again some of these results of psychological research as they apply to your personal or organizational growth. Perhaps you could call it a Humanistic Manifesto.

Creative—Humanistic Manifesto

1. You and your organization can grow and develop.
2. You and your organization can become more human, and more creative.
3. You can learn to become a more creative problem solver.
4. Your company can help employees more effectively to increase productivity and reduce costs through creative methods.
5. You can strive to lead a more creative, more human, more mentally healthy, self-actualized life.
6. Your organization can become less bureaucratic, more humanistic and more profitable by promoting the personal growth and development of employees.
7. The primary responsibility for your personal growth is **yours**.
8. Your organization's growth depends on the development of each member, and the responsibility lies with the CEO and all top executives.
9. You can learn to become more responsible, more creative, and more human both at work and outside of work.
10. You can become a more creative risk taker.
11. You can expect of yourself more creative efforts for better results and personal growth.
12. You can expect more of yourself in all situations.
13. You can realize increasingly more of your growth potential.
14. You can surpass yourself.
15. You can do it **now**.
16. You can do it **today**, without excuses.
17. You **can** become the person you want to be.

134

PART IV

USE OF BEHAVIORAL SCIENCE CONSULTANTS IN SELECTED INDUSTRIES

Well-informed managers and successful top corporation executives have long known that the company's best assets are its human resources. Researchers have consistently shown that developing human resources of employees can economically and financially improve the company's position (Dauw, 1966, 1968, 1971). Yet great strides remain to be taken to apply more fully all the behavioral science techniques available to management.

This report discusses research results of a study recently completed within the furniture and foundry industries on a nationwide basis.

Research Method

The questionnaire consisted of 16 items each having from 3 to 6 responses. In each industry, 220 questionnaires were distributed. Of the 440, 144 were returned (33%), 96 from foundry executives and 48 from furniture executives.

The main objectives of the questionnaire were to determine what percentage of those firms surveyed used professional assistance in the application of behavioral science to management; what percentage actually applied behavioral science techniques; what percentage offered internal assessment programs; what percentage offered supervisory or management seminars; and what percentage offered any form of vocational counseling and executive re-direction for those "de-hired" or "out-placed."

The questionnaire was also designed to provide a comparison between the 2 industries themselves, as well within each industry in relation to number of employees. Responses were also analyzed by number of employees in each firm: 500 or more, 300-500, 100-300, and 100 or less employees.

The statistical test used to compare the differences in proportions was the hypergeometric probability distribution test (Taro, 1964).

Results

Table I reports the statistically significant differences in the number of firms using vocational career guidance techniques. Table II reports the statistically significant differences for firms who did not employ or retain counselors. Table III shows the probability values of the sampling of management seminars content. There are significant differences in the number admitting no seminars were offered.

Table IV reports significant differences (.01) between industries where firms offer no assessment or evaluation programs of any kind. Internal consistency of measurement for the questionnaire was shown by the responses on subsequent questions (not reported here in tables). These questions considered the standards for measuring employee performance and differentiating between men and women. Naturally, all the firms reporting no program also reported no differences between norms or standards for the sexes.

All these results reported in the tables suggest that employee movements such as promotions, transfers, demotions or firings were done by methods other than suggested by the questionnaire, i.e., they were most probably arbitrary and capricious uses of human resources.

Considering the distribution for both industries, most did not retain any consulting psychologists, psychiatrists or mental health workers in any capacity. The percentages naturally vary by size, with the largest firms using them more than smaller firms. Of the firms with more than 500 employees, 17.5% did use consultants, but none of the firms with less than 100 did so.

Table I

Comparison of the Use of Vocational Career Guidance Techniques Within the Foundry and the Furniture Industries

	Foundry		Furniture		Probability Value
	Number	Percent	Number	Percent	
No	72	74.8	35	72.8	
Do not know	0	0	0	0	
Yes, transfers are possible	0	0	8	16.6	.0002
Yes, transfers receive consideration	0	0	5	10.4	.007
No answer	24	25	0	0	.00004

Table II

Comparison of the Number of Employees Referred to Vocational Counselors

	Foundry		Furniture		Probability Value
	Number	Percent	Number	Percent	
10 or less	9	9.36	8	16.6	
10-20	4	4.16	6	12.4	
20-30	0	0	0	0	
30 or more	4	4.16	0	0	
No counselors employed	57	59.2	18	37.4	.02
No answer	22	30.8	16	35.2	

Table III

Course Content of Management Seminars

	Foundry		Furniture		Probability Value
	Number	Percent	Number	Percent	
Human Relations	43	44.7	28	58.2	
Technical	28	29.1	14	29.1	
Administration	33	34.3	13	27.0	
Do not know	0	0	1	2.08	
None offered	35	36.4	7	14.5	.02
No answer	11	11.4	9	18.7	

Table IV

Categories of Assessment

	Foundry		Furniture		Probability Value
	Number	Percent	Number	Percent	
Male only	11	11.4	3	6.24	
Female only	1	1.04	2	4.16	
Male & Female segregated by sex	1	1.04	1	2.08	
Male & Female intermixed	32	33.2	18	37.4	
No program	41	42.6	10	20.8	.01
No answer	11	11.4	16	33.12	.005

Of all the 144 firms surveyed, 75.4 percent do not use any professional techniques in the recruiting, selecting or hiring of new executives, suggesting a random method leading to serious problems as discussed by Dauw (1968).

In summary, this research reveals that top executives in 2 industries are greatly lacking information about and use of behavioral science methods.

Implications

Industry can no longer afford such wide spread inattention to the growth and development of the human potential. We cannot be slow in either the recognition of the problems, or the coping with them. The success of the entire organization depends upon the abilities and attitudes of its members. The traditional company climate is killing more and more employees everyday, not physically, but creatively. If potential and initiative are not recognized and developed they will either become stagnant or seek an outlet. Those energies could very easily be channeled into contagious hostilities or they may be positively directed toward utilization in another company or industry.

The business climate is in danger of destroying the potential of those who are or can become great assets. The cure is not to build mental blocks against the employment market of today. The cure is not charging society with creating dissenters. One cure is helping managers understand and apply the behavioral sciences to management.

When an individual has a physical pain he does not attempt to perform surgery on himself, but rather he seeks professional diagnosis and prescribed medication. Similarly, the manager who has employee "pain" should seek professional assistance. Managing every day does not guarantee expertise. This concept is a management myth. It is vitally important to the organization that both those who make decisions and those who implement them be properly directed. This direction is of course lined with technical knowledge, but it is mostly filled with the knowledge of human behavior and potential.

As long as businesses insist on operating with antiquated employee selection techniques and as long as they continue to create a climate conducive to intellectual stagnation, that is how long they will continue to be drained of their key personnel.

Management needs to have greater application of psychological services in order to have a more effective organization. The organization can prove to be a stimulating and dynamic instrument in the area of human achievement and growth. As a direct consequence of this stimulation, the organization itself will prosper and achieve not only short-range goals, but also long-range stability.

References

1. Dauw, D.C. "Creativity in Organizations." *Personnel Journal*, 1966, 8:465-474.
2. ———. "Mental Health in Managers, A Corporate View." *Personnel Administration*, 1968, 31:42-46.
3. Dauw, D.C., and Fredian, A.J. *Creativity and Innovation in Organizations.* Dubuque: Kendall/Hunt Publishing Company, 1971.
4. Taro, Y. *Statistics: An Introductory Analysis.* New York: Harper & Row, 1964.

EVALUATING HUMAN RELATIONS TRAINING

Abstract

This research study tests whether an interaction rating scale can measure differences before and after human relations training. Four groups of subjects included:

a. 47 MBA graduate students.
b. 33 Government MBA grad students.
c. 29 Undergraduates.
d. 39 Roman Catholic nuns.

All subjects received similar training using structured interpersonal experiences. Statistically significant differences were found ($p < .05$). Conclusion was that the training produced changes measured by this instrument, a simple rating scale requesting actual and ideal ratings on the following scales: self-revelation, feelings, confrontation, response to confrontation, support, language, concreteness, response to support, genuineness, negative feedback and response to group exercises.

David Ogilvy is quoted in the New York Times for 6-11-72 as having said: "I believe it is more important for a reader in today's world to be trained in psychiatry than cybernetics." The authors contend the same statement would be even more appropriate, if one inserts *"LEADER"* for reader.

Certainly, leaders must be able to understand and deal with people better, if they are to become increasingly more effective. A basic problem, however, is not so much how to train executives, managers, administrators, and leaders to deal with people effectively, but rather how to measure the results of the training scientifically (Kerlinger, 1964. Laing, et al., 1966).

Harrison et al. (1967), detail the problems involved in performing research on human relations training and present an annotated bibliography of research. They emphasize how challenging is the task. Despite these challenges, Walker et al. (1972), were able to measure changes in self-judgments of self-disclosure after group experience.

The present research used a measurement method similar to that involved in the larger research project of which the Walker (1972) report was a part.

The purpose of this research project was to determine whether the trainees had improved their human relations skills as a result of the training, and whether real differences could be measured by this instrument (Appendix I).

Procedure

An Interaction Rating Scale (Appendix I), adapted from the research project by Walker (1972) was administered to four groups before and after human relations training.

The four groups included:

1. MBA graduate students in a private, co-ed university in a major urban setting.
2. Federal government employees seeking a similar degree in public administration at the same university.
3. Mature undergraduates employed full time seeking a business degree in the evening division.
4. Roman Catholic sisters involved in an organizational development project for their religious order. All the nuns had college degrees, and some had masters degrees. They were involved as teachers and administrators in various school systems in the Midwest.

These four groups all received similar training that involved structured, interpersonal experiences (Pheiffer and Jones, 1971).

Possible limitations of the research results reported below are that (1) items might be misunderstood by respondents despite clear instructions and explanations; (2) changes shown after the training might not be the sole results of the training. Strict experimental control groups were not used, but it was hypothesized that four highly diverse groups might in some way partially compensate for this factor (Kerlinger, 1964).

Results

The Walsh test (Siegel, 1956) was chosen, assuming the population is symmetrical. A one-tailed test was applied because the increase was expected in one direction.

Table I presents the data for the 39 nuns; Table II, for the 33 Government MBA's; Table III, for the 47 MBA's, and Table IV, for 29 undergraduates.

Table I

Average Ratings for Nuns (N = 39)

	Actual				Ideal			
Quality	Before	After	Diff.	Diff. ranked	Before	After	Diff.	Diff. ranked
Self-revelation	5.28	6.00	0.72	0.23	7.46	8.12	0.66	0.34
Feelings	5.35	5.58	0.23	0.49	7.46	8.00	0.54	0.36
Confrontation	3.89	4.69	0.80	0.54	6.97	7.84	0.87	0.36
Response to Confrontation	4.71	5.35	0.64	0.56	8.10	8.58	0.48	0.38
Support	6.28	6.84	0.56	0.57	8.23	8.94	0.71	0.40
Language	5.92	6.46	0.54	0.64	8.23	8.71	0.48	0.48
Concreteness	5.76	6.58	0.82	0.72	8.38	8.76	0.38	0.48
Response to Support	6.10	7.02	0.92	0.80	8.48	8.84	0.36	0.54
Genuineness	6.05	6.62	0.57	0.82	8.47	8.81	0.34	0.66
Negative Feedback	4.66	5.15	0.49	0.84	8.31	8.71	0.40	0.48
Exercises	5.84	6.68	0.84	0.92	8.20	8.58	0.36	0.87
Average Increase			0.64				0.59	

Table II

Average Ratings for Government MBAs (N = 33)

	Actual				Ideal			
Quality	Before	After	Diff.	Diff. ranked	Before	After	Diff.	Diff. ranked
Self-revelation	5.2	6.0	0.8	0.2	7.4	7.9	0.5	0.1
Feelings	5.5	6.1	0.6	0.4	7.4	7.7	0.3	0.2
Confrontation	5.0	5.7	0.7	0.6	6.8	7.4	0.6	0.2
Response to Confrontation	5.5	6.2	0.7	0.6	8.1	8.3	0.2	0.2
Support	6.8	7.2	0.4	0.7	8.0	8.1	0.1	0.3
Language	6.4	7.0	0.6	0.7	8.4	8.6	0.2	0.3
Concreteness	6.4	6.8	0.2	0.8	8.3	8.5	0.2	0.5
Response to Support	6.2	7.1	0.9	0.9	7.9	8.6	0.7	0.6
Genuineness	5.8	6.7	0.9	0.9	8.1	8.4	0.3	0.7
Negative Feedback	5.0	6.0	1.0	1.0	7.6	8.3	0.7	0.7
Exercises	5.2	7.1	1.9	1.9	7.6	8.3	0.7	0.7
Average Increase			0.79				0.40	

Table III

Average Ratings for MBAs (N = 47)

Quality	Actual				Ideal			
	Before	After	Diff.	Diff. ranked	Before	After	Diff.	Diff. ranked
Self-revelation	5.6	6.7	1.1	0.3	7.9	8.3	0.4	0.2
Feelings	5.6	6.8	1.2	0.4	7.4	8.3	0.9	0.2
Confrontation	4.6	5.6	1.0	0.5	6.7	7.7	1.0	0.2
Response to Confrontation	5.3	6.3	1.0	0.7	8.3	8.6	0.3	0.3
Support	6.1	6.9	0.8	0.7	8.0	8.5	0.5	0.3
Language	6.2	6.5	0.3	0.8	8.4	8.6	0.2	0.3
Concreteness	6.0	6.7	0.7	1.0	8.2	8.6	0.4	0.4
Response to Support	6.6	7.1	0.5	1.0	8.2	8.5	0.3	0.4
Genuineness	5.8	6.5	0.7	1.1	8.2	8.4	0.2	0.5
Negative Feedback	5.2	5.6	0.2	1.2	8.2	8.4	0.2	0.9
Exercises	5.3	6.9	1.6	1.6	8.3	8.6	0.3	1.0
Average Increase		0.91				0.42		

Table IV

Average Ratings for Undergraduates (N = 29)

Quality	Actual				Ideal			
	Before	After	Diff.	Diff. ranked	Before	After	Diff.	Diff. ranked
Self-revelation	5.4	7.7	2.3	0.1	7.2	8.9	1.7	0.4
Feelings	5.5	6.9	1.4	1.1	7.3	7.7	0.4	0.4
Confrontation	4.5	5.6	1.1	1.2	6.5	7.7	1.2	0.6
Response to Confrontation	4.8	6.7	1.9	1.4	7.8	8.5	0.7	0.7
Support	6.2	6.3	0.1	1.4	7.8	8.6	0.8	0.7
Language	5.4	6.8	1.4	1.6	7.8	8.6	0.8	0.8
Concreteness	5.4	7.0	1.6	1.9	8.0	8.6	0.6	0.8
Response to Support	6.0	7.2	1.2	2.3	7.7	8.1	0.4	1.1
Genuineness	4.4	6.9	2.5	2.4	8.1	8.8	0.7	1.2
Negative Feedback	4.3	6.7	2.4	2.5	6.4	8.6	2.2	1.7
Exercises	5.1	7.6	2.5	2.5	7.8	8.9	1.1	2.2
Average Increase		1.67				0.91		

Table V

Movement in the Gap between Actual and Ideal

	Ratings	
	Before	After
MBAs	2.3	1.9
Govt. MBAs	2.5	1.7
Undergraduates	2.3	1.5
Nuns	2.7	2.4

Statistically significant differences were found ($p < .05$) for all groups on both the actual and ideal ratings. Although the trends for all groups both before and after training follow the same patterns, some traits merit a closer inspection.

Generally speaking, the actual ratings fall between 5 and 7 on the rating scale, with the exception of qualities 3, 4, and 10. On the ideal ratings the same pattern occurs with the range being limited mainly between 7 and 8.5. For qualities 3 and 4, all groups fall below 7. Only the undergraduates fall below 7 on quality number 10 of the ideal scale.

One possible cause for the troughs on qualities 3, 4, and 10 is most probably associated with values, attitudes, or personality traits common to all groups, or associated with societal norms and culture. Social or group values result from society's expectations of the individual, as well as the individual's learned responses to societal pressures (Bradford, 1964).

Qualities 3, 4, and 10 have one commonality—all involve confronting and criticizing others as well as accepting such confrontations. These qualities all relate to the most personal intimate aspects of the individual and his interactions with others. These data seem to suggest the trainees tend to avoid confronting and criticizing others, preferring the same treatment for others in return.

Table V reveals the movement in the gap between Actual and Ideal ratings. Before training, a larger difference exists between the actual and ideal ratings. After training, however, a smaller difference exists.

Discussion

These data seem to suggest that the experience offered to the trainees led to some changes in their interpersonal relationships and that these changes could be measured statistically by this instrument. Future research might be designed with rigorous control groups and with diverse experiences specifically designed to cover the confrontation aspects (Scales 3, 4, and 10) where less movement was measured by this instrument.

Within the framework of the limitations previously discussed, it was found that the nuns changed less than the other groups. The undergraduates showed the highest rate of increase in all aspects. The undergraduates' ratings were lowest on most scales before training, but soared up to the top after training. Additionally, the gap between their actual and ideal ratings decreased considerably more than all other groups.

The traits that involve confronting and criticizing others and in return accepting criticisms and confrontations from others are areas with the lowest ratings for all groups. These results may have been influenced by the social milieu or cultural norms common to all groups.

Finally, the narrowing of the gap between the actual and ideal suggests the training was able to achieve its goals of enabling the trainees to relate more effectively.

Bibliography

Bradford, L., et al. *T-Group Theory and Laboratory Method.* New York, John Wiley and Sons, 1964.

Harrison, R., Durham, L.E., Gibb, J.R., and Knowles E.S. *Problems in the Design and Interpretation of Research on Human Relations Training.* Washington, D.C. NTL Institute for Applied Behavioral Science, 1967.

Laing, R.D., Phillipson H., and Lee A.R. *Interpersonal Perception.* New York, Harper & Row, 1966.

Pfeiffer, J.W., and Jones J.E. *A Handbook of Structured Experiences for Human Relations Training.* Volumes I, II, III. Iowa City: University Associates Press, 1971.

Siegel, S. *Non-Parametric Statistics.* New York: McGraw-Hill, 1956.

Walker, R., Shack J.R., Egan G., Sheridan K., and Sheridan E. "Changes in Self-Judgments of Self-Disclosure After Group Experience." *J. of Applied Behavioral Science,* 1972, 8:248-251.

Rate yourself on the left-hand scale according to how you actually see yourself at this time. On the right-hand side rate yourself according to how you would like to be—the ideal you. Use a nine point scale, with 1 indicating an extremely low degree of the quality examined, 5 indicating an average or moderate degree, and 9 indicating an extremely high degree.

Actual
Rating
(1-9)

Ideal
Rating
(1-9)

_____ 1. *Self-revelation.* To what degree are you open about yourself; that is, engage in self-revelation of some kind? 1. ___

_____ 2. *Feelings.* To what extent do you express your feelings openly and honestly? 2. ___

_____ 3. *Confrontation.* To what extent do you confront others, invite them to self-examination? 3. ___

_____ 4. *Response to Confrontation.* To what extent do you respond positively and growthfully, rather than defensively, to confrontation? 4. ___

_____ 5. *Support.* To what extent do you give support to others? 5. ___

_____ 6. *Language.* To what extent do you use language as an honest expression of yourself instead of engaging in cliches? 6. ___

_____ 7. *Concreteness.* To what extent do you speak concretely, addressing yourself directly to another rather than speaking generally and to no one in particular? 7. ___

_____ 8. *Response to support.* How well do you respond to the support given by others? 8. ___

_____ 9. *Genuineness.* How genuinely do you participate in meetings? 9. ___

_____ 10. *Negative feedback.* How well do you react to criticism and other negative feedback? 10. ___

_____ 11. *Exercises.* To what degree do you involve yourself in the exercises performed in the group? 11. ___

HUMAN RELATIONS I.Q.

Goals: (1) Learn more about human relations.

(2) Become more aware of how differently executives/managers/supervisors rank important job factors when compared to how employees rank them.

(3) Help you learn which issues are most important to you and what to do about them.

Procedure: Study the brief introduction below. Then, fill out the ten blank spaces for yourself. Finally, turn to the page following where the research shows executives guessed their employees would respond and contrast your own answers with the ways the employees actually answered.

A few years ago, a group of psychologists, whose objective was to measure employee attitudes toward various on-the-job morale factors, visited 24 business and industrial plants in various parts of the United States.

Each employee who was interviewed was handed a list of ten items and was asked to arrange them in what he/she considered their order of importance. Executives were given the same list and invited to predict how their subordinates would answer.

You can take the same test here and then compare your answers with those given by the above mentioned groups. Although there are no "correct" answers, how you reply will tell you quite a bit about yourself: how much sympathy you have for the aspirations of others; your grasp of what makes people tick; your opinion of your fellowman; in short, your human relations I.Q.

In the spaces below, enter the items in what you consider to be the descending order of importance to the **employees**:

Feeling "in" on things   1. _____

Full appreciation of work done   2. _____

Good wages   3. _____

Good working conditions   4. _____

Interesting work   5. _____

Job security   6. _____

Personal loyalty to workers   7. _____

Promotion and growth in company   8. _____

Sympathetic help on personal problems 9. _____

Tactful disciplining   10. _____

***Note: Do not turn to answers until you have filled in the blanks.**

Now, compare your listing with these two:

This is the way the executives assumed their employees would answer

1. Good wages
2. Job security
3. Promotion and growth in company
4. Good working conditions
5. Interesting work
6. Personal loyalty to workers
7. Tactful disciplining
8. Full appreciation of work done
9. Sympathetic help on personal problems
10. Feeling "in" on things

This is the way the employees actually answered

1. Full appreciation of work done
2. Feeling "in" on things
3. Sympathetic help on personal problems
4. Job security
5. Good wages
6. Interesting work
7. Promotion and growth in company
8. Personal loyalty to workers
9. Good working conditions
10. Tactful disciplining

Did your list approximate the one drawn up by the workers, or the one by the executives? Did you assume that workers respond most favorably to material rewards, or did you correctly predict their preference for "psychic income?" Did you list "good wages" either first or second, or do you realize in- stinctively that to many a worker, money is only of "middle interest?" Realization of what counts with the people under your supervision will result in increased cooperation and all-around better performance.

146

FAKING IN PERSONNEL SELECTION: AN EVALUATION OF ONE TECHNIQUE

Abstract

Psychologists have generally emphasized the important need for research validation of any psychological tests, inventories or instruments, regardless of the setting in which they are used (Fleishman, 1961). This urgency is especially important in corporations where a particular instrument may strongly influence a manager's decision to hire an individual applicant. Thus, the present research attempts to see how job applicants describe themselves when applying for a position, and to investigate how they tend to change their self-descriptions under various directions by the employers.

Personalities usually develop a style of life that places more emphasis on certain traits or qualities than on others. This gradual learning process depends in large measure upon the reactions of others to an individual's efforts to set up his own personal mode of living (Sullivan, 1953, Rogers, 1951, Rogers, 1961). One parent, for example, may encourage a son to be more dominant and more socially extroverted than another child, a daughter.

From all these efforts evolves a self-image or self-concept that the person strives to maintain and enhance in actual behavior (Lecky, 1945), while he also seeks out roles and jobs that are in keeping with this self-concept (Sarbin, 1954, Super, 1957). Thus a girl who sees herself as being oriented more toward people than things may feel a strong social service need to become a nurse or a teacher. The final result is a moderate degree of self-consistency for many people that provides more basis for predicting a normal individual's reactions.

However, developing a technique or instrument to describe or measure this self-concept with any degree of accuracy and within a framework providing for comparability is not an easy task. The difficulties in this area have been reviewed by Wylie (Wylie, 1961) from both a methodological and substantive viewpoint. Yet in the history of personnel selection, one usual approach of trying to understand a person's self-image from the impressions of interview are especially hazardous. Research into the preemployment interview has frequently demonstrated its lack of validity (Ulrich, 1965, Mayfield, 1964). In fact, all the research in person perception has outlined the problems involved in developing techniques that are valid and reliable without training, structuring, and clear definitions (Allport, 1961, Bronfenbrenner, 1958, Brunner, 1958, Cronbach, 1955).

Perhaps one of the most well-known self-report instruments is the activity vector analysis (AVA), whose proponents have apparently claimed practical value for test procedures when the statistical evidence does not bear out their contentions (Dunnette, 1962). Test users (who are very often skilled as businessmen but perhaps less proficient as "amateur" psychologists) have paid little heed to the frequently made injunction that validity should not be inferred from relationships that are statistically significant, but useless for practical predictive purposes (Biesheuvel, 1965). Locke and Hulie (Locke and Hulie, 1962) reviewed all the research on activity vector analysis. They found that all but two out of nineteen studies had adopted procedures that were inadequate for the validation of an industrial selection technique. One of the exceptions showed that for the particular subjects concerned (insurance salesmen), AVA had no practical value. The other was a cross-validation with such a large overlap between successful and unsuccessful salesmen that only scores at the extremes of the distribution could be used for predictive purposes. Locke and Hulie concluded that AVA research had failed to demonstrate any practical utility for this device in industrial selection, and thus the AVA flatly contradicted the confident claims that had been made on its behalf.

Development of Instruments

While most authorities recommend forced-choice techniques (Zavala, 1965), Dauw (Dauw, 1966) found a straight-forward adjective checklist useful to assist certain creative personalities in their self-descriptions. Since all self-report instruments are open to conscious and unconscious distortion, precautions must be taken to control the "social desirability" factor (Edwards, 1957, Newman, 1957). An adjective checklist may further avoid the problem of "response set" (Couch, 1960) or "response style" (Jackson, 1958) that can arise in inventories with only two response alternatives (yes or no—true or false—etc.).

The instrument used in the present research is a self-administering, forced-choice adjective checklist consisting of twenty-four tetrads of descriptive words. Directions and a simple tetrad follow.

> "The following descriptive words are grouped in sets of four. Examine the words in each set. Put an "X" under column M next to the word that is most like you in each set. Put an "X" under column L next to the word that is least like you in each set. Be sure to check only one word M and only word L for each set" (Donelly, 1965).

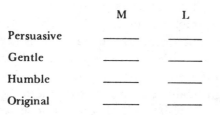

The profile measures four personality dimensions considered valuable in understanding self-concepts: dominance, inducement, steadiness and compliance. Wicas and Mahan (Wicas and Mahan, 1965) found the instrument useful for their research, and some validity data has been reported (Cleaver, 1959, Donelly, 1965, 1969).

The validity and reliability of an instrument is based on two assumptions made about those (e.g., job applicants) who use it: 1) that they know themselves well enough to describe their self-image; 2) that they are motivated to do so honestly. The extent to which people seeking new jobs can and will do this, however, is unknown, and, therefore,

to such a degree is the validity of this particular instrument also unknown. Donelly (1965) reports the "fakeability" of this instrument under special directions to appear good in applying for a personnel manager's job, but it is not known how many applicants tend to do so in applying for every job.

Research Method

The present research was designed to provide some clues as to how many job applicants might tend to change their self-reports if provided an opportunity to do so. The principal research precautions used are those listed by Dunnette and Kirchner (1962). They show how inadequate research techniques were used to influence businessmen into assuming a similar instrument validly predicted success in selecting insurance agents.

In a large corporate personnel office, 100 male applicants for various jobs were asked to complete the "self-description" Cleaver (1959), under standard conditions. Shortly thereafter, when all application blanks had been completed, each applicant was asked to complete the self-report again, with these instruments: "Please complete this same form again to try to make yourself appear in a more favorable manner that might better enable you to get hired for the job you are seeking." In other words, each job-seeker understood that, while his previous results may have been adequate, and there really was no problem involved, he could still try to make another attempt that might help him or make him appear better. Since the vast majority of the candidates were college graduates seeking exempt positions, there were no misunderstandings involved, and all seemed eager to comply.

Results

Table 1 summarizes the mean scores and the variances of each scale in the Cleaver "self-description" for both the first and second test administration. These statistics (Dixon, 1957) can be more easily interpreted in the light of the following additional data. Using a criterion of at least a ten percentage point increase on a scale, 55 percent of the applicants wanted to appear more compliant. Only 31 percent strove to appear steadier while 49 percent increased on the inducement scale (influencing people to act favorably).

Table 1

Comparisons of Mean Scores of Self-Discription Scales for
100 Job Applicants Under Different Instructions

Profile Dimensions of Cleaver "Self-Discription"	Administration (N = 100)				
	First		Second		Level of Significance
	M	S^2	M	S^2	(t-test)
Total Scores					
Dominance	.70	37.40	.99	36.90	.33
Inducement	.96	17.10	1.59	9.27	1.47
Steadiness	.37	34.96	4.38	6.27	11.39**
Compliance	.77	14.57	.23	12.88	1.07
Most Scores					
Dominance	6.01	1.04	7.35	1.19	9.43**
Inducement	3.73	4.44	4.20	3.97	1.67*
Steadiness	5.90	1.06	4.16	6.74	12.16**
Compliance	5.18	4.61	5.72	3.79	1.97*
Least Scores					
Dominance	6.59	11.49	6.46	9.86	.29
Inducement	4.68	5.67	4.46	4.53	.73
Steadiness	5.36	8.33	6.09	7.11	1.94*
Compliance	5.57	5.13	5.44	5.58	.40

*$p < .05$.
**$p < .01$.

Considering each applicant's profile change from the first to the second testing (again using a criterion of at least a 10 percentage point spread), 32 greatly changed one scale; 90, two scales; 88, three scales; and 60 people greatly changed all four scales.

Out of the 100 job applicants, only 26 produced similar profile patterns that would lead one to interpret the results as being sufficiently comparable. Another 48 percent of the profiles on both first and second testing tended to be invalid by the definition of the test authors (scales in the blue zone).

These results emphasize and help clarify the data in Table 1, that there are statistically significant differences in mean scores between first and second testing on six of the twelve scales.

Discussion

These research results seem to indicate that self-descriptions of job applicants as measureed by an instrument of this kind may be altered by the candidate trying to "fake good." The literature on self-concept theory, however, shows that normal people actually do react and behave consistently in their daily experiences (Sullivan, 1953, Rogers, 1951, Rogers, 1961, Lecky, 1945). But when seeking new jobs, three possibilities arise: (1) applicants either do not understand their self-images very well; or (2) do not choose to report their self-descriptions honestly; or (3) can be easily influenced by differing instructions to disregard the two previous alternatives and change their results. For in this sample of 100 people, 74 individuals easily modified their test results to present a completely different picture of their "surface behavior" as this instrument purports to measure it. It is not clear, of course, whether (1) the vast majority of these job-seekers (74%) really did understand themselves consistently and/or honestly; or (3) whether they could be easily influenced to produce new results. This particular instrument did not distinguish on only the first testing between the 26 percent who later chose to respond consistently and 74 percent who either did not understand themselves or did not choose to report their self-images as they see themselves, or changed their statements.

In fact, even if one were to assume that the 26 percent who responded consistently really did know their behavior and self-concepts, one still could not assume that this consistent self-image was honestly reported. Since this instrument does not have validity scales to measure lying as some personality inventories have, it may be that the 26 percent were merely consistent in their dishonesty.

Thus, these data seem to suggest that some self-description instruments may be more valuable in post-employment counseling or managerial motivation situations than in preemployment selection.

An instrument of this kind may have greater value *after employment* for the following reasons. First, managers schooled in its interpretations could develop a common language for interpreting employees' behaviors. Semantic difficulties could be minimized because all managers might have a common frame of reference and presumably be able to agree on, for example, what is highly dominant or highly compliant behavior. Secondly, in employee evaluations, managers may be attuned to the fact that some standards and measures of objectivity are important. Thus, managers may hopefully focus on attempting to interpret behavior itself, rather than allowing themselves to be biased by physical appearances (e.g., blond hair or skin color halo effects and all the other common sources of error in interpreting human behavior and interactions). These two good advantages result from using such a self-description technique *after employment decisions have already been made* on the basis of other information. But such an instrument certainly has less value in employee selection itself. Human personalities are so very complex, dynamic and highly individualized, that the authors do well insisting persons cannot be completely encapsulated in four dimensions measured by 96 words (Donelly, 1965, 1969).

Bibliography

1. Fleishman, E.A. (ed.). *Studies in Personnel and Industrial Psychology.* (Homewood, Ill.: Dorsey Press, 1969).
2. Sullivan, H.S. *The Interpersonal Theory of Psychiatry.* (New York: Norton, 1953.)
3. Rogers, C.R. *Client-Centered Therapy.* (Boston: Houghton-Mifflin Co., 1951.)
4. ———. *On Becoming a Person.* (Boston: Houghton-Mifflin Co., 1961.)
5. Lecky, P. *Self-Consistency: A Theory of Personality.* (New York: Island Press, 1945.)
6. Sarbin, T. Role Theory. In G. Lindzey (Ed.), *Handbook of Social Psychology.* (Cambridge, Mass.: Addison-Wesley, 1954), pp. 223-258.
7. Super, D. *The Psychology of Careers.* (New York: Harpers, 1957.)
8. Wylie, Ruth. *The Self-Concept.* (Lincoln, Nebr.: Univ. of Nebraska Press, 1961.)
9. Ulrich, L., and Trumbo D. The Selection Interview Since 1949. *Psychological Bulletin* (1965), 63: pp. 100-116.
10. Mayfield, E.C. The Selection Interview—a Re-Evaluation of Published Research. *Personnel Psychology* (1964), 17: pp. 239-260.
11. Allport, G.W. *Pattern and Growth in Personality.* (New York: Holt, Rinehart and Winston, 1961.)
12. Bronfenbrenner, Y., Harding, J., Gallwey, M. The Measurement of Skill in Social Perception. In D.C. McClelland et al. (Eds.). *Talent* and *Society.* (Princeton, N.J.: Van Nostrand, 1958), pp. 29-111.
13. Brunner, J., Shapiro, D., and Tagiuri R. The Meaning of Traits in Isolation and in Combination. In R. Tagiuri and L. Petrello (Eds.), *Person Perception and Interpersonal Behavior.* (Stanford, Calif.: Stanford Univ. Press, 1958), pp. 277-288.
14. Cronbach, L.J. Processes Affecting Scores on "Understanding Others" and "Assumed Similarity." *Psychological Bulletin* (1955), 52: pp. 177-193.
15. Dunnette, M.D., and Kirchner, W.K. Validities, Vectors and Verities. *J Appl. Psychology* (1962), 46: pp. 296-299.
16. Biesheuvel, S. Personnel Selection. *Annual Review of Psychology* (1965), 16: pp. 296-324.
17. Locke, E.A., and Hulie C.L. A Review and Evaluation of the Validity Studies of Activity Vector Analysis. *Personal Psychology* (1962), 15: pp. 25-42.
18. Zavala, A. Development of the Forced-Choice Rating Scale Technique. *Psychological Bulletin* (1965), 63: pp. 117-124.
19. Dauw, D.C. Personality Self-Descriptions of Original Thinkers and Good Elaborators. *Psychology in the Schools* (1966), 4: pp. 78-79.
20. Edwards, A. *The Social Desirability Variable in Personality Assessment and Research.* (New York: Dryden, 1957.)
21. Newman, S., Howell, Margaret, and Harris, F. Forced Choice and Other Methods for Evaluating Professional Health Personnel. *Psychological Monographs* (1957), 71: pp. 1-27.
22. Couch, A., and Keniston, K. Yeasayers and Naysayers: Agreeing Response Set as a Personality Variable. *J. Abnormal and Social Psychology* (1960), 60: pp. 151-174.
23. Jackson, D.N., and Messick S. Content and Style in Personality Assessment. *Psychological Bulletin* (1958), 55: pp. 243-252.
24. Cleaver, J.P. *Evaluation Techniques.* (Princeton, N.J.: J.P. Cleaver Co., 1959.)
25. Donelly, N.E. Behavioral Self-Analysis. *Personnel Administrator* 1969 (Nov.-Dec.).
26. Donelly, N.E., Mahan, T.W., Jr., and McManus, L.F., Jr. Self-Description: A Technical Manual. (Princeton, N.J.: J.P. Cleaver Co., 1965.)
27. Wicas, E.A., and Mahan, T.W., Jr. Characteristics of Counselors Rated Effective by Supervisors and Peers. *Counselor Educ. and Supervision* (1966), 6: pp. 50-56.
28. Dixon, W.J., and Massey, F.J. *Introduction to Statistical Analysis.* (New York: McGraw-Hill, 1957.)

MBO AND CREATIVITY

Management by objectives is a structural system and technique. Ideally under MBO an individual's job is defined in terms of end points—each employee has a *written* statement of his or her job goals and objectives. The issue I am going to discuss in this brief paper is the extent to which the structure inherent in MBO inhibits or promotes creativity, especially in terms of solving problems and making innovations.

The Organizational Legitimation of Creativity

Individuals are creative. Enterprises are not. In terms of creativity, an enterprise can represent an environment which frees up or inhibits the individuals within its jurisdiction. The MBO goals represent a contract between the organization and the individuals in that enterprise. If these contracts include innovative and problem-solving goals, the individuals with these kinds of objectives are committing themselves to "creativity." If individuals in enterprises do not have such goals, they do not have specific authorization to work on creative activities. These individuals are being paid to work on other activities—and any creativity on their part is not sanctioned or encouraged by the organization.

Through the acceptance of problem solving and innovative objectives, the organization is making a formal commitment to innovation. Individuals are officially authorized to spend time and devote energy to creative activities—the organization is formally budgeting time to the creative process. Time for creativity does not have to be stolen from other activities.

The Individual in the Enterprise

But remember, the organization can only foster a creative environment. By having a stated set of goals, a person has boundaries set on the projects on which he or she will work during a time period. Limits are then set on the areas in which creativity is encouraged—the person's attention is focused toward prescribed areas of problem solving and innovation by his or her stated objectives. The disadvantage of MBO is that if the individual experiences creativity outside these boundaries, he or she receives no payoff from the organization.

An individual also is forced to complete projects and groups of activities because of the commitments implied by his or her MBO objectives. In effect, the time pressure inherent in MBO can facilitate a closure on ideas in order to meet the MBO deadlines. There is a tension to complete projects which might otherwise stay as just vague ideas. Some creative people, who are low in n/ach (achievement motivation), may in fact learn the usefulness of setting and accomplishing short-term goals and milestones. Creative ideas and projects which might otherwise be lost are finalized because of the time pressure of the MBO period. Again, there is of course a danger of premature closure.

Guidelines for the Creative Use of MBO

Just because MBO has the potential of fostering creativity does not mean the automatic unlocking of this potential. Following are some guidelines to facilitate the creative process through MBO. Individuals in organizations should be:

1. encouraged but not required to set creative objectives.
2. allowed to establish qualitative verifiable objectives that are not overly precise in terms of specific requirements.
3. given constructive positive feedback during the performance period and specifically during progress and end-period reviews.
4. encouraged to set their creative objectives for appropriate periods of time. The main danger is setting MBO goals too far into the future.
5. allowed a much higher percentage of failure than with other types of goals.

Summary

Enterprises are not inherently creative, but constructive use of MBO can foster creativity through the establishment and achievement of problem solving and innovative objectives. On the other hand, by not setting these goals and not properly administering these objectives, MBO can retard innovation. Proper use of MBO can structure and more precisely focus the creative process in an enterprise.

PART V

FACT-FINDING, PROBLEM-FINDING, IDEA-FINDING, SOLUTION-FINDING, AND ACCEPTANCE-FINDING— APPLYING THE TOTAL PROCESS

"We can have facts without thinking but we cannot have thinking without facts."

John Dewey

The instructor will conduct a demonstration of the entire creative problem-solving process as applied to a specific problem. He will thus outline the precedures which members will use in their problem-solving sessions during the remainder of the course.

* * *

In problem-solving, the fact-finding process calls for careful observation, with all senses, in order to discover the relevant facts that are involved. These relevant factors provide the raw material upon which our imagination can feed in generating new ideas. The relevant factors must be a springboard from which our imagination can leap, rather than a floor upon which our imagination can rest.

If we allow bias to distort the relevant factors we discover, the resultant ideas will be distorted. The feeding of one's brain with biased factors may be like feeding a computer with incorrectly programmed sets of cards. In both cases the resultant answers would be incorrect.

We tend to base the interpretation of our observations upon past experience. Hence, finding raw, unbiased factors is difficult because we so often color the ideas to conform with our comfortable expectations. By way of illustration, there is the story about the psychiatrist's patient who insisted that he was dead. The psychiatrist asked him if he would agree that dead men don't bleed. The patient agreed. The psychiatrist thereupon pricked the patient's finger, drawing bright red blood. "Well I'll be darned," the patient exclaimed, "Dead men *do* bleed after all!" The patient interpreted a fact to justify his bias.

We must remember that circumstances surrounding facts do change and we must be ready to recognize these changes when they occur. Just as the tailor cannot always use the same measurements in the final fitting of a suit (even for the same man) so, to insure fact-finding accuracy, we need to seek additional information. The more new facts we can feed to our imagination, the more likely we are to generate new ideas. This is why questioning—discovering relevant factors—is so vital in generating creative means of meeting a challenge. Realizing this, the mother of a Nobel-prize scientist inquired of her son after school each day, "Did you ask any good questions today?"

When we raise good questions, however, we must be sure to seek the answers. In creatively approaching a problem, there will always be practical limits to our questioning, since we are unlikely ever to acquire *all* the facts that might be relevant. But, within the limits of time and circumstances, we try our best to discover all possible facts that may pertain to our problem. Like physicians diagnosing the illness of a patient, we must try, in an objective way, within the limits of time and practical considerations, to discover all relevant factors. As to how much time we should spend on gathering relevant factors, this depends on questions such as: "How important is the problem?" "How many people does it affect?" etc.

It is worth noting that a challenge may often be met by "creative" discovery of relevant factors. The creativity in this case consists of devising ideas for uncovering pertinent data.

Research scientist, Lewis Walkup, emphasizes,

"If it is legitimately a problem—and not just some known fact of nature that he is not acquainted with—the researcher will still be faced with it after this data-gathering process." On the other hand, if the solution to a problem is merely a known fact with which we may not be familiar, then during the data-gathering process, the problem may sometimes solve itself. In any case, as emphasized earlier, the process of discovering relevant facts provides fuel for empowering our imagination.

The questions we raise regarding a problem may be of different types. Some questions seek information (facts) while other questions call for judgments. "What is your phone number?" is a question which asks for a fact (or in some cases a quick decision: "Should I give it to him or not!?"). Another fact-finding question might be, "What is the cost of the tickets to the game?" However, "Should we go?" calls for a judgment, rather than a fact.

Fact-finding questions call for and lead to facts while decision-finding questions call for and lead to judgments. On the other hand, some questions call for new ideas rather than either facts or judgments. For instance, "In what new ways might we use a brick?" This question calls for new ideas (or facts out of which to create ideas; or judgment as to the relative appropriateness of the ideas).

Sometimes the changing of just one word will convert the emphasis of a question from sheer fact-finding or decision-finding to an emphasis which can suggest more idea-finding as well. For instance, "How did he go?" seems to emphasize a fact-finding, while "How might he go?" allows for idea-finding, as well as the possibility of additional fact-finding and ultimately decision-finding. "What ways have been used to get this done?" is a fact-finding question, while an idea-finding question would be "In what new ways might this be done?"

The verb itself often determines the nature of the question. "Should" often indicates a decision-finding question. "Is" and "does" often indicate a fact-finding question. The word "might," as we have used it, suggests an idea-finding question.

Different types of questions emphasize either facts or ideas or judgments, and time should be taken for each.

* * *

You will now have the opportunity to practice fact-finding as an integral part of the entire procedure of creatively meeting a challenge. You will approach a challenge in a methodical way, using all of the procedures covered in this and previous sessions—namely, Fact-Finding, Problem-Finding, Idea-Finding, Solution-Finding (Evaluation) and Acceptance-Finding (Implementation).

The worksheets on the next pages are intended to serve as flexible guidelines—"basic road maps." They are to be used as creative approaches to problems, not as restricting boundaries. The "spirit," not the "letter" of each worksheet is the important thing. There can be no rigid structure for so dynamic a process as creative problem-solving. Each student should adapt the sheets to suit the special needs of his own particular challenge.

While the five phases or steps provide a helpful guide, they are not meant to be an inflexible formula. For example, while working on the idea-finding step you may recognize the need for additional fact-finding. Such change of sequence may occur during any of the suggested steps. Therefore, as the process unfolds we recommend a continual review and amplification of earlier worksheets.

However, in your first attempt at using this total method, as outlined by the worksheets, you will probably find it advantageous to follow each procedure rather explicitly, as in learning any new skill. These sheets are designed to enable you to demonstrate to yourself how you can apply creativity at each stage of a methodical attack upon a problem.

The main emphasis is upon *piling up alternatives* throughout each of the five stages of the process (Fact-Finding, Problem-Finding, Idea-Finding, Solution-Finding and Acceptance-Finding). And, of course, the worksheets provide for *exercise—* practice in the deliberate and systematic use of your imagination at every stage. Recent research has demonstrated that this practice does much to develop creative ability, in the same way that practice develops other types of skills.

The proper use of the worksheets will help you to break the *habit* of approaching problems in a conventional way; they will help you acquire the *habit* of approaching your challenge creatively.

Sample Worksheet Set

Problem

The problem presented below, which is the one being attacked on this set of sample worksheets, was taken from Alex F. Osborn's "Supplementary Guide" for instructors. Study these illustrative pages (opposite each Worksheet you will use) to see how the worksheets are utilized in this sample illustration.

What Should the Bus Driver Do?

On a public bus the driver can eject rowdies. On a school bus he cannot do this, and must deliver the children safely no matter how badly they behave. On one school bus, an eight-year-old boy struck and hit other children and kept the entire busload in a noisy, confused state. Due to the disturbances, the driver nearly had several accidents. He pointed this out, but the boy jeered and continued behaving the same way. When the boy's victims complained, the school principal tried to punish the rowdy by keeping him at recess. This had no effect, nor did appeals to his parents. The driver reported that he was as bad as ever—and was cautioned by the principal that anyone who spanked him might be sued or prosecuted.

I. Fact-Finding

Concentrate on column 1 *first;* then go on to columns 2 and 3.

What other facts would you like to have about the problem? (List *Fact-Finding questions,* not judicial or creative ones. Don't worry whether or not you can get the information; if you would *like* it, raise the question.)	Where might the answers to the most significant questions be obtained? For each of the *circled* questions, list all conceivable sources of information.	When you are able, investigate your circled sources for further information on the problem. Meanwhile, assuming you cannot do this now, move on to Worksheet II.
① *Does he have personal or family problems that might account for his actions?*	a. *parents* ⓑ *principal* ⓒ *school psychologist* d. *teachers* e. *other boys* etc. *boy himself*	*No undue problems uncovered. Parents are very permissive in their manner of raising children.*
② *How does he act in the school building?*	a. *school psychologist* b. *teachers* ⓒ *custodian* d. e. etc.	*No serious misconduct reported in school building itself.*
③ *What are his special interests?*	a. *boy himself* ⓑ *gym teacher* ⓒ *other boys* d. e. etc.	*Most sports, particularly baseball.*
4. *Does he have*	a. b.	

II. Problem-Finding

List all the creative type questions (problems or challenges) suggested by the problem. (Such as: "How might I . . .?", "What ways might I . . .?", "What ideas might I produce to . . .?", etc.) If "fact-finding" or "judicial" type questions occur to you, convert them to "creative" types by stating as, "How might I find out . . .?", or "How might I decide . . .?"

1. *How might I settle this boy down?*

2. *How might I make the parents more responsible?*

3. *What might I do to obtain a better understanding of the boy?*

4. *What might I do to become well liked by the children?*

5. *What might I do to isolate "problem children" from the others?*

Stop a moment and ask, "What is the *real* problem?" "What is my basic objective?" "What do I want to accomplish here?" Ask "Why" of each problem you have listed. ("Why do I want to do this?") As a result of these questions you ask yourself, try to restate and broaden your problem. For example, you will recall the illustration where asking "Why" of the problem, "How might I catch the mouse?" led to the restatement, "How might I get rid of the mouse?" Try, similarly, to find problem statements (questions) that allow you the largest number of possible approaches. Try paraphrasing, changing the verbs in your statements, etc. Keep listing as many additional "How might I" questions as you can about the situation.

6. *How might I maintain order on the bus?*

⑦ *How might I achieve peace on the bus?*

8. *How might I gain greater pleasure and satisfaction from my job?*

etc.

Now circle the best, most promising problem statement for creative attack (from all listed). Perhaps it is the one that would give you the greatest leeway, the largest number of approaches or areas for exploration—the one that includes most of the other ones. Or it may be one of the narrower statements that is really the crux of the situation. In any event, choose the one which is *most* significant to you—the one most in need of creative attack.

Note: You may want to go back and consider additional fact-finding on the first Worksheet, now that you have restated your problem. With the new wording, you may have other fact-finding questions that you would like to note for further exploration.

(Use additional pages as needed.)

III. Idea-Finding (deferred judgment)

Problem Statement selected on previous sheet: (Be sure your statement is clear, concise, as brief as possible, worded as a "telegram"; also, be sure that it starts with words such as "What ways might I . . .?")

Write Statement Here:

How might I maintain peace on the bus?

Ideas (tentative leads to solution):

1. *Get troublemakers expelled from school.*
2. *Don't let the boy on the bus (make his parents furnish trans.).*
3. *Get one of the boy's parents to ride with him.*
4. *Equip the bus with seat belts.*
5. *Have a teacher assigned to ride the bus to keep order.*
6. *Keep the boy separated from the other children.*
7. *Punish all the children everytime someone "acts up."*
8. *Have the children decide what should be done with troublemakers.*
9. *Appoint the boy as a monitor to keep order.*
10. *Have the children study during the bus ride.*
11. *Arrange the route so the boy is picked up last and dropped off first.*

etc.

Now go back and circle the ideas that seem to offer the best potential *(judgment)*.

Note: If your original problem statement was quite broad, you may find that your ideas listed on this sheet are really "subproblems." For example, consider the problem, "How might I increase sales of our yearbook?" You might list ideas such as "interest more students," "step up advertising," etc. In cases like this you could choose one of these "approaches" at a time, and then probe for more *specific* ideas. ("*How might* I interest more students?"; "*How might* I step up advertising?"; etc.) In such cases you will want to repeat this Worksheet (using one of the more specific "approaches" as the problem statement each time), and follow all subsequent Worksheet procedures for *each* of these approaches, or for the one *best* approach. (Use additional pages as needed.)

IV. Solution-Finding

First, list criteria (read explanation); next proceed as mentioned at bottom.

Evaluation Criteria: What are the "yardsticks" by which you can mentally test the effectiveness of each of your ideas? These criteria are really a further measure of your sensitivity to problems—problems that might be implicit in changes that would be brought about by each idea. Try to anticipate all effects, repercussions, consequences. Look over the facts of the situation for leads as to important criteria.

	effect on objective	effect on boy	effect on the children	school policies and laws	cost (in time, money and/or energy)	Use Now	Hold	Reject	Modify (How?) (Try to improve ratings on criteria.)
1.									
2.	G	G	G	P	F			✓	
3.	F	P	F	P	F			✓	*Maybe suggest all mothers take turns riding*
4.									
5.	G	F	F	F	P	✓			
6.	F	P	G	F	P		✓		*Maybe make a seating plan where he is less likely to get*
7.	F	F	P	P	F	✓			*Combine into the idea of motivating the children*
8.	G?	G	G	F	G	✓			*to squelch the troublemaker*
9.									
10.									
11.	F	F	G?	P	F?		✓		

Tear this page out and lay it alongside your ideas on the previous Worksheet. *Evaluate* those circled on Worksheet III as offering the best potential. For each of these ideas, indicate a rating in each block [e.g., G ("good"), F ("fair"), P ("poor"), DP ("doesn't pertain"), etc.]. *Then make a decision regarding each* of the *circled ideas* (based on its ratings under the various criteria) by checking or commenting in one of the boxes under "Decision."

V. Acceptance-Finding

Note: This sheet is designed to help you use creative thinking in preparing to put an idea into effect. This should be followed for *each* idea you select for use. *First idea* (or combination of ideas) to be developed—(Select from previous Worksheet).

(Write *Motivate children* Idea *to squelch* Here): *troublemaker*	DO NOT FILL IN THESE COLUMNS UNTIL FINISHED WITH FIRST COLUMN (See bottom of page)	
Column A Ways of implementing, carrying out, accomplishing, gaining acceptance for, insuring effectiveness of, improving, etc.— the above idea (deferred judgment)	**Column B** Who, when and/or where?	**Column C** How and/or why? (How gain acceptance and enthusiasm of others for ideas)
1. *Disc* 2. ____ 3. *Ap* 4. *Hav* _In this problem dealing with the constantly changing human element, the results cannot be assured as reliably as in types of problems which deal with a mechanical breakdown. Hence the driver will probably be wise to consider a variety of ideas to insure the achievement of his objective. Even though No. 6 below solved the problem for him, at least for a time, he might also want to use other approaches and ideas such as suggested below and on previous sheets. This would tend to insure that his problem remains solved._		
⑤ *Set up* *to decide on action*		*for best alternative means of accomplishing if problem still persists.*
⑥ *Stop bus when rowdyism occurs. Refuse to start 'til settled down.*	*on way home on a hot day* **before an afternoon ball game* *near a policeman*	*with warning* **without warning* **suddenly pull out magazine and start reading*
⑦ *Have children propose ideas for group activities during bus ride.*	*Have contest throughout school. Have parents enter in. *Have*	*Ask them to think about. Bring portable tape recorder, have them record ideas.*
8.	*teachers conduct class brainstorming session for ideas*	**Put up suggestion box. Give prize for best suggestion. (have children vote.)*

Now go back and circle the best ones in Column A (Judgment); then, for *each circled* one, *list further thoughts* re: the who, when, where, how and why, as indicated in Columns B and C. Search for several *alternatives* in Columns B and C for each item circled in Column A. *Then circle* the best alternative(s) in each case.

Sidney J. Parnes

APPLICATION OF TOTAL CREATIVE PROBLEM-SOLVING PROCESS TO PRACTICE PROBLEMS

Subgroups will be guided through the procedures demonstrated in previous sessions. Members will learn to define problems so as to insure maximum likelihood of effective solution. Practice will be provided in dividing major problems into their various subproblems. Participants will consider a copious list of tentative ideas, and will then begin to develop tentative solutions and make plans for their implementation. The results will then be summarized and evaluated in preparation for each member's subsequent attack on his own problem.

* * *

After reaching the broad, idea-finding statement of a problem, the next step is to break down the comprehensive, general challenge into its subproblems. We might call these subproblems the approaches toward solving our overall challenge. As we think of ideas pertinent to the broad challenge, it becomes apparent that there are many methods of meeting the challenge.

We can delve deeper into almost any general idea that we think up, and turn it into a subproblem by asking, "*How* might I carry out this idea?" Thus, each general idea (approach) that comes to mind regarding a problem can subsequently be converted into a subproblem (for attack in depth) simply by asking "How?" or "In what ways?"

By listing all conceivable approaches toward solving a broad, overall problem, we can convert each such approach into a subproblem for idea-finding in depth. We are then able to start with a creative attack on the particular subproblem that seems to offer the most promise. Thus we will at least have looked at all possible approaches, and will not have jumped blindly at the first solution that came to mind. It might well be that our tenth or twentieth or thirtieth approach would prove much more fruitful to explore than the first ones listed.

Specific questions, as opposed to broad ones, tend to spur the imagination because we usually have not thought of these more specific approaches before. Hence, we don't have ready-made answers for these questions. Thus, we force our imagination to create new ideas.

A helpful technique of thinking up subproblems is to consider the reasons why the broad problem cannot be solved effectively. For example, if the challenge is to speed up service in the cafeteria, the fact that there is not enough help might be one reason why this cannot be done. Therefore, one approach or subprobelm to the challenge of speeding up service becomes:

"How might we provide more help?" or "How might we make more effecient use of the present employees?"

Another technique for discovering subproblems is to ask the causes of the situation which created the general or overall problem. These causes, of course, are related to our observations—our information—about the challenge. The causes are thus the facts of the case. In other words, we can regard the available facts relating to the general, overall problem as a source of further subproblems.

Consider this example: If we had the general challenge of how to get more students to attend a dance, we might ask, "What are the reasons for poor attendance?" If the facts showed us that one cause was "lack of interest," a subproblem might accordingly be stated as "How to create more interest."

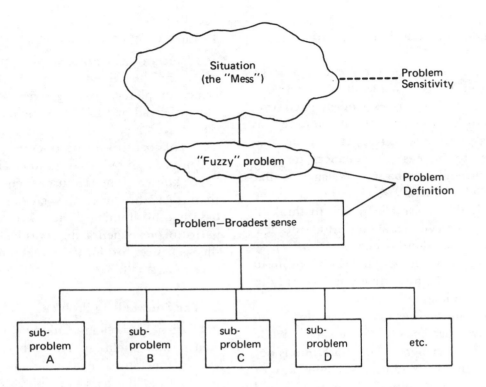

We studied earlier how to discover many statements of a problem, including statements more basic than those which might first come to mind. Now, we have explored how to break down a very broad or overall problem into a variety of subproblems.

Restudy the diagram above.

You will now have the opportunity to practice "breaking down" a problem as an integral part of the entire procedure of creatively meeting a challenge. In an earlier session, you used a five-page set of worksheets which covered the five phases involved in a methodical, yet creative attack upon a challenge: Fact-Finding, Problem-Finding, Idea-Finding, Solution-Finding and Acceptance-Finding.

Again, we must stress the fact that one cannot supply a rigid structure for so dynamic a process as creative problem-solving. While the five phases or steps provide a helpful guide, they are not an inflexible formula for meeting a challenge. They should be adapted to suit the special needs for each particular problem. Therefore, feel free to add or substitute blank pages for the worksheets at any stage where the blank page seems more comfortable to you than the printed guides.

The creative process is a fluid and flexible one, during which one may find it advisable or necessary to back-track at any particular phase and to repeat one or more phases before continuing. Thus, there should be continuous review and amplification of earlier worksheets as the process unfolds.

As in the previous set, emphasis here is upon piling up alternatives at each of the five steps, by deferring judgment first, evaluating later. Research has shown that extended effort in approaching a challenge creatively leads to a larger percentage of good ideas, as more and more alternatives are produced. Like the person who invests money to obtain greater rewards later, the creative person foregoes the immediate reward of applying his first idea, in expectation of a better solution (greater reward) ultimately.

Remember—there is never a best solution in approaching a challenge creatively—only a "best" solution so far as you have gone. A suitable solution may actually be found at any stage of the process, in which case some of the worksheet steps may become academic. However, by expending more effort probing into each of the steps, you are likely to reach a solution closer to the "perfect" one.

Theoretically there is no limit to the number of alternatives that might be listed on each of the worksheets. The amount of time you should consciously spend on a problem, therefore, becomes a matter of practical judgment. On the other hand, you will want to be forever alert to possible improvements upon your solution, even after it is put into effect.

Throughout all stages of the creative process, incubation can prove as valuable and productive as the more "deliberate" effort expended. Therefore, you will want to keep your "mental computer" as fully loaded as possible with respect to your challenge, in order to increase the chances for new ideas to occur through incubation. We suggest that you occasionally review all of your notes on the challenge. See if this doesn't help you to think of new ideas later—ones you can enter into your idea-notebook any time they occur to you. These thoughts should then be studied in relation to those already listed, the next time you are ready to "work" on the problem.

The stimulation of other minds can also be introduced to advantage in any of the stages. While the counsel of another person or of a group is not essential, it can be an extremely valuable way of enriching our own background of knowledge and experience, just as reading, travel, observation, etc., can help enrich our minds. Many problems you will undoubtedly attack without any formal group assistance; in others you may wish to draw heavily from the results of team or group cross-fertilization.

"Many ideas grow better when transplanted into another mind than in the one where they spring up." Oliver Wendell Holmes

On the previous set of worksheets, we provided you with a problem that was an "opportunity" problem. Nothing *had* to be done about the situation; but there was opportunity to develop interesting and valuable ideas to help the situation.

This time, you will work on an "obstacle-type" problem. This problem will be rather specific, and one wherein some action must be taken. The sample problem given in the adjacent pages of the worksheets is also of this type. Furthermore, the sample problem happens to be one of a technical nature. It has been chosen in order to illustrate the diversity of application of the creative process.

The first four of the following problems are from the "Supplementary Guide" of exercises, compiled by Alex F. Osborn:

1. Lucy Godby's Problem

"Recently, in Mississippi, a pilot trainee took off from the Greenville Air Force Base, and became completely lost by sunset. As darkness shut down, he radioed his his home base: 'Help me find out where I am. I can't see any landmarks at all'.

"The control-tower operator knew the cadet had no radar or radio navigational aids, and wouldn't have known how to use them had they been there. At the time, this civilian-contact training base had no homing device. It could only send out patrol planes when a flier was lost, and in this case their chances of locating the trainee would have been very small."

2. The Snowballing Problem

"When Cornell and Columbia met on snow-covered football field last November, some exuberant young spectators in the stands began throwing snowballs at the bass horn players in the band, the cheerleaders and the campus police. Soon these unguided missiles were crashing with enough force to threaten injury. The public-address system blared, 'Will the person or persons throwing snowballs please stop'?

"The snowballing ceased. A few minutes later it was resumed with greater volume and force than ever. The loud-speaker bellowed, 'It is the custom at Cornell for students and guests to heed requests made over the public-address system! Will the persons throwing snowballs please stop'?

"Instead of stopping, however, the snowballers indulged in a wild flurry of flinging. Some of their victims began wincing and screaming."

3. Mrs. Sears' Problem

"Our neighbor's chickens had a perfectly good yard of their own, but gypsy-like they ignored it for ours. Each spring, just after we got our garden well started, they would come over and would stage scratching contests to see which one could dig up the most seeds and young plants. Between matches they rested under our shed, gathering strength for a new attack.

"My husband and I chased them and complained to the neighbors; but, except for one measly egg that a hen laid in our feed trough, we got no compensation and no results. We couldn't afford to fence our yard, and we didn't want to go to court. Yet the chickens were ruining both our garden and our tempers."

4. Subway Company Problem

Youngsters in this big city delighted in stealing bulbs from subway cars, often leaving a car in semi or total darkness by the end of a run.

The subway company could not afford to hire more personnel simply to watch for bulb-snatchers. The police department also could not afford to station men in subway cars.

5. Forgotten Invitations Problem

You have planned a party. After all preparations are made and the evening has arrived, you await the arrival of your guests. As you sit in the living room awaiting, your eyes fall with horror on the lower shelf of your bookcase. There are the invitations to your party! All twenty of them are sealed, stamped and held by a rubberband!

Note: Regarding these sample worksheet illustrations, the problem is presented at the bottom of this page.

Worksheet Set

I. Fact-Finding

Concentrate on column 1 *first;* then go on to columns 2 and 3.

What other facts would you like to have about the problem? (List *Fact-Finding questions*, not judicial or creative ones. Don't worry whether or not you can get the information; if you would *like* it, raise the question.)	Where might the answers to the most significant questions be obtained? For each of the *circled* questions list all conceivable sources of information.	When you are able, investigate your circled sources for further information on the problem. Meanwhile, assuming you cannot do this now, move on to Worksheet II.
1. *What has been done under similar circumstances in the past?* 2. *How much did the float cost?* 3. *What would happen if the float were not repaired quickly?* 4. *Where can the*	a. *foreman* b. *engineers* c. *"oldtimers"* d. *superintendent* e. *manufacturer* a. *engineers* b. *foreman* c. *supt.* d. *workers in other dept.*	*Never happened before.* *An expensive shutdown is threatened.*

Problem

The problem below, which is the one being attacked on this set of sample worksheets, was taken from Alex F. Osborn's "Supplementary Guide" for instructors. Study these illustrative pages (opposite each Worksheet you will use) to see how the worksheets are utilized in this sample illustration.

How Should the Welder Solve the Problem?

A valve-control float, a stainless steel cylinder of about a gallon size, made especially for its job in a chemical plant, had very gradually lost buoyancy. It was detected just in time to avoid serious trouble. Until fixed, it could not be relied upon.

A welding shop worker received orders to repair the leak immediately. On shaking the float, about a quart of water could be heard sloshing around inside. But none came out anywhere. Even under careful inspection the leak was invisible.

Worksheet Set
(Note sample set on left)

I. Fact-Finding

Concentrate on column 1 *first;* then go on to columns 2 and 3.

What other facts would you like to have about the problem? (List *Fact-Finding questions,* not judicial or creative ones. Don't worry whether or not you can get the information; if you would *like* it, raise the question.)	Where might the answers to the most significant questions be obtained? For each of the *circled* questions list all conceivable sources of information.	When you are able, investigate your circled sources for further information on the problem. Meanwhile, assuming you cannot do this now, move on to Worksheet II. (You will note in the sample problem that some of the answers were found.)
(Go back and circle the most significant questions.)	(Go back and circle the best sources.)	

(Use additional pages as needed.)

II. Problem-Finding

List all the *creative*-type questions (problems or challenges) suggested by the problem. (Such as: "How might I . . .?", "What ways might I . . .?", "What ideas might I produce to . . .?", etc.) If "fact-finding" or "judicial" type questions occur to you, convert them to "creative" types by stating as, "How might I find out . . .?" or "How might I decide . . .?"

After listing several statements, stop a moment and ask, "What is the *real* problem?" "What is my basic objective?" "What do I want to accomplish here?" Ask "Why" of each problem you have listed. ("Why do I want to do this?") As a result of these questions you ask yourself, try to restate and broaden your problem. For example, you will recall the illustration asking "Why" of the problem, "How might I catch the mouse?" led to the restatement, "How might I get rid of the mouse?" Try, similarly, to find problem statements (questions) that allow you the largest number of possible approaches. Try paraphrasing, changing the verbs in your statements, etc. Keep listing as many additional "How might I" questions as you can about the situation.

1. *How might I find the leak?*

2. *How might I get the hole sealed?*

3. *What sealant might I use to coat the entire float without bothering to find the hole?*

4. *How might I keep the water out?*

5. *How might I weld the hole shut?*

6. *How could hole be kept at top, so water would not seep in?*

7. *How might I repair the float?*

8. *How might I prevent loss of buoyancy?*

9. *How restore and maintain buoyancy?*

After having broadened the problem, what other creative aspects or approaches ("subproblems") can you see that you didn't list earlier? What are some of the causes of the problem? Convert these into additional "How might I" questions as you did in Part A of this session.

10. *How maintain control of valve?*

11. *How might I eliminate the valve?*

12. *What else might be substituted or adapted satisfactorily to replace the float?*

13. *How might the hole be enlarged so it might be found?*

14. *How might the float be modified to cause the hole (and water already in it) to be of no concern?*

Now circle the best, most promising statement for creative attack (from all listed). Perhaps it is the one that would give you the greatest leeway, the largest number of approaches or areas for exploration—the one that includes most of the other ones. Or it may be one of the narrower statements that is really the crux of the situation. In any event, choose the one which is *most* significant to you—the one most in need of creative attack.

Note: You may want to go back and consider additional fact-finding on the first Worksheet, now that you have restated your problem. With the new wording, you may have other fact-finding questions that you would like to note for further exploration. (Use additional pages as needed.)

II. Problem-Finding

List all the *creative*-type questions (problems or challenges) suggested by the problem. (Such as: "How might I . . .?", "What ways might I . . .?", "What ideas might I produce to . . .?", etc.) If "fact-finding" or "judicial" type questions occur to you, convert them to "creative" types by stating as, "How might I find out . . .?" or "How might I decide . . .?"

After listing several statements, stop a moment and ask, "What is the *real* problem?" "What is my basic objective?" "What do I want to accomplish here?" Ask "Why" of each problem you have listed. ("Why do I want to do this?") As a result of these questions you ask yourself, try to restate and broaden your problem. For example, you will recall the illustration asking "Why" of the problem, "How might I catch the mouse?" led to the restatement, "How might I get rid of the mouse?" Try, similarly, to find problem statements (questions) that allow you the largest number of possible approaches. Try paraphrasing, changing the verbs in your statements, etc. Keep listing as many additional "How might I" questions as you can about the situation.

After having broadened the problem, what other creative aspects or approaches ("subproblems") can you see that you didn't list earlier? What are some of the causes of the problem? Convert these into additional "How might I" questions as you did in Part A of this session.

Now circle the best, most promising statement for creative attack (from all listed). Perhaps it is the one that would give you the greatest leeway, the largest number of approaches or areas for exploration—the one that includes most of the other ones. Or it may be one of the narrower statements that is really the crux of the situation. In any event, choose the one which is *most* significant to you—the one most in need of creative attack.

Note: You may want to go back and consider additional fact-finding on the first Worksheet, now that you have restated your problem. With the new wording, you may have other fact-finding questions that you would like to note for further exploration. (Use additional pages as needed.)

III. Idea-Finding (deferred judgment)

Problem Statement selected on previous sheet: (Be sure your statement is clear, concise, as brief as possible, worded as a "telegram"; also, be sure that it starts with words such as "What ways might I . . .?")

Write Statement Here:

   In what ways might the buoyancy be restored and maintained?

Ideas (tentative leads to solution):

1. *Look for hole under Microscope.*

2. *Use a block of wood or other material for a temporary float.*

3. *Replace with a rubber or plastic float that can be thrown away when it is damaged.*

4. *X-Ray the float to find the hole.*

5. *Drill a hole in the float and fill it with detergent and watch for bubbles.*

6. *Drill a hole in the float and fill it with colored liquid—watch for seepage.*

7. *Drill out hole to empty water—weld shut; then paint the entire float with liquid metal.*

8. *Drill small hole at one end; too small for water to drain out without an air hole inlet. Then run hand all around until water stops flowing because hand is covering pin hole.*

If you are "running out" of ideas, look at some of your more specific problem statements ("subproblems") on the previous page for fresh approaches in your search for ideas.

9. *Put entire float into a rubber balloon to seal hole shut.*

10. *Drill a hole, look into it under a strong light to seek pinpoint hole.*

11. *Heat the float. This will cause steam to escape and indicate the hole.*

12. *Drill hole, empty water, insert strong perfume, smell for hole.*

13. *Drill hole, then blow through, feel for air escape.*

14. *h.h. Blow in air under pressure.*

   Now go back and circle the ideas that seem to offer the best potential *(judgment).*

   Note: If your original problem statement was quite broad, you may find that your ideas listed on this sheet are really "subproblems." For example, consider the problem, "How might I increase sales of our yearbook?" You might list ideas such as, "interest more students," "step up advertising," etc. In cases like this you would choose one of these "approaches" at a time, and then probe for more *specific* ideas. ("*How might* I interest more students?", "*How might* I step up advertising?", etc.) In such cases you will want to repeat this Worksheet (using one of the more specific "subproblems" as the problem statement each time), and follow all subsequent Worksheet procedures for *each* of these approaches, or for the one *best* approach. (Use additional pages as needed.)

III. Idea-Finding (deferred judgment)

Problem Statement selected on previous sheet: (Be sure your statement is clear, concise, as brief as possible, worded as a "telegram"; also, be sure that it starts with words such as "What ways might I . . .?")

Write Statement Here:

Ideas (tentative leads to solution):

If you are "running out" of ideas, look at some of your more specific problem statements ("subproblems") on the previous page for fresh approaches in your search for ideas.

Now go back and circle the ideas that seem to offer the best potential *(judgment)*.

Note: If your original problem statement was quite broad, you may find that your ideas listed on this sheet are really "subproblems." For example, consider the problem, "How might I increase sales of our yearbook?" You might list ideas such as, "interest more students," "step up advertising," etc. In cases like this you would choose one of the "approaches" at a time, and then probe for more *specific* ideas. (*"How might* I interest more students?"; *"How might* I step up advertising?"; etc.) In such cases you will want to repeat this Worksheet (using one of the more specific "subproblems" as the problem statement each time), and follow all subsequent Worksheet procedures for *each* of these approaches, or for the one *best* approach. (Use additional pages as needed.)

IV. Solution-Finding

First, list criteria (read explanation); next proceed as mentioned at bottom.

Evaluation Criteria: What are the "yardsticks" by which you can mentally test the effectiveness of each of your ideas? These criteria are really a further measure of your sensitivity to problems—problems that might be implicit in changes that would be brought about by each idea. Try to anticipate all effects, repercussions, consequences. Look over the facts of the situation for leads as to important criteria.

	Time	Cost	Reliability	Durability	Availability of materials	Safety	Use Now	Hold	Reject	Modify (How?) (Try to improve ratings on criteria.)
2.	G	G	F	P	F	G	✓			
3.	P	G	F	F	F	G	✓			
7.	F	G	F	P	G	G		✓		
8.	P	G	F	G	G	G		✓		
9.	G	G	F	P	F	G	✓			
10.	F	G	P	G	G	G		✓		
11.	G	G	G	G	G	P	✓			
										heat while rotating in tub of water to avoid danger of explosion
14.	F	G	G	G	F	F		✓		

Line this margin up with your ideas on previous Worksheet. *Evaluate* those circled on Worksheet III as offering the best potential. For each of these ideas, indicate a rating in each block e.g. G ("good"), F ("fair"), P ("poor"), DP ("doesn't pertain"), etc. *Then make a decision regarding each* of the *circled ideas* (based on its ratings under the various criteria) by checking or commenting in the columns under "Decision."

IV. Solution-Finding

First, list criteria (read explanation); next proceed as mentioned at bottom.

Evaluation Criteria: What are the "yardsticks" by which you can mentally test the effectiveness of each of your ideas? These criteria are really a further measure of your sensitivity to problems—problems that might be implicit in changes that would be brought about by each idea. Try to anticipate all effects, repercussions, consequences. Look over the facts of the situation for leads as to important criteria.

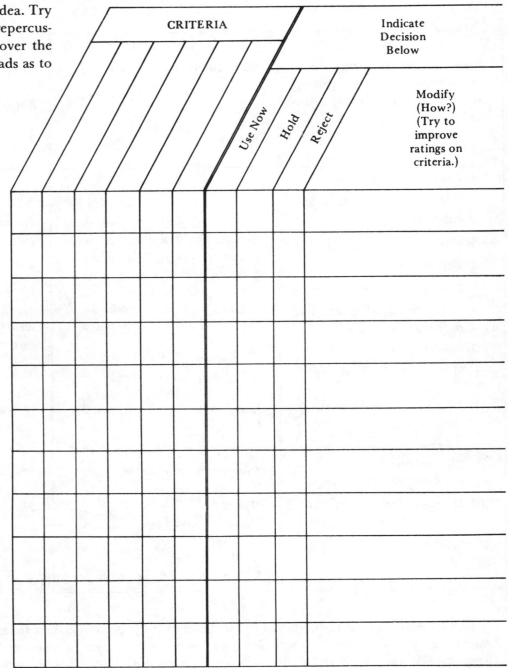

Line this margin up with your ideas on previous Worksheet. *Evaluate* those circled on Worksheet III as offering the best potential. For each of these ideas, indicate a rating in each block e.g., G ("good"), F ("fair"), P ("poor"), DP ("doesn't pertain"), etc. Then make a decision regarding each of the circled ideas (based on its ratings under the various criteria) by checking or commenting in the columns under "Decision."

V. Acceptance-Finding

Note: This sheet is designed to help you use creative thinking in preparing to put an idea into effect. This should be followed for *each* idea you select for use.

First idea (or combination of ideas) to be developed—(Selected from previous Worksheet).

Write Idea Here: *Heat float while rotating in tub of water, to cause jet of steam to escape, then weld shut.*

Column A	Column B	Column C
Ways of implementing, carrying out, accomplishing, gaining acceptance for, insuring effectiveness of, improving, etc.—the above idea (deferred judgment)	Who, when and/or where?	How and/or why? (How gain acceptance and enthusiasm of others for idea)
1. *Explain to foreman* 2. *Take necessary safety precautions* 3. *Place on stove* 4. *Boil in tub of water* 5. *Heat with welding torch* 6. *Force most of water out before welding shut* 7. *Drill hole when find spot, empty water out and weld shut.*	Because of the nature of the problem, the who, when and where seem to be myself, here and now! (for nos. 1, 2, 5 and 6)	*Roll in water while heating till see steam play flame back and forth across float* *Mark spot where you see steam. Weld after most of water steams out.*
8. *Look closely for additional holes* 9. *Suggest obtaining a replacement float to have on hand for emergencies* 10. *Develop a system of automatic detection of future leaks.*	*Have someone else watch for holes with me.* *To foreman in the department* *Suggestion committee Myself *Couple of buddies Foreman *At lunch at my home *After work 1/2 hr. each day*	*Watch for any jets of steam as rotate all surfaces of float in the water* *Suggestion box* *Think through together*

Now go back and circle the best ones in Column A (Judgment); then for each *circled* one, list further thoughts re: the who, when, where, how and why, as indicated in columns B and C. Search for several *alternatives* in columns B and C for each item circled in Column A. *Then circle* the best alternative(s) in each case.

V. Acceptance-Finding

Note: This sheet is designed to help you use creative thinking in preparing to put an idea into effect. This should be followed for *each* idea you select for use.

First idea (or combination of ideas) to be developed—(Selected from previous Worksheet).

Write Idea Here:

Column A	Column B	Column C
Ways of implementing, carrying out, accomplishing, gaining acceptance for, insuring effectiveness of, improving, etc.—the above idea (deferred judgment)	Who, when and/or where	How and/or why? (How gain acceptance and enthusiasm of others for idea)

Now go back and circle the best ones in Column A (Judgment); then for each *circled* one, list further thoughts re: the who, when, where, how and why, as indicated in columns B and C. Search for several *alternatives* in columns B and C for each item circled in Column A. *Then circle* the best alternative(s) in each case.

NOTES

SAMPLE TEST A

There are many ways to test psychologically an individual's creative thinking abilities. Here is one example. On these pages are drawn a number of circles. Draw as many different, unique pictures or objects as you can, in the fastest time. The circles should be included in whatever you make. You can put markings inside and outside—wherever you wish. Try to think of things no one else might draw. Finish as many different pictures or objects as you can and put as many ideas as you can into each one. Have them tell as complete and interesting a story as you can. Add names, captions, or titles below the objects.

183

SAMPLE TEST B

There are many ways to test psychologically an individual's creative thinking abilities. Here is one example. On these pages are drawn a number of lines. Draw as many different, unique pictures or objects as you can, in the fastest time. The lines should be included in whatever you make. You can put markings wherever you wish. Try to think of things no one else might draw. Finish as many different pictures or objects as you can and put as many ideas as you can into each one. Have them tell as complete and interesting a story as you can. Add names, captions, or titles below the objects.

191

195

197

199

PART VI

Dean C. Dauw
Helen LaVan
Iris Jasieniecki

The Influence of Young Executives' Values and Self-Esteem on Decisions

What are some of the most basic decisions of and about young managers? Do these decisions affect or reflect their values and self-esteem? What are the relationships or differences between values and self-esteem of younger male and female managers? These are a few of the issues involved in this research project about young male and female executives' values and self-esteem.

Rokeach (1968, 1973) pioneered many initial studies into values, and developed the inventories used and described later in this study. Brown (1976) recently summarized twenty-seven (27) relevant studies on values, but none considered younger managers as in the present research.

Managers, executives and academicians already have much information available on which to base their decisions about employees' motivations, values and job satisfactions. Relatively little investigation, however, has been made into the relationship between self-esteem and values.

Dauw and Fredian (1976) summarized extensive studies about self-esteem of creative people, suggesting that more creative executives have significantly higher levels of self-esteem than do less creative managers. And Dauw (1977) has shown relationships between career success and self-esteem.

Self-esteem, according to some (Barksdale, 1972, 1974) is extremely important in everyone's daily decisions. One's self-esteem can be accurately measured psychometrically and action-growth programs can be developed by individuals to improve it. Hill (1976) correlated high self-esteem and effective leadership, revealing that effective managers characteristically have high confidence in their abilities and high expectations of subordinates. Hill also cited various studies correlating effective leadership and high self-esteem.

In other recent research, LaVan, Dauw, and Jasieniecki (1977) studied the self-esteem differences between younger male and female executives. No significant differences were found between the sexes on self-esteem, but there existed a strongly significant relationship between levels of self-esteem, salary and other variables.

The Sample

This study sampled 167 young (mean age of 22) men and women employed in various corporations in a large, Midwestern metropolitan area. The 120 men and 47 women were enrolled in evening graduate and undergraduate business programs. These students were all gainfully employed in beginning or mid-management levels, and were very different from the typical, young, day-school undergraduates seen in most colleges. In age distributions, 120 were between ages 20 and 29, 36 were between ages 30 and 39, and six were between ages 40 and 49.

The young managers sampled here had a mean income level of $12,250. They are full-time employees, and part-time students in evening programs, 107 of whom are in an MBA program.

What the Inventories Measure

The self-esteem inventory is a 50-item scale developed by L.S. Barksdale and Associates at the Barksdale Foundation (1972, 1974). The respondent achieves a score ranging from -75 to $+75$ by rating oneself on a scale from 'zero' (not true), through 'one' (somewhat true), 'two' (largely true) and 'three' (true). Previous studies by Dauw revealed mean scores of $+22$ for undergraduates and $+28$ for MBAs. In this study, the mean score was 27.33 for all 167 respondents.

Rokeach's value inventories (1968, 1973) measure 18 instrumental and 18 terminal values. Respondents ranked their personal-work values on each list from 1 through 18.

The Results

There were statistically significant differences in various aspects of this study, as measured by the gamma statistic.

Table I shows the overall list of instrumental values, and Table II, the terminal values, along with results from various samples. In this apparently homogenous sample, only three sex-values differences appeared. Women ranked the instrumental value "Forgiving — Willing to Pardon Others" much more highly than men, to a statistically significant degree ($p < .001$). But, on terminal values, men ranked "Equality — Brotherhood, Equal Opportunity for All" much higher than women ($p < .04$) and also "Family Security — Taking Care of Loved Ones" much higher than women ($p < .003$).

Differences also exist in levels of self-esteem and values. Respondents were grouped into thirds based on self-esteem scores, the lowest group from -12 to $+18$, the middle group from $+19$ to $+35$, and the highest group on self-esteem measured from $+36$ to $+75$. Those with the highest levels of self-esteem ranked "an exciting life — a stimulating, active life" more highly ($p < .05$).

Those with the lowest levels of self-esteem ranked "happiness — contentedness" more highly ($p < .03$) as well as "national security — protection from attack" ($p < .03$).

In instrumental values, "independence — self-reliant, self-sufficient" was ranked more highly by those highest in self-esteem ($p < .03$).

Discussion

Every day, executives make decisions about, for, and with younger male and female managers. These decisions could lead to more effective actions, if they were better informed with information about employee's values and self-esteem.

Executives need to understand more clearly that men and women basically do not differ in self-esteem, just as other research has shown women are not more emotional than men, nor are men more rational than women.

In fact, considering the instrumental values, such as "logical" or "intellectual," no sex differences existed. In only one minor area did sex make a difference in instrumental values, where the young women managers valued "forgiving — willing to pardon others" more highly than men.

Whereas sex led to only one difference in values, levels of self-esteem certainly had more impact. Managers with higher self-esteem have different values and impact than those with lower self-esteem.

The differences on Tables I and II between this group and national samples may be explained by the fact that most of the 107 respondents here are highly achievement-oriented MBA candidates, a unique and homogeneous group.

Top executives in any organization are becoming increasingly more aware that human resources are their greatest assets. To increase the worth of these assets, higher-level executives need to become increasingly more aware of subordinates' values, self-esteem and other traits. Providing more effective management development programs has always been a primary concern. Perhaps in the future, more of these programs might also focus on values' clarification and programs to enhance employees' self-esteem. Managers with higher self-esteem will make better decisions, and become more productive for any organization.

Finally, everyone may be reminded that every decision contains both factual and value elements, because values play a major role in the lives of everyone. Most behavior in organizations, individual or group, as well as the behavior of our nation and society, is based on the values we hold. A major source of conflict and aggression between individuals, groups and peoples is incompatibility between, or failure to understand and accept, the values and value systems of others.

Table I

Rank Order of Instrumental Values: Various Samples*

	1 Yours	2 National Sample	3 Men	4 Women
1. Ambitious (hard-working, aspiring)	_____	2	2	4
2. Broadminded (open-minded)	_____	5	4	5
3. Capable (competent, effective)	_____	9	8	12
4. Cheerful (lighthearted, joyful)	_____	12	12	10
5. Clean (neat, tidy)	_____	8	9	8
6. Courageous (standing up for your beliefs)	_____	6	5	6
7. Forgiving (willing to pardon others)	_____	4	6	2
8. Helpful (working for the welfare of others)	_____	7	7	7
9. Honest (sincere, truthful)	_____	1	1	1
10. Imaginative (daring, creative)	_____	18	18	18
11. Independent (self-reliant, self-sufficient)	_____	13	11	14
12. Intellectual (intelligent, reflective)	_____	15	15	16
13. Logical (consistent, rational)	_____	17	16	17
14. Loving (affectionate, tender)	_____	11	14	9
15. Obedient (dutiful, respectful)	_____	16	17	15
16. Polite (courteous, well-mannered)	_____	14	13	13
17. Responsible (dependable, reliable)	_____	3	3	3
18. Self-Controlled (restrained, self-disciplined)	_____	10	10	11

The rankings above are those of: col. 1, yourself; col. 2, a national sample of 1419 adult Americans; col. 3, men from national sample; and col. 4, women from national sample.

*Source: Milton Rokeach, *The Nature of Human Values*, Free Press, New York, 1973. The data presented above were derived from various tables in the book. Reproduced by permission.

205

Table II

Rank Order of Terminal Values: Various Samples*

	1 Yours	2 National Sample	3 Men	4 Women	5 Students
1. A Comfortable Life (a prosperous life)	_____	9	4	13	13
2. An Exciting Life (a stimulating, active life)	_____	18	18	18	12
3. A Sense of Accomplishment (lasting contribution)	_____	10	7	10	6
4. A World at Peace (free of war and conflict)	_____	1	1	1	10
5. A World of Beauty (beauty of nature and the arts)	_____	15	15	15	17
6. Equality (brotherhood, equal opportunity for all)	_____	7	9	8	11
7. Family Security (taking care of loved ones)	_____	2	2	2	9
8. Freedom (independence, free choice)	_____	3	3	3	1
9. Happiness (contentedness)	_____	4	5	5	2
10. Inner Harmony (freedom from inner conflict)	_____	13	13	12	8
11. Mature Love (sexual and spiritual intimacy)	_____	14	14	14	5
12. National Security (protection from attack)	_____	12	10	11	16
13. Pleasure (an enjoyable, leisurely life)	_____	17	17	16	18
14. Salvation (saved, eternal life)	_____	8	12	4	14
15. Self-Respect (self-esteem)	_____	5	6	6	15
16. Social Recognition (respect, admiration)	_____	16	16	17	4
17. True Friendship (close companionship)	_____	11	11	9	7
18. Widsom (a mature understanding of life)	_____	6	8	7	3

The rankings above are those of: col. 1, yourself; col. 2, a national sample of 1419 adult Americans; col. 3, the 665 men of the national sample; col. 4, the 744 women of the national sample; and col. 5, 298 Michigan State University students.

*Source: Milton Rokeach, *The Nature of Human Values*, Free Press, New York, 1973. The data presented above were derived from various tables in the book. Reproduced by permission.

References

Barksdale, L.S. *Building Self-Esteem*. Idyllwild, Calif.: Barksdale Foundation, 1972.

Barksdale, L.S. *Daily Program for Building Self-Esteem*. Idyllwild, Calif.: Barksdale foundation, 1974.

Brown, N.A. Values — A necessary but neglected ingredient of motivation on the job. *Academy of Management Review*, 1976, 1, 15-23.

Dauw, D.C. *Up Your Career, 3/E*. Prospect Heights, Ill.: Waveland Press, 1980.

Hill, N. Self-esteem: The key to effective leadership. *Administrative Management*, 1976, 37, 24-25 +

LaVan H., Dauw, D.C., and Jasieniecki, I. "Values and Self-Esteem, Differences of Male and Female Executives." Paper presented at Academy of Management Midwest, Milwaukee, April, 1977.

Rokeach, M. *Beliefs, Attitudes and Values*. San Francisco: Jossey-Bass, Inc., 1968.

Rokeach, M. *The Nature of Human Values*. New York: The Free Press, 1973.

Helen LaVan
Dean C. Dauw
Iris Jan Jasieniecki

VALUES AND SELF-ESTEEM DIFFERENCES OF MALE AND FEMALE EXECUTIVES

What do younger business executives value today? Are there differences between values of young business women and men? How are these values related to their self-esteem? Do their values and self-esteem affect their career decisions? How are all these related to the ways they perceive their future career success? These are only a few questions and issues researched in the present study.

Recent research by Brown (1976) summarized 27 relevant studies on values, but none cited experimental studies on younger managers, as in the present research. Rokeach (1968) (1973) performed many initial studies on values, and formulated the values' inventories used and described extensively later in this present study.

Although much work has been done on managerial motivations, values, job satisfactions and the like, relatively little has been done on their self-esteem especially on the interrelationship between work-related values and self-esteem.

Previous research by Dauw and Fredian (1976) summarized extensive studies about self-esteem of creative people, suggesting that more creative managers tend to have significantly higher levels of self-esteem than do less creative administrators. And Dauw (1977) has shown relationships between self-esteem and career success.

Research done by Ondrack (1973) on student values has revealed that occupational values have changed from the business executives' values as found by Kilpatrick (1964) and the graduates entering industry as found by Manhardt (1966-1970) to the values of college teachers as found by Kilpatrick (1964). According to Ondrack, students are no longer concerned with the conventional climb up the hierarchical ladder and authoritarian supervision but rather with individual achievement, independence, responsibility and equality among peers.

Research done by White and Ruh (1973) was done to investigate the effects of individual values of workers on the relationship between job attitudes and participation (in decision-making). White and Ruh found that personal values had no effect on the relationship between job attitudes and participation. (The values in this study were measured against the Rokeach Value Study.)

Consultant Norman Hill (1976) has correlated effective leadership with high self-esteem. He has cited that effective leaders have two distinct characteristics: confidence in their abilities and high expectations of their subordinates. He has also cited several studies which have correlated effective leadership with high self-esteem.

This study focuses on what is absent from these studies — that is, the relationship between work-related values and self-esteem as well as the relationship between self-esteem and short term career goals. Male-female differences in values and self-esteem will also be examined.

The Data

The present study sampled 167 young (mean age 22) men and women employed in various positions in corporations in a large, Midwestern metropolitan area, and enrolled in both graduate school and undergraduate business programs. There were 120 men and 47 women. In age distribution, 125 were between 20-29, 36 between 30-39, and six were between 40-49.

The young managers involved in this study had a mean income level of $12,250. While most of the students (N = 107) were completing an MBA, 60 were finishing an undergraduate bachelor's in business degree in the evening division. What is being controlled for in this study is educational background, which is obviously the same for both sexes, but different for undergraduates and graduates. The subjects are part-time students and full-time employees.

The Inventories and What They Measure

The self-esteem measure is a 50-item inventory developed by L.S. Barksdale and colleagues at the Barksdale Foundation (1972) (1974). By rating onself on a scale from zero (not true) through one (somewhat true), two (largely true) to three (true), the respondent achieves a self-esteem score ranging from −75 to +75. Previous studies by Dauw revealed mean scores of +22 for undergraduates and +28 for MBA graduate students. The mean score of all 167 participants in this study was 27.33.

Value inventories were adapted from the research by Rokeach (1968, 1973), measuring 18 terminal and 18 instrumental values. Participants were asked to rank their personal values on each list from one through 18.

An additional, brief questionnaire developed by the present authors sought information on present majors, current and projected career levels as well as current and projected salaries. Seven major fields of study were represented: accounting (N = 65), economics (N = 9), finance (N = 11), marketing (N = 15), personnel management (N = 28), social sciences (N = 10) and other (nonbusiness majors) (N = 27).

These respondents were divided into nine categories of positions: clerical (15), administrative (nonclerical) (28), sales, (1), professional accountants, engineers, teachers) (72), lower management (38), middle management (3), upper management (1), self-employed (1), and other (6).

Results

There were statistically significant differences in varius aspects of this study. The higher the level of measured self-esteem, the higher the earnings. Table 1 shows the relationships between salary and self-esteem.

Table 1
Relationships Between Salary and Self-Esteem

	Over $25,000	Under $25,000	
Lower 25%	0	40	40
Middle 50%	3	84	87
Top 25%	4	36	40
	7	160	167

Chi-square = 5.23

For example, none of the managers in the lowest 25% of self-esteem had salaries over $25,000, but four members of the top 25% in self-esteem earned more than $25,000 (p > .07). This study suggests a definite statistical relationship between self-esteem and salary levels, although no causal relationship is posited.

Higher levels of self-esteem also are associated with higher levels of projected earnings, as revealed in Table 2. When asked to project their income levels in five years, only seven in the lowest 25% on self-esteem projected earning more than $35,000 annually, whereas 13 of the top 25% in self-esteem projected they would be earning more than $35,000 (p > .08).

Table 2
Relationships Between Projected Salaries and Self-Esteem

	Over $35,000	Under $35,000	
Lower 25%	7	33	40
Middle 50%	32	55	87
Top 25%	13	27	40
	52	115	167

Chi-square = 4.80
Probability   0.0893

Higher self-esteem also is associated with markedly higher levels of projected executive positions, as shown in Table 3. For example, 80 respondents have either poorly defined or definitely lower career goals. Of the lowest 25% in self-esteem, only 14 hoped to be in middle or upper managerial levels in the future, whereas 24 of the top 25% in self-esteem expected promotions.

Table 3
Relationships Between Projected Executive Job-Levels and Self-Esteem

	Middle, Upper and Self	Other	
Lower 25%	14	26	40
Middle 50%	49	38	87
Top 25%	24	16	40
	87	80	167

Chi-square = 6.31
Probability   0.04

There were **no** statistically significant differences between the ways men and women ranked their values, in the present study, although earlier research by Rokeach (1968, 1973) had reported definite differences between men and women. Young managers in this study ranked as their top three terminal values, a sense of accomplishment, freedom and happiness. As their top three instrumental values, they ranked ambitious, honest and independent.

Statistically significant correlations existed between self-esteem and values. Higher self-esteem was significantly correlated with values of honesty (p > .05), independence (p > .03) and freedom (p > .004).

By contrast, in a national sample, the top three terminal values (Rokeach, 1973) were "a world at peace," "family security," and "freedom," whereas in this sample, the top three were a sense of accomplishment, freedom and happiness. Also, by contrast, in this national sample, the instrumental values were honest, ambitious, responsible; whereas here they were ambitious, honest and independent.

These differences may result.from the fact that MBA-type managers are more achievement-oriented (terminal value) and ambitious (instrumental value).

Discussion

The present study uncovers some data of interest to managers, executives, academicians and researchers at all levels.

Women's libertarians may find value in the fact that no measured differences in values nor in self-esteem existed between the men and women in this sample. Business executives may become increasingly aware of their younger managers' values as one means of increasing their motivation and productivity. Certainly, as executives become increasingly more aware of their employees' values, they will become more effective in managing them.

A better understanding of the concept of self-esteem is useful for executives and researchers alike. Younger managers, men and women, who have lower levels of self-esteem earn less and expect fewer promotions or career successes. Certainly, this aspect of their self-concept affects their daily human relations and job satisfactions. Most top executives consciously or unconsciously take an employee's self-esteem into consideration when considering promotions and raises. It is not clear here whether an employee expects promotions and higher earnings levels because one is already more self-confident, but much evidence exists in managerial literature that self-confidence is a trait of successful executives. It is doubtful if a manager with lower self-esteem will be promoted as readily as one who acts and appears self-confident.

More research is needed, of course. But certain implications are clear here. Younger managers need to become increasingly more aware of their levels of self-esteem and how self-esteem affects their future career perceptions. Higher level executives need to adopt programs to assist younger employees in enhancing their own self-awareness and self-esteem as one important way to assure greater motivation and productivity. Volumes have been written on the need for management development to achieve corporate goals. Hopefully, more can be done in the future to raise employees' levels of self-esteem as an intermediate variable, to ultimately increase their career success and corporate goals.

References

Barksdale, L.S. *Building Self-Esteem*. Idyllwild, Calif.: Barksdale Foundation, 1972.

Barksdale, L.S. *Daily Program for Building Self-Esteem*. Idyllwild, Calif.: Barksdale Foundation, 1974.

Brown, N.A. Values — A necessary but neglected ingredient of motivation on the job. *Academy of Management Review*, 1976, 1, 15-23.

Dauw, D.C. *Up Your Career, 3/E*. Prospect Heights, Ill.: Waveland Press, 1980.

Hill, N. Self-esteem: The key to effective leadership. *Administrative Management*, 1976, 37, 24-25 +

Ondrack, D.A. Emerging occupational values: A review and some findings. *Academy of Management Journal*, 1973, 16, 423-432.

Rokeach, M. *Beliefs, Attitudes and Values*. San Francisco: Jossey-Bass, Inc., 1968.

Rokeach, M. *The Nature of Human Values*. New York: The Free Press, 1973.

White, J.K. and Ruh, R.A. Effects of personal values on the relationship between participation and job attitudes. *Administrative Science Quarterly*, 1978, 18, 506-514.

AN EXPERIMENTAL BEHAVIOR MODIFICATION PROGRAM TO INCREASE YOUNG EXECUTIVES' SELF-ESTEEM

Introduction

Along with "intelligence," "self-esteem" may be the primary attribute of individuals most typically discussed in both professional and managerial evaluations of executive talent, personality and social functioning. Whereas libraries of research have been done on intelligence, relatively little has been written on self-esteem.

This research project is part of a continuing series of research studies on self-esteem attempting to understand the role of self-esteem in managerial development. The primary question asked here was "Can an executive learn to modify his/her self-esteem?" What techniques or methods, used in which ways, with what kinds of managers, would lead to what results in developing personal self-esteem.

Wells and Marwell (1976) have provided an overview of self-esteem's conceptualization and measurement. They clearly emphasize that establishing self-esteem is a precondition for self-actualization. In satisfying one's esteem need a person is not trying to actualize an inborn potential, but to establish superiority over others. As a result of this, Maslow's notion of self-esteem was identified with the concept of "dominance-feeling" — a kind of sureness, pride, sense of mastery, or feeling of superiority when dealing with other people and objects. (Maslow, 1937, 1942, 1954). Clearly, increasing one's self-esteem is required before a person can begin or attempt to become self-actualized.

Aside from the notion of one's personal growth and development, the concept is valuable from the corporate need for executive development. Hall and Morgan (1977) and Dauw (1977) explained the place of self-esteem in career planning, and as having an important role in the career success cycle.

Lewin (1936) and Argyris (1964) have described the conditions under which effective task performance will lead to increased self-esteem. For example, (1) if a woman sets a challenging goal for herself, and (2) the woman determines her own means of attaining that goal, and (3) if the goal is central to her self-concept, then she will experience psychological success upon attainment of that goal. This sense of personal success will lead to an increased involvement in the task. This increased involvement will then lead the person to set additional goals in the same task area and to set higher levels of aspiration. (Porter and Lawler, 1968).

Hall and Morgan's theory suggests that success breeds success. This cycle of events can be self-reinforcing and can be generalized beyond simple tasks to people's careers; and, then, beyond self-esteem to self-actualization. When a person experiences a success cycle at work, she may develop greater enthusiasm for the career represented by the successful activity. She may experience and express "really finding herself" or "being turned on" by her work. This cycle, then leads to increased self-esteem as a necessary step toward self-actualization. In other previous research, Dauw and LaVan (1977) and LaVan, Dauw and Jasieniecki (1977) have investigated the relationship between self-esteem and values in executives.

Methodology

Following the concepts clearly outlined by Williams and Long (1975), an experimental program was developed using both three (3) experimental and three (3) control groups of young executives, mostly evening graduate students, who were

212

employed full time during the days in advancing their managerial careers. A pre- and post-test of self-esteem was administered to measure first their initial base line position and then subsequent growth. The experimental program was initiated by introducing the participants to the concept of self-esteem, an issue they freely volunteered was foreign to their thinking. The self-management model was described in detail: (1) Selecting a goal; (2) Monitoring target behaviors; (3) Altering setting events; (4) Arranging consequences; (5) Focusing on contingencies; (6) Using covert control — all as outlined by Williams and Long (1975). Group Dynamics sessions were developed wherein some students acted as consultants to facilitate other students' program development. Then, roles were switched so that each had an opportunity to function as either a client or as a consultant. Participants were encouraged to continuously enhance and refine their personal-action-growth-and-development programs by daily implementation. In succeeding meetings during the ten (10) week quarter of classes, they were continuously reminded, cajoled, and exhorted by the experimenter to continue their efforts for personal growth and increasing self-actualization until the post-test was administered at the end of the ten (10) week quarter. In confidential, anonymous evaluations, the participants overwhelmingly approved the program and related examples of the insights, results and successes achieved in improving their daily lives, both in actual job performance and in personal relationships outside of work.

Sample

Three experimental and three control groups were developed, with 146 subjects in the three experimental groups (N = 48, 32, & 66) and with 80 subjects (N = 32, 16, & 32) in the control groups. The average age of the youngest group was 23, and the average age of the oldest group was 28 with a range from 21 to 44. Only one experimental and one control group were graduate students, studying for an MBA degree in the evening and working as young managers and executives during the day. The same statement is true about the other experimental and control groups who studied in the evening division on an undergraduate degree, while still employed during the day. (One of the latter students, for example, was a very high level executive earning $50,000 annually.) The sample was extremely heterogeneous in terms of career responsibilities and income.

Inventory and What It Measures

The self-esteem measure is a 50-item inventory developed by L.S. Barksdale and colleagues at the Barksdale Foundation (1972, 1974). By rating oneself on a scale from zero (not true) to "one" (somewhat true), to "two" (largely true), to "three" (true), the respondent achieves a self-esteem score ranging from −75 to +75. Previous studies by Dauw revealed mean scores of +22 for undergraduates and +28 for MBA graduate students in various samples.

Results

Table One

Groups

SEI Scores Experimental		SEI Scores Control	
pre X = 24	t = 5.3*	pre X = 25	t = 1.63
1. post X = 40	p < .005*	A. post X = 33	p < .05
df = 48		df = 32	
pre X = 22	t = 4.57	pre X = 25	t = .35
2. post X = 46	p < .005*	B. post X = 27	p = N.S.
df = 32		df = 16	
pre X = 25	t = 4.35	pre X = 34	t = .41
3. post X = 40	p < .005*	C. post X = 36	p = N.S.
df = 66		df = 32	

p = N.S.

Table I reveals statistically significant differences in all three experimental groups, almost to the same degree (p < .005). Little or no change was manifest in two control groups from pre to post test scores; with some minor change in one control group. This latter change was in the undergraduate group that had a large amount of overlap and interaction with the undergraduate experimental group. Since the graduate and evening students generally have fewer or no classes in common and no personal interaction, there was no opportunity for them to discuss various class developments, and activities with friends, which situation is not true among the more relatively intimate undergraduate day students, who typically discuss among themselves events in other classes.

Anecdotal evidence from the confidential evaluations include some of the following:

I feel that there are two major reasons for this increase in my self-esteem (1) this course. I have had the opportunity to turn my thoughts inward and analyze myself; **Who** am I, **Where** am I going, and **How** am I going to move from where I am to where I am going. In addition, the self-change project and the work-change project have had a profound effect on my self-esteem. (2) Coupled with the experience I have had in this course, I have just left the only company that I have ever worked for on a full-time basis (eleven years), and started a new job in a different, but related, field. This change came about partly from insights I gained in reading *Up Your Career* (Dauw, 1977) about ten months ago. The effect of this job change has been that (a) my level of frustration has decreased, (b) my self-confidence has increased and (c) my own feelings of self-worth have increased."

"I feel good about it. Part of what I intend to do is given in my "change program" progress report and the most important aspect of my intent is to simply be aware of the fact that something can be done—that there is a theory to apply. I intend to make a conscious effort to keep O.D. as part of my daily work habits."

"I feel pleased about my score and score increase. I plan to continue to increase my self-esteem—because you never stop learning in life and striving to improve yourself."

"Class exercises have enabled me to feel less vulnerable to others' openness and to thereby believe in *myself* more. This result makes me feel very good and I intend to keep working on certain areas which are still weak, such as belittling my own achievements.

"I feel that my increase has been due to my realization that I control my destiny. I should be pleasing myself first, then others."

"The primary reason for the increase is that I have stopped worrying about what other people think with regards to me, my actions, and my opinions. This change in my attitude was largely initiated by the discussions held in class, particularly those of the group of which I was a member for the 'fun learning exercises.'"

"I intend to strengthen those elements within myself that lead to higher self-esteem because I believe in it. My actions are improved when I am feeling good about myself. I sincerely feel it is very important."

"I feel improvement has been made in my personality and ability to deal effectively with others. I know that as far as confidence goes, mine has increased in holding to my own opinion and in conversing." I hope to continue with my change project both for myself and at work. It has made life more interesting!"

"I feel really good about it!! It makes me feel that I have achieved greater emotional freedom. I will try to maintain and enlarge this freedom through readings and, above all, by trying to be honest with myself. + 16 is far from + 75."

Discussions

The experiments in this research clearly show that younger managers can significantly increase their levels of self-esteem, and learn to feel more positively about themselves. This procedure can definitely enhance every aspect of their daily lives, leading to greater productivity at work, as well as personal satisfaction at home.

These research results have valuable implications both for organizations and individuals. On the organizational level, an increasingly greater awareness of the concept of self-esteem can enable executives to make better decisions in personnel selection, management training and development, performance appraisals and the like. For example, more valid selection of appropriate talent can enable managers to make their organizations more productive.

On the level of individual development, it provides more evidence for personal growth and development. If a manager cannot personally grow, how can a person presume to develop the talent to be managed. One of the main reasons managers fail to increase organizational results is because they do not know how to, or try to improve themselves personally. Hopefully, they can become increasingly more aware of their personal needs to increase their own self-esteem and that of others.

References

Argyris, C., *Integrating the Individual and the Organization*. New York: Wiley, 1964.

Barksdale, L.S. *Building Self-Esteem*. Idyllwild, California: Barksdale Foundation, 1972.

Barksdale, L.S., *Daily Program for Building Self-Esteem*. Idyllwild, California: Barksdale Foundation, 1974.

Dauw, D.C., *Up Your Career, 2/E.* Prospect Heights, Illinois: Waveland Press, 1977.

Dauw, D.C., H. LaVan, and I Jasieniecki, "Influence of Young Executives' Values and Self-Esteem on Decisions." Research presented to the Illinois Sociological Association, October, 1977.

Hall, D.T. and M.A. Morgan, "Career Development and Planning" in Hamner and Schmidt *Contemporary Problems in Personnel*. Chicago, Illinois: Saint Clair Press, 1977.

LaVan, H., D.C. Dauw, and I. Jasieniecki, "Values and Self-Esteem Differences of Male and Female Executives." Proceedings of the Academy of Management — Midwest. Milwaukee, Wisconsin, 1977.

Lewin, K., "The Psychology of Success and Failure." *Occupations*. 1936, 14, 926-930.

Maslow, A., "Dominance-Feeling, Behavior and Status." *Psychological Review*. 1937, 44: 404-429.

Maslow, A., "Self-Esteem (Dominance-Feeling) and Sexuality in Women." *Journal of Social Psychology*. 1942, 16: 259-294.

Maslow, A., *Motivation and Personality*. New York: Harper, 1954.

Porter, L.W. and Lawler, E. E. III., *Managerial Attitudes and Performance*. New York: Irwin-Dorsey, 1968.

Wells, L.F. and G. Marwell, *Self-Esteem: Its Conceptualization and Measurement*. Beverly Hills, California: Sage Press, 1976.

Williams, R.L. and J.D. Long, *Toward a Self-Managed Life-Style*. Boston: Houghton-Mifflin, 1975.

NO HIDDEN MEANINGS

Sheldon Kopp, Ph.D. is a psychotherapist in Washington, D.C. He has written many well acclaimed books on therapy. One is entitled *"No Hidden Meanings* (published by Science and Behavior Books, 1975; 701 Welch Road, Palo Alto, California 94306.

One day he wrote up his Eschatological Laundry List of Eternal Truths. "I did not have to search for them. They arose from my unconscious as in a dream, taking form more quickly than I could write them down. This was to be a zany spoof, a way of tenderly making fun of myself. Instead, what emerged was a fragment of a cosmic joke, a visionary list of the truths which, at my best, shape my life, provide answers to unasked questions, and give insights too powerfully simple to be grasped finally and forever."

Goals

(1) To learn what these "**Truths**" mean.

(2) To integrate them into your daily behavior and your interpersonal relationships.

(3) To use them to increase your level of self-confidence.

(4) To help you become more aware of the challenges of life.

Procedure:

(1) First check off those you especially agree with: True.

(2) Put a question mark next to those you do not fully understand.

(3) Finally, break up into small groups of two or three participants to discuss, interpret, etc.

Statements

1. This is it!
2. There are no hidden meanings.
3. You can't get there from here, and besides there's no place else to go.
4. We are all already dying and we will be dead for a long time.
5. Nothing lasts!
6. There is no way of getting all you want.
7. You can't have anything unless you let go of it.
8. You only get to keep what you give away.
9. There is no particular reason why you lost out on some things.
10. The world is not necessarily just. Being good often does not pay off and there is no compensation for misfortune.
11. You have a responsibility to do your best none-the-less.
12. It is a random universe to which we bring meaning.
13. You don't really control anything.
14. You can't make anyone love you.
15. No one is any stronger or any weaker than anyone else.
16. Everyone is, in his own way, vulnerable.
17. There are no great men.
18. If you have a hero, look again; you have diminished yourself in some way.
19. Everyone lies, cheats, pretends (yes, you too, and most certainly I myself).
20. All evil is potential vitality in need of transformation.
21. All of you is worth something, if you will only own it.
22. Progress is an illusion.
23. Evil can be displaced but never eradicated, as all solutions breed new problems.
24. Yet it is necessary to keep on struggling toward solution.

25. Childhood is a nightmare.
26. But it is so very hard to be an on-your-own, take-care-of-yourself-cause-there-is-no-one-else-to-do-it-for-you grown-up.
27. Each of us is ultimately alone.
28. The most important things each man must do for himself.
29. Love is not enough, but it sure helps.
30. We have only ourselves, and one another. This may not be much, but that's all there is.
31. How strange, that so often, it all seems worth it.
32. We must live within the ambiguity of partial freedom, partial power, and partial knowledge.
33. All important decisions must be made on the basis of insufficient data.
34. Yet we are responsible for everything we do.
35. No excuses will be accepted.
36. You can run, but you can't hide.
37. It is most important to run out of scapegoats.
38. We must learn the power of living with our helplessness.
39. The only victory lies in surrender to oneself.
40. All of the significant battles are waged within the self.
41. You are free to do whatever you like. You need only face the consequences.
42. What do you know...for sure...anyway?
43. Learn to forgive yourself, again, and again, and again and again.

INCREASING YOUR SELF-ESTEEM

In all the people who contact SECS — Sexual Enrichment Counseling Services (Chicago) — for any reason, a glaring lack of self-esteem is obvious. The same lack of self-esteem is apparent in all patients seeking therapy from any psychologist, or other mental health professional.

To understand how your lack of, or diminished, self-esteem is related to your career or your personal growth, please fill out the following questionnaire. Try to answer it as quickly as possible, without thinking too much about a particular question. Usually, the first idea that enters your mind is the most correct one. Be as honest and open with yourself as you possibly can, because no one else has to know your score. (If you try to lie to yourself, you have an even bigger problem!)

Remember, whatever you score, you can always be a **Winner**. Fortunately, now you can become an even **bigger** winner by doing something about it.

After you finish the questionnaire, follow the directions on how to score it.

Do not be concerned about your Self-Esteem score, no matter how low it may be. For your Self-Esteem simply is what it IS, the automatic product of your heritage and total life experience; and thus nothing to be ashamed or embarrassed about. It is important, however, that you understand each statement and be completely honest with yourself in order to obtain as valid a score as possible. Furthermore, do not confuse any concepts or ideals you may hold with how you actually function. For your beginning Self-Esteem Index (SEI) is an important reference point for gauging your progress in building Self-Esteem. Remember that no matter how low your SEI may be, you can bring it up to any desired value by conscientious effort. You may also find comfort in the fact that lack of sound Self-Esteem is a universal problem that varies only in degree. It is, however, often so well camouflaged by false fronts that only a trained observer can detect it.

Score as follows:　　　　"0" If not true　　　　"2" If largely true
　　　　　　　　　　　　"1" If somewhat true　　"3" If true

SCORE		*STATEMENT OF PRESENT CONDITION OR ACTION*
____	1.	I usually feel inferior to others.
____	2.	I normally feel warm and happy toward myself.
____	3.	I often feel inadequate to handle new situations.
____	4.	I usually feel warm and friendly toward all I contact.
____	5.	I habitually condemn myself for my mistakes and shortcomings.
____	6.	I am free of shame, blame, guilt and remorse.
____	7.	I have a driving need to prove my worth and excellence.
____	8.	I have great enjoyment and zest for living.

____	9.	I am much concerned about what others think and say of me.
____	10.	I can let others be "wrong" without attempting to correct them.
____	11.	I have an intense need for recognition and approval.
____	12.	I am usually free of emotional turmoil, conflict and frustration.
____	13.	Losing normally causes me to feel resentful and "less than."
____	14.	I usually anticipate new endeavors with quiet confidence.
____	15.	I am prone to condemn others and often wish them punished.
____	16.	I normally do my own thinking and make my own decisions.
____	17.	I often defer to others on account of their ability, wealth or prestige.
____	18.	I willingly take responsibility for the consequences of my actions.
____	19.	I am inclined to exaggerate and lie to maintain a desired image.
____	20.	I am free to give precedence to my own needs and desires.
____	21.	I tend to belittle my own talents, possessions and achievements.
____	22.	I normally speak up for my own opinions and convictions.
____	23.	I habitually deny, alibi, justify or rationalize my mistakes and defeats.
____	24.	I am usually poised and comfortable among strangers.
____	25.	I am very often critical and belittling of others.
____	26.	I am free to express love, anger, hostility, resentment, joy, etc.
____	27.	I feel very vulnerable to others' opinions, comments and attitudes.
____	28.	I rarely experience jealousy, envy or suspicion.
____	29.	I am a "professional people pleaser."
____	30.	I am not prejudiced toward racial, ethnic or religious groups.
____	31.	I am fearful of exposing my "real self."
____	32.	I am normally friendly, considerate and generous with others.
____	33.	I often blame others for my handicaps, problems and mistakes.
____	34.	I rarely feel uncomfortable, lonely and isolated when alone.
____	35.	I am a compulsive "perfectionist."
____	36.	I accept compliments and gifts without embarrassment or obligation.
____	37.	I am often compulsive about eating, smoking, talking or drinking.
____	38.	I am appreciative of others' achievements and ideas.
____	39.	I often shun new endeavors because of fear of mistakes or failure.
____	40.	I make and keep friends without exerting myself.
____	41.	I am often embarrassed by the actions of my family or friends.
____	42.	I readily admit my mistakes, shortcomings and defeats.
____	43.	I experience a strong need to defend my acts, opinions and beliefs.
____	44.	I take disagreement and refusal without feeling "put down," or rejected.
____	45.	I have an intense need for confirmation and agreement.
____	46.	I am eagerly open to new ideas and proposals.
____	47.	I customarily judge my self-worth by personal comparison with others.
____	48.	I am free to think any thoughts that come into my mind.
____	49.	I frequently boast about myself, my possessions and achievements.
____	50.	I accept my own authority and do as I, myself, see fit.

____ SELF-ESTEEM INDEX, i.e., your "SEI."   Date_____

TO OBTAIN YOUR SELF-ESTEEM INDEX: Add the individual scores of all *even* numbered statements (i.e. Nos. 2, 4, 6, 8, etc.). From this total subtract the sum of the individual scores of all *odd* numbered statements (i.e. Nos. 1, 3, 5, 7, etc.). This *net score* is your *current* Self-Esteem Index, or SEI. For example: If the sum of all the individual scores of the even numbered statements is 37 and the sum of all the individual scores of the odd numbered statements is 62, your SEI is 37—62 or a *minus* 25. The possible range of one's Self-Esteem Index is from —75 to +75. Experience shows that any score under +65 is handicapping; a score of 35 or less is seriously handicapping, and a Zero or a minus score indicates a truly crippling lack of Self-Esteem.

NOTE: The Barksdale Foundation, an internationally known pioneer in the field of building Self-Esteem, conducts periodic Self-Esteem workshops throughout the United States. The Foundation also produces a number of self-help booklets and cassette tapes on building Self-Esteem. Call or write The Barksdale Foundation, P.O. Box 187, Idyllwild, CA 92349 — Tel. (714) 659-3858.

Please do not read beyond this point until you have scored your results and double-checked them. Your score should range somewhere from a — 75 to a + 75.

In various studies that we have conducted, we discovered the mean (average) score for a typical college graduate is + 22. The mean (average) score for a typical MBA executive is a + 28.

If your score is somewhere between — 75 and + 22, you will have to work harder than someone whose score is between + 22 and + 75. But even if your score exceeds. + 22, you will still feel much better about yourself by developing an action-oriented growth program, outlined in previous chapters and below here.

Try, right here and now, to outline your own program to improve your self-esteem. Please remember that you will need to raise your own level of self-esteem. There is no magic pill anyone can give you. A tranquillizer will never do it. Nor is there any magic wand that some guru can wave over your head. Only you can raise your own level of self-esteem.

It's hard work, daily, but the results will pay off one thousand fold, at least. First, your pay off will be in the way you feel about yourself. You will be giving yourself more warm fuzzies instead of cold prickly feelings. Besides these more positive feelings you will have when alone, you will receive more warm feelings whenever you relate to the people you live with. Thirdly, it will pay off for you at work in all your human relations. You will doubtlessly earn more money and get bigger and better promotions.

Here is one way to initiate a concrete, explicit, definite program that you **must** become **committed** to. First, turn back and look at all the odd-numbered items on the Self-Esteem Questionnaire (#1, 3, 5, 7, 9, etc.). Item #9 is usually rated high

for many folks with low self-esteem: "I am much concerned about what others think and say of me." Now, if you have given yourself a score of 2 or 3, it may mean this can be a problem for you.

Pete, for example, should have learned an important idea when he was young, but he never realized it until he underwent therapy: here is the idea — "you can be completely happy and successful, even if there is one dumb S.O.B. out there who doesn't like you."

Most people can become very neurotic worrying because a boss passed their desk without handing out a raise. Or, a co-worker passed you by at the water cooler without applauding you. Or, if your next-door neighbor was in too big a hurry to talk. So, you have worried about it too much. O.K. Now's your chance to do something about it.

(1) **Select a goal**: For example, "From now on, I will **not** permit myself to be upset or worry because Don, my boss, snubs me at 9:00 a.m. (probably because he has bigger problems!)" You must pick a definite person, and time, and place where this usually occurs.

(2) **Record quantity and circumstances of behavior**: For example, is this person my boss more than anyone else? Or, my husband/wife, lover, parents? Where does this typically occur? You will want to determine mostly when, where and who.

(3) **Change setting events**: Try not to put yourself in those places and times recorded in step #2 above. But, if you have to be there, then try not to let these negative thoughts, doubts, worries and/or fears take hold. Resolve to put these cold pricklies out of your mind immediately.

(4) **Establish effective consequences**: As soon as you are able to be aware of harboring these negative thoughts, and you **do** put them out of your mind, you can then give yourself a positive rein-

forcer, a reward. A good reward, for example, might be money (25¢, 50¢, or $1.00) in a kitty for your next new item of clothes. Or, if you catch yourself dwelling on the negative thought too morosely for too long a time, you could consciously do something distasteful, e.g., go clean a closet.

(5) **Focus on contingencies:** Make a sign or note describing the desired behavior and its consequences and place it where you will see it, e.g., on your desk, mirror, or kitchen table, and write down: "I will not dwell on feelings and thoughts about what others (my boss, husband/wife, etc.) may incorrectly be thinking about me."

(6) **Achieve covert control:** Tell yourself the negative consequences of the harmful behavior to be avoided ("People who always look backwards over their shoulders can't see where they are going." "Monday morning quarterbacking every day doesn't help me do better next time."). Then, tell yourself the positive consequences of what you really want ("Greater self-confidence will help me earn more money." "Women like self-confident men more.") For some people, it is very helpful to focus on the ultimate consequences of being totally lacking in self-esteem. ("If I don't like me, neither will anyone else." "Lack of self-esteem leads to loneliness, serious depressions and suicide in the long run.")

After you have tried that growth program for some time, write yourself another one. Take item #5, for example: "I habitually condemn myself for my mistakes and shortcomings."

(1) **Select a goal:** "Stop self-blaming."

(2) **Record quantity and circumstances of behavior:** "Where, when and with whom do I usually catch myself blaming myself? Is it everytime I say the wrong thing to a customer, or client, or patient, or child? Is it everytime I ejaculate prematurely, or don't get erect at all?"

(3) **Change triggering events:** "I will not attempt to work with customers and the like when overly tired later than 8:00 p.m. after a twelve-hour day. I will go home early."

(4) **Establish effective consequences:** "If I leave work before 8:00 p.m. after completing a ten or twelve-hour day, I will reward myself by having a beer or cocktail. If I work late again, I will donate money to my favorite charity."

(5) **Focus on contingencies:** "I will call attention to whatever seems to cause me to blame myself and make up a sign or note about it. The note will say: 'What causes a person to be blaming him/herself? _____ event is not sufficient to be causing me to be blaming myslef.' "

(6) **Achieve covert control:** Keep telling yourself that "self-blamers are no fun to do things with." Or, from the positive viewpoint, "I must love myself first before anyone else can do so." Wanting love from others should be enough to motivate me to love rather than blame."

By now it is clear for you. You know how to make up your own action-oriented personal growth program about self-esteem. Our suggestion right here and now is for you to do exactly the same as we did for you in the two previous examples just given. Please do make up another program for yourself. Take one of the odd-numbered items in the Self-Esteem Questionnaire (#1, 3, 5, 7, etc.) that seems to be a problem for you and then construct a written program about it.

(1) **Select a goal:** _____

_____

_____

_____

_____

_____

_____

_____

(2) **Record quantity and circumstances of behavior:** _____

_____

_____

_____

_____

_____

_____

_____

(3) Change triggering events: _____

_____

_____

_____

_____

_____

_____

_____

(4) Establish effective consequences: _____

_____

_____

_____

_____

_____

_____

_____

(5) Focus on contingencies: _____

_____

_____

_____

_____

_____

_____

_____

(6) Achieve covert control: _____

_____

_____

_____

_____

_____

_____

_____

_____

Now that you have been able to measure your own level of self-esteem, and develop programs about it, you may be wondering how we define self-esteem.

The Barksdale Foundation publishes a large number of outstanding books and pamphlets on self-esteem. One of their best is *Building Self-esteem.* Here is how "Barks" describes it:

Our basic need and urge is to "feel good" about ourselves, mentally, physically, and **emotionally**. This need is responsible for our ultimate motivation. For regardless of our immediate objective, everything we do is to achieve a sense of total well-being. Unfortunately, few if indeed any of us, have sufficient awareness to know always what will make us feel really good about **ourselves**. Herein lies our crucial need for good self-esteem. For we cannot possibly feel good and at peace with ourselves without a significant sense of adequacy and self-worth."

All our goals, hopes, and aspirations are based on this fundamental need. The more limited and distorted our awareness, the more misleading and unfulfilling are our efforts."

Please look at it this way for a moment. People smoke, take drugs, drink booze, and seek love and sex in all its phases. Other people may compulsively have needs to win, or appear better than others. We have needs to help others We are motivated to avoid mistakes. Rich people are constantly motivated to hoard more wealth than they can ever use. Just continue to think for a moment about all the typical human motives and needs you experience in one day, especially our desperate urges to love and be loved, to be approved and accepted, and to be respected and looked up to. The ultimate motivation behind all these above mentioned urges or needs is the universal human need for "feeling good." That's the need we have to increase our self-esteem.

Self-Esteem: What Is It?

Barksdale defines self-esteem, on a subtle and often unconscious level as how one actually **feels** about oneself, based on your own individual sense of personal worth and importance. How much do you value yourself? The answer to that question is your level of self-esteem.

The main reason why it is hard to make or perform the self-esteem programs described earlier is because your present level of self-esteem is the result of your entire life's history. From our earlier childhood we have developed subtle and non-conscious feelings that have become fixed in our awareness. Thus, you have to learn to modify feelings that have become unconscious factors in your awareness.

High self-esteem principally comes from your accepting complete responsibility for your personal well being and taking complete charge of your own life. High self-esteem basically means you have to learn to accept yourself completely as an inherently valuable person, regardless of past mistakes, problems, and non-achievement of your goals.

Low self-esteem, on the other hand, can come about because of unrealistic comparisons and/or irrational beliefs about perfection. For example, you can be happy today even if you are not as rich as Rockefeller. you do not have to be comparing yourself with billionaires. You can be a desirable woman today, even if your bosom is not as perfect as a Playmate of the Month. You need not and must not be constantly comparing yourself to others You can be very successful today, even if you are not a president of a company. You need not be always making comparisons in every way. These ideas, then, can provide another basis for you to be making a different self-esteem growth program. Select a goal: "I will not make comparisons all day between myself and _____ or any other person(s).

Many people have developed unconscious irrational beliefs about their need for perfection. So, you may be haunted daily by feeling that you are not **really** worthy; that you **must** or **should** be better. And, of course, you may not really know why, at a conscious level, you must be perfect.

Low self-esteem typically results from many negative feelings and negative emotional reactions that have in turn led you to feel dependent, inferior, or badly about yourself. Your parents, for example, may have repeatedly made statements to you like "children should be seen and not heard." Or, they may have said: "Mom or Dad knows best." Similar comments could have led you to feel poorly as if you are too lacking to be treated with respect.

Just as beauty is in the eyes of the beholder, so does your self-esteem brighten or darken your perception of your surroundings. In the same way, your self-esteem influences all your emotional responses, moods or attitudes, which includes your feelings about your career success. If you have low self-esteem, you will tend to feel inferior, and thus have difficulty accepting a compliment. So you may suspect whoever gives you a compliment as a hypocrite or a manipulator, because you yourself **know** how bad you really, really are.

You can begin now to see the inklings of another growth program. Select a goal: " I will always accept a compliment and say 'Thank you'."

Your self-esteem is **not** an intellectual, cognitive idea but rather a **feeling** of a whole host of feelings deeply hidden. Most people do not even give conscious attention to their feelings of self-esteem. In fact, in one management development seminar, every executive wrote on the final, confidential evaluation form that they never once had previously given any attention to their level of self-esteem. Needless to say, many of them had very low levels of measured self-esteem.

What Self-Esteem Is Not

Sometimes you can understand concepts better by looking at their opposites. Self-esteem is **not** a kind of egotistical self-love. On the contrary, the most obvious, crucial symptoms of people with low self-esteem is their inordinate need to boast or puff themselves up. Deep down inside you, if you have good self-esteem, you know your own self-worth and can appreciate it. But most people do not. They really need to work at it.

If you have difficulties accomplishing what has just been described here, you may need more professional help from any therapist you can trust or become more open and honest with.

Jim was a good example of a young man who disliked himself. He actually used the word "loathed." He came for therapy, stating his goals were: (1) to get over his total lack of self-confidence, (2) reduce his extreme fear of women, (3) learn how to function in bed with a woman, and finally, (4) understand how to develop intimate relationships as a way to reduce severe loneliness.

For Jim, his self-esteem was not an enumeration of his abilities on an intellectual level. A person can have great talents and yet not esteem oneself. Skid rows (and all of recorded history) are filled with gifted people who have succumbed to drugs, alcohol, and suicides to escape themselves. One essentially has to learn how to accept oneself on an emotional level.

INCREASING YOUR SELF-ESTEEM BY AN INVENTORY OF STRENGTHS

Many people lack the greater level of Self-Esteem that they may want or deserve because they are not aware of all their strengths.

You **can** increase your self-esteem by many methods, some of which are described elsewhere in this volume. (You should take the Self-Esteem inventory first before you proceed with this exercise, so that you may appreciate both these exercises more fully.)

This exercise is an attempt to aid you in becoming increasingly more aware of **all** your good strengths, abilities, good qualities, and the like.

First, before reading further, please take as much time as you feel you need (at least 5-10 min.) and write down on the spaces below:

(1) The date _____ _____
                    Month   Day   Year

(2) As many strengths, abilities and good qualities as you can recall:

Now that you have written down as many good qualities, strengths and abilities as you can recall, please study all these following categories and ask yourself why you may have initially omitted these points. Then, continue to expand on these categories and lists until you have accomplished more for yourself. You will need to remind yourself of all these issues more frequently and more fully as one good method to increase your level of self-esteem.

Inventory of Strengths

Instructions:

To make an inventory of your strengths and resources, write each of the following headings, which indicate various areas of strength, on a separate sheet of paper and list under each heading your assets in that area. Anything that you have done well in the past which still interests you or which you still enjoy doing represents a strength and should be listed.

Sports and Outdoor Activities

Hobbies and Crafts

Expressive Arts

Health

Education, Training and Related Areas

Work, Vocation, Job or Position

Special Aptitudes or Resources

Strengths Through Family and Others

Intellectual Strengths

Aesthetic Strengths

Organizational Strengths

Imaginative and Creative Strengths

Relationship Strengths

Spiritual Strengths

Emotional Strengths

Other Strengths:

Humor

Liking to adventure or pioneer

Ability to stick your neck out

Perseverance or stick-to-it-iveness

Ability to manage finances

Knowledge of languages or cultures

Ability to speak in public

Making the best of your appearance

STEPS FOR SELF-HYPNOSIS

There are three stages toward completely believing you will be, can be and actually are as successful as the next person in business, love, sex, and any other endeavor.

Stage #1

First you have to set your goals. Carefully select goals that are **positive, achievable, important, measurable** and **explicit.**

Use verbs in future tense:

1. **I will** become as self-confident as possible.
2. **I will** become as successful as I possibly can become.
3. **I will** become as effective as others whom I admire.
4. **I will** raise my self-esteem (and self-confidence) to the highest levels.
5. **I will** become a more creative risk-taker in all aspects of my life.
6. **I will** become the person I want to be.
7. **I will** develop more rewarding interpersonal relationships.
8. **I will** learn how to relate better to members of the opposite sex.
9. **I will** take more creative risks today, now, with people I want to become closer to.
10. **I will** strive to live more in the **here** and **now.**
11. **I will** not worry about past mistakes or faults.
12. **I will** not project doubts and fears onto future situations.
13. **I will** make every effort right **here and now** to set some goals.
14. **I will** right **here and now** do what seems best for me and not all other possible people.
15. **I will** not fret over how others judge me.
16. **I will** strive harder to accept responsibility for my own life, decisions and feelings.
17. **I will** give myself credit for all my good qualities, traits and accomplishments.
18. **I will** not be constantly seeking others' approval.
19. **I will** ask for what I need from others.
20. **I will** not deny myself valid, legitimate wants and needs that do not hurt others.
21. **I will** right **here and now** do what's best for me.

Please fill in other relevant goals.

22. I will _____

_____

23. I will _____

_____

24. I will _____

_____

25. I will _____

_____

After you have fully memorized the above positive statements, you must affirm them every day. Perhaps you could paste them on your mirror, put them in your top desk drawer **on top,** or in your purse, briefcase, or wherever you will see them. Repeat daily until you feel better.

Stage #2

After you have completed the tasks described above, then begin all over, using the word **can** instead of **will**. "**I can** become as self-confident as possible."

Stage #3

After you have repeatedly accomplished what is outlined in Stages #1 and #2 above, go on and insert **am** instead of **can** (Stage #2). Then, you will finally be saying "**I am** the person I want to be."

These stages will obviously all take different times for each individual. One person may have to spend sixty days on Stage #1, thirty days for Stage #2, and only fifteen days on Stage #3.

The important thing is that you do it for yourself, daily, right here and now.

RISK-TAKING

Bill came to see a sex therapist at SECS — Sexual Enrichment Counseling Services (Chicago) — and when asked what he wanted, Bill replied: "I am horribly lonely. I have never had a date with a woman in my entire life. Loneliness is the worst way to live, and yet it is the only way I know how to live." With tears streaming down his cheeks, he quivered: "Can you please help me?"

The therapist asked what he had been doing about his problem. Bill opened a large envelope and pulled out a foot-thick computer print-out, listing names and phone numbers of eager women from a dating service. Then he stated: "I am afraid to call anyone of them."

Bill was definitely not a risk-taker. Yet, most people might admit they would like to learn to take bigger risks, to attain their goals and satisfy their needs. Risk-taking behavior is one way to "stretch yourself" to achieve personal growth goals. Risk-taking has been defined as behavior you would not usually engate in at this time in your life. You typically have not done a certain thing or engaged in a particular behavior you see as posing a possible threat to you. It may not appear to be a real threat to some other people, but you surely do fear it. Usually, what seems to be a risk for you is new behavior or skills you have not yet learned. In Bill's case, he had not yet learned to phone women and deal with the potential fear of rejection.

Risk-taking, then, involves a subjective sense of danger that one must learn to overcome.

Creative risk-taking can be learned. It can become an important way to increase your variety of possible responses available to you. By owning a larger repertoire of responses, you have more freedom of choice. You will not be restricted by fears or inhibitions.

Then you can have greater spontaneity of action. You can become more flexible in relating to all people.

The purpose of the following questionnaire is to see where you are presently. Are you a risk-taker or not? Do you want to learn more risk-taking behaviors to avoid loneliness, or to obtain more love and friendship and the like? You can see how you compare with others. You can also stimulate your thinking about risks. Hopefully, this can be discussed seriously with others who are important to you.

Please read the following statements and rank them as to how much personal subjective risk you feel might be involved. Use any reference group you prefer, such as the people you live with or work with. Put down your first answer as quickly as possible, because it will most likely be your most honest answer. Do not spend time thinking or rationalizing about it. Write the appropriate number from the scale next to each item.

Remember, whatever you score, you can always be a **winner**. Fortunately, now you can become an even **bigger winner** by doing something about it.

Risk-Taking Evaluation

Score:

        0 — Would be no risk for me
        1 — Would be a small risk for me
        2 — Would be a moderate risk for me
        3 — Would be a high risk for me

_____ 1. Disclosing certain events about my past to people.

_____ 2. Revealing definite negative feelings about myself to others.

_____ 3. Breaking out of a familiar routine.

_____ 4. Expressing anger toward anyone.

_____ 5. Getting involved with someone even though there may be rejection.

_____ 6. Showing affection toward someone.

_____ 7. Seeking help with my problems from others.

_____ 8. Starting something new (and feeling very happy about it!)!

_____ 9. Receiving affection from someone.

_____ 10. Asking, rather than just wondering, if my partner **really** loves me.

_____ 11. Asking for feedback from significant members of a group.

_____ 12. Making up my mind quickly about a major life decision and sticking to it.

_____ 13. Touching someone else physically.

_____ 14. Putting up bail-bond money for my best friend without question.

_____ 15. Having someone else touch me.

_____ 16. Becoming personal and close with another in a group.

_____ 17. Risking money for the sheer excitement of gambling.

_____ 18. Making statements that might anger someone else.

_____ 19. Expressing sexual attraction for someone.

_____ 20. Typically driving too fast, swerving into and out of traffic.

_____ 21. Walking out of a group while under stress.

_____ 22. Actively betting on events, from sporting activities to politics.

_____ 23. Admitting openly that someone has hurt my feelings.

_____ 24. Telling others to leave me alone or get off my back.

_____ 25. Becoming the center of attention in a group.

_____ 26. Giving another person or group member some negative feedback.

_____ 27. After receiving money in an unexpected legacy, risking half the capital.

_____ 28. Expressing my confusion or uncertainty in the presence of others.

_____ 29. Accepting a new job for less money initially, but with better prospects for outstanding performance.

_____ 30. Expressing and handling conflicts with another individual.

_____ 31. After winning the jackpot on a fruit machine ("one-armed bandit"), feeding the coins right back in.

_____ 32. Revealing my feelings about my physical traits in a group.

_____ 33. Sharing my feelings about another's physical traits in a group.

_____ 34. Showing indifference to other members of a group.

_____ 35. Making no provisions for retirement in the early stages of work life.

_____ 36. Telling another person that he/she has become important to me.

_____ 37. Revealing a fantasy about some member or a whole group.

_____ 38. Discussing sexual feelings in a group.

_____ 39. Admitting an error I made to a group.

_____ 40. Expressing anger or dissatisfaction with a group member.

_____ 41. Admitting I feel badly for letting others down.

_____ 42. Choosing a delightful lover, even if I know it could never last.

_____ 43. Admitting I was wrong about another group member.

_____ 44. Attempting mountaineering or stock car racing, if given a chance.

_____ 45. Risking my life for some person or cause very important to me.

_____ 46. Risking my reputation for some person or cause very important to me.

_____ 47. Risking my money for some person or cause very important to me.

_____ 48. Constantly risking new experiences in a consistent search for stimulation.

Please count up your scores now and add them up. **Do not** read further until you have a score. Remember, whatever score you have, you are a winner! But, you can improve your score and become a bigger winner, if you wish. You must put in some effort and energy to develop a growth program.

The important thing is what you really feel about yourself right here and now. If, for example, you are lonely and want more love and affection, you may begin to realize you must take risks to get what you want. All growth requires change. All change requires risk-taking.

Believe it or not, some individuals have obtained a score of zero on all forty-eight items. Obviously, they are big risk-takers. Others, at the opposite end of the extreme, obtained a score of 192, which means they are not risk-takers, but strong seekers of security. You should not worry about your score, but actively strive to do something about it.

Here are some possible analyses. Remember that there are definite degrees in any kind of measurement. Also, standard errors of measurement do exist. And finally, you could be some kind of exception.

Score: **Under Thirty**. This score is very low, suggesting you are definitely a risk-taker. You may even be jeopardizing your financial, social or domestic life. It is very likely you are involved in gambling so that your pocket suffers. Risk-taking may be fun for you, but those closest to you may judge you as reckless or foolish. Consider asking yourself why you may seem to be so fearless. You are surely not lonely for want of asking, but possibly because no one can accept it.

Score: **30 - 70**. You may not be the world's greatest risk-taker, but you surely do take chances. As a car driver, you may be too aggressive. You may be intrigued by gambling, but respond more to the thrill of it rather than hoping to win the lottery. Some people may see you as too unreliable, or erratic. Fortunately, you may have sufficient common sense so as not to seriously hurt yourself. You may not have as much action as those who score less than 40, but you probably are not lonely. you might strive harder to work on your common sense.

Score: **70 - 100**. You are not a high risk-taker, but you take chances from time to time. You may have a rather well-balanced approach in the eyes of the majority, but the high-risk-taker may see you as well below average. You may see yourself, however, as moderating your normal inclination to take a chance with a healthy degree of common sense. If your better judgment advises against taking a risk, you will surely turn down the temptation.

Score: **100 - 120**. You may be rather inhibited. you may be pretty lonely and missing out on a great amount of joy and fun. You may even be harming your career by not taking risks, even though it may seem secure on the surface. Others may reject you because you cannot make commitments to them. Then, you may be lonlier because they may want a commitment but you cannot take enough risks. You need a growth program to take more chances, somewhere, somehow, anytime.

Score: **120-144**. If you have answered honestly and scored the questionnaire correctly, you are too rigid, too inflexible, and too passive. You are not any kind of a risk-taker. Others may judge you as being unable to take any chances ever. You have allowed yourself to become too handicapped. You definitely need to seek some professional help.

BECOMING MORE SUCCESSFUL

Almost every person wants greater success, regardless of how you define it. For you, success may mean becoming president of an organization or company. Success for your friend may mean becoming rich. Another person may define success as accomplishing other goals.

Procedure: (1) Read the following statements. (2) Rank them in terms of their value or meaning to you. (3) Discuss the more meaningful issues with a friend or colleague. (4) Try to integrate them into your life in the most valuable manner. For one person, it would mean memorizing them. For another, using them in a self-hypnosis fashion. Develop your own creative method that is meaningful to you.

Action Idea 1
Only by developing a creative, inquisitive mind and a passionate love of learning and growth, can you ever expect to succeed.

Action Idea 2
You may not be able to begin with your ideal goal, but you can begin today, *here and now*, by working toward it. Everything you learn and do *today* can be applied tomorrow.

Action Idea 3
Discover *all* of your great potential, by using more of your talents and abilities today.

Action Idea 4
Become more of a self-starter. Take more initiative. Don't wait for someone else to make the suggestions first. *You can.*

Action Idea 5
Keep an on-going list of things you want to accomplish. Get a little notebook for your purse or pocket and entitle it: *Action-Plans*.

Action Idea 6
Big thinkers are specialists in developing optimistic, positive images in their own minds and in the minds of others. Use words and phrases that create big, positive mental images.

Action Idea 7
Look at things not as they are, but as they can become. Your visualization can add value to anything. Big thinkers always project images of what can be done in the future. Don't be stuck with any bad aspects of the past or present.

Action Idea 8
Develop habits of *stretching*...and producing more and really making yourself do a little more this week than last week. Develop images of how much more effective you can become five or ten years from now. Write id down. Begin here and now.

Action Idea 9
Continuously set challenges for yourself. keep working on your goals until you reach them.

Action Idea 10
Don't define it as a problem, but rather as a challenge or opportunity to help you grow.

Action Idea 11
Don't rest on your laurels, or mesmerize yourself that you have it made. Continue learning to stay abreast of your field.

Action Idea 12
Work is love made visible.   Kahlil Gibran

Action Idea 13

Work is the real essence, concentrated energy.
Walter Bagehot

Action Idea 14

Work is a high human function, the most dignified thing in the life of a man.

David Ben-Gurion

Action Idea 15

Work is a remedy against all ills.
Charles Baudelaire

Action Idea 16

Work is the grand cure for all the maladies and miseries that ever beset mankind.

Thomas Carlyle

Action Idea 17

Work is the finest expression of the human spirit.
Walter Courtenay

Action Idea 18

Work is the significance of the individual.
Jean Paul Sartre

Action Idea 19

Be more conscious of the quality rather than quantity. Work smart.

Action Idea 20

Find the movers and shakers who are making things happen. Try to get hired or transferred into their departments, so you can be in a better position to move ahead.

Action Idea 21

Be resourceful and creative in whatever you do, especially by associating yourself with the right mentors in your organization.

Action Idea 22

You can become as big a winner as you want to be. Losers merely talk themselves into becoming losers.

Action Idea 23

After you discover what you're good at and what you care about, *decide*. Then give good quality work or service. You won't have any competition.

Action Idea 24

Persistence and endurance will always pay off, even in the face of a temporary discouragement. You can find or develop greater markets.

Action Idea 25

People can do what they want, if they will only *decide* and *start*. That start could even be a carefully chosen volunteer effort.

Action Idea 26

Be as enthusiastic as you can possibly be. No one wants to hire or work with a deadbeat.

Action Idea 27

Set a goal to accomplish at least one worthwhile thing a day.

Action Idea 28

Trial and error doesn't work. Develop a plan and set goals — both long and short range.

Action Idea 29

Forget about age! Do what you want or need to do, regardless of how old you will be when you achieve it. The important thing is to achieve it.

Action Idea 30

Friends can give you open and honest feedback about your potential. Talk to them about your hopes and dreams, but don't let a pessimist slow you down.

Action Idea 31

You can learn from people everywhere, in any position. Jot down ideas and names in your notebook for future reference.

Action Idea 32

Give yourself credit for *all* your talents and traits. Appreciate them. Then figure out how to use them better.

Action Idea 33

Everyone has at least one hidden talent or unused ability. Maybe you have more. Try today to discover and use.

Action Idea 34

Try harder to please your bosses. If you can't find any redeeming qualities in them, get out fast.

Action Idea 35

If you haven't been promoted in the past three years, ask yourself or your boss *why?* Then do something about it.

Action Idea 36

Accomplish as much as you can to become better and better. Most people only know about or use a minor fraction of all their talents and abilities.

Action Idea 37

Never underestimate your chances after you get your first "foot-in-the-door" opportunity. Keep on looking up at those who can promote or transfer you into a more rewarding position.

Action Idea 38

Your best incentive could be a picture of yourself as the higher level executive, manager, or officer you want to become. Keep on imagining yourself at the top!

Action Idea 39

Do anything you can and try to make that what really counts.

Action Idea 40

Small kids demand of Mommy: "I want it now." Mature adults make long-range plans.

Action Idea 41

A competitive field merely means you need a more positive approach — the same optimistic, "can-do" attitude you should have anyway, all the time.

Action Idea 42

There is no laundry list of the wisest aphorisms — only the positive, unlimited potential inside you. Actualize it.

Action Idea 43

Priorities are what really matter. Secondary things can always be taken care of later. Convince yourself you're a bigger winner and put first things first.

Action Idea 44

Think about the most important things you must do today. Don't worry about the future.

Action Idea 45

The past is gone. The future is imaginary. *The only thing* you have is *here* and *now*. Do that well and your future will be better.

Action Idea 46

Don't believe in good luck. Trust rather in *yourself*, good planning and hard work.

Action Idea 47

Keep looking creatively in new directions. There will always be a better idea for you to use, if you can only find or develop it.

Action Idea 48

One great way to get ahead is to convince people you have the personality and willingness to do the job. This works in every career at any level.

Action Idea 49

Bosses can't read your mind. Speak up for what you need to do your job and what you want for your future. Assert yourself tactfully, not aggressively.

Action Idea 50

Remind yourself daily: you can succeed. You can find the right career. You can advance as high as you want to go.

Action Idea 51

Value your time and manage it well. Almost everyone can develop ways to invest time more profitably.

Action Idea 52

Your self-image is one of your most priceless possessions. You can improve yours by remembering that everything you do, say, or write contributes to it.

Action 53

Your self-esteem can be improved. You can have a more valid basis for it. Keep telling yourself every day, you can feel better about yourself. You can become the person you want to be.

Action Idea 54

Life is the survival of the fittest. So is the world of work. You can become as fit as you want to be.

Action Idea 55

Life is a succession of choices. Don't say "you'd love to have time to do that." Make time.

Action Idea 56

Just as the fog creeps in on little cats' feet, so also your success is a series of little steps. Create a picture of the success you want, and set goals to work at it, step by step.

SELF-MANAGEMENT PROJECTS: GOAL-SETTING FOR PERSONAL GROWTH AND DEVELOPMENT TOWARD SELF-ACTUALIZATION

"And in keeping yourself with labour you are in truth loving life, And to love life through labour is to be intimate with life's inmost secret."

From Gibran's — *The Prophet*

Introduction

Since almost everyone will admit at one time or another to some personal goals, the chief challenge is essentially how to achieve them (e.g., lose weight, stop smoking, get promoted, earn more cash, and the like).

William and Long have spelled it out most clearly in their book, *Toward a Self-Managed Life Style* (Boston, Houghton-Mifflin, 1975). Our ultimate hope is that you will develop a self-management outlook on life. Instead of giving in to self-pity, the self-manager seeks out factors contributing to a problem and then changes those factors. Not many people manage their lives this way. But, hopefully, you may be willing to take the less travelled road this time.

Example No. 1

Consider this example:

(1) **Select a goal**: To cut down frequency of snacking.
(2) **Record quantity and circumstances of behavior.** Keep a daily record of everything eaten, conditions, calories, and weight.
(3) **Change setting events.** Consume snacks only at kitchen table. Remove all cookies, candies and the like from house. Store only foods requiring preparation.
(4) **Establish effective consequences.** Keep a point system. Earn points for good record-keeping, eating snacks at kitchen table, and not exceeding a specific level of snacking behavior. Cash in a definite number of points for a special weekend privilege. (No, not more wining and dining.) Giving yourself appropriate rewards and/or punishments is the key. Rewards are positive reinforcers. Punishments are aversive consequences.
(5) **Focus on contingencies.** Attach notes describing the desired behavior and its consequences where food is kept.
(6) **Achieve covert control.** Verbalize the negative consequences of the undesired behavior and then the positive consequences of the desired response, usually of an immediate nature. For some, perhaps, focusing on the ultimate consequences of obesity is essential to weight control. By pairing thoughts of those consequences with pro-eating thoughts, you will develop an aversion to certain types of eating. For some weight-watchers, humiliation was more effective than data on heart disease, high-blood pressure or diabetes. One sad soul confessed he had gotten so overweight he could hardly engage in sexual activity! That would doubtlessly qualify as an ultimate aversive consequence!

Example No. 2

(1) **Set a goal.** Stop Smoking. Quit, cold turkey, or reduce frequency of cigarettes smoked by ½/day; or hold number constant, but reduce amount smoked per cigarette.
(2) **Record circumstances and quantity of behavior.** Record number smoked per day or record number smoked in various situations.

236

Will you record events that precede and follow smoking? Will you record the amount smoked per cigarette?

(3) **Change setting events.** Identify one or two places where you smoke. Can you try to arrange circumstances that would prevent reflexive smoking?

(4) **Arrange consequences.** Will you use an aversive strategy, such as shock or stimulus satiation? (Satiation is a strategy of repeatedly indulging in a reinforcing activity until that activity is no longer reinforcing. In doing this strategy, however, you *must* be sure satiation is really reached, or else the behavior may become even *more* resistant to change.) Or, will you try to strengthen *non*-smoking behavior through reinforcement? Will you give all the contingencies yourself or will you formulate a mutual contract with someone else who has a smoking problem?

(5) **Focus on consequences.** Will you leave written "threats" in places where you are most inclined to smoke?

(6) **Apply covert control.** Will you use covert sensitization to attach an aversive connotation to smoking? (You would emit a thought that is incompatible with the desire to smoke. For example, "smoking costs too much," "smoking makes me stink" "my lover dislikes bad smoking breath," "smoking will increase chances of cancer" and the like.) *Coverant* is a contraction for covert operant. *Operant* is a term in behavioral psychology referring to behavior that has an effect on the environment (e.g., causing good things to happen). The coverant pair, then, is designed to become a new link in the stimulus-response chain, a link that hopefully will prevent the target behavior from occurring.

Example No. 3

Here is another example of a self-management project. How can you get an old love off your mind? How can you stop being so depressed?

(1) **Select your goal.** (Remember, it must be (a) important, (b) measurable, (c) external, (d) attainable and (e) positive. In this instance, your goal may be two-pronged. You may want to cut down the amount of time you worry over the lost romance (or lost job, or lost whatever is bugging you). And, at the same time, you may want to increase your contacts with members of the opposite sex (or employers, or whatever).

(2) **Record quantity and circumstances of behavior.** You might try recording the names of the people and places that resurrect the undesirable memories.

(3) **Change setting events.** Use the information gained by recording (in number 2 above) to change or avoid setting events that cause your brooding, depression, worry or whatever. Identify other setting events that will lead to added exposure to fun-seekers of the opposite sex.

(4) **Establish effective consequences.** You know your own reinforcement priorities, e.g., watch TV, go to a movie, enjoy an extra cocktail or whatever.

(5) **Focus on contingencies.** What would make you more consciously and consistently aware of the payoff for pursuing new relationships?

(6) **Achieve covert control.** Work on thought-stopping for old memories and covert reinforcement for imagining better, more creative methods of interaction.

PART VII

CONTRACTS FOR INTIMACY

We human beings want to be more than we are. Are you becoming the person you have always wanted to be?

For most of us caught up in daily life — in the midst of all our activities and thoughts involving work and family, bills and money matters, friends and social life, education, public affairs, a changing panorama of problems, — still there is a vague awareness of an inner person urging to be recognized, realized, and fulfilled. There are potentials to be activated. There are inner conflicts to be resolved. There are new and enriching dimensions to be added to our mental, our emotional and our physical lives. If only we could find a way to unlock them.

It is curious, isn't it, that while all of us have these potentials that lead to rich and satisfying lives, few of us develop them as much as we'd like. Many reasons account for this. Growth involves change. And changing from the old to the new may often be a complex process requiring real work. And once we are willing to make the needed effort, we need reliable knowledge and techniques to guide our progress. Without these, many of us hesitate, unsure of how to proceed.

Consider drawing up your own contract (agreement) for intimacy. It can be an extremely valuable technique whether you are marrying, married, cohabiting, or involved in any relationship you want to be fairly permanent. Even managing! Yes, managing. Many supervisors want employees to communicate better. In business, for example, most communication is from the top down, whereas greater openness and honesty from the bottom up would be more rewarding in many ways.

For the moment, consider what kind of marriage or intimacy contract you would like to have. (Later, you can generalize and adapt to your business, work or professional relationships.) Only when marrying do people sign a contract in which words are unwritten, boundaries unspecified, terms unclear and penalties not clarified.

Reasons and causes for termination are often unilateral, unpredictable, unexamined and unexplained. Because specific performance criteria do not seem to exist, are not set up and examined, a breach of contract (or expectations) is not defined. Even acts of God, like serious accidents or disabling illnesses, cannot be considered excuses for non-performance. Restitution is not clear, but divorce lawyers can require "exposure" of the personal "faults" of the intimate partner, forcing a partner to become an adversary in a public court of law. The transition from marital to martial is not a Martian leap. It can be quite a surprise, shock, catastrophe!

Each partner acts as if the other can read minds; as if the other magically knew all of his or her unrevealed assumptions, expectations, and hidden ground rules. Meanwhile, no methods for the resolution of possible conflicts are ever spelled out or agreed upon. As both partners progress through the passages of life in the development of their relationship, each weathers different storms from within and without. Whatever unspoken rules were made in the past can now be changed without notice or even discussion. The only major expectation agreed upon seems to be that of all the popular songs like "love conquers all," "love means forever," "love means never having to say you're sorry."

Divorce statistics are increasing. The state's interest in upholding legal marriage is declining. Laws change. The personal needs of two unique individuals naturally should become more important than legal contracts binding couples as abstract entities. Thus, marriage is evolving more into a "social understanding" cemented by the fragile bond of emotional satisfactions. Many simply choose to live together without heavy legal hassles.

People are expecting more than ever from relationships and marriages, yet relationship-contracts are increasingly unclear, unspoken and unmade.

Change is more inevitable than even death and taxes; because taxes are annual, death occurs once, but change is a daily dynamic. One hint is the increasing omission of the promise to "obey" from marriage ceremonies. As older social forms pass, **people need to highlight clearly what they expect from one another**. People now seek both change and permanence, freedom **and** emotional security, flexibility **and** structure.

Intimacy Contract: The following sample is one possible model agreement intended as an outline stimulus for mutual investigation and ultimate negotiation, so that both parties can be bigger winners, with less chances of having two losers. (Many divorced people insist they were both losers turned into adversaries unnecessarily by the two attorneys who were the only big winners.)

Many provisions discussed here are to help clarify and are not legally enforceable. Legal agreements can be made about exchanging money, property and gifts, but you must consult your local attorney. (#1) see references.

Some may argue these suggestions are too idealistic. You must decide what is more practical: an explicitly defined statement of what you want and need or an "unclear assumption" about what you think your partner "may expect" today and tomorrow.

Romanticists may be turned off by plain words that look too legal or are called "too legalistic" by an avoider seeking a cop-out. If a possible partner is too defensive about involving oneself in this valuable exercise, ask yourselves what that avoidance behavior really means. Here is what psychologists have found. Avoidance may mean lack of true commitment. Couples married for ten years, rating their marriages above average in happiness, described their felt experiences of intimacy as including a sense of: acceptance, respect and admiration, understanding, friendship and companionship, ease in communication, sharing, caring and concern, desiring to please, striving for mutual goals, interdependence, trust, pride,

belonging together, similarity of thought, feeling and action, indebtedness, gladness and peace, expansion, reciprocity, and a feeling that sexual experiences expressed and aided their total relationship. These experiences and feelings can be most aided by explicity-making agreements and by resolving conflicts through negotiated compromises.

Procedure: Design your own contract. Use some or all the ideas listed below. Modify what you might like to improve. Add your own better ideas. Discuss details with relatives, friends and work associates who know you best. Then, negotiate with your partner and spell out **all** your expectations, needs and deepest hidden desires. Be as open and honest as you possibly can. Then, take a bigger risk and open up more.

(1) Contractors use three copies of this agreement; one each for a workbook and a final draft for the agreement.

(2) Initially, each partner works alone to avoid being influenced by the other's apparent reservations or feelings, noting ideas on left-hand column.

(3) Together, take each idea, paragraph, or section separately, one at a time, discussing priorities.

(4) Separate again, perhaps even for days, to meditate on the feelings that emerged, considering possible, subtle conflicts, and what you are willing to give to get, in return.

(5) Meet together to discuss possible differences and negotiations. (It may be necessary to have to repeat step 4 more than once.) In this step, you must feel more open, experience more honesty, hopefully leading to more trust. If you do not take some risks to express deeper, hidden feelings, you may be making a mistake.

(6) After negotiating each actual issue, record all agreements on the final copy to be signed, witnessed, notarized and specially kept for safekeeping. This will be your own unique contract/agreement.

INTIMACY CONTRACT

FOR

COHABITING OR MARRIED ADULTS

AN EXPLICIT AGREEMENT

MADE THIS   **DAY OF**   19

BETWEEN

hereinafter known as "FIRST PARTNER"

and

hereinafter known as "PRIME PARTNER"

(which numbers do not infer priority)

INTIMACY CONTRACT

Notes Column   WHEREAS, we desire to continue loving one another, making our relationship stronger through openness and honesty;

WHEREAS, we state we are of legal age, free, independent individuals with no obligations prohibiting this agreement;

WHEREAS, we seek a primary relationship that is responsible, loving and nurturing while simultaneously desiring autonomy as unique individuals requiring personal time, space and freedom;

WHEREAS, we recognize we both influence one another in various ways as to who can do what, where, when, how much and to whom; and that we are often unaware of this subtle, shaping behavior;

WHEREAS, we understand that each of us has a unique history and experiential viewpoint from which disagreements are ineluctable, and these could cause either blaming and bad feelings or mutual acceptance and positive growth;

WHEREAS, we agree that when expectations, motives, goals and behavior are not clearly stated and explicit, one partner can make faulty projections and assumptions leading to negative feelings, unfulfilled expectations and needs that jeopardize love and trust;

WHEREAS, we know that change is inevitable in our society and our lives, and that agreements made at one time may not be appropriate for a later time;

WHEREAS, we are convinced an increasingly satisfying relationship only results from a mutual investment of awareness, openness and responsiveness;

WHEREAS,

THEREFORE, We hereby agree to make our expectations clear and not to impose on one another terms that are not outlined herein; and we agree to continue modifying and updating our negotiations as new needs and expectations emerge.

Negotiations for Daily Living Together

(1) We will invest every effort in our principal relationship, devoting time and energy to improve our love and esteem, through sharing and companionship.

(2) We will each be responsible for our own needs, attitudes and feelings, realizing that we may influence one another but can only be responsible for our own individual happiness.

(3) We **will** air any ill-feelings and grievances as soon as we recognize problems rather than submerge them; and quickly give them open and complete consideration.

(4) Without encouraging unhealthy dependency, we will offer support, nurturance and love in all its phases when our partner needs and asks for it.

(5) We will not expect the other to guess our needs and feelings, but will request what we want; and we will have no cause for resentment, if we do not ask.

(6) We will actively resist any parental or in-laws' interferences in our primary relationship in any way; and support our partner's needs and feelings.

(7) We will foster the good reputation of our partner with all others; and hold private, personal matters as confidential information.

(8? Although some disagreements may seem not easily resolvable, we will accept them as growth opportunities, avoid judgmental criticism, strive to resolve these conflicts, and enlist a third-party negotiator if necessary.

(9? We will avoid embarrassing one another in public by any inconsiderate behavior; neither alcohol nor anger will be an excuse.

(10) We will expect our relationship **not** to mean possession nor any licenses over the other; but rather an opportunity to express our feelings and valid needs.

(11) Remembering that responding in kind only fosters more conflict, we will strive to avoid revenge.

(12) An important investment/sacrifice/favor can be expected to be returned (e.g., putting a partner through school). In return for _____

_____, then I will _____

_____

(13) We will allow each other privacy (space and time alone), without requiring control or accountability.

(14) We will take responsibility that no unplanned nor unwanted pregnancies occur and agree with one another about contraceptive measures.

(15) If we have children, we will maintain our primary relationship, despite demands of children.

(16) We will invest every effort in the best psychological methods to develop the children; letting each one accept his/her own responsibility for relationships with them nonexclusively.

(17) We will hold one another free from debts owed a third party, maintaining separately our own personal properties and financial assets, especially all those gained before initiating this partnership.

(18) As a partnership, we will keep one another informed of financial matters, and conceal no income.

(19) We especially agree not to spend more than $_____ without consulting one another.

(20) Without accounting to one another, charge accounts will not exceed $_____/mo; each may spend $_____/mo; and if each partner has income, common bills will be apportioned equitably: first partner paying

_____

prime partner paying _____

(21) Our mutual, total indebtedness will be negotiated regularly.

(22) Considering our present relationship, each partner is willing to make these adjustments:

first partner will _____

_____

_____

_____

_____

prime partner will_____

_____

_____

_____

_____

(23) These arrangements will be agreed to in principle now and modified as needs occur:

	First Partner	Prime Partner
A. Days Off	_____	_____
B. Evenings Out	_____	_____
C. Children-Sitting	_____	_____
D. Children-Sitting Provided For:	_____	_____
E. Vacation Time	_____	_____
F. Privacy Time	_____	_____
G. Other	_____	_____
	_____	_____

(24) Friendship with either sex will be arranged so as not to jeopardize the partner, the relationship, the marriage, or one's reputation. We will not select intimate friends from the partner's special confidantes. And if any friendship seems to threaten our primary relationship, we will face the issue as soon as it occurs.

(25) If only one partner is employed outside the home and/or provides a disproportionate share of services not covered in article #20 above, the _____ partner agrees to pay the _____ partner $ _____/mo; and if required, fulfill all governmental tax or other benefits such as social security; **or** in lieu of, _____

_____

_____ then _____

_____

(26) Additional Agreements:

_____

_____

_____

_____

_____

_____

Agreements for Separation/Divorce

(1) If we begin or seem to grow apart, we will immediately endeavor to understand and discuss the process and allow time for appraisal/curing/reconciliation.

(2) We will never use intimidations, manipulations or threats of divorce to resolve conflicts.

(3) We will never separate nor take legal actions until we have confronted the partner and enlisted a neutral third-party negotiator.

(4) If one partner still insists then on separation, we will fully participate in at least 10 or _____ counseling sessions with a professional psychologist of our choice. No unilateral decisions will be made until after the counseling period.

(5) If the above methods fail, we will agree to _____ months trial separation period before legally ending the partnership. Intentions will be put in writing and separate maintenance provided.

During this period, if a partner needs to initiate certain business ventures, these will not be hindered nor used to hold the other partner liable.

(6) During reconciliation efforts or after separation/divorce, we will not injure one another's reputation, nor financial ventures.

(7) We will make every effort to be qualified to child-custody, have equitable rights to custody; both can provide a nurturing home and developmental discipline.

(8) The career development and earnings potential of each partner is to be respected. Thus, for example, if the wife has been involved in full-time homemaking, the separation or divorce arrangements will be equitably negotiated to cover her investment, but not to such an extent as to force a partner to sell a home, business or investments and the like at a loss.

(9) If the relationship/marriage ends, each party will endeavor not to use the children as a manipulative tool; nor engender harmful feelings in them toward one another.

(10) The guardian-parent will provide for convenient, regular vistis by the other, without jeopardizing the other parent's love and discipline. If geographical closeness is not possible, we will agree to an equitable _____ weeks/ months Summer vacation each year.

(11) Cost figures agreed upon for maintenance and the like will be mutually adjusted regularly as each partner's financial picture (audited) (?) changes and as inflation occurs, etc.

(12) Each partner agrees to maintain a $_____ life insurance program that is owned by the other partner for tax purposes.

(13) Additional provisions:

WE AFFIRM THIS AGREEMENT

INCLUDES ALL PROVISIONS BETWEEN BOTH PARTIES: WILL BE GOVERNED BY THE LAWS OF THE STATE OF _____ ; WILL CONTINUE IN EFFECT UNTIL_____ ; OR CAN BE CANCELLED BY EITHER PARTY WITH A MINIMUM OF _____ DAYS NOTICE; AND MAY BE ADJUSTED BY WRITTEN AGREEMENT. WE WILL SET ASIDE RENEGOTIATION TIMES AT LEAST _____

WE ESPECIALLY AGREE DISABLING ACCIDENTS OR ILLNESSES CANNOT BE CAUSE FOR RENEGOTIATION.

_____   _____
First Partner   **Prime Partner**

Dated _____

Notarized _____

Witnesses _____

_____

Additional Issues for Possible Inclusion

(1) Career Development Priorities;
   decisions re: moving, five-year plans, etc.

(2) Personal Growth Commitments;
   re: social, religious, economic and all value systems.

(3) New ventures: consents and conditions.

(4) Special provisions for education, job layoffs, disabilities.

(5) Methods of Conflict Resolution:
   ground-rules; compromises; penalities; binding arbitration alternatives and the like.

(6) Division of labor: household, part-time, etc.

(7) Provisions for child-care;
   parents or in-laws' illnesses; former spouses, debts, medical, etc.

(8) Financial: savings; debts;
   responsibilities for recordkeeping.

(9) Personal: agreements re: gambling, drinking, wide range of all behaviors.

(10) Inheritance/gifts received.

(11) Insurance and/or medical details:
   for whom, by whom and how much.

(12) **Wills and Inheritance Rights** during and after contract periods; provision for children of this or former relationships.

(13) Responsibilities for debts of parents, relatives and the like.

(14) Sabbaticals: trading time for special projects, personal growth, etc.

(15) **Termination**: grounds for, no-fault; periodic renewal, or indefinite time, etc.

References

Weitzman, L.J., C. Dixon, et al: "Contracts for Intimate Relationships: A Study of Contracts Before, Within and in Lieu of Legal Marriage." *Alternative Lifestyles*, 1978, 1: 303-379. (Sage Publications, Inc. Beverly Hills, CA 90212).

INTIMACY QUOTIENT

Objectives

— To clarify and understand attitudes, feelings, needs and desires regarding a specific person or partner of the opposite or same sex.

— To rank order fifteen feelings, attitudes, needs and desires listed here in the Intimacy Quotient that are the clearest sign(s) of your love.

— To use these ideas and conclusions to expand your concept of Intimacy.

Theory or Rationale:

The infinite cannot be measured. Love or intimacy are such meaningful and important issues/concepts that they are hypothesized to be beyond measures. Perhaps you have seen a small child telling a parent that her love is "this much," as she holds her arms as wide as possible.

Method:

Below is a list of statements regarding love/intimacy. First read all items carefully.

Respond on the basis of your own feelings without discussing with any other person(s). Write in the space provided on the left, your own rating:

$$0 = \text{Absent}$$
$$1 = \text{Weak}$$
$$2 = \text{Strong}$$

Rate only your own feelings, needs, values and the like, regarding one person. If you are not 'madly in love' at this time, try to imagine your ideal. For example, if your willingness to accept responsibility for the other person's behavior is absent, write '0' — if weak, write '1' — if strong, write '2'.

Remember, each item should reflect **only** your own feeling. Perhaps you can develop some additional items.

After rating them, you may find it helpful to discuss your results with others to enhance your own learning.

_____ 1. Willingness to accept responsiblity for the other person's behavior.

_____ 2. Experiencing feelings of loyalty.

_____ 3. Feeling as if we were really one.

_____ 4. Loneliness when apart.

_____ 5. Desire to be together always and forever.

_____ 6. Assisting my partner financially, if needed.

_____ 7. Need for my partner as a source for my security.

_____ 8. Putting my partner's needs ahead of mine.

_____ 9. Feeling of intellectual unity with my partner.

_____ 10. Need to share religious values.

_____ 11. Giving security to my partner.

_____ 12. Preferring to experience things together.

_____ 13. Overall emotional dependence on partner.

_____ 14. Agreeing on financial decisions.

_____ 15. Desire to do most things together.

_____ 16. Making sacrifices willingly.

_____ 17. Accepting financial limits and expecting what is possible.

_____ 18. Sharing my partner's sadness.

_____ 19. Aiding my partner's self-actualization.

_____ 20. Valuing my partner's opinions.

_____ 21. Accepting my partner's views on family size.

_____ 22. Investing efforts in relationship's growth.

_____ 23. Sharing partner's interests.

_____ 24. Giving as unselfishly as possible.

_____ 25. Aiding in sickness.

_____ 26. Seeking joy in partner's successes and happiness.

_____ 27. Agreement about division of labor.

_____ 28. Enjoying just being with one another.

_____ 29. Taking pride in your partner.

_____ 30. Offering moral support.

_____ 31. Accepting partner's concept of child rearing.

_____ 32. Helping solve partner's problems.

_____ 33. Doing things for the partner; friends and relatives of the partner.

_____ 34. Avoiding things that could hurt the relationship.

_____ 35. Taking risks for the partner.

_____ 36. Being patient when problems arise.

_____ 37. Enjoying just talking with partner.

_____ 38. Forgiving faults and weaknesses.

_____ 39. Accepting faults and weaknesses.

_____ 40. Boosting partner's ego.

_____ 41. Reinforcing partner's weaknesses.

_____ 42. Trusting in any event.

_____ 43. Willingness to resolve conflicts constructively.

251

_____ 44. Eagerness to share responsibilities.

_____ 45. Willingness to plan together.

_____ 46. Being as open as possible.

_____ 47. Accepting my partner's goals.

_____ 48. Sharing my daily experiences.

_____ 49. Respecting my partner's behavior.

_____ 50. A need to be desired by partner.

_____ 51. Assisting "my other" to feel important.

Score: 0 = No Love

      102 = Strongest Love

In a group setting, one member of the group or dyad could detail a ranking on the blackboard from the least of the fifteen feelings, attitudes needs and desires chosen to the strongest, e.g. from the need to share religious values on the bottom line to the highest point, unselfish giving, as shown in the diagram below.

1. unselfish giving
2. . . . .
3. . . . .
et cetera
15. need to share religious feelings

EXPERIENCES IN EMOTIONAL INTIMACY

Every human being desperately needs, wants and seeks emotional intimacy daily. A good resource book is: *The Stranger In Your Bed: A Guide to Emotional Intimacy* (Dean C. Dauw, Ph.D., Chicago: Nelson-Hall Publishers, 1979). Until you read this book, however consider these exercises.

Procedure

(A) First, study the ten steps (listed below) toward Emotional Intimacy. (B) Underline those areas that may be important issues, or possible stumbling blocks at this time in your life. (C) Then discuss each step and issue with a partner. Use this experience here and now as a kind of preparatory role play for a later time, when you will discuss it with someone more important to you. (D) After your initial discussion here in dyads or triads, a general summary will follow.

Steps Toward Emotional Intimacy

1. Reveal as much as you can about yourselves as you really are, such as your feelings, values, needs, and the like. Do not succumb to inner or outer pressures to meet someone else's expectations.
2. Receive your partner's statements and give your own comments as your **own feelings**, rather than as judgments or demands.
3. Experience whatever differences or conflicts that arise as opportunities for growth and development.
4. As you pass through all these stages, do not misinterpret another's feelings as being any possible rejection.
5. During these stages or steps, remain aware and committed so that each of you feels openly heard, understood, and hopefully, accepted, at least to some minimal degree.
6. Become increasingly more aware of your own limitations and boundaries so that you can be responsible for your **own needs**. Then, you will feel less need to blame your partner.
7. Respect whatever you can, and as much as you can, about your partner's apparent weaknesses or limitations.
8. Make a clearer committment; even if you unintentionally irritate or offend or disappoint one another, you do not deliberately intend or desire to hurt your partner.
9. Do not ever accept manipulation or punishment as a possible alternative, no matter how tempting it may seem.
10. Develop a mutual feeling or committment to give everything you can to your partner whenever possible without at the same time hurting yourself.

SELF DISCLOSURES FOR INTIMACY

Learning about intimacy is a challenging task, because we were never taught how to do it, because few people know how to teach it, and perhaps, because it is so ineffable.

Sidney Jourard's *The Transparent Self* (New York: D. Van Nostrand Co., 1971, p. 60) entire volume is worthwhile.

The person who reads or listens to the hitherto concealed experience of another is enriched by it. To learn of another's experiencing is to broaden and deepen the dimensions of one's own experience. Authentic writing is psychedelic for the reader — it turns him on.. In ways that we do not yet fully understand, at least in a scientific sense, the disclosed experience of the other person enables us to see things, feel things, imagine things, hope for things that we could never even have imagined before we were exposed to the revelations of the discloser."

The following exercise is to help you identify and further develop new strategies and issues for gaining greater intimacy.

Objective: To Spotlight Statements or Strategies For Gaining Greater Intimacy, Love or Zest For Life

According to Jourard, (p. 19) "To disclose means to unveil, to make manifest, showing yourself so others can perceive you." One method of disclosing yourself is to reveal your feelings about intimacy, love or life in speech or writing. In this exercise, you will be asked to disclose your feelings to another by sharing a statement or concept that has special meaning and value to you.

In the following blank spaces after the initial examples, write down some results from your partners or friends. Perhaps you could keep a notebook in the future for new ideas and phrases that you will find.

Disclosures

1. Leo Buscaglia: "Life is not the goal, it's the trip."

2. Dean C. Dauw: "Some of life's greatest satisfactions, joys, and happiness come from the process of setting meaningful goals and then developing growth programs to achieve them."

3. Charles Baudelaire: "Love, the need to escape from oneself."

4. Max Gralnick: "Love is a non-possessive empathy and respect for the feelings of the loved one."

5. _____

6. _____

7. _____

8. _____

9. _____

10. _____

254

DEVELOPING RELATIONSHIPS FOR GREATER INTIMACY

There are many possible growth exercises that you could use to improve your relationships, regardless of what the relationships are or on what level you wish them to be. This is a very valuable concept: as a normal human being you probably do not overly "compartmentalize" your relationships. Therefore, what you learn about relationships can be applied to those at work, at home or wherever. Two forms or outlines are offered here, the first Form A, could be best used to think about relationships at work or more casual relationships. Form B should be used for more romantic or intimate liaisons. After you have filled out both forms A and B, you may then wish to compare the final summary statements. (We usually do not like to give examples here because more dependent persons may not stretch themselves to discover their own best answers.) You might consider our statement elsewhere in this volume: "My Convictions — Relationships."

Form A: Part I

Please outline ways or methods you want colleagues or peers to express their relationships or involvements with you. List at least 5, and no more than 10.

_____

_____

_____

_____

_____

_____

_____

_____

_____

Form A, Part II

Now, list ways or methods in which you actively express your relationships or involvements with your colleagues or peers.

_____

_____

_____

_____

_____

_____

_____

_____

_____

Form A, Part III

Finally, make comparisons between what you have detailed in Part I and II. (You should see if you can find any patterns, omissions or significant differences. Then discuss them openly with the significant others involved.)

_____

_____

_____

_____

_____

_____

_____

_____

_____

_____

Form B, Part I

Please outline ways or methods you want lovers to express their more intimate relationships or involvements with you. List at least 5 and no more than 10.

_____

_____

_____

_____

_____

_____

_____

_____

Form B, Part II

Now, list ways or methods in which you actively express your love, intimacy and involvements with your most significant other(s).

_____
_____
_____
_____
_____
_____
_____
_____
_____
_____

Form B, Part III

Finally, make comparisons between what you have detailed in Part I and II. (You will look for any patterns, omissions, or significant differences. Then, discuss them openly with the significant others involved.)

_____
_____
_____
_____
_____
_____
_____
_____
_____
_____

Form C

Now, please make comparisons between your conclusions in Form A, Part III and Form B, Part III. Follow same instructions and conclusions as outlined in Form B, Part III.

_____
_____
_____
_____

INTIMACY IN LIFE-STYLES

For every couple getting married today in states like California and New York, another couple is getting divorced. Some couples are advocating communal living. Other married couples insist on spouse-swapping. People in general are experimenting with alternate life styles, to such a degree that there is even a professional journal *Alternative Life-Styles* published by Sage Publications, Inc., Beverly Hills, California 90210.

Objective: List life styles in your order of preference, discuss and defend your ranking.

Method: Divide your group into subgroups of four or five members. Below is a list of nine choices. Rank your choices on the list from one to nine, with #1 being where you would like to be in five years, and with #9 being one that, possibly, you would never want to experience.

1. _____ a. Traditional marriage.

2. _____ b. Polygamy; more than one spouse.

3. _____ c. Swinging single: many relationships with the opposite sex.

4. _____ d. One-to-one intimacy relationship with someone.

5. _____ e. Communal living: all married couples; partner swapping.

6. _____ f. Married; swapping partners.

7. _____ g. Communal living; all single; one relationship with everyone.

8. _____ h. Single; one-to-one relationship with opposite sex; not living together.

9. _____ i. Single; one-to-one relationship with opposite sex; living together.

k. Another option? _____

EXERCISES

1. USE OF AUTOBIOGRAPHY AS AN AID IN PERSONAL PROBLEM SOLVING

Many individuals often feel they have various sorts of problems. And they attempt to solve these problems by methods which are more or less effective, depending on (1) whoever is approached for help; and (2) whichever means he uses to assist the client in attempting to resolve the problems.

The word "problems" can actually embrace a large number of issues. We might use the word "problems" when we actually mean such things as: setting goals in life, determining a particular course of action, deciding about changing jobs, resolving an emotional issue, and the like.

Many people in the "helping professions" also define problems in different ways. For example, a minister, priest, or rabbi may tend to focus on the spiritual aspects of a problem, both as to how the problem arose in the first place, as well as how to solve the problem. On the other hand, some psychologists, psychiatrists, social workers, counselors, and the like may tend to focus on other aspects of a problem.

All these individual members of the various helping professions, then, may also employ various techniques in assisting a client, counselee, parishioner, or patient who seeks a friendly ear.

The autobiography is *only one means* that may be useful for a particular individual, *regardless* of the problem and also *regardless* of the kind of person in the helping professions that he may approach for aid. (Of course, the exact extent of its value and all the other related issues can be investigated more extensively if you wish, by referring to: Dr. A.P. Annis, "The Autobiography," *Journal of Counseling Psychology,* 1967, 14: 9-18.)

The main point here is this: *any individual can gain much profit from writing and studying his own autobiography even if he has no special problems.* It follows, then, all the more clearly, that if you have a particular problem, issue, difficulty, (or whatever you want to call it) that you want to resolve, the autobiography can be of especially good value for you. And this is also true, no matter who you wish to seek out for help in resolving your difficulties.

Our second main point here is merely to help you get started in writing it out. Naturally, we do hope you will take our word for it, that an autobiography will be helpful. All the research indicates this fact. Just how helpful or valuable it will be for you depends on **YOU!!**

If you really want to understand yourself better, you will be motivated to put some effort into the project. Then, once you have written it out, the next step will depend on what you do with it. You should not put it away in a drawer and forget about it. But you *can* use it yourself alone or in your talks with someone else.

All the various uses of your brief autobiography will be discussed later. Consider now how you should compose it.

Basically, an autobiography is an individual's personally written report of his own life. It makes you look inwardly. It should help you answer questions like: "What I think I am like"; "How other people see me"; "What I would like to be like."

If these questions sound too structured for you, you could try others: "What kind of person am I?"; "How did I get that way?"; "What do I hope to become?"

In writing your autobiography you might possibly adopt one of these four distinct orientations:

1. The *chronicler* who deals only with the external events of his life.
2. The *self-defender* who focuses primarily upon defending his activities and points of view.

3. The *confessant* who may write feelings never expressed before.
4. The *self-analyst* who makes a special effort at self-analysis.

Regardless of your orientation, you are bound to communicate some information about your psychological makeup. However, the last two (3 and 4) usually find the exercise to be more profitable.

Please don't worry so much about the method or techniques you use, but rather, concentrate on *really expressing your honest feelings* about various situations in your life. Thanks. You won't regret it.

AUTOBIOGRAPHY
"Hung Up"

Sitting down to write the paper, I have one feeling running through my mind, and that is frustration. To be young, healthy, but frustrated, I feel is a sad commentary. Why am I frustrated, but most important, why does it bother me so much. The truthful answer, whether I like to admit it or not is, I am not getting what happens to be extremely important to me. This intangible substance is thought about by many but really talked about by few, and that is sex.

I need, want, and crave sex, but I cannot satisfy my desires. Not satisfying my desires, not getting what I need sexually I feel truly makes me why I am the way I am. This may seem funny or childish, or selfish, or maybe even stupid to most of you, but I really don't give a damn, because it is important to me.

I consider myself basically a very emotional type of person and not fulfilling my needs causes me to have problems. These feelings of frustration not only effect my sex life, but they effect my thoughts and dealings outside the bedroom.

To better understand, I have to explain my upbringing. My parents felt that sex lessons and an understanding of sex should be taught at home and not in the street. Because of this, I was exposed to explanations of sexual relations before I was nine years old. I don't know how other kids reacted, but I do remember what I said. When my parents explained intercourse to me, all I did was scream, "If that's what I have to do when I grow up, I am

never going to get married." Then I ran from the room. I am not saying that sexual exposure at an early age is bad, but I can say that it had a profound effect on me.

Besides an early exposure, I had a mother who was determined to impart unto me the importance of satisfying my partner's desires. This is to say that I was taught to always make sure my partner was completely and totally whipped. I was taught the importance of foreplay and also that most girls really needed and truly enjoyed it. The importance of being sensual and uninhibited was also passed along.

All of this knowledge was passed on before I was one year into high school. Needless to say, I began putting into practice what I had learned. I must stop and say that I really feel all this knowledge was given to me for use when I grew up and got married, but it sort of backfired because I didn't wait. As I stated earlier, I began to experiment, and the more I tried, the more I liked, and the more I liked, the more I tried. Besides believing in the ideas I learned, I found myself truly enjoying them. I no longer used foreplay to just satisfy the girl, but I used it because I liked it. I found that the more I satisfied my date, the more satisfied I became. Later on all of these traits which I acquired would backfire on me when I got married.

I must now explain some of my philosophies about sex and the married man. No matter how many relations I had when I was younger, I always told myself that when I got married, my wife would be the only person I would have sexual relations with. I could not understand how some of the married men I know could have relations with other women and not think anything of it. I had this fantasy that when I got married, my wife and I would be totally uninhibited and that we would make love any time and anywhere (anywhere meaning anywhere in the house). I would not need another woman because my wife would satisfy me completely.

Even though I had overpowering sex drives, I felt convinced that I would marry a girl that would match me drive for drive. I felt this way because I rationalized that if I tried as hard as I could to satisfy her and she enjoyed it then she would want more. This sort of follows the crackerjack theory which is the more you eat, the more you want. Therefore, if my wife really enjoyed sex and had great orgasms, then she would crave more. Because of all these feelings, when I got married, I was convinced that my sex life would be great.

I married a girl who I felt fit all the categories I want in a woman. She had a great personality, a great sense of humor, she was intelligent, warm and good-natured. But also she was put together the way I like a woman to be put together. Needless to say, she had a great body.

I must say that all through our relationship before we were married, I always felt my desires would be fulfilled. There is one catch though—my wife told me that she wanted to stay a virgin until she got married. Because I loved her so much, and it was so important to her, I decided that no matter how badly I wanted to have complete relations, I would just wait until we were married. This waiting and drawing lines not only caused problems before we were married, but it caused problems after.

After we were married, my wife and I enjoyed a very healthy sex life. Being newlyweds, we thought nothing of indulging any time we felt like it. But, as time went on my desires for sex increased, while my wife's decreased. This is not to say that she did not enjoy sex, but only that her drives were of a lesser degree and also came at much greater intervals.

As we went along, my wife's inhibitions began to show. Because of having to wait and draw those lines, she developed hangups, while I did not. Because of these hangups, she was not able to completely let herself go. Letting oneself go is the magic dream in my house. To be able to let oneself go I feel is the ultimate. To be able to completely block out the world, block out other thoughts and just totally concentrate on sex is my ideal situation. The problem began to develop in that my wife could not let go, she could not block out the world. I always have the feeling that she expects her mother to walk in and ball her out for being in bed with a man. This may sound funny to some, but to us it is not.

I could go on into further detail, but I don't see any need to. I feel a need to draw all the ends together and come up with a final total picture.

As I have stated before, I have these great sexual desires along with these ideals about my behavior after marriage. These turn out to be contradictory and in the end a great and bitter frustration

for me. Because my wife is inhibited and cannot let go, we have found ourselves growing further and further apart in bed. This effects other aspects of our life. We have found that we have polarized at opposite ends of the sexual pole. My wife now feels that she could never satisfy me no matter how hard she tries. Her logic is that no matter how much we make love, it will not be enough and I will want more, so why try. Because of this logic, she has given up trying to satisfy me and only takes what she needs to be satisfied. This logic totally goes against my feelings which polarizes us even more.

I cannot understand how a person who is young and healthy like her can have such few and far between drives. Because of this, I find myself becoming more frustrated than ever. To me making love is one of the greatest joys in the world. As a matter of fact, I cannot think of too many other great feelings other than that of sexual gratification and fulfillment. I find sex to also be an escape hatch for me. When I get depressed and want to hide from the world, all I want to do is go to bed and make love. When I am in bed, I can truly block out everything else and therefore escape from reality into enjoyment. I find sex to be a great tranquilizer. The most important aspect is that I truly enjoy making love with my wife. To me there is nothing greater than making love with my wife. I told her a long time ago that when I married her, she was the only one and that all I wanted was her. You have to understand that I don't need or want anyone else as long as I can have her because I love her.

Now this brings up another aspect, and that is the emotional and psychological fulfillment involved. To me just making love for the sake of release is not totally fulfilling. I must know that my wife is fulfilled and that she is satisfied before I am happy. (This has to do with my early teachings.) The final problems arise because of all this. If what I have just said is true, then as long as my wife is satisfied, then I should be, but that is not the case. I need more sex than my wife can give. Because I do not believe in looking elsewhere for fulfillment, I must get it at home, but I am not. Even if I am frustrated and come home looking for release, I still have the knowledge that I will probably be turned down. That effects my actions before we even get together. In some cases, I even defeat my own purpose because of presupposed ideas that I feel my wife has before I even get home. All of this ends up to be a vicious cycle. The more I want, the more frustrated I become, and the more frustrated I become, the more nasty I become, and the more nasty I become the less willing my wife becomes which makes me more frustrated, etc.

My wife has called me sick and demented, while I have accussed her of being undersexed and sick because of her lack of drives. Who knows—maybe we both are sick. The fact is that our inability to get together has caused me to be a frustrated and unhappy person. Being frustrated and unhappy in bed has caused me to react and respond differently out of my home life. This frustration has leaked over into other areas of my life. I am now questioning myself in many areas because I feel I have failed as a lover.

This feeling of inadequacy has effected me in many ways. I no longer have the confidence I once had. Where I never questioned my drives before, I am now questioning whether something is wrong with me. Am I sick. Are my views and desires so different that I am considered a deviate. Is my wife normal. Are her drives like most of the people. All these questions and all these problems caused by them I feel effect me greatly every day. If and when they are worked out, I feel I will be able to find greater peace with myself that will allow me to look at life differently and possibly cause me to have different feelings on why I am the way I am. Because, as you can see from this paper and everything expounded in it, that I am one "Hung Up Individual" looking for help and understanding to my problems.

AUTOBIOGRAPHY

"Born in Detroit"

I was born in Detroit. My father was born in Detroit; my mother came from Europe. I'm the oldest; I have a brother and a sister.

My mother's family is quite cultured; they appreciate the better things in life, such as art, good music, the stage and so forth.

My father's side of the family is quite the opposite . . . rough and tumble. My grandfather drove in some of the first cross-country automobile races. My father was involved in both automobile and boat racing. At one time, he held a world speed record. The family has been involved in either fighting, wrestling, or boxing all the way back. My grandfather, a little guy, was a bantam weight champion. My dad's younger brother worked his way through engineering school with his boxing.

My father's family also includes a branch that were wild west characters and Indian fighters. My father would sometimes talk about how they would sometimes visit Detroit when he was a boy. They would bring their handguns with them. This was taking place less than sixty years ago.

When I was a child, for no reason that I could understand, I would get the hell knocked out of me all the time. I can still remember the feeling of struggling and being helplessly knocked senseless. I would hide whenever my father was around. I am still outwardly, a very quiet person. I didn't overcome my fear of people until I was physically large enough to demolish people myself. I felt a compulsion to "go after" guys that were larger than myself; usually, I would fight more than one at a time. This is not the proper behavior for the twentieth century. I learned that my father was raised the same way. Because I understand how I was raised to react physically, I have learned to temper my overt behavior.

I didn't like my mother any better. Before I was of school age, someone gave me some old scientific books. I would love to read them. My mother would punish me by throwing these down the stairway. I would repair the ripped covers and try my best to hide them. After my mother burned these books, I didn't talk to her for several years.

My parents liked music, so they bought me an accordion. I began to play professionally at the age of twelve. I started out with just myself and a drummer. My parents would let me stay out until three or four A.M. to play weddings, clubs, school dances, et cetera. I played five instruments. As I think back, it seems funny that they never worried about me.

I never had any problems with intelligence in school. Usually, I was the brightest child in the room, if not the school. I would get a bang out of astounding people with my test scores. I caused a good deal of trouble in the later grades. For some reason, the principal liked me. He let them put my name on the honor roll any time my citizenship reached a "C." I graduated from high school at fifteen.

I always had the feeling that I was some kind of "special" person. There wasn't any real reason for this feeling; it was something that was inside of me. A lot of this feeling has been knocked out of me by others, but I keep trying to do the spectacular. I have tried a lot of things but, to date, I haven't lived up to my potential. I'll probably keep trying; I would rather be dead than be ordinary.

When I started going to college, my father was in the hospital and my family was having a tough time. I worked full-time to help out as well as to go to school. The band jobs were usually only on weekends, so I got another job during the week. Usually, I worked as a truck driver. (I got a driver's license that showed I was eighteen.)

I had some pretty interesting jobs, too. I worked as a lifeguard, resort musician, stevedore, and I worked as a test driver for X Corporation. This job was actually very dull. I worked with a relay of drivers that would run a car hour after hour at top speed, until the car broke down mechanically. We were hired by an outside organization and signed a statement that waived responsibility for anything that happened to us. I didn't like what I saw happen in a couple of cases, so I went back to driving trucks.

I prepared an Austin Healy for time trials and did okay with it. I made money by buying beat-up sports cars, repairing them and selling them. I liked Jaguars the best. I was unsuccessful in finding a sponsor for all out racing.

One time I put a hundred dollar deposit down on a three-year-old Ferrari. John Johnson of Johnson Foods had traded it in on a Buick and I could have got it for one-third of its real value. It handled like a dream. You didn't have to horse it around the curves like the cars I was used to. It would slide wherever you imagined it to; it was as if the car could read your mind. However, I knew that I couldn't have afforded to repair the car if I damaged it. For example, John's mechanic showed me that he had paid $90.00 (each) for the front wheel bearings. The car was illegal for the highway. My mother threatened to do away with me if I brought it home.

I started out in pharmacy school because we have a friend of the family that is a pharmacist. There wasn't enough time to take the required lab courses. I changed over to Business Administration and majored in advertising.

In advertising, I liked to try everything. I worked in media, copywriting, research, as an account executive and in straight advertising sales. My work took me to Chicago, New York, Los Angeles and back again.

But, I had the love for race cars and danger that my father had. I thought that I could sublimate these feelings by becoming an airline pilot. In college, I was in Air Force ROTC but, when they increased the enlistment requirements for pilot training to five years, I got out. (a mistake) I joined the Michigan Air Guard and was trained as a jet aircraft mechanic. This was the Chanute Air Force Base in Illinois.

I applied for fighter pilot training with the Air Guard. This was for twenty months of training in F-100s, then a return to guard unit to fly. This was more like it. I went to Fort Wayne, Indiana, for the physicals. I took the mental tests in Michigan. I set some kind of record for correct answers; I ace'd everything. Then, the damn guard bumbled around with the paper work for over a year—until it was too late. They sent me a letter saying I was over-age. I was furious.

I decided to train myself. I seemed to be a "natural" at flying. I have spent more thousands of dollars on this training than I would care to say. Today, I have about 700 of the required 1000 hours. Toward the end of my self-training program, it became evident that there was no longer a demand for new pilots. The airlines were in fact, cutting back. I had put everything I had into a dead end. If I could be anything I wanted, I'd still want to be an airline pilot. There is an honesty about the job that is lacking in so many areas of our life. There is no faking, either you know or you don't know what you're doing.

The biggest mistake of my life was meeting a girl in Chicago that wanted to open an art gallery. At the time, I was working as an account executive D Company. I was in advertising sales, and while I wasn't making a spectacular amount, I was taking care of everybody.

The girl and I opened an art gallery on Oak Street. I did the decorating after work; the girl helped to do some of the work too. She was a good sales person. We started out okay. We made several nice sales on our first show. I sold one customer four paintings for over six thousand dollars.

Things were going good. I was pretty lucky with advertising and publicity. One of our sculptors had a piece of his work accepted into the

White House. I got Joe Serico to write a page story about it in the Z Newspaper.

We sold everything the artist ever made in forty-five days. Gradually, I raised the prices from $350.00 to $1,000.00. It was the only way we could hold on to any. Things were rolling. At work, one of the vice presidents got smart and I threw him out of my office. I left the advertising job to sell art full-time.

Then, the recession hit in May of 1970. The luxury goods market dried up as the stock market dived to 630. Sales went down to nothing. People wanted to return items. But, the overhead continued. There were no advertising jobs . . . everybody was being let go. We had to close our doors in January of 1971. The recession had killed us.

I went from champagne to beer and then to water. I had sold everything to keep the business going. After all, it was a good business and Nixon had promised to have a recovery in the fall. There wasn't.

When the business closed, I was completely flat. I didn't have enough money to eat every day. In November and December of 1970 and January of 1971, I didn't have a dime to buy a newspaper.

I wasn't eating every day. I would go through my pants in the closet and look for enough change to buy a box of Creamettes. When things got tough in November, the girl moved in with another guy.

When I left my advertising job in February, I was making a good couple of thousand dollars a week selling artwork. Now, the recession was on. I had been looking for another advertising job since April. In my field, everybody was being let go. I was interviewing for five-figure a year jobs in the loop and I didn't have enough for either laundry or carfare. I would wash out a shirt by hand for each interview. I was too proud to tell anybody.

By hard perseverance and determination, I was selected as the best candidate for two different jobs. Several months later, I was told the first opening had been eliminated. The second job was filled by someone already in the firm. (They were sorry.) I continued to seek after and to follow up those interviews I could walk to.

I started substitute teaching in mid-January of 1971. The day of my first pay in February I had my first full meal in some time. Until that time, I was really miserable. At lunch time, I would walk out on the street or on the play ground. I didn't have enough change to buy anything in the cafeteria.

I applied for a job with The Post Office, just to insure that I would have something for a last resort in the summer time. It was about the only civil service opening. I went after the "good" jobs again. Nothing came through. I ended up driving a cab. In spite of what you hear, this pays about twenty dollars a day for twelve hours work. I looked forward to the fall when I could teach again.

Fall came. They weren't hiring provisional teachers. I was flat broke again. I couldn't work enough hours in a day to pay all my bills. I owed thousands of dollars and I was about to be evicted from my apartment. But, I was healthy . . . I was eating now.

The Post Office job came through. It was a real blessing. It saved me from being evicted from my apartment by one day. I showed my landlords in writing that I had a starting date for a civil service job . . . and they didn't evict me. Two years ago, I never would have dreamed that I'd be doing this kind of work but, it pays the bills. Now, I am getting my head above water.

Last September, after the civil service job came through, a girl loaned me $200.00 so that I could complete the fifteen hours of education I need in order that I may teach again in January. This will be of help because fifty hours of teaching equals the pay for 100 hours of the work I am doing now, although I have been working overtime. If there is another recession in 1980, I'll be ready. I'll be prepared with more than one speciality.

Things are looking a good deal better now. In January, I'll look for a job in my field again. If things "aren't ready," I'll continue working my midnight to eight-thirty job and I'll teach afterwards, during the day. My little sister is starting prelaw school; I have to get situated so that I can help her.

After I have some capital again, and if things are better, I'll start another business . . . provided that the Republicans aren't in. If things continue to be relatively tough, I'll either go to law school or go for a PhD . . . maybe in psychology. I wouldn't want my seventeen-year-old sister to get ahead of me.

There is only one thing that really frightens me . . . and that is . . . no money. I detest being poor. I intend to do my best to insure that it never happens again.

AUTOBIOGRAPHY

"Scarves"

I cannot remember everything about my childhood. My parents' philosophy of child-rearing seemed to be "Don't bother us, but don't go out of the yard"—a life sentence to a head trip: my fantasy world and fetishes.

I can remember before the age of five, sneaking into the closet to take my mother's head scarf. I would stick it in my pants and beat off. At first, my fantasies were always in the third person, and "he" always died at orgasm. For the next ten years, my mother and I played "hide and seek" with the scarves (until a shrink advised her to let me have them) but it was never talked about.

At age five I began kindergarten, already convinced I was worthless. I let one of my schoolmates bully me for six years without once fighting back. Finally I belted him in the nose, then cried for the rest of the day.

Crying all or part of the day was not uncommon until about age twelve. If someone tried to help, I would push him away: others would kick me as I laid on the floor and I would cry harder.

Meanwhile at home, my fantasies continued. I had found a pair of large leather mittens. I would hang over the edge of our neighbor's porch with these mittens, letting myself gradually slip until I fell to the ground. "He" would be hanging over a cliff and slipping to his death. Sometimes I masturbated while doing this.

Somewhere as I grew older, my fantasies changed to first person. Every night before I fell asleep, I thought of getting polio so they would take care of me.

As I reached puberty, the scarves went around my head or neck instead of in my pants. As my mother became more adept at hiding them, I started stealing them from school or out of stores. I even considered knocking out ladies on the street to steal their scarves, but never did so.

About the time I started to notice girls, the death fantasies stopped, and were replaced by a girl who either punished me or I her, with scarves: the orgasm was the punishment. If the girl was being punished, I was the girl: sometimes, I dressed in my mother's or sister's clothing.

When I was about fifteen or sixteen, my parents were concerned enough to want to send me to a psychiatrist. (I think they panicked when I started playing some blues music that told of suicide.) The first one I saw only once. The second I saw for about two or three months. One day I was depressed while at a session. He asked if I felt bad enough to go to a hospital. I was shocked and afraid that I would never come back, or if I did that no one would ever associate with me. I did not see him more than once or twice afterwards. I often went into a stupor if pressed on the subject of my illness, but I never, then, considered myself sick: the problem, as I saw it then, was that I was worthless, and feeling bad was my just reward.

At age nineteen, my fantasies took another switch. Instead of general maso-sadistic torture, my fantasies became specifically centered on spanking and hanging. This change occurred shortly after seeing a picture of a female breast for the first time. (Sex was very suppressed at home. I did not know there was a difference between boys and girls until nine or ten. When adolescent sexual curiosity began, the medical books were quickly hidden.) The hanging fantasies ceased after one episode while home from college. I was in the shower with a scarf over my head and two scarves tied as a diaper. My head was through a noose while I beat off. During previous episodes, I slid out of the noose after orgasm into the water. But this time, I remained suspended by the neck. A picture I cannot now remember flashed before me. I screamed, than sank down into the tub. It must have been a half-hour before I got out of the bathroom to my bed.

A second scene under similar conditions happened recently. I was in the tub with a wet scarf and diaper. I stood up to look at myself in the mirror. A sharp pain in my gut started as I beat off. I stopped: it stopped: I started: it started, and continued until orgasm. The spanking fantasies have continued to the present time. (I remember once my sister telling me that I was going to get a surprise when I got home: when I got home hours later, the surprise was a spanking. Once my mother got mad at me, and told me I was going to be spanked. I ran away, but stopped to make her stop screaming at me, and got it. I was bad in church, and told I would be spanked. On the way home, my mother said, "You sure are happy for a boy who's going to get a spanking when we get home." Once when my younger brother got himself spanked, my sister and I were ecstatically elated.)

My mother has a split personality. She would scream hysterically at us kids, then be laughing a quarter-hour later, when company arrived. I watched her waver from one personality to the other once just before someone came to our house, but I can't remember the look on her face. I cannot focus on the face of either of my parents in my mind's eye, even though I saw them only several days ago. To this day, she will freak out at the least annoyance, and she will completely disintegrate if a bird flys near her.

I haven't said anything about my father. I quickly learned to avoid him. He would not or could not communicate with me: I was always wrong. He would always walk so fast when I was small that I was dragged behind. I ran away from home once at about fourteen or fifteen. When my father was called to take me home, he cried and told me he loved me for the first and only time. I did not react: I was in a stupor.

I feel that these episodes are mere fractions of what went on day to day. I can remember vividly every inch of our house, but to see my parents in my mind's eye in the same way is impossible: they are ghosts. I can even remember "things" back to two or three years of age, but no people.

Certain things that I cannot remember, but have been told to me may be significant. When I was first born, my mother fed me whenever I cried. I was fat and pudgy. The doctor said I needed to be fed only three times a day. Shortly afterwards, I became allergic to my milk formula and lost considerable weight. I have been thin ever since. I would not be surprised if my problems started during this period. I am told that I grunted and kicked during my sleep as a baby.

It has been only lately that I have come to the conclusion that I am sick. The patterns of my life since I have left home eight years ago have become all too aparent. Every girl I have ever had a relationship with has been just as spaced out as I; I doubt that I could get myself into any other type of relationship. I have never dated a girl until I had planned to leave an area. The more concrete the plans, the more concrete the relationship as a rule. This has happened four times now, and is happening now with my current girl friend. Almost without exception, I have been attracted to a girl with boyish characteristics. Recently I had a homosexual dream (interrupted unfortunately), and did entertain homosexual feeling while drunk. The only girl I have ever had sex with was a slut off the street at twenty-two. I fantasized that I was punishing her before I could come.

If this is not sufficient reason for wanting treatment, there is my current psychosomatic systems: asthma, restless sleep, poor eating and digestion, the dull knot in my stomach, and the constant stream of phlegm from my lungs, especially in the morning. I do not know how much longer I can keep the lid on.

2. "DAYS OF OUR LIVES"
A WIFE'S VIEW OF HER HUSBAND
FOR A CONSULTING PSYCHOLOGIST

First off, I'd like to say that this project is not an easy one. I have given it much thought and will do my best to help you understand my husband. Therefore, I will go back to our meeting and courtship days.

In January, 1964, Joe was standing up as best man in his cousin's wedding and I was maid of honor for my girlfriend. (At the time, Joe had just broken his engagement with another girl and I was seriously dating another boy with the thought of getting engaged.) Joe and I first met at the rehearsal dinner. I was very impressed with him and was hoping for a chance to get to know him. Joe was very handsome to me and also *extremely* quiet. As I am a very outgoing and aggressive individual and had never met any guy as quiet as Joe; he presented a challenge to me and I simply had to find out what made him tick! I had to go back to college and our first somewhat blind date was arranged over Easter vacation. To my disappointment, I became ill (with mono!) and couldn't keep our date. Needless to say, Joe thought I made up an excuse and didn't want to keep the date. Anyway, we finally got together in July for the first time, but not for a second date until September. Joe had been hurt very badly by this other girl and he was thoroughly against getting serious again for a long time. It was *very* hard for me to get him to open up but in time I succeeded. Naturally, I fell in love with him first and it took him a long time to finally come out and admit it to me and to himself! While dating and for four years after we were married, I was secretary to a Personnel Manager. Being in the same field—Personnel—helped me help Joe by discussing our work at home. By doing this and in other ways, I feel I helped Joe to let out some of his thoughts and to try to be more outgoing. I know I have had a tremendous influence on Joe, especially our first five years of marriage, in many ways, but especially on his career and jobs.

Joe's first job with X company was a beginning, but not a good one. Joe graduated in June, we were getting married in August, and he was having a tough time finding a job in Personnel. I tried to encourage him to wait and he'd find something but he jumped at this job as a Sales Service Representative for $525.00 a month. Being in Personnel myself and being responsible (as secretary) for the hiring of college graduates, I knew the salary was between $50. and $75. below the norm and it upset me that Joe would settle for less; this and the fact that it was not a job in Personnel. After working there for awhile, it seemed as if they would have office parties for any number of reasons—and the majority of the girls were cute and single! Being very insecure as I was then, this upset me a great deal. So—because of the position he had, the money, et cetera, I encouraged him to seek another job—in Personnel—his major in college. My work experience helped me to give suggestions for his resume, letter, et cetera.

Again, he was having a tough time finding a company that was willing to give him a chance in Personnel. After several rejections and interviews, he seemed to be liked at Y corporation. If I remember correctly, it was down to a matter of selecting him or one of three or four other candidates. I was telling my father about this and he asked if I felt it was a good job and if Joe really wanted it. I told him yes, of course. Well, my dad knew the President of Y corporation and said he would make a call to insure Joe of the job. Needless to say, Joe got the job. Only—to this day he thinks he got it on his own. I *never* told him at the time about my father's call because he and my father never got along and because Joe was so pigheaded at the time that he didn't want help from anyone. I guess he was trying to prove that he didn't need anyone—he could stand on his own. About a year ago, I mentioned my father's call and

Joe still refused to believe that it had any bearing on his being hired.

Y corporation was a fairly good company, except for one thing—money. When it came to raises, they were terrible! One raise I'll never forget—it was over six months, maybe ten, since his last raise, and it was at least $50. a month. If it had been me, would have gone into my boss that day and discussed how I felt. But Joe was still rather shy and introverted at the time and he felt uneasy about doing it. Finally I convinced him to mention it to his boss. He did, but got no where because it was too late to do anything and because he probably didn't know how to quite handle the situation. Anyway, because the money didn't get much better and because the advancement wasn't that great, we decided he should again start job hunting.

The next job was at Q company. I feel this was a good job because Joe was given the opportunity to handle all phases of Personnel work on his own. He had to get final approval from the Plant General Manager, but at least he could organize things the way he wanted. Joe did have a slight problem with the General Manager. He was known to go out for a lunch and have quite a few drinks. When he would come back to the office, his attitude was a little bit hostile and it was hard to reason with him. Instead of things getting better, Joe found it increasingly harder to talk with him. The money was satisfactory, but there did not seem to be much of a future, except maybe in New York. Again, I had influence on this because of all places to move, I did *not* want to move there. Also, the increase he would have received with the move would not have enabled us to keep our same style of living as New York is so much higher than Chicago. We also knew if he turned that offer down, there was nothing else available.

So again comes job hunting. Joe had received the Master's Degree in February of 1970, but had started answering ads in November, 1969. He wanted a good company that offered advancement and whose compensation was very good. He wanted a long-range future with his next company so that he would finally feel secure.

It took over ten months to find what we both felt was an excellent company with good opportunity. It sounded as if Joe would have more responsibility and that promotions would be forthcoming. I remember at the time that he said he might have some problems with Mr. Peterson because he formerly worked in manufacturing, did not have the education and basically knew very little about Personnel. Joe felt that he knew more than his boss, because of getting an education in this field and he felt he would have a hard time working with Mr. Peterson without stepping out of line in ideas of projects he would mention. Mr. Peterson was very similar to one of my bosses (Personnel Manager also) who wanted to do everything himself and never gave the others a chance to prove themselves. When something wasn't done on time he would always blame his subordinates, even though he was at fault. I feel Mr. Peterson did the same thing with Joe, only I'm afraid Joe probably let his feelings show too much which didn't go over well. Also, Joe felt something was wrong but *never* mentioned it in detail to anyone. If he had sought advice or maybe gone to Peterson's boss, maybe he wouldn't be in this situation today. My father has tried for seven years to talk to Joe about business and work in general, but Joe would *never* open up. There are probably several reasons why, which I will attempt to explain.

As long as we've known each other, Joe and my father have never hit it off well; the main reason probably being that they are exact opposites. My father is very outgoing and aggressive and he comes on *very* strong. (He has also been very successful considering his background.) Well, for some reason, Joe doesn't seem to hit it off with this personality type (his boss at Q company was very much like my father). He always felt my father was prying when he would ask Joe about his job and Joe felt it was none of his business. All Dad was trying to do was to find a topic of conversation. After all, they are both in the business world even though my father is in Sales and Joe is in Personnel. I don't know if Joe felt Dad was too successful and above him and in a way resented it. Or, maybe Joe felt he had to live up to being as successful as him for my sake. Joe also feels Dad is somewhat conceited and has an inflated ego and he definitely does not like this attitude in people. So—for many years, it was a bad scene whenever my parents were around. It got so bad that Joe would go outside if we were in; leave the table to play with Tommy while we sat and talked, et cetera. To this day, I do not fully understand why. But he *definitely* let his feelings show and my father certainly was aware of it. Joe claimed there was never anything to talk about, but God knows Dad tried. Joe even started to give my brother the cold shoulder when he was around. I came from a rather close knit family where we always talked and Joe's background was entirely different. He was not that close to his brothers—maybe because Joe was the only one to go onto college—and his father runs a tavern and could never give much advice. So I guess Joe felt alone and that he could manage on his own. I've always been one to seek advice and talk over problems. It was difficult to get Joe to do this with me, but because I worked, I knew some of his problems and could discuss it intellectually with him. The one point I'm trying to make here is that if he could treat my father and brother and sometimes my mother that way, did he do this at work, too? I really don't know . . . .

Anyway, when Joe was given the news about being layed off, he was the one to tell my father about it over the phone. (My parents live in California.) They talked for quite awhile and then my father had to make a business trip to Kentucky and he wanted to know if he should stop here to see Joe. For the first time, Joe said "Yes, the sooner the better!" Dad was here for a whole weekend. Joe scooted me out of the room that Friday night and he and my father talked for *six* hours in one night—six hours in seven years!! Needless to say, the weekend went well and he finally confided in my father. Even my father said to Joe that for the first time he's actually smiling around him! I'm sorry that it took this to bring them together, but something had to because the situation was not a pleasant one. This is why I feel Joe shows his emotions at work and if he does, he's in trouble.

Another example would be the Vice President of Personnel at Z Corporation—John Marshall, who is over Joe and Mr. Peterson. He's a young man (in his late 30's?) and he does not have much of a personality, just a great deal of intelligence. I know because I was at a couple of parties when he was there. You would think John would want to get to know the men under him for future considerations and at least talk to Joe at the parties. John caught my eye several times (and Joe's) but never came over to introduce his wife to us or to meet me. So we never met. Joe probably should have been more aggressive at this time and taken me over to meet them, but he didn't. Sometimes I think Joe feels people should go out of the way for him because he's something special and that it isn't up to him to go up to them. Also, it seems as if Joe is uneasy about someone higher than he is and he's not sure what to say to them. When John would be in town and in Personnel, I feel Joe should have tried to start small conversation with him, but he didn't go out of his way to do so. I know Joe doesn't like John, but sometimes you have to do things you don't like and be friendly to those you don't like just to get ahead. I don't mean be two-faced—just play a little politics. Another example of his attitude was with my best girl friend and her husband. We used to do many things with them but we've grown apart over the last two years or so. They were over one night and the guy seemed to become rather conceited lately over his success, et cetera. He, too, came from a background similar to Joe's— he was the only one in his family to go to college and he has done quite well for himself. Even though some people are like this, you should still be friendly and talkative to them if they're your guests. This couple also has different views than we do on many topics but I like to discuss different ideas and opinions and maybe learn something that may change my mind. Joe is *extremely* opinionated and won't budge from his thinking even if he may be the one who is wrong. It's very hard for me to get through to him when his feelings and ideas are strongly made up. This is when he begins to lose his temper and I quit the conversation. When we were first married, he had a terrible temper. It has cooled considerably, but he does fly off the handle every now and then. All this is based on how I know and see Joe at home. Whether he acts this way at the office or not is hard for me to say. Most of what I have written so far I feel I could not tell Joe face to face because of his pride and ego. He would feel I was putting him down and would probably get bitter towards me and this I don't want. I love my husband very much and just want to help him. So please tread on light water when mentioning some of these things to him—for the sake of our marriage.

Now for some other points. Joe has turned out to be a very good husband, father and provider. Again, Joe was very unsure of himself around our son, Tommy, when he was born and up until he was a year old. Then, when Joe wanted to start helping with feeding, et cetera, it was almost too late because Tommy wanted me all the time. Just within the past year have these two really gotten acquainted, Joe still doesn't know how to play with Tommy in a constructive and learning way (building blocks, line up cars, et cetera), but I'm sure he'll improve as time goes on. I *always* change Tommy, feed him, put him to bed, et cetera, until I finally convinced Joe to take a bath with him which our son dearly loves. Even though Joe didn't help much with Tommy, he is exceptionally considerate and helpful around the house. When I worked, Joe *always* helped with the housework which was great. He will watch Tommy while I go shopping; he helps when I'm sick or have several things to do and he's even considerate in the bedroom—understanding when I'm not in the mood. Of course, there are times I don't even know he wants sex because he's not overly aggresive. When we were first married, I wanted sex too much (so he claims!) and he didn't! Lately he wants it more and I have calmed down. What an odd situation. I have been a little uptight about his layoff and have it on my mind quite a bit and therefore have just not been in the mood. Another great quality of Joe's is his neatness and cleanliness—about his body, his clothes and his appearance. He always looks great! Also, from what I have gathered, Joe is considerate of others at work, is friendly, helpful, cooperative, understanding, sympathetic and a good listener to other people's problems. He is well liked by almost all at Z Corporation with the exception of his two bosses. Joe is also a very hard worker—at home and at work. When he starts a project, he likes to stick to it until it gets done. This is good in itself, but sometimes he gets upset if he gets interrupted or has to put it off for another day. When he has a slow time at work he always asks for additional projects and is very interested and willing to learn new things and take additional responsibility. Joe wants very much to get ahead and I feel he's willing to work hard to get there, if only he'd be given the chance to prove himself. I truly wish he could find a company that could provide him with some real challenge and a good chance for promotions and success. I also hope he can find a job with a company that he can plan to stay with for the next ten years or so. Joe had good reasons for each one of his job moves, but he really needs to develop stability in his work pattern. Just to mention a few other fine points—

Joe is a completely honest person, is down to earth, is trustworthy, sincere, loving, and—I'm glad I'm his wife an; he's my husband.

Now we'll go on to where and how I would like to live. To tell you the truth, I'm perfectly happy right where we are for this stage and time of our life. We have a beautiful, four-bedroom ranch, air-conditioned, two baths, et cetera, and I feel we're doing very well for our age. For a fact, we are much better off than all our friends and most of our relatives. We have better than average furniture and I would say that our whole style of living is definitely better than average. I am very happy living in a suburb of Chicago as we do. In fact, I really can't think of a better place to live. I think the Mid-west and this metropolitan area in particular (Chicago) has so many things to offer—good schools, definitely good job opportunities with all the companies located here, good housing, good environment, great access to a variety of activities (night life, zoos, museums, theatres, restaurants and everything fairly easy to reach), good shopping and definitely a good class of people. I really wouldn't mind living in this area for many years to come. BUT—I am also willing to move wherever the best opportunity may arise for Joe—now when he's seeking employment, or in the future because of a promotion. I'm used to moving (I was in seven different schools by the time I was in eighth grade so I do know what moving is about!) and am sure I could adjust to almost anywhere, except maybe New York (I feel the cost of living, et cetera, would be too high for us to come out ahead).

Now for how I would like to live. Basically, the way we are now with the hope that Joe's income will increase as our family grows and our needs for our family increase. I did not mind working full-time but would prefer to be able to stay home where I feel my child (and hopefully—children) need me. I enjoy being able to come and go as I please and not have to worry financially about food (although I feel I'm very economical), clothing, gifts, social activities, et cetera. I would like our children to grow up in a good environment and attend good schools. I would like to be able to financially offer them college and many of the things they would like, along with such things as a good family background and home life. I want to do things as a family—I want our children *to know their father and their father to know them.* My father is in sales and he really was never around when my brother and I were growing up. His job was—at the time—more important then his family. Now my father is regretting the fact that he missed out with us. I *definitely* do not want this to happen to Joe. I want Joe to be happy in his work and I want him to be successful according to the goals he has set for himself. But I don't want him to be knee-deep buried in his work so much that he misses out on his family. If he has to work late during the week or travel quite a bit, I won't mind—as long as he has his weekends for us. I realize that the better the job and the higher he goes up the ladder, the more hours he'll have to devote to work. I don't even want to hold Joe back or cause him to lose out on a promotion because of me. I know if Joe is happy, we'll be happy and this is my goal for our family. I may be asking for too much, but I feel we can reach our goals if Joe and I stick together and both try our best.

Well, this report certainly turned out longer than I expected. I just hope some of these things will help you better understand Joe and give him the advice he needs. The only area I wish you wouldn't mention unless he does, is about his relationship with my parents and brother, especially my father, unless he brings it up first. Joe and I have been over this so many times and I would rather not have it brought up again, mainly because he and my father are *really* hitting it off for the first time. I would hate to jeopardize a good thing.

Again, I hope you can help Joe, because if you help him, you're helping us . . . .

If you have any questions or need additional information, please feel free to contact me.

3. DEVELOPING LIFE PLANS

I. Who Am I?

It is a part of our culture to explain things chronologically. Therapy deals with the past, while sensitivity training deals with the present, the here and now. Probably the most important thing about behavior that is occurring here and now is that it has consequences for here and now, plus past explanations, and future eventualities. So, today, we will work on the right hand side of the check mark you have made on your life line, and look at that part of your life that hasn't happened yet. We will investigate the right hand side of your line as much as we can, rather than slip back to the left side. Write-on ten separate pieces of paper—ten separate answers to the question, "Who am I?"

You have your own way of thinking about yourself. You may think of yourself in terms of your role, or in terms or in terms of qualities that you have. You may think of yourself in terms of your negative attributes. Or you may think of yourself as a mixture of all of these different frameworks. Whatever framework your life has had, try to find different answers to the question, "Who am I?" and write them down. When you are done, I want you to review the ten answers and think about what you would be if you eliminated any one of them.

Rank them.

II. Life Inventory.

A. Peak Experiences.
B. Things I do well.
C. Things I do poorly.
D. Things I would like to stop doing.
E. Things I would like to learn to do well.
F. Peak experiences I would like to have.
G. Values to be realized.
H. Things I'd like to start doing now.

III. Project Planning Phase.

The next phase begins the formulation of projects that combine a number of the desires expressed in the life inventory. This is difficult, and there are few procedures or patterns. Instead of thinking of goals with a separate set of strategies, think of projects that provide opportunities to allow you to learn what you want to learn or that move you towards the peak experiences you want to have. In each project, try to realize as many of these values, goals, and desires as you can. Try to develop an overall picture that lets you feel alive and satisfied. I can make these three suggestions:

A. Think of vocational or avocational projects to which you are already committed. Consider the parts of these projects that provide you opportunities to learn what you want to learn, that move you toward the peak of experience you want, or that allow you to reach the values, goals, and desires you want. Think about these projects in terms of what you can add or subtract from them so they will provide you with increased fulfillment.

B. Then list projects you have in mind to which you have not yet made a commitment. Consider these in terms of those which are likely to be most fulfilling for you. Make some plans for these.

C. Another thing you might do is brainstorm possible projects with your group. Make a list without evaluating each item. Rotate around the team, first one person then another. After the list is made, each person can evaluate each project for himself.

This phase of the process is where the "pay off" will take place. This part of the design will take at least one hour or more. At the end of this time the trainer may want some general discussion with the total group on such questions as:

Which aspects of the design seem to be most difficult?

Which aspects of the design seemed most meaningful?

What surprised you the most?

What are some of the obstacles you might encounter in accomplishing your projects?

This will provide a valuable release, evaluation and channeling of the learning experience to their ongoing life experience.

_____
_____
_____
_____

4. CAREER GROWTH PLAN

Planning is one major growth element in your career program. This outline can help you to devise a plan that definitely increases your career opportunities. Answer each question as specifically as you can. Consult with your boss, colleagues, and others who can help you to develop your best choices.

I. *Self-evaluation (skills inventory)*

1. Describe at least five of your best skills (manual talents, communications, supervision of others, handling figures and details, for example).

2. Areas of growth potential. Describe some of your underdeveloped or only partially developed abilities.

_____

_____

_____

_____

_____

3. What are your ambitions—long- and short-range goals? Describe as specifically as possible what you would like to be, achieve, or attain.

_____

_____

_____

_____

_____

II. *Outline information about your job*

1. Detail the main functions (duties and responsibilities) of your present job.

_____

_____

_____

_____

_____

2. Compare your abilities with those actually required in your job.
   a. List capabilities not being used effectively.

_____

_____

_____

_____

_____

b. List job functions or skills in which you can or should improve.

_____

_____

_____

_____

_____

3. Performance improvement.
   a. Describe specifically how you plan to carry out each job function more effectively. (Set specific objectives such as 20% increase in sales; 30% increase in inventory turnover; 15% cut in rejects; installation of cost controls.) Then, in each case, add a deadline by which these improvements will be made. This may seem difficult, but do it anyway.

_____

_____

_____

_____

   b. Specify additional assignments and responsibilities you will seek, and when.

_____

_____

_____

_____

With the above information spelled out, you can now go on to specify additional payoff goals.

III. *Short-range goals* (6 months to 2 years, approximately)
   1. Job goals (list additional assignments, new job areas, responsibilities, higher job title, and the like).

_____

_____

_____

_____

2. Training and development goals.
   a. New knowledge, skills, techniques.

   _____

   _____

   _____

   _____

   _____

   b. Educational (courses and studies of a formal nature).

   _____

   _____

   _____

   _____

   c. Professional areas (clubs or societies to join or become more active in; books; publications, papers, or theses to write).

   _____

   _____

   _____

   _____

3. Salary objectives.
   a. Amount of increase desired.

   _____

   _____

   b. Within (time period).

   _____

   c. Accomplishments you must achieve to show increase is deserved.

   _____

   _____

   _____

   _____

d. How you must present evidence of job accomplishments that justify your increase.

———————————————————————————————
———————————————————————————————
———————————————————————————————
———————————————————————————————
———————————————————————————————

VI. *Long-range goals* (3 to 6 years. These steps cover the same elements as for short-range planning, but goals should express your most optimistic self.)

1. Job goals (specify additional assignments, new job areas, higher job title, and so on).

———————————————————————————————
———————————————————————————————
———————————————————————————————
———————————————————————————————
———————————————————————————————

2. Training and development goals.
    a. New on-the-job duties, responsibilities, skills, and techniques you want to acquire.

———————————————————————————————
———————————————————————————————
———————————————————————————————
———————————————————————————————
———————————————————————————————

    b. Education, new skills (courses and studies of a formal nature, or even on TV college).

———————————————————————————————
———————————————————————————————
———————————————————————————————
———————————————————————————————

    c. Professional areas (clubs, or societies to join, or become active in; books, publications, papers or theses to write).

———————————————————————————————
———————————————————————————————

5. DYADIC ENCOUNTER

Goal

To explore knowing and trusting another person through mutual self-disclosure and risk-taking.

Group Size

Any number of paired participants.

Time Required

A minimum of thirty minutes. The time period allowed should be open-ended.

Materials Utilized

One booklet for each participant.

The exercise beginning on the following page should be reproduced in the form of a booklet which presents one question at a time. The format of the questions as they appear in this book will illustrate where each new page begins. The format has been designed to accommodate one page for every quarter of an 8 1/2 by ll inch sheet of paper. Copies of this booklet may be ordered from University Associates for the cost of duplication and handling. Allow seven days for receipt of booklets.

Physical Setting

Participants are seated facing each other.

Process

I. Participants are asked to follow the instructions indicated in the booklet.

II. The facilitator may choose to conduct an open discussion of the encounter after the experience has been completed.

1

Read silently. Do not look ahead in this booklet.

A theme that is frequently voiced when persons are brought together for the first time is, "I'd like to get to know you, but I don't know how." This sentiment often is expressed in encounter groups and emerges in marriage and other dyadic relationships. Getting to know another person involves a learnable set of skills and attitudes. The basic dimensions of encountering another person are self-disclosure, self-awareness, non-possessive caring,

---
2

risk-taking, trust, acceptance, and feedback. In an understanding, non-evaluative atmosphere one confides significant data about himself to another, who reciprocates by disclosing himself. This "stretching" results in a greater feeling of trust, understanding, and acceptance, and the relationship becomes closer, allowing more significant self-disclosure and greater risk-taking. As the two continue to share their experience authentically they come to know and trust each other in ways that may enable them to be highly resourceful to each other.

3

This dyadic encounter experience is designed to facilitate getting to know another person on a fairly intimate level. The discussion items are open-ended statements and can be completed at whatever level of self-disclosure one wishes.

The following ground rules should govern this experience:

4

All of the data discussed should be kept strictly confidential.

Don't look ahead in the booklet.

Each partner responds to each statement before continuing. The statements are to be completed in the order in which they appear. Don't skip items.

You may decline to answer any question by asking your partner.

Stop the exercise when either partner is becoming obviously uncomfortable or anxious. Either partner can stop the exchange.

Look up. If your partner has finished reading, turn the page and begin.

5

My name is . . .

6

My titles are . . .

7

My marital status is . . .

8

My hometown is . . .

9

The reason I'm here is . . .

10

Right now I'm feeling . . .

11

One of the most important skills in getting to know another person is listening. In order to get a check on your ability to understand what your partner is communicating, the two of you should go through the following steps *one at a time.*

Decide which one of you is to speak first in this unit.

The first speaker is to complete the following item in two or three sentences:

12

When I think about the future, I see myself . . .

The second speaker repeats *in his own words* what the first speaker has just said. The first speaker must be satisfied that he has been heard accurately.

The second speaker then completes the item himself in two or three sentences.

The first speaker paraphrases what the second speaker just said, to the satisfaction of the second speaker.

13

Share what you may have learned about yourself as a listener with your partner. The two of you may find yourselves later saying to each other, "What I hear you saying is . . ." to keep a check on the accuracy of your listening and understanding.

14

When I am in a new group I . . .

15

When I enter a room full of people I usually feel . . .

16

When I am feeling anxious in a new situation I usually . . .

17

In groups I feel most comfortable when the leader . . .

18

Social norms make me feel . . .

19

In ambiguous, unstructured situations I . . .
Listening check: "What I hear you saying is . . ."

20

I am happiest when . . .

21

The thing that turns me on the most is . . .

22

Right now I'm feeling . . .
Look your partner in the eyes while you respond to this item.

23

The thing that concerns me the most about joining groups is . . .

24

When I am rejected I usually . . .

25

To me, belonging is . . .

26

A forceful leader makes me feel . . .

27

Breaking rules that seem arbitrary makes me feel . . .

28

I like to be just a follower when . . .

29

The thing that turns me off the most is . . .

30

I feel most affectionate when . . .

31

Establish eye contact and hold your partner's hand while completing this item.
Toward you right now, I feel . . .

32

When I am alone I usually . . .

33

In crowds I . . .

34

In a group I usually get most involved when . . .
Listening check: "What I hear you saying is . . ."

35

To me, taking orders from another person . . .

36

I am rebellious when . . .

37

In a working meeting, having an agenda . . .

38

Checkup: Have a two- or three-minute discussion about this experience so far. Keep eye contact as much as you can, and try to cover the following points:

How well are you listening?

How open and honest have you been?

How eager are you to continue this interchange?

Do you feel that you are getting to know each other?

39

The emotion I find most difficult to control is . . .

40

My most frequent daydreams are about . . .

41

My weakest point is . . .   42

42

I love . . .

43

I feel jealous about . . .

44

Right now I'm feeling . . .

45

I am afraid of . . .

46

I believe in . . .

47

I am most ashamed of . . .

48

Right now I am most reluctant to discuss . . .

49

Interracial dating and/or marriage make me feel . . .

50

Premarital or extramarital sex . . .

51

Right now this experience is making me feel . . .

52

Express how you are feeling toward your partner without using words. You may want to touch. *Afterwards,* tell what you intended to communicate. Also, explore how this communication felt.

53

The thing I like best about you is . . .

54

You are . . .

55

What I think you need to know is . . .

56

Right now I am responding most to . . .

57

I want you to . . .

58

Time permitting, you might wish to continue this encounter through topics of your own choosing. Several possibilities are: money, religion, politics, race, marriage, the future, and the two of you.

6. INTIMACY EXPERIENCE

Goals

I. To accelerate the getting-acquainted process in groups.

II. To study the experience of self-disclosure.

III. To develop authenticity in groups.

Group Size

Unlimited.

Time Required

Approximately one hour and a half.

Materials Utilized

Intimacy Experience Guidelines.

Physical Setting

Room large enough for dyads to talk privately without disrupting noise.

Process

I. The facilitator introduces the exercise with a brief lecturette on self-disclosure and the building of trust. He explains the goals of the exercise.

II. Group members pair off, preferably with people whom they know least.

III. Intimacy Game Guidelines are described, the group rules are explained, and the forms are then distributed.

IV. Pairs meet for approximately one hour.

V. Groups of three or four dyads are formed to process the experience.

VI. The total group hears reports from each of the small groups.

Intimacy Experience Guidelines

Directions: During the time allotted for this experience you are to ask questions from this list. The questions vary in terms of their intimacy, and you may want to begin with some relatively less intimate ones. You may take turns initiating the questions. Follow the rules below.

1. Your communication with your partner will be held in confidence.
2. Any question that you ask your partner you must be willing to answer yourself.
3. You may declind to answer any question initiated by your partner.

How important is religion in your life?

What is the source of your financial income?

What is your favorite hobby or leisure interest?

What do you feel most ashamed of in your past?

What is your grade-point average at present?

Have you ever cheated on exams?

Have you deliberately lied about a serious matter to either parent?

What is the most serious lie you have told?

How do you feel about couples living together without being married?

Have you ever experienced premarital or extramarital sex?

Do you practice masturbation?

Have you been arrested or fined for violating any law?

Have you any health problems? What are they?

Reprinted by permission from *A Handbook of Structured Experiences for Human Relations Training*, Vol. III, pg. 70, by J.W. Pfeiffer and J.E. Jones. Copyright 1971 by University Associates, San Diego.

Have you ever had a mystical experience?

What do you regard as your chief fault in personality?

What turns you on the most?

How do you feel about interracial dating or marriages?

Do you consider yourself a liberal or conservative with regard to political parties?

What turns you off the fastest?

What features of your appearance do you consider most attractive to members of the opposite sex?

What do you regard as your least attractive features?

How important is money to you?

Are you or your parents divorced? Have you ever considered divorce?

To what clubs do you belong?

What person would you most like to take a trip with right now?

Do you drink alcoholic beverages?

How do you feel about swearing?

Have you ever been drunk?

Do you smoke marijuana or use drugs?

Do you enjoy manipulating or directing people?

Are females equal, inferior, or superior to males?

How often have you needed to see a doctor in the past year?

Have you ever been tempted to kill yourself?

Have you ever been tempted to kill someone?

Would you participate in a public demonstration?

What emotions do you find it most difficult to control?

Is there a particular person you wish would be attracted to you? Who? (Give name.)

What foods do you most dislike?

What are you most reluctant to discuss now?

To what person are you responding the most and how?

What's your IQ?

Is there any feature of your personality that you are proud of? What is it?

What was your worst failure in life, your biggest disappointment to yourself or your family?

What is your favorite TV program(s)?

What is your most chronic problem at present?

What is the subject of the most serious quarrels you have had with your parents?

What is the subject of your most frequent daydreams?

How are you feeling about me?

What are your career goals?

With what do you feel the greatest need for help?

What were you most punished or criticized for when you were a child?

How do you feel about crying in the presence of others?

What activities did you take part in in high school?

How could you improve your present living arrangement?

Do you have any misgivings about the group so far?

What is your main complaint about the group?

Have you ever engaged in homosexual activities?

Do you like your name?

If you could be anything/anyone—besides yourself—what/who would you be?

Who in your group don't you like?

Steps Toward Emotional Intimacy

The first step is to reveal yourselves as you are without bending to inner or outer pressure to fulfill someone else's conceptions.

The second step is to give and receive each other's expressions as statements about yourselves rather than demands or judgments.

The third step is to experience and express your differentness and conflict as chances for growth and learning, rather than as rejection.

The fourth step is to be committed to sticking with any feelings that arise until each of you feels openly heard and understood.

The fifth step is to be responsible for your own boundaries and limitations so that you do not pass the blame for what you do onto your partner.

The sixth step is to respect each other's limitations.

The seventh step is to understand that though you may unintentionally irritate or disappoint each other, you do not intend or want to hurt each other, and you do not see manipulation or punishment as even a possibly productive alternative.

The eighth step is the mutual feeling that your intent is to give all you can to each other wherever you can without hurting your own selves.

Shirley Luthman, *Intimacy: The Essence of Male and Female,* Freeport, New York: Nash Publishing Company.

NOTES

On the use of "Intimacy Experience":

7. IMPROVING WORK RELATIONS— A GROWTH EXPERIENCE

This dialog is one of the most effective ways you can improve your work relationships anywhere, on the job or off, by communicating better. This means sharing your feelings openly and honestly. The more you can open up, the better you can understand yourself and others.

This dialog will also hopefully enable you to analyze any assumptions you make about yourself and work. Please try to encounter yourself and another *human* person, by investing as much of yourself as possible. You will find your level of trust will grow in proportion to your risking more openness and honesty.

These suggestions may facilitate your progress:
1. All issues discussed here are confidential.
2. Do not jump ahead or omit any items.
3. Please have one partner initiate an item; each person respond; and then the second partner initiate the second item.

1. My job is essentially . . .

2. My responsibilities make me feel . . .

3. Your responsibilities seem to be . . .

4. I am the type of individual who usually . . .

5. My impression of you so far (honestly, HERE AND NOW) is . . .

6. When problems arise, I feel . . .

7. Conflicts usually make me feel . . .

8. I'd like to become more . . .

9. I can help you by . . .

10. I most enjoy . . .

Improving your ability to *LISTEN* will aid you greatly in your job and at home. Try following these guidelines. Complete the next item and all the following ones, in two or three sentences of *feeling*. The listener then should repeat in his/her own words the feelings-content. Do not parrot. But *reflect* the feelings rather than any fact-content. You may begin your reflection of feelings by saying . . . "You seem to be saying," or "You seem to be feeling . . ."

11. My main feelings about you here and now are . . .

12. In my work, I'm best at . . .

13. On my job, I need to improve . . .

14. Conflict for me means . . .

15. My best boss made me feel . . .

16. In managing others, I like . . .

17. In managing others, I feel . . .

18. My worst colleague (or subordinate) made me feel . . .

19. The best colleague (or subordinate) I ever had . . .

20. Negative criticism makes me feel . . .

21. I need positive reinforcement whenever . . .

22. I get positive reinforcement when . . .

23. The pressures of a deadline make me feel . . .

24. So far, what I like about you . . .

25. This encounter . . . — — — LISTEN: "I hear you saying . . ."

26. My most common feeling in the past few months . . .

27. My next short-range (2-3 months) goal is . . .

28. My best long-range (3-5 years) goal is . . .

29. My overall feeling about you . . .

30. My favorite coworkers are . . .

31. Feedback for me . . .

32. What surprises me about you . . .

33. What I most want to know about you is . . .

34. I've been fantasizing about you . . .

35. Right here and now I feel . . .

36. My worst important career development need is . . .

37. The one thing about you that would enable me to open up more is . . .

PLEASE DISCUSS HOW YOU BOTH FEEL ABOUT EACH OTHER HERE

38. Here's a real situation facing me. What do you think I feel like and actually did?

39. I'd most like to see you involved in . . .

40. I keep hoping . . .

41. I "suppose" you see me as . . .

42. If only . . .

43. My most secret goals are . . .

44. You and I can . . .

45. You and I should . . .

Please try to use this exchange at work, later *sometime*, and make a contract now to meet again for more mutual support. Also, try to do this again with the same person in less than six months.

8. THE MPI INVENTORY

DIRECTIONS

This inventory contains various pairs of statements about tasks and things you may or may not like; about ways you may or may not feel. Consider this example:

A—I am constantly seeking to improve methods and systems on my job.

B—If I clearly see no chances to advance or make progress in my career, I would move on to another situation.

Which of these two statements is more typical of how you act or feel? Please choose one that is most characteristic of you.

You will have to choose either A or B, even if you like both. If you like both A and B, please choose the one you like most. If you dislike both A and B, please choose the one you dislike less. In each case, your choice should be made in terms of what you like and how you feel at the *present* time, and not in terms of what you think you should like or how you think you should feel.

So this is *not a test*. There are *no right or wrong answers*. So your choice should be an honest one of how you really feel. Please make a choice for every pair of statements and do not skip any.

Please do not make any marks in this booklet, but rather on the separate answer sheet. Please make sure you check to see that numbers in the booklet correspond with numbers on the answer sheet.

Published by
HUMAN RESOURCE DEVELOPERS, INC.
112 W. Oak Street
Chicago, Ill. 60610
and
MANAGEMENT PROGRAMS, INC.
P.O. Box 72
Glen Ellyn, Ill. 60137

THE M P I INVENTORY

1A I am constantly seeking to improve systems and methods on my job.

 B If I clearly see no chances to advance or make progress in my career, I would move on to another situation.

2A I like to experiment and try out novel things.

 B I am rarely permitted to complete anything to my perfect satisfaction.

3A I want my friends or others to support me when I meet with difficulties or failure.

 B The most important aspect of a product or service is the quality.

4A I like to believe the best way to deal with people is to tell them what they want to hear.

 B Acquiring maximum skill in my job or career is the best way to succeed.

5A I like my standard of living to be as high as possible.

 B I would like to learn to do things better than I do now.

6A I would rather do one thing very well, than many things adequately.

 B I am constantly seeking to improve systems and methods on my job.

7A Acquiring maximum skill in my job or career is the best way to succeed.

 B I like to be involved in new fashions, fads or projects.

8A I like people to treat me kindly.

 B I enjoy doing new things and going to different places.

9A When I ask someone to do something for me, I sometimes do not give the real reasons for wanting it but reasons that carry weight.

B I prefer to experience novelty and change in my daily life.

10A I like my standard of living to be as high as possible.

B I like to try new and different jobs or tasks rather than continue the same old things.

11A I am rarely permitted to complete anything to my perfect satisfaction.

B I prefer to have people make a fuss over me when I'm ill.

12A I enjoy doing new things and going to different places.

B I need understanding and sympathy when I have problems.

13A I feel anyone who completely trusts anyone else is asking for trouble.

B I like people to sympathize with me when I'm ill.

14A I believe its hard to get ahead without cutting corners here and there.

B I like friends to aid me when I have a problem or challenge.

15A Money is more than just a symbol of success to me.

B I prefer friends to perform small favors for me cheerfully.

16A The most important aspect of the product or service is the quality.

B I feel anyone who completely trusts anyone else is asking for trouble.

17A I prefer to experience novelty and change in my daily life.

B I believe its hard to get ahead without cutting corners here and there.

18A I prefer to have people make a fuss over me when I'm ill.

B I feel safest in assuming all people have a vicious streak that will come out when they are given a chance.

19A I like to insist on my viewpoint whenever anyone attacks it.

B I believe its hard to get ahead without cutting corners here and there.

20A I like my standard of living to be as high as possible.

B I like to believe one should take action even if unsure its morally right.

21A Acquiring maximum skill in my job or career is the best way to succeed.

B Even if I were already very wealthy, I'd still work hard for all the money I could earn.

22A I like to try new and different jobs or tasks rather than continue the same old things.

B Money is more than just a symbol of success to me.

23A I need understanding and sympathy when I have problems.

B I like to think all the wealthy people I've read about still want more money.

24A I feel safest in assuming all people have a vicious streak that will come out when they are given a chance.

B I like to enjoy all the finer things that only money can buy.

25A I feel anyone who completely trusts anyone else is asking for trouble.

B If I had the capital to invest, I would begin my own business primarily to make more money.

26A I would like to learn to do things better than I do now.

B I enjoy forming new friendships.

27A I like to try out new and unusual restaurants.

B I prefer deep relationships with my friends.

28A I like friends to aid me when I have a problem or challenge.

B I enjoy sharing with my friends.

29A I like to believe one should take action even if unsure its morally right.

B I prefer to make as many new friends as possible.

30A My superiors or peers have always said I'm worth more than I've been paid.

B I like to have deep intense attachments to my friends.

31A The old saying "Anything worth doing is worth doing well" is especially needed today.

B When I think my superiors have done well, I like to tell them.

32A I enjoy traveling to new places in this country and abroad.
B I enjoy reading about great men.

33A I prefer friends to perform small favors for me cheerfully.
B I prefer to conform and avoid anything people I respect might view as extraordinary.

34A I do not believe most people are basically good and kind.
B I enjoy praising anyone I respect and admire.

35A I believe successful executives are motivated more by money than by love or authority or their own ego needs.
B I enjoy doing what's expected of me in following orders.

36A One cannot possibly learn all there is to know about a subject.
B I like to be able to earn as much money as possible.

37A I would like to live in different parts of the country.
B I like to be rewarded financially more so than in any other way.

38A I like my friends to show a lot of affection to me.
B Money means more to me than to most of my friends or peers.

39A I believe sometimes you may have to lie to someone for his own good.
B I would do just about anything for the money involved.

40A I like to think other executives and managers work mostly for the money, regardless of what they may say.
B I like money for its own sake.

41A I feel sorry to see human potential unused in our society.
B I want to be able to say I've performed well on a different task.

42A I like to find new, improved ways to perform my job better.
B I like to resolve problems or puzzles others find difficult.

43A When I am depressed I need friends to sympathize and cheer me up.
B I strive to be able to accomplish things better than others can.

44A I believe most men forget more easily the death of their father than the loss of their property.
B I like to perform tasks that others insist require great skill and effort.

45A If I had the capital to invest, I would begin my own business primarily to make more money.
B I strive to be a success in all things I do.

46A The quality expended is an effort is more important than merely finishing the project or task.
B I want others to esteem me as a leader.

47A I prefer never to do the same thing in the same old way.
B I like to tell others how to do their jobs better.

48A I want my friends or others to support me when I meet with difficulties or failure.
B I prefer to lead and direct the actions of others wherever and whenever I can.

49A I believe in general people won't work hard unless they're forced to do so.
B I like to insist on my viewpoint whenever anyone attacks it.

50A I like my standard of living to be as high as possible.
B When I'm with others in a group, I prefer to make the decisions on what we'll do.

51A If I clearly see no chances to advance or make progress in my career, I would move on to another situation.
B Sometimes I get so angry I feel like throwing or breaking things.

52A I am constantly seeking to improve systems and methods on my job.
B I feel like making fun of people doing what I view as dumb and stupid.

53A I like people to treat me kindly.
B I enjoy reading or hearing accounts of violence.

54A I like to believe the best way to deal with people is to tell them what they want to hear.
  B When things go wrong for me, I prefer to blame others.

55A I prefer my superiors to be more receptive to my ideas rather than give me more money.
  B When I disagree with someone, I will tell him off.

56A I would rather do one thing very well, than many things adequately.
  B I prefer not being interrupted when working.

57A I like to experiment and try out novel things.
  B I like to work very hard on anything I do.

58A I like people to sympathize with me when I'm ill.
  B I like to keep on working late to finish a job.

59A When I ask someone to do something for me, I sometimes do not give the real reason for wanting it but reasons that carry weight.
  B I like to complete any project or action that I begin.

60A I like my standard of living to be as high as possible.
  B Even if it may seem I'm not making much progress on a project, I like to stick to it anyway.

61A I enjoy forming new friendships.
  B The old saying "Anything worth doing is worth doing well" seems especially needed today.

62A I like to discover what outstanding leaders did about problems of my interest.
  B One cannot possibly learn all there is to know about a subject.

63A I like to be able to earn as much money as possible.
  B I feel sorry to see human potential unused in our society.

64A I would like to achieve something of outstanding significance.
  B The quality expended in an effort is more important than merely finishing the project or task.

65A I like to be one of the leaders in the company, organization or group.
  B If I clearly see no chances to advance or make progress in my career, I would move on to another situation.

66A I prefer deep relationships with my friends.
  B I like to try out new and unusual restaurants.

67A I prefer to follow orders and do what is expected of me.
  B I enjoy traveling to new places in this country and abroad.

68A I like to be rewarded financially more so than in any other way.
  B I would like to live in different part of the country.

69A I would like to be a renowned expert in some field, profession or career.
  B I like to find new, improved ways to perform my job better.

70A When working on a committee, I like to be elected or appointed chairperson.
  B I prefer never to do the same thing in the same old way.

71A I enjoy sharing with my friends.
  B I like my friends to show a lot of affection to me.

72A When I think my superiors have done a good job, I like to tell them.
  B When I am depressed I need friends to sympathize and cheer me up.

73A Money means more to me than it does to most of my friends and peers.
  B I want my friends or others to support me when I meet with difficulties or failure.

74A I want to be able to say I've performed well on a difficult task.
  B I like people to treat me kindly.

75A I want others to esteem me as a leader.
  B I like people to sympathize with me when I'm ill.

76A I prefer to make as many new friends as possible.
  B I do not believe most people are basically good and kind.

77A I enjoy reading about great men.
 B I believe sometimes you may have to lie to someone for his own good.

78A I would do just about anything for the money involved.
 B I believe most men forget more easily the death of their father than the loss of their property.

79A I like to resolve problems or puzzles that others find difficult.
 B I believe in general people won't work hard unless they're forced to do so.

80A I like to tell others how to do their jobs better.
 B I like to believe the best way to deal with people is to tell them what they want to hear.

81A I like to have deep, intense attachments to my friends.
 B My superiors or peers have always said I'm worth more than I've been paid.

82A I prefer to conform and avoid anything people I respect might view as extraordinary.
 B I believe successful executives are motivated more by money than by love or authority or their own ego needs.

83A I like money for its own sake.
 B I like to think other executives and managers work mostly for the money, regardless of what they may say.

84A I strive to be able to accomplish things better than others can.
 B I like to be a trader (not an investor) in stocks so I can make more money.

85A I prefer to lead and direct the actions of others wherever and whenever I can.
 B I prefer my superiors to be more receptive to my ideas rather than give me more money.

86A I feel safest in assuming all people have a vicious streak that will come out when they are given a chance.
 B I enjoy doing things with my friends rather than alone.

87A I enjoy praising anyone I respect and admire.
 B I prefer to be in groups where members have deep, warm feelings for one another.

88A The best measure of my personal success is the money I earn.
 B I enjoy assisting my friends when in difficulty.

89A I like to perform tasks that others insist require great skill and effort.
 B I like to be generous and do small favors for my friends.

90A I like to insist on my own viewpoint whenever anyone attacks it.
 B I like to forgive my friends who may offend me.

91A I prefer to be in groups where members have deep, warm feelings for one another.
 B I enjoy accepting leadership from people I respect.

92A I do not believe most people are basically good and kind.
 B I enjoy doing what's expected of me in following orders.

93A I feel more strongly about money than just about anything else, except perhaps sexual behavior.
 B When organizing something, I like to ask opinions from people I admire.

94A I strive to be a success in all things I do.
 B When in a group, I prefer to accept the leadership of someone else.

95A When I'm with others in a group, I prefer to make the decisions on what we will do.
 B I like to discover what outstanding leaders did about problems of my interest.

96A I enjoy assisting my friends when in difficulty.
 B The best measure of my personal success is the money I earn.

97A I enjoy accepting leadership from people I respect.
 B I feel more strongly about money than just about anything else, except perhaps sexual behavior.

98A I believe sometimes you may have to lie to someone for his own good.
 B I prefer a raise in pay rather than have my superior be receptive to my ideas.

99A I would like to write a great novel or play or compose a hit song.
  B I'd prefer more money in my present job rather than more responsibility in a field of lesser prestige.

100A I like to motivate and persuade others to do it my way.
  B I feel money is more important to me than prestige or power.

101A I like to be generous and do small favors for my friends.
  B I would like to write a great novel or play or compose a hit song.

102A When organizing something I like to ask opinions from people I admire.
  B I like to perform at the utmost in everything I do.

103A I'd prefer more money in my present job rather than more responsibility in a field of lesser prestige.
  B If I had the capital to invest, I'd begin my own business so I could have a greater feeling of accomplishment.

104A I believe sometimes you may have to lie to someone for his own good.
  B I like to perform at the utmost in everything I do.

105A I like to be asked to mediate disagreements and arguments between others.
  B I would like to achieve something of outstanding significance.

106A I like to forgive my friends who may offend me.
  B I like to motivate and persuade others to do it my way.

107A When in a group I prefer to accept the leadership of someone else.
  B I like to be asked to mediate disagreements and arguments between others.

108A I feel money is more important to me than prestige or power.
  B I prefer to set my own goals rather than have them set for me.

109A If I had the capital to invest, I'd begin my own business so I could have a greater feeling of accomplishment.
  B I prefer to lead and direct the actions of others wherever and whenever I can.

110A I feel anyone who completely trusts anyone else is asking for trouble.
  B I prefer to set my own goals rather than have them set for me.

111A I enjoy showing a good amount of love and affection toward my friends.
  B When I disagree with someone, I will tell him off.

112A I like to discover what outstanding leaders did about problems of my interest.
  B I like to fight points of view different from mine.

113A I am more easily motivated by money than anything.
  B If someone deserves it, I will critically reproach him publically.

114A I would like to achieve something of outstanding significance.
  B I do not hesitate telling others what I think of them.

115A I like to be one of the leaders in the company, organization or group.
  B Sometimes I get so angry I feel like throwing or breaking things.

116A I prefer to relate to other people with warmth and kindness.
  B I like to finish one single project or task at a time before taking on others.

117A I prefer to follow orders and do what is expected of me.
  B When I have something to do, I like to keep on it until it is finished.

118A I would prefer a higher salary rather than various kinds of fringe benefits.
  B I like to keep working a puzzle or project until I solve it.

119A I would like to be a renowned expert in some field, profession or career.
  B I prefer not being interrupted when working.

120A When working on a committee I like to be elected or appointed chairperson.
   B I like to work very hard on anything I do.

121A I like to fight points of view different from mine.
   B I would rather do one thing very well than many things adequately.

122A I like to work very hard on anything I do.
   B I am rarely permitted to complete anything to my perfect satisfaction.

123A If someone deserves it, I will critically reproach him publically.
   B I am constantly seeking to improve systems and methods on my job.

124A I like to keep on working late to finish a job.
   B I like to experiment and try out novel things.

125A I do not hesitate telling others what I think of them.
   B I prefer to have people make a fuss over me when I'm ill.

126A I like to complete any project or action I begin.
   B I need understanding and sympathy when I have problems.

127A Sometimes I get so angry I feel like throwing or breaking things.
   B When I ask someone to do something for me, I sometimes do not give the real reasons for wanting it but reasons that carry weight.

128A Even if it may seem I'm not making much progress on a project, I like to stick to it anyway.
   B I feel anyone who completely trusts anyone else is asking for trouble.

129A I feel like making fun of people doing what I view as dumb and stupid.
   B If I had the capital to invest, I would get in my own business primarily to make more money.

130A I like to finish one single project or task at a time before taking on others.
   B I like to be a trader (not an investor) in stocks so I can make more money.

131A I enjoy reading or hearing accounts of violence.
   B I enjoy showing a good amount of love and affection toward my friends.

132A When I have something to do I like to keep on it until it is finished.
   B I prefer to relate to other people with warmth and kindness.

133A When things go wrong for me, I prefer to blame others.
   B I prefer to follow orders and do what is expected of me.

134A I like to keep working a puzzle or project until I solve it.
   B When I think my superiors have done a good job, I like to tell them.

135A I feel like revenge when someone has hurt me.
   B I am more easily motivated by money than anything.

136A I prefer not being interrupted when working.
   B I would prefer a higher salary rather than various kinds of fringe benefits.

137A When I disagree with someone, I will tell him off.
   B I would like to be a renowned expert in some field, profession or career.

138A Even if it may seem I'm not making much progress on a project, I like to stick to it anyway.
   B I want to be able to say I've performed well on a difficult task.

139A I like to fight points of view different from mine.
   B I like to insist on my own viewpoint whenever anyone attacks it.

140A I like to finish one single project or task at a time before taking on others.
   B I prefer to set my own goals rather than have them set for me.

141A I believe in general people won't work hard unless they're forced to do so.
   B If someone deserves it, I will critically reproach him publically.

142A When I have something to do I like to keep on it until it is finished.

B I feel like making fun of people doing what I view as dumb and stupid.

143A I do not hesitate telling others what I think of them.

B I like to keep on working late to finish a job.

144A I do not believe most people are basically good and kind.

B I like to keep on working on a puzzle or project until I solve it.

The MPI Inventory—By Dean C. Dauw, Ph.D.

Name

Age   Sex   Date

	MPI	R.	C.	RS
1.				
2.				
3.				
4.				
5.				
6.				
7.				
8.				
9.				
10.				
11.				
12.				

For each numbered item in the booklet, select either A or B and circle it.

1. A B	6. A B	11. A B	16. A B	21. A B	26. A B	31. A B	36. A B	41. A B	46. A B	51. A B	56. A B
2. A B	7. A B	12. A B	17. A B	22. A B	27. A B	32. A B	37. A B	42. A B	47. A B	52. A B	57. A B
3. A B	8. A B	13. A B	18. A B	23. A B	28. A B	33. A B	38. A B	43. A B	48. A B	53. A B	58. A B
4. A B	9. A B	14. A B	19. A B	24. A B	29. A B	34. A B	39. A B	44. A B	49. A B	54. A B	59. A B
5. A B	10. A B	15. A B	20. A B	25. A B	30. A B	35. A B	40. A B	45. A B	50. A B	55. A B	60. A B
61. A B	66. A B	71. A B	76. A B	81. A B	86. A B	91. A B	96. A B	101. A B	106. A B	111. A B	116. A B
62. A B	67. A B	72. A B	77. A B	82. A B	87. A B	92. A B	97. A B	102. A B	107. A B	112. A B	117. A B
63. A B	68. A B	73. A B	78. A B	83. A B	88. A B	93. A B	98. A B	103. A B	108. A B	113. A B	118. A B
64. A B	69. A B	74. A B	79. A B	84. A B	89. A B	94. A B	99. A B	104. A B	109. A B	114. A B	119. A B
65. A B	70. A B	75. A B	80. A B	85. A B	90. A B	95. A B	100. A B	105. A B	110. A B	115. A B	120. A B
121. A B	123. A B	125. A B	127. A B	129. A B	131. A B	133. A B	135. A B	137 B	139. A B	141. A B	143. A B
122. A B	124. A B	126. A B	128. A B	130. A B	132. A B	134. A B	136. A B	138. A B	140. A B	142. A B	144. A B

9. SOUNDS AND IMAGES

Part I.

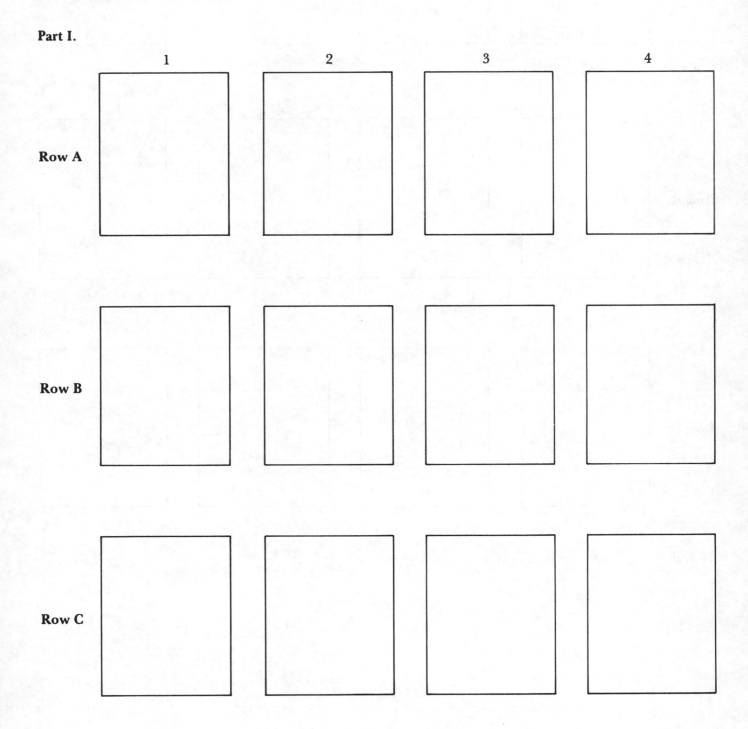

Part II.

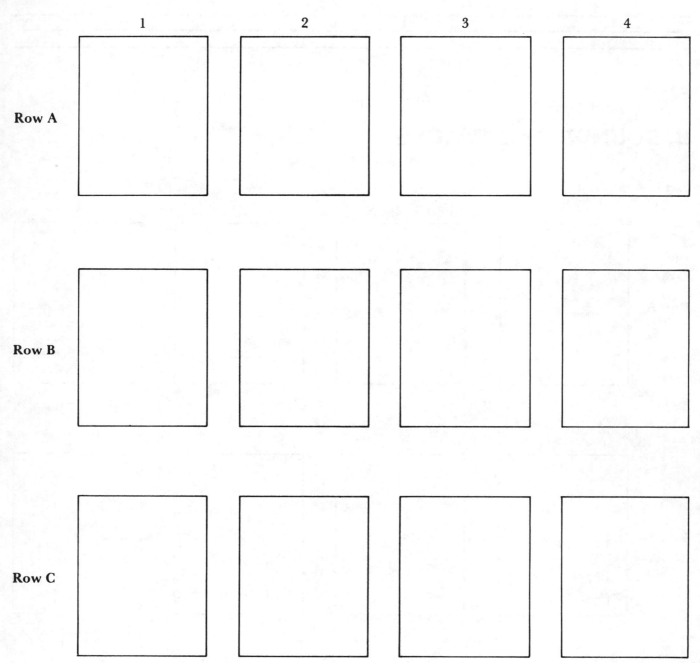

10. T-P LEADERSHIP QUESTIONNAIRE

Goal

To evaluate oneself in terms of task orientation and people orientation.

Group Size

Unlimited.

Time Required

I. Lecturette: open.
II. Questionnaire: ten minutes.
III. Scoring: ten minutes.
IV. Discussion: open.

Materials Utilized

I. T–P Leadership Questionnaire for each participant.
II. Pencil for each participant.
III. Leadership Style Profile Sheet for each participant.

Physical Setting

Participants should be seated comfortably for writing, preferably at tables or desk-chairs.

Process

I. Without previous discussion, the facilitator asks participants to fill out the T–P Leadership Questionnaire.
II. Before scoring the questionnaire, the facilitator will present a brief lecturette on shared leadership as a function of the combined concern for task and people.
III. The facilitator announces that in order to locate oneself on the Leadership Style Profile Sheet, group participants will score their own questionnaires on the dimensions of task orientation (T) and people orientation (P).

IV. The facilitator instructs the participants in the scoring as follows:
   A. Circle the item number for items 8, 12, 17, 18, 19, 30, 34, and 35.
   B. Write a "1" in front of the *circled items* to which you responded S (seldom) or N (never).
   C. Write a "1" in front of *items not circled* to which you responded A (always) or F (frequently).
   D. Circle the "1's" which you have written in front of the following items: 3, 5, 8, 10, 15, 18, 19, 22, 24, 26, 28, 30, 32, 34, and 35.
   E. Count the circled "1's." This is your score for concern for people. Record the score in the blank following the letter "p" at the end of the questionnaire.
   F. Count the uncircled "1's." This is your score for concern for task. Record this number in the blank following the letter "T."

V. The facilitator distributes Leadership Style Profile Sheets and instructs participants to follow the directions on the sheet. He then leads a discussion of the implications that members attach to their location on the profile.

From *A Handbook of Structured Experiences for Human Relations Training* by J.W. Pfeiffer and J.E. Jones. Revised Version of Questionnaire reprinted by permission of University Associates, San Diego.

309

T–P LEADERSHIP QUESTIONNAIRE

The following items describe aspects of leadership behavior. Respond to each item according to the way you would be most likely to act if you were the leader of a work group. Circle whether you would be likely to behave in the described way always (A), frequently (F), occasionally (O), seldom (S), or never (N).

If I were the leader of a work group . . .

A F O S N _____ 1. I would most likely act as the spokesman of the group.

A F O S N _____ 2. I would encourage overtime work.

A F O S N _____ 3. I would allow members complete freedom in their work.

A F O S N _____ 4. I would encourage the use of uniform procedures.

A F O S N _____ 5. I would permit the members to use their own judgment in solving problems.

A F O S N _____ 6. I would stress being ahead of competing groups.

A F O S N _____ 7. I would speak as a representative of the group.

A F O S N _____ 8. I would needle members for greater effort.

A F O S N _____ 9. I would try out my ideas in the group.

A F O S N _____ 10. I would let the members do their work the way they think best.

A F O S N _____ 11. I would be working hard for a promotion.

A F O S N _____ 12. I would be able to tolerate postponement and uncertainty.

A F O S N _____ 13. I would speak for the group when visitors were present.

A F O S N _____ 14. I would keep the work moving at a rapid pace.

A F O S N _____ 15. I would turn the members loose on a job and let them go to it.

A F O S N _____ 16. I would settle conflicts when they occur in the group.

A F O S N _____ 17. I would get swamped by details.

A F O S N _____ 18. I would represent the group at outside meetings.

A F O S N _____ 19. I would be reluctant to allow the members any freedom of action.

A F O S N _____ 20. I would decide what shall be done and how it shall be done.

A F O S N _____ 21. I would push for increased production.

A F O S N _____ 22. I would let some members have authority which I could keep.

A F O S N _____ 23. Things would usually turn out as I predict.

A F O S N _____ 24. I would allow the group a high degree of initiative.

A F O S N _____ 25. I would assign group members to particular tasks.

A F O S N _____ 26. I would be willing to make changes.

A F O S N _____ 27. I would ask the members to work harder.

A F O S N _____ 28. I would trust the group members to exercise good judgment.

A F O S N _____ 29. I would schedule the work to be done.

A F O S N ____ 30. I would refuse to explain my actions.

A F O S N ____ 31. I would persuade others that my ideas are to their advantage.

A F O S N ____ 32. I would permit the group to set its own pace.

A F O S N ____ 33. I would urge the group to beat its previous record.

A F O S N ____ 34. I would act without consulting the group.

A F O S N ____ 35. I would ask that group members follow standard rules and regulations.

T _____   P _____

LEADERSHIP STYLE PROFILE SHEET

Indicating a Leadership Style:

Directions: In order to indicate your style of leadership, find your score on the *concern for task* dimension (T) on the left-hand arrow. Next, move to the right-hand arrow and find your score on the *concern for people* dimension (P). Draw a straight line that intersects the P and T score; the point at which that line crosses the *team leadership* arrow indicates your score on that dimension.

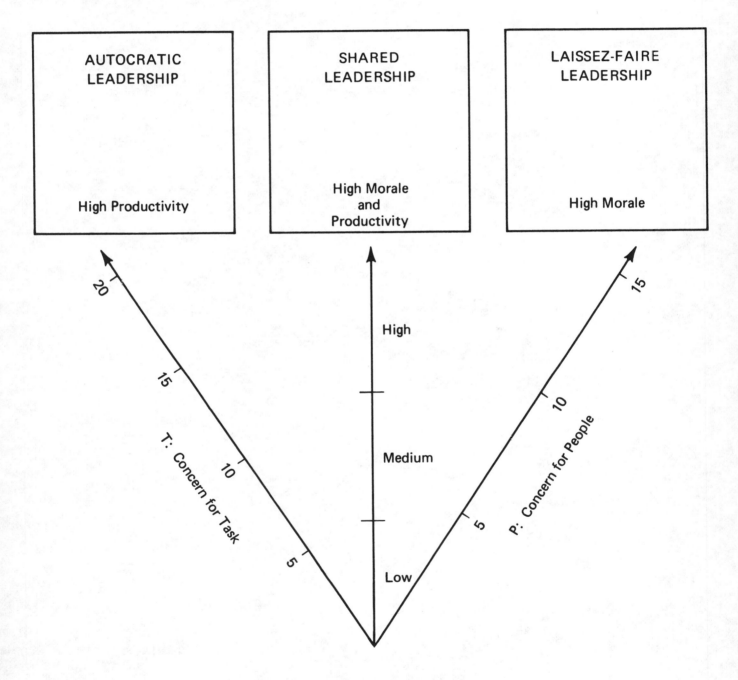

Shared Leadership Resulting from
Balancing Concern for Task and Concern for People

11. THRUST-COUNTER THRUST

Part I. Problem Specification.

Think about a problem that is significant in your back-home situations. Respond to each item as fully as needed so that another participant will be able to understand the problem.

1. I understand the problem to be specifically that . . .

2. The following people with whom I must deal are involved in the problem:

   Their status of involvement is . . .

   They relate to me and to the problem in the following manner:

3. I consider these other factors to be relevant to the problem:

Reprinted by permission from *A Handbook of Structured Experiences for Human Relations Training*, Vol. II, pg. 83, by J.W. Pfeiffer and J.E. Jones. Copyright 1970 by University Associates, San Diego.

4. I would choose the following aspect of the problem to be changed if it were in my power to do so (choose only one aspect):

Part II: Thrusting and Counter Thrusting Forces.

5. If I consider the present status of the problem to be a temporary balance of opposing forces, the following would be on my list of forces providing thrust toward change:

—— a. _____

—— b. _____

—— c. _____

—— d. _____

—— e. _____

—— f. _____

—— g. _____

—— h. _____

6. The following would be on my list of forces in counter thrust to change:

—— a. _____

—— b. _____

—— c. _____

—— d. _____

—— e. _____

—— f. _____

—— g. _____

—— h. _____

7. In the spaces to the left of the letters in item 5, quantify the forces on a range from one to five in the following manner:

   1. it has almost nothing to do with the thrust toward change in the problem;
   2. it has relatively little to do with the thrust toward change in the problem;
   3. it is of moderate importance in the thrust toward change in the problem;
   4. it is an important factor in the thrust toward change in the problem;
   5. it is a major factor in the thrust toward change in the problem.

8. Fill in the spaces in front of the letters in item 6 to quantify the forces in counter thrust to change.

9. Diagram the forces of the thrust and counter thrust quantified in question 7 by drawing an arrow from the corresponding degree of force to the status quo line. For example, if you considered the first on your list of forces in item 5 to be rated a 3, draw your arrow from the 3 position in the left hand column of numbers indicating thrust up to the status quo line.

Counter Thrust

```
      /    a   /   b   /   c   /   d   /   e   /   f   /   g   /   h   /
  5 ------------------------------------------------------------------------
  4 ------------------------------------------------------------------------
  3 ------------------------------------------------------------------------
  2 ------------------------------------------------------------------------
  1 ------------------------------------------------------------------------
```

Status Quo ==

```
  1 ------------------------------------------------------------------------
  2 ------------------------------------------------------------------------
  3 ------------------------------------------------------------------------
  4 ------------------------------------------------------------------------
  5 ------------------------------------------------------------------------
      /    a   /   b   /   c   /   d   /   e   /   f   /   g   /   h   /
```

Thrust

Part III. Strategy for Changing the Status Quo.

Detail a strategy for decreasing two or more counter thrust elements from your list from item 6.

12. DECISION STEMS

Instructions: Complete the following decision-making steps according to how you actually feel about each item. Ignore the urge to put down the theoretically "best" answer. What is typical is more important to self-development.

1. Decision making is . . .

2. Decisions make me feel . . .

3. In making decisions, I . . .

4. If there are no clear-cut guidelines for deciding, I . . .

5. Putting off decisions . . .

6. When I make a decision, my boss . . .

7. For me the best part of decision making is . . .

8. When I see a decision-making situation, I . . .

9. When people get into a decision-making situation I faced, I . . .

10. When forced to make a decision in an area for which I have no authority, I . . .

11. From my experience the best way to decide is . . .

12. In making people decisions I . . .

13. When people get into a decision-making situation they usually . . .

14. My subordinates privately feel my decisions . . .

15. The best way to gain acceptance of decisions is . . .

16. In implementing decision I . . .

13. CONFLICT RESOLUTION

Resolving conflict is a challenge for everyone. There are numerous theories about how to assess the sources of conflict and how to resolve them. Below are listed some stems that you should fill in, usually with the first idea that comes to mind. Then, discuss them for greater insights into your own present ways of approaching or handling conflict. Then see if you can consult with others about ways of improving your present methods.

1. Conflict is . . .

2. For me, the exhilarating aspect of conflict is . . .

3. The most depressing aspect of conflict for me is . . .

4. When I see a conflict situation coming, I . . .

5. In the last important conflict I experienced, I . . .

6. My usual feeling about conflict is . . .

7. The best thing you can say about conflict is . . .

8. The worst aspect about conflict for me is (do not repeat what you wrote in #3 above) . . .

9. When people get into a conflict situation, they usually . . .

10. From my experience, the best way to resolve a conflict is . . .

11. Others mostly seem to resolve conflicts by . . .

12. In the future, I will try to handle conflicts better by . . .

14. ROLE IDENTIFICATION FORM

Instructions: Place check marks in the column identifying the roles each member has played in the group.

Roles   Members

Group Task Roles	A	B	C	D	E	F	G	H	I	J	K	L
1. Initiator Contributor												
2. Information Seeker												
3.. Information Giver												
4. Coordinator												
5. Orienter												
6. Evaluator												
Group Growing and Vitalizing Roles												
7. Encourage												
8. Harmonizer												
9. Gatekeeper and Expediter												
10. Standard Setter or Ego Ideal												
11. Follower												
Anti-Group Roles												
12. Blocker												
13. Recognition Seeker												
14. Dominator												
15. Avoider												

Reprinted by permission from *A Handbook of Structured Experiences for Human Relations Training*, Vol. II, pg. 76, by J.W. Pfeiffer and J.E. Jones. Copyright 1970 by University Associates, San Diego.

323

15. "MASLOW HIERARCHY OF NEEDS"

Needs	Expression	Threat	Action
Self-Fulfillment	Realizing Potential Creativity Self-Development of talents Self-Projection of Ideas	Inflexible Policies Narrow Definitions of job tasks No Interest in Job Enrichment	Boss Trust (Credit Bank) Progressive Business Climate Creating Opportunities Tolerating Individualism Management Development

Ego Needs	Self (Competence)—
	Esteem Mastery
	    (Self-Confidence)
	    (Independence)
	    (Achievement)
	Theory Y Management
	Reputation (Recognition)
	    (Appreciation)
	    (Respect)
	    (Personal Identity)
		Job fractation
		Careless Criticism
		Failure to Praise or Reward
		Centralization of: Authority
		Theory X Management
		Accoutrements of Office
			Consultation
			Use of Rewards & Recognition
			Job Enlargement & Influence
			Boss Feedback
			Visibility & Exposure

Social Needs	Belonging Association Acceptance Giving and Receiving Attention Friendship Love and to Be Loved	Unfriendly Associates & Management Office Cliques & Rejection Poor Communications Boss Ostracism	Recreational Programs Participation in Management Morale and Opinion Survey Communications & Special Bulletin Project Management

Safety Needs	Protection against
	  a. Danger
	  b. Threat (arbitrariness)
	  c. Deprivation
	  d. Insecurity
	Unpredictability in Environment
		Arbitrary Action By Management
		Sudden Changes
		Poor Communications
		Lack of Policy & Procedure
		Favoritism & Discrimination
		No Benefits
			Performance Appraisal
			Written Policies and Procedures
			Position Guide
			House Organ
			Bulletin Board
			Meetings
			Union & Grievance Process

Physiological Needs	Air, Food, Water, Space Rest and Exercise Protection from the Elements	Inadequate Benefits Poor Pay No Break (Coffee) Poor Conditions (Cramped) Poor Facilities Excessive Hours	Sound & Effective Salary Program Good Working Environment Work Planning and Scheduling Rest, Lunch, and Holiday Periods Shorter Work Week

16. GENERAL PERSONALITY DESCRIPTION

1. You have a great need for other people to like and admire you.

2. You have a tendency to be critical of yourself.

3. You have a great deal of unused capacity which you have not turned to your advantage.

4. While you have some personality weaknesses, you are generally able to compensate for them.

5. Your sexual adjustment has presented problems for you.

6. Disciplined and self-controlled outside, you tend to be worrisome and insecure inside.

7. At times you have serious doubts as to whether you have made the right decision or done the right thing.

8. You prefer a certain amount of change and variety and become dissatisfied when hemmed in by restrictions and limitations.

9. You pride yourself as an independent thinker and do not accept others' statements without satisfactory proof.

10. You have found it unwise to be too frank in revealing yourself to others.

For more information, please see:
    Blumenfeld, W.S., and Leveto, G.A., "Gullibility's Travels." *Academy of Management Journal,* 1975, 18:370-374.
    Stagner, R., "The Gullibility of Personnel Managers." *Personnel Psychology*, 1958, 11:346-352.

11. At times you are extroverted, affable, sociable, while at other times you are introverted, wary, reserved.

12. Some of your aspirations tend to be pretty unrealistic.

13. Security is one of your major goals in life.

17. SEAT AND SOURCE OF POWER EXERCISE

Role play involves situations to understand:

1. differences in sources of power (eg. Internal-personal or External-role).
2. How evaluate (1) and resolve conflict (eg. was it done thru Internal or External).
3. understand feelings during 1 and 2.

INTERNAL

1. trust and openness
2. knowledge and skill
3. charisma—charm
4. responsibility for self
5. interdependence and mutual concern
6. leveling
7. self-confidence
8. initiative
9. likeability and warmth
10. personal style
11. body language
12. humor, etc.

EXTERNAL

1. degrees
2. status of school where 1
3. visibility in community
4. professional association and status
5. office location
6. social license and control
7. publishing status
8. power to evaluate others
9. political-social power of professional role

SITUATIONS

1. Two grad students want to marry but he has job in New York City, she, California.

2. Professor gives grades on paper but student thinks it should be based on his great growth.

3. Therapist-client hassle on felt vs. value received.

4. Boss promoted over *friend* now has to evaluate friend's poor work.

5. Parents leave on trip and fourteen-year-old daughter wants her boyfriend to stay.

6. Man-woman in each of five above or in unique situation due to sex only.

18. DEVELOP YOUR OWN LEARNING EXPERIENCES

If you want to become more self-actualized, or increasingly more successful (by whatever criteria you may choose—more money, higher level promotions, and the like), you must work at it. Becoming more self-actualized, as many researchers have shown, is no easy matter. It requires work. Like anything else in life, the more effort and energy you invest, the more you can get out of it.

In your past life, you may have already developed many of your own learning experiences. Some women, for example, teach themselves how to cook, knit, crochet, macrame, or any hobby. Some young men have taught themselves how to repair motorcycles or cars. Some older men have taught themselves, as true entrepreneurs, how to set up their own companies.

Many future entrepreneurs might use this exercise to take a small risk, stretch themselves, and practice now on a small scale what they could do later on a larger scale.

Peter Weaver has written *You, Inc.,* a detailed escape route to being your own boss. (Garden City, N.Y.: Doubleday and Company, Inc., 1973) You can get similar information from Dean C. Dauw's *Up Your Career.* Prospect Heights, III: Waveland Press, 1975. (P.O. Box 400, Prospect Heights, 60070.)

In this exercise, you are being asked to try to outline any creative learning experience of your own. For example, you might fantasize you were fired today and could not get the same job or a higher level position elsewhere. What would you do? Try to think about it creatively for a few minutes. Check the Business Opportunities ads in the local papers (Sunday's *Tribune* or the *Wall Street Journal*). Could you buy an already existing business? Could you set up your own company?

The author has had myriads of experiences, trying to find a cleaning lady for his home. Some apartment-cleaning firms are called Merry Pop-In, Broom Hilda, XYZ Cleaning Service, et cetera. No luck. Could you set up your own company to provide responsible and reliable cleaning services? How would you do market research? How soon could you go to your favorite bank's lending officers or Small Business Bureau for loans? How do you feel as you read this right here and now? (Scared, doubtful, fearful, self-confident?) Do you want or need a partner? If so, what kind? What does this tell you about yourself?

Or, perhaps you can creatively approach this experience from a different viewpoint, perhaps because you are already convinced (rightly or wrongly) you would not like your own business. Imagine you have employees to train. If not today, chances are very good you will in the future.

Creating a complex learning experience is itself a problem or a challenge in creative problem solving. You can surely enhance your own creativity. One process for increasing human creativeness is described in *Supplementary Guide,* a publication of the *Creative Education Foundation* (Chase Hall, State University College, 1300 Elmwood Avenue, Buffalo, New York, 14222).

You must first look at the needs of the trainees. Research has shown they will accept much more readily what you have in mind, if they are involved in the learning or planning for learning. (At this point, you might want to study a text on Educational Psychology, Principles of Learning, or How to Train. One good example in paperback is *Preparing Instrumental Objectives* by Robert F. Mager. Palo Alto, Ca: Fearon Publishers, 1962.)

In creating your own complex learning exercise, please consider the following points:

1. State the purposes or objectives. This is done to maintain a focus, as you brainstorm for ideas to achieve your goals.

2. State operational parameters of the setting. This includes "remindertype" data on group size, maximum training time, nature of the group (strangers or friends) and related facts.

3. Set any arbitrary numerical goal for exercise's ideas. At least ten is sufficient.

4. A smaller, more intimate group usually yields best and quickest results in brainstorming. Thus, you should seek the aid of a colleague in generating the forced growth of exercise ideas. Use a blackboard or large flip chart. Do not *reject* or *judge* any ideas, regardless of how weird they may seem on initial impression. Encourage additions and changes to ideas as a second step of brainstorming.

As you brainstorm, put yourself in the trainees' place. Why are they in training? What do they hope to get out of it? Then allow some time to elapse so ideas can incubate. Sleep overnight on ideas and new ones will spring up. Your goal should be to generate the *form* of the learning exercise. Once you have developed that, working out the more specific details is as easy as dressing a mannikin in a store window.

19. FALL OUT SHELTER EXPERIENCE

You are a committee to decide who goes into the shelter.

You cannot go yourself.

You must choose six out of ten possibilities.

1. A pregnant high school drop-out of dubious I.Q.
2. A 28-year-old ex-policeman who was thrown off the force for police brutality.
3. A female M.D., 37 years old who has had an hysterectomy.
4. A 75-year-old rabbi (Reformed).
5. An architect, 31 years old who is an ex-con. He was convicted of pushing narcotics.
6. A 25-year-old law student. He is an Ivy League graduate but he's married and won't go without his wife. If you choose him, you've chosen two people.
7. The law student's wife who is 26 but has a terminal disease which is believed to be hereditary. She won't go without her husband.
8. A retired prostitute who is living on her annuities. She is 37 years old.
9. A 20-year-old black militant who is very angry. He has no particular skills that we know of.
10. A 45-year-old male violinist who is extremely artistic and creative but is suspected of homosexuality.

*As you discuss this learning experience, please (1) try to get in touch with your own feelings; (2) listen to others feelings and value systems; (3) observe the roles others are playing as outlined in section on Role Identification Form.

20. DYAD-AID OR A HELPING DYAD OR HELPING PAIRS

The innovative technique or method of teaching described below has these primary goals (objectives) for you to obtain:

1. to build helping relationships of the kind needed daily in management, administration, small group behavior and the like.
2. to give participants an opportunity to experience new behavior within a dyadic relationship.
3. to provide participants with ways to check out their perceptions of and reactions to various interpersonal experiences.

Process:

Several variations have been developed for using helping pairs within laboratory learning or other related educational experiences.

A. *RISK-TAKING PAIRS:* Partners meet as often as is recommended by the facilitator to tell the other what sensitive, interpersonal risk(s) he is going to take during that day (or immediate future). Then partners meet again (later on same day; or, next class, or whenever) to check out what occurred. Partners counsel with each other to specify what is a risk for the individual person and support each other in trying new behavior.

B. *GOAL-ASSESSMENT DYADS:* Partners meet at least three times during the life of the group or class (or whenever is the formal time arrangement)—the beginning for an initial assessment of their goals, about the middle of the experience for a continuing assessment, and toward the end of the experience. They follow instructions on the Assessment Forms listed below.

C. *NO-EXIT DYADS:* Partners meet daily, weekly or on some mutually-agreed upon regular basis for at least 30 minutes. Time is used any way they prefer. The only requirement is that they meet regularly throughout the learning or laboratory experience.

This exercise is intended to simulate other or "back-home" dyadic relationships that are permanent. It offers you an opportunity to experiment with making changes (hopefully risky ones) in no exit relationships in which you are involved.

D. *INTERVIEWING PAIRS:* Participants choose a partner and take turns interviewing each other according to The Interview Guide (or any valid similar method) listed below. Later, you should be prepared to give a brief report on the results of interviewing this partner.

Goal Assessment Form

Initial Assessment

Step 1. Please write on a separate sheet of paper five to ten answers to the following question:

"WHAT DO I MOST WANT TO LEARN FROM THIS EXPERIENCE (LAB, CLASS, ETC.)?

Step 2. Revealing and Clarifying Personal Goals. Take turns going through the following procedure:

a. Read aloud your answers to the question in Step 1.
b. Discuss these goals using the following guidelines:

1. Is the goal specific enough to permit direct action and planning?
2. Is the goal personally involving, i.e., does it require personal effort and some commitment?
3. Is the goal realistic? Can significant progress be made in the time available?
4. How can others located here or elsewhere help you on these goals?

(At this point each of you may need to revise your goal statements so that they make better sense to you. Rewrite them and save them.)

Second Assessment

Earlier you prepared your initial statement of some personal goals for this experience (lab or course or program, etc.).

A purpose of this session is to reexamine your goals now in the light of your experience so far. Use the questions under Step 2 (Revealing and Clarifying Personal Goals) to help modify your goal statements.

Please take turns reassessing and discussing your goals. Describe how you have tried to make progress in attaining your goals. When you have finished, write your modified and/or reconfirmed goals.

Interview Guide

1. Decide who will be interviewed first.
2. Conduct a 15-minute interview, focusing on questions below. The interviewer should take notes and feed back to the interviewee a paraphrase (NO PARROT-ING, please) after each question. Seek openness and accurate listening.
3. Repeat the process by switching roles.
4. Take about 10 minutes to talk about the interviewing experience.
5. Later, you may be asked to give a brief report on YOUR FEELINGS about the person interviewed.

Interview Questions

1. What personal goals do you have that you could work for in this group?
2. What concerns or anxieties or feelings do you have about this group so far? (Be as specific as possible.)
3. What personal concerns or issues or feelings would you be willing to share with the group right now?
   (e.g., concerns about particular group members, about how you see yourself, about your impact on this group-program or class—your interpersonal relationships, etc.)

21. EXERCISE ON CONSULTATION

(O-P-Q-R)

Instructions: O

1. Listen thoughtfully to the problem as presented.
2. As you observe the discussion between P and R note:
   a. What you think were the unspoken feelings of each as the talk went along.
   b. Which proposals from R seemed helpful to P and which were duds. Try to distinguish between P's polite appreciation and his real feeling of progress on the problem.
3. As you observe the discussion between P and Q note:
   a. What you think were the unspoken feelings of each as the talk went along.
   b. Which questions from Q seemed to bring real insight to P and which were just unproductive cross-examination. Again, distinguish between courteous thanks and a real change in orientation.
4. You are also to be time-keeper throughout the exercise. Don't be too rigid: listen for an appropriate stopping place at about the time indicated on the flow chart.

(O-P-Q-R)

Instructions: P

1. Choose a problem on which you would like help. It may lie in your personal life, family, job, or community affairs. It should meet the following criteria:
   a. *Urgent.* You really care. You have thought a lot about it. It is important. Something will have to be done about it when you go home.

b. *Human Relations.* It should be appropriate to the resources here. The heart of the problem should lie in relation with another person or with a group or groups.
   c. *Limited.* You will have 15 minutes to tell about it and a half-hour to discuss it. It should be simple enough to permit you to convey the issues clearly in the limited time.
   d. *Yours.* You should have a responsibility in dealing with the problem.
2. Join freely and genuinely in the discussion—first with R—later with Q. Try to get help from them. Test out their suggestions and explore their ideas. Ignore observer(s) and trainer.
3. Note your feelings as they change during the discussion; try to connect changes in feeling with what R and Z say and do.
4. After the discussion you will have 5 minutes to tell the small group how you felt as the conversation went on, and what ideas you now judge to be fruitful and helpful to you for dealing with this problem.

(O-P-Q-R)

Instructions: Q

1. Listen thoughtfully to the problem as presented.
2. Your task is, by raising questions, to help P diagnose his difficulty. Refrain from giving any advice or citing any experience of your own or of others. Keep probing to bring out new angles. Keep responsibility for the answers on P himself. You will have succeeded if you enable him to redefine his problem, seeing the difficulty as due to rather different factors than those originally presented.

It is not easy to ask helpful questions. This is not a cross-examination to fix blame. It is not necessary to dig for every factual detail. It is better to ask "open-end" questions rather than those which can be answered "Yes" or "No." The idea is to help P keep thinking aloud. Your mood should be luminative and reflective, not aggressive or argumentative. Begin in accord with his present line of thought and move along with him.

(O-P-Q-R)

Instructions: R

1. Listen thoughtfully to the problem as presented.

2. Respond with either of the following types of help:

a. Recall and describe a similar experience you or someone you know had to deal with. Tell what you or he did to solve it. If P doesn't accept this, and you still see it as a good solution, explain further.

b. Recommend, in order, the steps you would take if you were in his situation. If P doesn't accept some of these, make other proposals until you hit on something he finds helpful. Be constructive.

22. HIDDEN AGENDA EXERCISE

Alfco Mfg. Company

Alfco Mfg. Co. is the oldest division of Alfco Consolidated Industries a transnational, diversified conglomerate with sales in excess of $5 billion. This division manufactures automotive replacement parts and has sales of over $100 million.

Alfco Mfg. has been a rugged, male-dominated organization. Blacks and other minorities have advanced, but women have not. There are two women in top management which on the surface is impressive but they are not officers. Furthermore, there is an enormous gap between them and the masses of women at the clerical level.

James Androni, VP of Finance and chairperson of the Executive Coordinating Council has called a meeting in an effort to get a single policy statement to which all members of the Council might subscribe regarding career opportunities for women at Alfco.

The meeting is to last twenty minutes.

The attendees are:

Mr. Jim Androni—Vice President of Finance
Mr. Jack Farson—Vice President of Personnel
Ms. Bee Walters—Manager of Administration
Mr. Joe Brandt—Vice President of Production
Ms. Pat Clausen—Manager of Marketing

Instructions for Role Players

1. Participants should not look at each other's roles.
2. Each person should read his part carefully and play the role conscientiously.
3. Put yourself in the role that you are given.
4. Participants should not over-act.
5. Be natural, but emphasize behavior aimed at fulfilling your role.

Jim Androni, V.P. Finance

You, Mr. Androni, were just named President of Alfco but, because you believe only the Board knows, you want to avoid doing anything which would show your hand ahead of the announcement.

You are also the Chairperson of the meeting and want to get a committment from the group within 20 minutes on a policy for hiring and promoting females.

Your knowledge of the subject is very sketchy but you don't want to show any weakness in front of this group. Therefore, you will make vague generalizations in an authoritative way. For example, say: "Our company has always done the right thing." "We are leaders in corporate responsibility." "People get ahead on merit." etc.

One side objective you have is to get others to talk so that you can assess their problem identifying and solving skills.

You are, however, to strive for a consensus statement within the established time frame, but you want the statement to come from the group not from yourself.

Bee Walters — Manager of Administration

You are Bee Walters, a long service employee who has gotten ahead through brilliance and hard work. You disdain Pat Clausen who moved up rapidly through sex appeal and female militancy. You are proud to have made it on your own in a "man's world" and to have a reputation for being competent. (Furthermore, you have recently been told in confidence by Farson, the Personnel VP, that you have been appointed Vice President-Administration.) You feel that women who are advanced as a result of a "policy" or the law would detract from your achievements. Instead of a specific statement

on women or minorities you want a statement about Alfco being committed to total utlization and promotion of qualified and competent personnel.

Joe Brandt — VP Production

You are Joe Brandt. You came up through the ranks. You attended night school to get a degree in industrial engineering and eventually an MBA. You are highly task oriented and concerned about running an efficient plant. You are of the opinion that women supervisors would not be respected by their male and female subordinates and that they have an inordinate need to be liked. You, therefore, are opposed to any policy which would encourage the advancement of females into managerial responsibilities.

You like to be thought of as hard hitting and direct. Today you are your usually blunt self, except you don't want to upset Pat Clausen with whom you have been having an affair. Therefore, for every statement you make, you want to indicate that Ms. Clausen is an exception.

You will strive to avoid any articulate or specific statement on women's opportunities.

Jack Farson — VP Personnel

You are Jack Farson, a person who is very knowledgeable in the field of personnel management and affirmative action. You are the prime technical resource within the committee. You know the laws and the statistics. For example, the company has done an excellent job of hiring and advancing minorities but has neglected the female issue. Except for the two who are in top management, few have positions outside the clerical area.

You are aware, as a result of an insider, that Androni has been named President by the Board. No one else on the committee knows except Androni, of course. You believe your posture in the meeting should be one of non-committal until Androni makes a move and then you will support him all the way hoping to make. a favorable impression. You believe that you must avoid taking a stand because, up to this point, you don't know anything about Androni's views on the subject.

The following Exercises are included to aid you in your personal growth and development toward self-actualization.

23. SELF-EVALUATION
THROUGH YOUR OWN PERSONAL JOURNAL

Whenever people gather together, whether at parties, classes, meetings or groups of any kind for any reason, many events occur. Because some events or behaviors go unexamined, we lose many valuable opportunities for personal growth and development.

Here, you are asked to keep a personal journal, or notebook. The reasons or goals are clear:
  a. You will intensify your awareness of the flow of events and the concomitant emotional development.
  b. You can develop your own resources for future learnings.
  c. You can development your own resources for future learnings.

Method

In developing your own notebook, you could use the left-hand pages for an objective description of events, processes, or behaviors. Then, on the right-hand page, you can note as openly and clearly as possible, your own subjective feelings and reactions.

The more you can focus in on your accurate, honest feelings, the more you will be enabled to expand your own awareness and use it for personal growth. The important thing is what you invest in it for what you hope to get out of it.

Example

EVENT

My boss chewed me out about --------

FEELINGS

Feel angry at first, then more hostile, then calmed down and feel more hopeful for progress.

EVENT

My lover, partner, spouse or friend rejected me.

FEELINGS

Feel frustrated, sad and upset.

24. MODIFY YOUR OWN BEHAVIOR

Do you want to stop smoking? Or cut down? Are you eager to eat less? Can you, hopefully, increase your sexual potential? Do you want to reduce some stress in your life? These are some of the many areas, major or minor, in which people would like to change in some way or another.

Fortunately, there is much any person can do on his/her own, without recourse to a professional therapist or behavior modifier. Reed Mencke (1972) has recently shown how he developed an effective self-help program for younger people of college age that fortunately applies to people of all ages, regardless of their situation or problem or objectives for desired growth and development.

The major idea underlying the self-help program is B.F. Skinner's explanation of self-control. The early Greeks advised people to "know thyself." Since behavior is usually assumed to be controlled by events around you, this can be clarified by saying "Know thy behavior," "Know thy environment," and "Know the actual relationship between the two." These relationships are to help you focus more on explicit, clearly defined behaviors rather than feelings and thoughts. The emphasis is on developing methods you can use to get yourself to do what you really want to do but find hard to accomplish. The emphasis here is also not on getting you to change your goals by some external forces or pressures. Rather, to help you get it on your own.

There are four fundamental concepts you must get clear:

1. *Commitment.* This is absolutely necessary for all changes, large or small. You really have to have a strong, clear, active, positive commitment—night and day. These commitments are stronger if you can make them public, like telling a friend and having him/her help you by inquiring, coaching, and/or reminding.

2. *Observable Behavior.* You need to restate your goals in terms of behavior that is clearly defined so that you can observe them clearly. This method makes your goals more specific. Sometimes it even begins to suggest a solution. It also helps to clarify it in your own mind as well as for anyone you may wish to communicate it to. It is good to have a spouse, partner, relative, friend or boss to help coach you. One way to start is by telling that person clearly what to look for. It is a good test to give yourself. You will want them to help reward you anyway whenever these changes occur. (Hilgard, and Bower, 1966: Bandura, 1969)

3. *A Gradual Step-By-Step Method to Change.* Many people fail to change or grow because they bite off too much to chew. So, you have to pick small parts of your behavior to change gradually. You must learn to float or kick before swimming. You ought to learn to swim before diving. Learning to masturbate comes before learning intercourse (Kohlenberg, 1974). Skinner called it "shaping." Wolpe calls it "desensitization." Gagne called it "learning programs." There is impressive evidence cited by all these authors as to why and how it works.

4. *Changing Behavior is Best Done by Rewarding Yourself.* Most humanists might disagree with this basic concept and ask you to get insight. In therapy, we like to think of ourselves as behavioral humanists, using these behavioral methods but with an overall humanistic orientation. To increase

strength and depth of a preferred response, the response must be rewarded (reinforced). But it must first occur even before it can be reinforced. To become a really self-actualized person, you must first practice being who you want to be (rather, a small part of who you want to be). (Mehrabian, 1970)

25. ACCEPTING OTHERS

Accepting focuses on two aspects—accepting oneself and accepting others. Accepting oneself means you can own up to your innermost needs, desires, thoughts, and feelings, and (this is the hard part) doing it without judging yourself or your feelings. Since all your feelings are a very real part of your person, you are entitled to the varied spectra of thoughts and feelings you may experience—from hate to love: anger as well as affection, fear as well as hope, and the like. By learning to accept the different parts of yourself, you can more easily accept others' feelings and motives without judging them. Research has shown acceptance to be an essential part of meaningful relationships.

Your willingness or ability to listen shows your acceptance. By listening intently to be sure you understand what another says, even if you disagree with the speaker, you show acceptance. By trying to accept others, you postpone evaluating them, and thus have a chance to learn from them. You avoid unneeded misperceptions and faulty stereotypes. By the same method, we learn about ourselves in stepping back and looking at ourselves without self-criticism. You cannot really cope with or change anyone's thoughts and/or attitudes without accepting them first.

This exercise has three goals: (1) to understand, explore and act out the concept of accepting oneself, (2) to learn more about accepting others, and (3) to see how acceptance can be applied in a real situation.

Part I

First, think about all your strengths, good qualities and abilities: any positive attribute, e.g., having a good sense of humor or being honest. In our culture, unfortunately, accepting oneself too often means admitting your failures or limitations, rather than your assets. As children, we were often discouraged from talking about our strengths. (You may find this difficult because you never did it before. Please take a small risk and do it anyway. Once you get into it with others involved; it gets easier.)

Having done the step above, form into small groups, from three to five or more, and share these assets with others, for one full minute. And *ONLY* then, others can suggest strengths they think he has, but which he or she *omitted* to mention. It is important for everyone to participate.

Part II

Please discuss *the way* the person expressed his/her strengths. Here an individual can receive as much useful feedback as he/she gave him/herself in initially listing the strengths. One example may be that someone was reluctant to participate, or held out to be last, or was embarassed when talking of his/her own assets. This is all valuable information that should be shared.

This procedure should be followed for each member: sharing strengths, receiving feedback and then discussion.

Part III

Please form trios or quartets. "Speaker" makes a statement to "listener" about his/her *strongest* feeling about listener. Use *only one sentence*. Listener then tries, using different words not like a parrot or tape recorder, to reflect the meaning of what was said. That is, listener states what was said and possibly why. Please use only one sentence. Speaker may then have to correct the interpretation of his/her original statement. This method may have to be repeated until the speaker and/or listener really feels he/she was understood correctly.

The important goal is not to learn paraphrasing but rather achieving mutual, clear communication. Then, the observer(s) describe the interaction. This exercise then is repeated with each person assuming a different role.

Part IV

Accepting others means: (1) understanding their points of view, values, etc., (2) seeing how and why they hold such beliefs, and (3) caring for them, despite disagreements. Accepting is really listening with caring. Milton Mayeroff has written a terrific book *On Caring*. (New York: Harper and Row, 1971. Perennial edition in paper, 1972.) He defines caring, in the most significant sense, is to help a person grow and become more self-actualized. Caring is a process, a way of relating to someone involving development, in the way that friendship only emerges in time through mutual trust and a deepening, qualitative transformation of the relationship. Caring does not mean always agreeing, but rather enables others to feel they can express themselves in a nonjudgmental atmosphere.

Part V

If you can creatively develop a more appropriate or meaningful experience, please try. This role-playing situation, however, may appeal to some.

Individuals should try hard to identify with the roles so that they can really put themselves into it. Although the interaction's content is important, the *most* important part is the way the role players listen and communicate. Try to reflect values and feelings. For example, it would not be consistant with the information given about the conservative father if he should instantly turn liberal. If he does change, it should be because his son's behavior and words motivated the change.

Roles

Son, first year college student, has academic problems. During the first semester, questionable friends. Dad is a very conservative civil engineer or accountant and has been unable to keep in touch with his son during school.

Intense arguing at Thanksgiving. Now, after not having seen each other at Christmas, they meet at the end of the semester.

* * *

Remember, there is no one right/wrong way. Everyone discuss after 20 minutes.

26. DIAGNOSING AND MANAGING STRESS

Stress is an unavoidable element in everyone's daily life. Some people have developed effective ways to handle stress, while others are relatively less successful. This exercise is an attempt to help you diagnose some stressful situations, to evaluate them, look at some hopefully more effective ways to handle them, and then get in closer touch with some of your own feelings about conflict, anxiety and tension.

Please think up, in a creative way, the most stressful situation you have ever had. Try to develop a role-play about it, so that you can explain it and share it with others. Some possibilities are suggested below, in the event you cannot here and now develop a better one. Then, process and discuss what happened. Look especially at *your own feelings, here and now.*

a. Silently circulate and mill about the room. Take any denomination of money you wish from your pocket. Give away coins and dollar bills to other participants. Be open to accept money from them. Do not expect to get it back but do expect to receive what is given to you.

b. Within a clearly defined time limit, please develop a rating scale on the following topics, or another topic of your choice that is controversial or designed to stimulate open display of feelings. Examples are: dimensions of successful managers, leadership behavior, qualities and/or motives needed for success, etc.

c. Encourage the group to develop any stressful task by creating an ambiguous situation without a leader.

d. Have each member choose from the group a mother, father, boss, husband, wife, or person you would most like to be shipwrecked with on a desert island. Explain why.

e. After the group has been together for enough time to develop loyalties and strong feelings, eliminate somebody.

f. Develop all possible triads from group members. Then, explain why two members differ from the third person.

g. Form any pattern (e.g., line or circle) wherein participants rank themselves on a dimension, such as smartest to dumbest, most to least influential, and the like.

h. Try harder to create a better exercise about stress and stressful situations.

27. GETTING IN TOUCH WITH YOUR FEELINGS AND DEFENSES

Personal growth toward self-actualization can progress more easily as you learn to get more in touch with your own feelings. In this exercise, you can focus on your own feelings and the defenses others use. You are asked to learn better how to take increasingly more responsibility for your own learning, because research has shown no one can really learn for you.

Method

1. Try to spell out as many feelings as you can, giving their opposites, e.g., love—hate. Try to stretch to list at least thirty-two. Then, rank which ones you are able to more easily get in touch with and express on a daily basis. Then, *only after you feel you have exhausted all efforts,* turn to the listing at the end of the book and check.

2. Do the same with your defense mechanisms (e.g., Lying: when my boss asked if I had done it, I said my secretary or subordinate was still collecting data.) Only after you have exhausted all creative efforts, turn to the listing at the end of the book.

3. Prepare a brief lecture, in a small group, about feelings and defenses. Someone must take notes.

4. A volunteer will be asked from each small group to explain what was prepared.

5. Please try to develop a more creative method than this one, if you can. Take a risk and stretch yourself.

----

love—hate

sadness—joy

affection—anger

hope—fear

hurt—relief

satisfaction—unfulfillment

frustration—contentment

superiority—inferiority

attraction—repulsion

community—lonliness

involvement—boredom

weakness—strength

rejection—support

clarity—confusion

trust—suspicion

shyness—curiosity

Adapted from the *Feel Wheel,* coauthored by Anthony L. Rose, Ph.D., Martin J. Thommes, Ph.D., Terry Van Orshoven, Ph.D., and Layne A. Longfellow, Ph.D., fellows of the Center for Studies of the Person, La Jolla, California. (Del Mar, Ca: CRM, Inc., 1972)

Ego Defense Mechanisms

denial of reality—protecting self from unpleasant reality by refusal to perceive or face it.

fantasy—gratifying frustrated desires by imaginary achievements.

repression—preventing painful or dangerous thoughts from entering consciousness.

rationalization—attempting to prove that one's behavior is "rational" and justifiable and thus worthy of self and social approval.

projection—placing blame for difficulties upon others or attributing one's own unethical desires to others.

reaction formation—preventing dangerous desires from being expressed by exaggerating opposed attitudes and types of behavior and using them as "barriers."

Coleman, J.C., *Abnormal Psychology and Modern Life.* Glenview, Illinois: Scott, Foresman and Company, 1972.

displacement—discharging pent-up feelings, usually of hostility, on objects less dangerous than those which initially aroused the emotions.

emotional insulation—reducing ego involvement and withdrawing into passivity to protect self from hurt.

intellectualization (isolation)—cutting off affective charge from hurtful situations or separating incompatible attitudes by logic-tight compartments.

undoing—atoning for and thus counteracting immoral desires or acts.

regression—retreating to earlier developmental level involving less mature responses and usually a lower level of aspiration.

identification—increasing feelings of worth by identifying self with person or institution of illustrious standing.

introjection—incorporating external values and standards into ego structure so individual is not at their mercy as external threats.

compensation—covering up weakness by emphasizing desirable trait or making up for frustration in one area by overgratification in another.

acting-out—reducing the anxiety aroused by forbidden desires by permitting their expression.

28. PEAK EXPERIENCES AS GROWTH EXERCISES

Self-actualized people in all walks of life, at all educational levels, seek new ways to become more fully-functioning. This exercise was developed to aid anyone accomplish these goals:

1. Learn more about your own positive feelings.
2. Develop a better, quicker system to elevate your mood when depressed, anxiety-ridden, or attempting to dispel worries.
3. Find easier, cheaper ways to enjoy life.
4. Emphasize a climate or atmosphere of growth rather than its opposite.

Try to analyze your peak stimuli. These are the things or events that you most enjoy smelling, tasting, touching, looking at and listening to, and doing. When you experience them, they tend to lift your general mood (i.e., accentuate positive feelings). Thus, they make you feel better here and now than you previously did. Since your tastes naturally differ from other people, you can make up your own list by filling these blanks.

1. The three things that I enjoy smelling the most are:

    1.

    2.

    3.

2. The three things that I enjoy tasting the most are:

    1.

    2.

    3.

3. The three things that I enjoy touching the most are:

    1.

    2.

    3.

4. The three things that I enjoy looking at the most are:

    1.

    2.

    3.

5. The three things that I enjoy hearing the most are:

    1.

    2.

    3.

6. The three things that I enjoy doing the most are:

    1.

    2.

    3.

Many people discover they need to give some thoughtful consideration to this issue. While you may be able to think of many things you like, you really need to focus on what you really like the *very best.*

For example, you may enjoy listening to music, but have to spend some time deciding on what selections you like the very most. The closer you can come to what you prefer the very most, the more effective will these stimuli be in helping

This technique was originally researched by psychologist Paul Binu rim, to whom credit is given and acknowledgement made. This exercise is adapted from his statement.

your growth experience. Take your time. It is worth it and *very important*.

After completing the list, you can use it in various ways. Privately, at home, assemble them for your own personal pleasure and use, whenever your mood requires it. For example, observing a terrific sunset may be enhanced by your soothing music, a sip of wine, and the like.

In a growth session, you may choose to share them with your favorite friends, or others. Some favorite items may not easily be brought to a party or public session. For example, you may enjoy the smell of sea air, but have no way to bring it. On the other hand, you may really enjoy the sound of the ocean that is taped or on a record that you could bring.

Please continue to work on your list, as you replace what you could bring to a session. The value of the group session will be enhanced, if you can bring your favorite items.

If you are using this exercise in a group session, rather than privately, please try to bring at least one item to smell, another item to taste, one item to touch, an item to look at, and one to listen to—whatever you need for an activity you enjoy. In a session, you will be asked to experience all items at the same time. Even though each item may have no relationship to another, the end result is to lift your mood more than if you just used one alone.

Elevating your mood as high as possible is necessary for a peak experience. One participant, for example, experienced a truly high mood elevation by eating chocolate, touching fur, listening to Mozart, smelling cologne, looking at a picture of a meadow and singing, all at the same time. Since each person is such a unique individual, you really must make your own selections and *bring your own things*.

29. GIVING JOY AND POSITIVE FEEDBACK

Have you ever noticed in our society and culture that much more negative feedback is given than positive feedback? In fact, if you do take a minor risk and give positive, warm compliments, the receiver feels uncomfortable, and falsely assumes you may be trying to manipulate him/her. Why do we have to wait until someone is dead to give him/her a rose? Do it NOW!

This exercise is intended to help you: (a) develop an atmosphere of trust, more self-affirmation, and greater feelings of self-esteem; (b) experience giving positive statements rather than negative feedback; and (c) risk giving small gifts of joy and happiness to someone.

Method

Please write down positive statements or messages to each person in the group. There is more than one possible approach. Keep an open mind and try.

1. Please try to avoid generalities and be more specific. Avoid "I like your personality" but consider: "I appreciate the way you look and talk in a friendly way when you sit down next to me."
2. Explain: (a) what you perceive to be this person's greatest strengths or best accomplishment, either here in the group or from prior knowledge; (b) what aspect of him/her you would like to know better; and (c) why you would like to know the individual better.
3. Include every person as much as possible. For example, even if you do not know as much as you would like, you might say something positive about a person's clothes, hair-style, and the like.
4. Try harder to make each message apply to the person rather than be applicable to more than one; and say what about him/her makes you happier or better.
5. Try harder to be more personal, using his/her name, and "I feel" or "I like."
6. You may sign your messages, but if you feel it is too big a risk, you can avoid signing.

Other Possible Variations

1. You could use this method or process for almost any content or purpose. You could do negative feedback first, then positive. You could focus on growth and change, like "I would like you to become more_____." "I can't say this to you,_____, because _____."
2. Actual gifts could be brought rather than the symbolic ones described above.

30. ASSERTIVENESS TRAINING

A large number of books have been written on assertiveness training. A good example is M. Smith's *When I Say No, I Feel Guilty!*

The goal of this exercise is to help you develop certain interpersonal skills, to develop greater self-respect, to satisfy your own needs, and to defend your own rights without controlling or abusing other people.

These skills give you an overall measure of your degree of assertiveness.

Try to visualize assertiveness as a continuum:

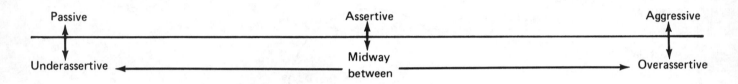

There are differences within the same person over time in various situations, as well as between individuals in their level of assertiveness.

Using Figures 2, 3, and 4, try to get a more explicit impression of the continuum above.

Figure 2

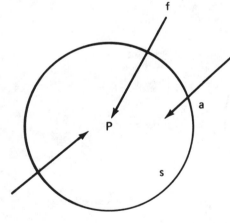

p = Person
s = Personal Space
f = Environmental Forces
à = Point of Assertion

Underassertion

This model assumes each individual has a certain amount of *personal space*. Included in this space is a feeling of one's sense of self-respect, self-worth and right to be treated humanly. Also included are their rights to pursue basic needs (e.g., self-protection). Even if there might be minor disagreement about what is included in this personal space, everyone agrees about its existence. This personal space is the sum of your ideas about how you wish to be treated.

Every person must be enabled to assert him/herself, to maintain self-respect and to avoid exploitation whenever outside forces (people or organizations) violate this personal space. These outside forces could be, for example, a business cheating you or an individual calling you derogatory names.

Please look at Figure 2. In this example, this person has not completely defended him/herself at the so-called "point of assertion." This is defined as underassertion.

Figure 3

Assertion

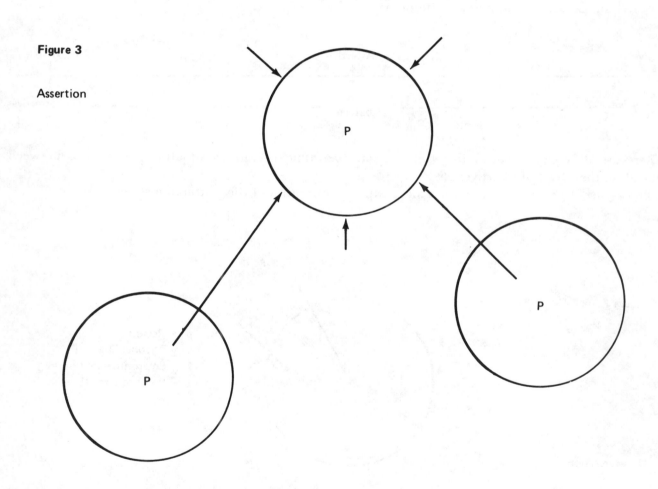

358

In Figure 3, however, there is a strong boundary. This individual has strong skills, enough to block any outside impinging forces. This is defined as assertion: defending your own rights and satisfying your own needs without violating any others' space.

Figure 4

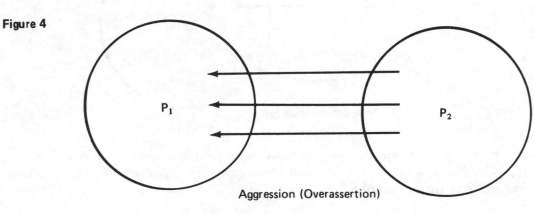

Aggression (Overassertion)

Figure 4 is an example of overassertion or aggression. P-2 is acting on P-1 in some way that is an attempt at control, manipulation, domination, abuse, or exploitation. When P-2 penetrates p-1's space, then P-2 is being aggressive.

In every situation where one person moves against another, there is either underassertion, assertion, or overassertion (aggression). See Figures 5, 6, and 7.

Figure 5

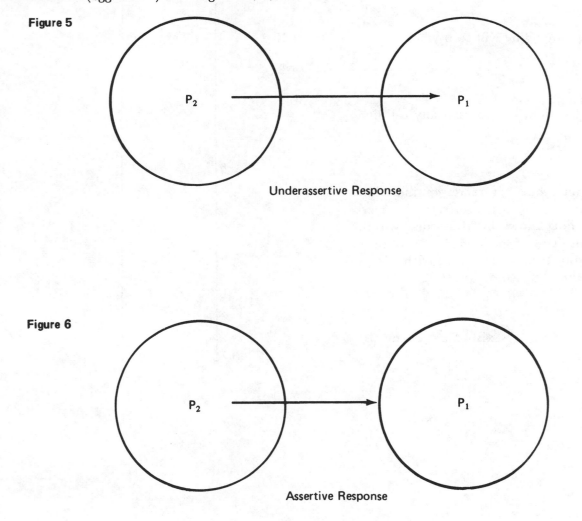

Underassertive Response

Figure 6

Assertive Response

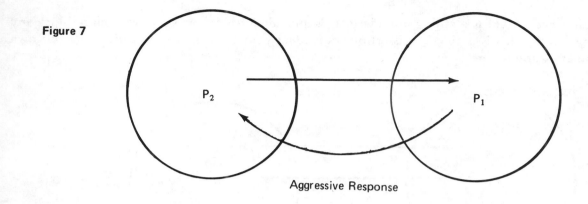

Figure 7

P_2

P_1

Aggressive Response

The only true assertive response is one that protects your space while avoiding the violation of others (Figure 6). People typically have, in the past, countered with aggression, because they see it as power or strength, without being aware of the option of an assertive response.

EXAMPLE ONE

On a new job, a male coworker refers to you as "chick," "baby," or "honey." You feel insulted and angry, preferring to be referred to as a woman.

	underassertive	assertive	aggressive
Response one You do nothing, hoping he will stop when he sees you upset.	X		
Response two Without an explanation, you sarcastically call him "boy."			X
Response three You confront him as one mature, responsible adult to another, with words to this effect: "I understand you did not know this, but such words, "chick," etc., insult me. I'd be glad to explain. I hope you can stop. If you want to be friends, you will have to use different words with me."		X	
Response four You denounce him as a "sexist—Male Chauvinist Pig" and walk away.			X

EXAMPLE TWO

When you come home emotionally drained, your partner wants to tell you his/her feelings and events of the day. You prefer not to listen, but have a need to talk about what happened to you.

	underassertive	assertive	aggressive
Response five You are torn up inside, but listen to your partner, thinking how selfish and unperceptive he/she is. "Can't you see how I feel?"	X		
Response six You tell your partner how drained you are. You explain your strong need and ask your partner if he/she could wait, unless there is something that cannot wait.		X	
Response seven You scream "How could you be so selfish and blind (etc.). You only think of yourself. My mother was right; you wouldn't take care of me!"			X
Response eight You listen for awhile and then begin getting drunk while pretending to listen.	X		

In responses #1 and #5, the person allowed to continue a situation violating self-respect or abusing needs, *without* even stating or giving a direct expression of feelings. This is common in underassertive behavior.

In responses #2, #4, and #7, the injured gave indications of feeling upset—but did not explain why. Instead, they attacked the other person with sarcsm, shouting, name-calling, overstatement (#7), generalizing (#7), and manipulation (#7). Hence, these are aggressive responses.

Response #8 reveals both underassertive and underaggressive styles, often called passive aggressive. The person is passive by not expressing needs or feelings; yet, the situation is allowed to progress while tuning the person out.

Responses #3 and #6 are clearly acts of assertion. Anger or other feelings are not allowed to boil up too high and then spill out as aggression. There is a clear sequence:

a. Person acted quickly, before anger builds too high. Feelings are protected from additional hurt.

b. Feelings and needs are strongly stated but . . .

c. . . . without blaming.

d. They did not demand or manipulate the first person who apparently was injuring. Future possible consequences were explained in #2.

By avoiding coercion, you let the initiator decide what to do next. You avoid violating the initiator's space in return.

Please note that responses #3 and #6 are assertive responses that begin an interaction. Depending upon the next stimulus, the encounter may be resolved. Or, the first person, the initiator, may up the ante and a further, escalated assertion may be required.

Most underassertive people do not realize they have the right to express how they are feeling and what their needs are. In most situations, that is all that is necessary.

When underassertive behavior becomes habitual, it is destructive. It has pervasive effects on your self-esteem, self-concept, and chances for growth and development.

Underassertive behavior can become part of a person's nonverbal behaviors, stance, posture or way of being. In varying degrees and ways, the underassertive individual is saying: "I do not count. I am not worth much. I do not have the right to stop you."

Aggressive behavior, by contrast, may seem good on the surface. Aggression often parries thrusts and fends off assaults on personal space. Whenever it is successful, aggressive behavior often satisfies the needs of some people to dominate, control or aggress against others. Usually, it is interpreted as strength, rather than a harmful response. It helps some insecure people bolster their self-esteem. A closer look, however, shows you how harmful aggressive behavior can be.

The aggressive person is hindered from having truly loving relationships with people. Instead of giving and receiving love, the aggressive person who deeply within wants love is only giving abuse, domination, manipulation and control. Good relationships are not built upon aggression. Rather, aggression can only lead to a relationship built on inequality and disrespect. Aggressive people will not be truly relating to individuals for whom they feel love and respect. An aggressive attitude keeps one from appearing vulnerable and thus receiving care or love.

A truly strong person need not have to "be strong," "be on top," or "be in control" at all times. An aggressive person lacks this strength, and thus cannot form true relationships.

On the other hand, consistently using assertive skills has great benefits:

1. Assertive personalities can grow more self-confident and less fearful as they increasingly become aware they can and will defend themselves.

2. Thus, by being less concerned with self-protection (since they know it is there when needed), more energy is freed for truly "seeing," "hearing," and "loving" others more readily. A person who is less defensive can give more.

3. Assertive people can be free of any need to manipulate, dominate or control others. They can permit themselves and others the freedom of choice.

4. Good knowledge of one's self is needed to be assertive. You must know what you are feeling and what your needs are. An assertive person is fully aware of his/her personal space.

5. An assertive person can affirm positive values of self-worth and the integrity of others by maintaining a clear conscience in dealing with them.

31. LIFE'S JOURNEY

You can interpret this exercise in many ways and use if for different experiences. Consider these possible procedures:

1. Use the following stimulus as a way to get to know and understand another person.
2. Use the issues to understand your own behavior.
3. Use these questions as a follow-up exercise to interpret any **other preceding** experience.

Please study the following and discuss with your partner after you have jotted down the first notes that come to your mind. As you get more involved, hopefully your discussions can follow the spiral of the following words. (Accolades for the following to Louis T. Brusatti, C.M.)

The journey of your life is a very personal and
  unique experience — an experience full of
      emotion reflecting the heights and depths
          of your being/becoming

Who you are is your history.
How we are one in the circus of life is your poem.

Poetry is built on history
          on personal experience.

Poetry is a generalization — writ large — for all to
  experience.

The following is for your reflection.
The following is intended that your history
  might become our poetry.

What is the journey of my life?
What are my life images?
What moments have been like no others?
How do I let life seduce me?
What is juicy and zestful in my life?

How does my life spiral?
What do I circle around?
What is central to me?
What does the **I Am** I speak mean to me?
Where are there stones in my life?
How do I dream?

What is it my life plants?
Where did life begin for me?
Who is with me on my life journey?
What do the clouds of my life mean?
What is the food of my life journey?
What way am I on?
What does my life want to say to others?

Louis T. Brusatti

32. GROWTH LEARNING EVALUATIONS

Name: _____

Exercise	Action-oriented Ideas Growth Expected	Implications of these action-oriented learnings for me as a person	Implications of these action-oriented learnings for me as a manager

33. DO I NEED PSYCHOTHERAPY
(Be Honest With Yourself, For Yourself, and For Others)

Life for most people has its good times and bad times. It's inevitable; we have ups and downs. Perhaps, in a down time, you have wondered if you need psychotherapy. How can you decide? What are some principal differences between the normal, expected ups and downs and the kinds of emotional difficulties that require therapy.

Psychologists agree it is time to seek assistance when you feel so badly you cannot function as well as you want; when your problems start hindering your daily activities, your job, your marriage, your sex life. When this situation occurs, your next question is, for how long? If you have been feeling bad in any area of your life for a few months or more, you could profit from some help.

Anyone can have a crisis, such as a death in the family, a divorce, or loss of a job that will upset anyone. But if you do not conquer a crisis as quickly as you want you may need therapy — if you do not have a crisis, but feel bad over a period of months, often for no apparent, obvious reason, then you can also profit from professional consultation.

These following questions may help you decide to consult a psychologist. Remember, there are no right or wrong answers. Answer quickly and honestly.

1. In new situations, such as parties where there are many strangers, or job interviews, do you feel fearful and expect failure?

   a) all or most of the time   b) frequently   c) occasionally   d) rarely or never

2. When asked to do something you do not wish to do, such as work late, or help out a friend, can you say no without feeling quilty?

   a) all or most of the time   b) frequently   c) occasionally   d) rarely or never

3. Do you ever totally lose your temper, realizing later you expressed more anger than the occasion deserved? For example, your partner has been delayed and arrives later than you expected.

   a) all or most of the time   b) frequently   c) occasionally   d) rarely or never

4. Can you get friends to listen when you have a suggestion, like choosing movies or restaurants?

   a) all or most of the time   b) frequently   c) occasionally   d) rarely or never

5. Do you have difficulties making decisions, such as choosing a new suit or deciding what to do over a week-end holiday?

   a) all or most of the time   b) frequently   c) occasionally   d) rarely or never

6. Are you reluctant to get involved in group activities? For example, do you most often avoid parties or stand alone?

   a) all or most of the time   b) frequently   c) occasionally   d) rarely or never

7. Do you need encouragement or approval for activities you do all the time, such as daily office matters or preparing meals for your family?

a) all or most of the time   b) frequently   c) occasionally   d) rarely or never

8. Can you state your dissatisfaction when others take too much advantage of you, such as force themselves ahead of you in line?

a) all or most of the time   b) frequently   c) occasionally   d) rarely or never

9. Are you pleased and content with your closest relationships?

a) all or most of the time   b) frequently   c) occasionally   d) rarely or never

10. Do you take a tranquillizer or a drink to increase your confidence before parties or job interviews?

a) all or most of the time   b) frequently   c) occasionally   d) rarely or never

11. Are you concerned about habits you can not control, such as eating, smoking or drinking to excess?

a) all or most of the time   b) frequently   c) occasionally   d) rarely or never

12. Do you have fears — such as crowded, small or wide open places — that you can not control or keep you from doing what you want?

a) all or most of the time   b) frequently   c) occasionally   d) rarely or never

13. When leaving your house, do you ever return to check the windows, doors, locks, or whatever?

a) all or most of the time   b) frequently   c) occasionally   d) rarely or never

14. How often are sexual experiences dissatisfactory for you or your partner?

a) all or most of the time   b) frequently   c) occasionally   d) rarely or never

15. Do you awaken more than an hour earlier or take more than an hour to fall asleep when you do not wish?

a) all or most of the time   b) frequently   c) occasionally   d) rarely or never

16. Have you recently lost weight without a diet or medical cause?

a) very little, if any   b) more than five pounds   c) more than ten pounds   d) more than fifteen pounds

17. Are you overly concerned with cleanliness or germs on yourself or objects that you might contact?

a) all or most of the time   b) frequently   c) occasionally   d) rarely or never

18. Do you see the future as hopeless, or do you ever imagine hurting yourself or committing suicide?

a) all or most of the time   b) frequently   c) occasionally   d) rarely or never

19. Do you ever hear, see or feel things that no one else is experienceing?

a) all or most of the time   b) frequently   c) occasionally   d) rarely or never

20. Do you believe you have superior powers or that others are using unknown forces against you?

a) all or most of the time   b) frequently   c) occasionally   d) rarely or never

Evaluating Your Responses

Remember, there are no right or wrong answers. We all occasionally feel dissatisfied with an intimate relationship. We all can lose our tempers over trivialities. In ordinary situations, the well-adjusted person will usually respond:

1. c or d	5. c or d	9. a or b	13. c or d	17. c or d
2. a or b	6. c or d	10. c or d	14. c or d	18. d
3. c or d	7. c or d	11. c or d	15. c or d	19. d
4. a, b, or c	8. a or b	12. c or d	16. a or b	20. d

Items #1 through #10 cover how well you express your feelings or how much self-esteem you have. If many of your responses differ from those listed above, it means you have difficulties expressing feelings or feeling confident about yourself. If you want to change some of these behaviors or feelings, psychotherapy will help you.

Items #11 through #14 consider behaviors that typically accompany emotional problems. If some of your answers differ from those listed above, and if you believe these problems hinder your daily life, it would be prudent to see a professional psychologist for an opinion.

Items #15 through #20 discuss behavior patterns that could be important early-warning signals of serious emotional difficulties. If some of your responses differ from those given here, you should see a psychologist soon. Therapy is always easier if not delayed.

You can have a confidential, no-cost appointment to talk to a therapist who cares at (312) 634-1920. Medical insurance is honored. It is also totally tax-deductible. Since our clients can all eventually and quickly be reimbursed from these two major sources, there is no *valid excuse* to keep someone from feeling better. Call Now. (312) 644-1920.